“Paul Sloan masterfully argues that the Synoptic Gospels present Jesus as a Jew intent on recalling Israel to renewed covenant faithfulness by repenting and then obeying, not abandoning, the Law that God had given. This illuminating and important book reminds us afresh that we cannot understand the Synoptic accounts of Jesus’s disputes about the Mosaic Law without putting them in dialogue with biblical texts, Jewish restorationist eschatology, and rabbinic legal reasoning.”

—**David M. Moffitt**, University of St. Andrews

“‘Who do you say that I am?’ the Jesus of the Synoptic Gospels asks. In *Jesus and the Law of Moses*, Sloan answers, ‘Jesus is God’s eschatological agent sent to Israel to unleash a renewed fidelity to both the covenant and the Law of Moses.’ If you want to understand the Synoptic portrayal of Jesus, you need to read this book!”

—**Matthew Thiessen**, McMaster University

“*Jesus and the Law of Moses* is one of the best and most important books on Jesus and the Gospels in decades. Sloan has accomplished the rare feat of producing a field-shifting book that is also accessible to readers outside the scholarly guild. This is a must-read for anyone wanting to understand Jesus and his message more fully—scholars and laypersons alike.”

—**Jason A. Staples**, North Carolina State University

“*Jesus and the Law of Moses* offers a significant and nuanced contribution to the complex question of the Gospels’ portrayal of Jesus’s teaching on the Law. By carefully situating Jesus’s instruction within the framework of apocalyptic expectations of restoration, Sloan demonstrates that Jesus’s legal teachings and disputes are not rejections of the Law but authoritative interpretations aimed at its full observance in the dawning eschatological age. In doing so, Sloan effectively challenges common scholarly misconceptions.”

—**Cecilia Wassén**, Uppsala University

“Jewish Law provided not the contrast to Jesus’s message but its context and much of its content. By reading closely in biblical and postbiblical Jewish texts, Sloan restores this dimension to the Synoptic Gospels’ representations of Jesus. *Jesus and the Law of Moses* is an exemplary work of scholarship.”

—**Paula Fredriksen**, Boston University (emerita)

"Christian readers of the Gospels often find themselves in the awkward position of explaining away sayings of Jesus about the Law, trying gymnastically to square them with theological axioms derived from elsewhere. Against such tortured efforts, Sloan shows in this lucid, readable book how it is possible—and indeed necessary—that Jesus means exactly what he says. Sloan's Jesus consequently stands much closer both to the prophets before him and to the rabbis after him."

—**Matthew V. Novenson**, Princeton Theological Seminary

"Sloan's work is a timely and welcome corrective to the persistent and dominant dichotomies that pit Jesus and the Gospel against Moses and the Law and mistakenly assume that Jesus canceled the so-called ritual or ceremonial commandments. I hope that this promising work will reach the widest possible audience. It showcases the exciting, innovative insights of a scholar who engages seriously with New Testament texts *qua* Jewish expressions of antiquity."

—**Isaac W. Oliver**, Bradley University

"In this incredibly helpful book, Sloan addresses several misguided interpretations of Jesus's relationship with the Law, ranging from ritual purity to sabbath observance, and in their place he provides a compelling alternative: as a faithful interpreter of the Law, Jesus heralds the restoration of the people of God."

—**Madison N. Pierce**, Western Theological Seminary

"Sloan makes a powerful argument that scholarly study of Jesus's teachings on the Law of Moses must attend much more closely to Jesus's alternative interpretations (not rejections!) of the Law as well as Jesus's eschatological conviction that he has inaugurated Israel's restoration. Truly a fresh, creative, and convincing argument!"

—**Joshua W. Jipp**, Trinity Evangelical Divinity School

JESUS AND THE LAW OF MOSES

JESUS AND THE LAW OF MOSES

The Gospels and the Restoration of Israel within First-Century Judaism

PAUL T. SLOAN

Baker Academic
a division of Baker Publishing Group
Grand Rapids, Michigan

Published by Baker Academic
a division of Baker Publishing Group
Grand Rapids, Michigan
BakerAcademic.com

Printed in the United States of America

Library of Congress Cataloging-in-Publication Data
Names: Sloan, Paul (Religious educator), author.
Title: Jesus and the Law of Moses : the Gospels and the Restoration of Israel within First-Century Judaism / Paul T. Sloan.
Description: Grand Rapids, Michigan : Baker Academic, a division of Baker Publishing Group, [2025] | Includes bibliographical references and index.
Identifiers: LCCN 2024054981 | ISBN 9781540966384 (paperback) | ISBN 9781540969200 (casebound) | ISBN 9781493450183 (ebook) | ISBN 9781493450190 (pdf)
Subjects: LCSH: Jesus Christ—Views on Jewish law. | Bible. New Testament.
Classification: LCC BS2417.L3 S46 2025 | DDC 232.9/54—dc23/eng/20250103
LC record available at https://lccn.loc.gov/2024054981

Cover art: *The Disciples Pluck Corn on the Sabbath*, by Gustave Doré / SuperStock

Baker Publishing Group publications use paper produced from sustainable forestry practices and postconsumer waste whenever possible.

26 27 28 29 30 31 7 6 5 4

For my dad

Contents

Acknowledgments

No book is written alone, and every project is helped by many unseen hands. I'm grateful to the many who have helped this undertaking along: my colleagues who endured unsolicited conversations on the Law; my dean and friend, Phil Tallon, who found ways to support my research and encourage me along the way; Chris Kugler, who, to get me to stop bothering him with observations, suggested that I just write a book instead (but sincerely, his encouragement got this project off the ground); Bryan Dyer, Wells Turner, Cody Hinkle, and the team at Baker, who have provided helpful insights throughout; the anonymous reviewer, whoever you may be: the book is stronger for your comments; Heights Church, where I serve as the teaching pastor, who listened to and engaged with a seed form of these ideas in Bible studies; all the participants in Houston Christian University's theology seminar who provided feedback on substantial portions of the arguments in this book; and my students, whose questions and insights over the years have nuanced many points.

Many colleagues and friends read portions or whole drafts of the book, and many more lent a listening ear throughout the process, for which I'm very grateful. My dad and brother, Robert and Michael, read whole drafts multiple times. An immense help. Kyle Sherling read portions and offered critical insights; Oren Hayon always offered a listening ear, armed with references; Yair Furstenberg listened and talked for hours over the shape of the whole project and the particulars of several arguments; David Moffitt was a source of encouragement and advice throughout.

I also owe special thanks to Jason Staples and Logan Williams. Jason provided invaluable feedback on several chapters and helpful conversation throughout the process; I hope he forgives me if the final product is not as punchy as he'd like. And Logan—with whom I converse daily, if not *hourly*, about all things related to the Law, restoration eschatology, Second Temple Judaism, and much else—sharpened my thoughts and this project. Though any errors are my own, the book is stronger from all their comments.

My parents, Robert and Sue, have offered endless support and encouragement. My wife, Meghan, and our three kids—Elijah, Kate, and Elizabeth—are a constant stream of joy and encouragement. Indescribable gifts.

Abbreviations

General and Bibliographic

[ ] or ( )	encloses alternate versification when different from English Bible verse numbering (e.g., Joel 2:28–32 [3:1–5 MT, LXX])	Eng.	English
BCE	before the Common Era	esp.	especially
ca.	*circa*, about	etc.	*et cetera*, and so forth, and the rest
CE	Common Era	frag(s).	fragment(s)
cent.	century	HB	Hebrew Bible
chap(s).	chapter(s)	i.e.	*id est*, that is
col.	column	NT	New Testament
cp.	compare	OT	Old Testament
e.g.	*exempli gratia*, for example	par.	parallel
		repr.	reprint
		trans.	translated by
		v(v).	verse(s)

Old Testament

Gen.	Genesis	Neh.	Nehemiah	Hosea	Hosea
Exod.	Exodus	Esther	Esther	Joel	Joel
Lev.	Leviticus	Job	Job	Amos	Amos
Num.	Numbers	Ps(s).	Psalm(s)	Obad.	Obadiah
Deut.	Deuteronomy	Prov.	Proverbs	Jon.	Jonah
Josh.	Joshua	Eccles.	Ecclesiastes	Mic.	Micah
Judg.	Judges	Song	Song of Songs	Nah.	Nahum
Ruth	Ruth	Isa.	Isaiah	Hab.	Habakkuk
1–2 Sam.	1–2 Samuel	Jer.	Jeremiah	Zeph.	Zephaniah
1–2 Kings	1–2 Kings	Lam.	Lamentations	Hag.	Haggai
1–2 Chron.	1–2 Chronicles	Ezek.	Ezekiel	Zech.	Zechariah
Ezra	Ezra	Dan.	Daniel	Mal.	Malachi

New Testament

Matt.	Matthew	1–2 Thess.	1–2 Thessalonians
Mark	Mark	1–2 Tim.	1–2 Timothy
Luke	Luke	Titus	Titus
John	John	Philem.	Philemon
Acts	Acts of the Apostles	Heb.	Hebrews
Rom.	Romans	James	James
1–2 Cor.	1–2 Corinthians	1–2 Pet.	1–2 Peter
Gal.	Galatians	1–3 John	1–3 John
Eph.	Ephesians	Jude	Jude
Phil.	Philippians	Rev.	Revelation
Col.	Colossians		

Old Testament Apocrypha / Deuterocanonical Works

Bar.	Baruch	1–4 Macc.	1–4 Maccabees	Tob.	Tobit
2 Esd.	2 Esdras	Sir.	Sirach	Wis.	Wisdom
Jdt.	Judith	Sus.	Susanna		

Old Testament Pseudepigrapha

Apocr. Ezek.	Apocryphon of Ezekiel	Ps.-Phoc.	Pseudo-Phocylides
2 Bar.	2 Baruch (Syriac Apocalypse)	Pss. Sol.	Psalms of Solomon
1 En.	1 Enoch (Ethiopic Apocalypse)	Sib. Or.	Sibylline Oracles
2 En.	2 Enoch (Slavonic Apocalypse)	T. Iss.	Testament of Issachar
Jos. Asen.	Joseph and Aseneth	T. Naph.	Testament of Naphtali
Jub.	Jubilees	T. Reu.	Testament of Reuben
LAE	Life of Adam and Eve		

Qumran / Dead Sea Scrolls

CD	Damascus Document	4Q387	Jeremiah C[b]
CD-A	Damascus Document[a]	4Q389	Jeremiah C[d]
1QS	Community Rule	4Q390	Apocryphon of Jeremiah
4Q37	Deut[j], the text of Deuteronomy	4Q504	Words of the Luminaries[a]
4Q159	Ordinances[a]	11QMelch	Melchizedek
4Q169	Nahum Pesher	11QT[a]	Temple Scroll[a]
4Q265	Serek Damascus		

Rabbinic and Hellenistic Jewish Sources

Abbreviations appearing before tractate names indicate the following sources: Mishnah (m.), Tosefta (t.), Babylonian Talmud (b.), and Jerusalem/Palestinian Talmud (y.).

Ag. Ap.	Josephus, *Against Apion*	Ber.	tractate Berakhot
Ant.	Josephus, *Antiquities of the Jews*	*Decalogue*	Philo, *On the Decalogue*

Git.	tractate Gittin
J.W.	Josephus, *Jewish War*
Lev. Rab.	Leviticus Rabbah (a midrash)
Migration	Philo, *On the Migration of Abraham*
Ned.	tractate Nedarim
Neg.	tractate Nega'im
Num. Rab.	Numbers Rabbah (a midrash)
Pesah.	tractate Pesahim
Rewards	Philo, *On Rewards and Punishments*
Rosh Hash.	tractate Rosh Hashanah
Sacrifices	Philo, *On the Sacrifices of Cain and Abel*
Shabb.	tractate Shabbat
Shev.	tractate Shevi'it
Spec. Laws	Philo, *On the Special Laws*
Tg. Jer.	Targum Jeremiah
Yad.	tractate Yadayim

Bible Texts and Versions

AT	author's translation
ESV	English Standard Version (2001)
LXX	Septuagint, Greek Old Testament
MT	Masoretic Text of the Hebrew Bible
NASB	New American Standard Version (2020)
NIV	New International Version (2011)
NRSV	New Revised Standard Version (1989)

Modern Secondary Sources

AB	Anchor Bible
AGJU	Arbeiten zur Geschichte des antiken Judentums und des Urchristentums
AJEC	Ancient Judaism and Early Christianity
ApOTC	Apollos Old Testament Commentary
AUSS	*Andrews University Seminary Studies*
BECNT	Baker Exegetical Commentary on the New Testament
BIS	Biblical Interpretation Series
BJS	Brown Judaic Studies
BRev	*Bible Review*
BTB	*Biblical Theology Bulletin*
BZABR	Beihefte zur Zeitschrift für altorientalische und biblische Rechtsgeschichte
BZNW	Beihefte zur Zeitschrift für die neutestamentliche Wissenschaft
CBQ	*Catholic Biblical Quarterly*
CCSS	Catholic Commentary on Sacred Scripture
CEJL	Commentaries on Early Jewish Literature
CNT	Commentaire du Nouveau Testament
DSD	*Dead Sea Discoveries*
EBC	Expositor's Bible Commentary
ECL	Early Christian Literature
EvT	*Evangelische Theologie*
FAT	Forschungen zum Alten Testament
FRLANT	Forschungen zur Religion und Literatur des Alten und Neuen Testaments
HeyJ	*Heythrop Journal*
HTR	*Harvard Theological Review*
ICC	International Critical Commentary
JBL	*Journal of Biblical Literature*
JJS	*Journal of Jewish Studies*
JPSTC	Jewish Publication Society Torah Commentary
JSHJ	*Journal for the Study of the Historical Jesus*
JSJ	*Journal for the Study of Judaism in the Persian, Hellenistic, and Roman Periods*
JSJSup	Supplements for the Journal for the Study of Judaism in the Persian, Hellenistic, and Roman Periods
JSNT	*Journal for the Study of the New Testament*

JSNTSup Journal for the Study of the New Testament Supplement Series
JSOTSup Journal for the Study of the Old Testament Supplement Series
JSQ *Jewish Studies Quarterly*
LCL Loeb Classical Library
LHBOTS Library of Hebrew Bible / Old Testament Studies
LNTS The Library of New Testament Studies
NAC New American Commentary
NCBC New Cambridge Bible Commentary
NICNT New International Commentary on the New Testament
NICOT New International Commentary on the Old Testament
NIGTC New International Greek Testament Commentary
NovT *Novum Testamentum*
NTS *New Testament Studies*
NTTSD New Testament Tools, Studies, and Documents
ÖBS Österreichische biblische Studien
OTM Old Testament Message
OTP *Old Testament Pseudepigrapha*. Edited by James H. Charlesworth. 2 vols. New York: Doubleday, 1983–85
PRSt *Perspectives in Religious Studies*
RBS Resources for Biblical Study
RevQ *Revue de Qumrân*
SBLMS Society of Biblical Literature Monograph Series
SCJR *Studies in Christian-Jewish Relations*
SHBC Smyth & Helwys Bible Commentary
SNT Studien zum Neuen Testament
SNTSMS Society for New Testament Studies Monograph Series
SNTW Studies of the New Testament and Its World
SP Sacra Pagina
SPCK Society for Promoting Christian Knowledge
SPNT Studies on Personalities of the New Testament
SR *Studies in Religion*
STDJ Studies on the Texts of the Desert of Judah
SUNT Studien zur Umwelt des Neuen Testaments
TBN Themes in Biblical Narrative
THNTC Two Horizons New Testament Commentary
TNTC Tyndale New Testament Commentaries
TSAJ Texte und Studien zum antiken Judentum
VT *Vetus Testamentum*
WBC Word Biblical Commentary
WUNT Wissenschaftliche Untersuchungen zum Neuen Testament
YJS Yale Judaica Series
ZECNT Zondervan Exegetical Commentary on the New Testament
ZNW *Zeitschrift für die neutestamentliche Wissenschaft und die Kunde der älteren Kirche*

Introduction

"Teacher, what good thing shall I do that I may obtain eternal life?" When a man asked Jesus this question, he answered plainly, "If you want to enter life, keep the commandments" (Matt. 19:16–17).[1] Despite clearly commending doing the Law to "enter into life," the Gospel Coalition published an online article in 2020 titled "Survey: Majority of American Christians Don't Believe the Gospel," in which the author wrote the following:

> The Gospel of Matthew tells of a rich young man who asked Jesus what good works he must do to inherit eternal life (Matt. 19:16). Jesus responded that if the man wanted to be judged by his works, then he must keep the entire Law—and do so perfectly. The young man thought he had done enough good works to earn a place in heaven because he was judging himself by man-made standards rather than the perfect standard of God. But that's not how it works. As the apostle James clarifies, "For whoever keeps the whole law and yet stumbles in one point, he has become guilty of all" (James 2:10).[2]

I confess that this strikes me as an odd reading of Matt. 19. Jesus did not contextualize the man's question as his desire "to be judged by his works." Instead, Jesus receives the question as a good faith attempt on the man's part to learn from one widely recognized as an authoritative teacher. Rather than assert that the man "must keep the entire Law—and do so perfectly," Jesus responded simply, "Keep the commandments" (19:17). His answer does not

1. Unless otherwise indicated, all OT and NT quotations are from the New American Standard Bible (NASB), though capitalization and some other typographic features have been adjusted to match current usage. Quotations from the so-called deuterocanonical OT books are from the NRSV unless otherwise indicated.

2. Carter, "Survey."

appear to be a stepping stone offered toward helping the man realize *instead* his need for grace. And Jesus does not say "the entire Law," but in response to the man's question, "Which ones?" he specifies a discrete body of commandments (19:18–21). And he does not say that the man would need to obey "perfectly." In the prior chapter, Jesus instructs the disciples how to respond to members in the assembly who commit transgressions (18:15–17), demonstrating that the commission of transgressions (thus, not "perfect" obedience) is an assumed aspect of the covenantal relationship between God and the assembly. Moreover, Jesus repeatedly and explicitly teaches that when the Son of Man comes, he will "repay every person according to his deeds" (16:27; cp. 25:14–46). Thus, it is not the man's desire "to be judged by his works" that compels Jesus to answer so; rather, Jesus's conviction that he, as the future judge, would judge "each person according to his work" conditions his directive to "keep the commandments." After affirming that he has kept the commandments, the man asks, "What am I still lacking?" (19:20), indicating that Jesus's instruction "Come, follow me" (19:21) does not negate but complements his previous answer regarding the commandments. Following Jesus, then, does not replace "keeping the commandments" but supplements it. Even more startling than the quoted reading of Matt. 19 from the Gospel Coalition is its presentation in an article that laments misunderstanding "the gospel." Based on the article's framing, one wonders, in light of my own reading offered above, whether Jesus would end up on the "wrong side" of this debate.

Frameworks like those on display in this article tend to describe Jesus's critique of his contemporaries (or his ancestral "religion") in terms of their "legalism," understood as a person's belief that he or she can "earn a place in heaven" by doing "enough good works." And though this article is published by the Gospel Coalition, views like it are typically downstream of historical theology and NT scholarship indebted to misinformed understandings of the Law and early Judaism. Moreover, some NT scholars continue to argue that "legalistic" (as just described) appropriately describes some Jewish groups of Jesus's day, including the Pharisees or other Jewish "leaders" in the Gospels,[3] but due to the landmark study by E. P. Sanders,[4] such claims are rarer. Sanders described the Jewish "pattern of religion" within the time of Jesus as "covenantal nomism": Israel is God's people, chosen by God and given the Law, and forgiveness for transgressions and maintenance of the covenant relationship is available through human repentance and the divinely

3. See, e.g., Hellerman, *People of God*, 113–14.
4. E. P. Sanders, *Paul and Palestinian Judaism*.

prescribed sacrificial system.[5] Thus, "legalistic" does not appropriately describe the Jewish "pattern of religion" for two reasons: First, a Jew was in the covenant by birth (not meritorious effort). Second, maintenance of his or her standing in the covenant did not depend on sinless, perfect obedience; rather, the commission of transgressions was an assumed aspect of the covenantal relationship, remedied regularly through the divinely prescribed sacrifices.[6]

But even if the specter of "legalism" is mostly banished in current biblical scholarship, it still haunts popular religious discourse in North America, wherein "Pharisee" is often a slur, Pharisees are employed as a foil for a supposedly Christian theology of grace, and any pontification about rules is denounced as "Pharisaical."[7] Such disjunctive depictions of Jesus and the Pharisees, or Jesus and his Jewish contemporaries, or even Jesus and the Law itself, are occasioned by controversies in the Gospels that appear to depict Jesus as either intentionally breaking the Law (e.g., his healings on the Sabbath) or teaching its abrogation (e.g., his supposed dissolution of the food laws in Mark 7:19). Such disputes encouraged scholarly explanations to the effect that Jesus was compassionate and gracious over against the legalistic Pharisees, or that Jesus enacted an authoritative abrogation of the divine law due either to his "enlightened" understanding of God's expectations and graciousness or to his understanding of salvation history.[8] These interpretative options often employ a certain (mis)reading of Paul as a lens by which to construe Jesus's disputes with the Pharisees, with the result that Jesus and Paul both are thought to promote a religion of grace and inclusivity over against a legalistic, particularistic Judaism.

Additionally, the notion that Jesus dispensed with cherished elements of his ancestral customs is enshrined both in the popular (American) conscience

5. E. P. Sanders, *Paul and Palestinian Judaism*, 17.

6. Novenson (*Paul and Judaism*, 115–21) ponders whether Sanders's contribution might have made a more radical criticism had he not ceded use of the term "legalism" to those who employ it pejoratively. Sanders chose the term "nomism" to describe his view, but as Novenson points out, etymologically there is no distinction between "legalism" (deriving from Latin *lex*) and "nomism" (from Greek *nomos*). Both mean "law-ism." However, the connotations of a word are always greater than the sum of its lexical seeds. So, while I agree with Novenson that if one could overlook the pejorative connotations (hypocritical, compassionless, etc.), "legalism" could be a useful descriptor of both Jesus's and the Pharisees' practice of their customs; however, the pejorative connotations of the term currently perdure. Hence, I will continue to use "nomism" to describe first-century Jewish practice of the Law. If Novenson's work turns that ship, I'll get on board.

7. For a thorough introduction to the Pharisees that corrects such misunderstandings and historically contextualizes their practices, see Sievers and A.-J. Levine, *Pharisees*.

8. "Salvation history" does condition Jesus's interpretations but not in the ways depicted by some.

and in many works of scholarly literature—even ones that insist upon "the Jewishness" of Jesus. While many have rightly concluded that "legalistic" (in the pejorative sense) misdescribes Jewish religion, ancient or modern, other equally misleading descriptors replaced it. Instead of legalism, Jesus supposedly critiqued the purity or sacrificial system per se, the external rituals and badges of Jewish identity, Jewish nationalism, or, to the degree that it reinforces the latter, the Law itself.[9]

For example, regarding Jesus's "critique" of his contemporaries, N. T. Wright states:

> To put it simply, the Temple cult, and the observance of sabbaths, of food taboos, and of circumcision were the key things which marked out Jew from Gentile, which (in other words) maintained and reinforced exactly this agenda [of national liberation], both political and religious, of the hard-line Pharisees. . . . And the object of [Jesus's] critique, I suggest, was the "zeal" that was leading Israel to ruin—and which was maintained and reinforced by precisely those aspects of Torah which marked out Israel over against her pagan neighbors.[10]

According to Wright, the Law had become a test of loyalty to Israel's aspiration of national liberation, reinforced by the victories won by zealous Law-keepers after the crisis of 167 BCE. To the degree that Jesus critiqued the zeal inherent in such aspirations (on Wright's view), Jesus made redundant the symbols—temple cult, Sabbath, purity codes, food taboos—that bolstered that zeal.[11]

But depictions in which Jesus critiques either legalism, external rituals, or a "nationalism" of sorts do not sit well with a Jesus who declares:

> Do not presume that I came to abolish the Law or the Prophets; I did not come to abolish, but to fulfill. For truly I say to you, until heaven and earth pass away, not the smallest letter or stroke of a letter shall pass from the Law, until all is accomplished. Therefore, whoever nullifies one of the least of these commandments, and teaches others to do the same, shall be called least in the kingdom of heaven. (Matt. 5:17–19)[12]

9. Wright, *Victory of God*, 384–85, 390, 395–96, 398.

10. Wright, *Victory of God*, 384–85.

11. So also Hellerman, *People of God*. In both Wright and Hellerman, a "new perspective on Paul" approach to the Law—which sees Paul setting aside the Law, understood as a sociological boundary marker between Jews and gentiles—is evinced not just by the canonical Gospels, but by "the historical Jesus" due to his intent to realize God's goal of a multiethnic "people of God."

12. This text is not discussed (nor is it in the index) in Hellerman, *People of God*. It is mentioned once in Wright (*Victory of God*, 289) in a parenthetical comment with no interpretation of particulars. One wonders how Jesus's insistence that "the least of these commandments"

One prooftext does not automatically falsify alternative accounts. But in addition to Matt. 5:17–19, consider the following:

> But woe to you Pharisees! For you pay tithe of mint and rue and every kind of garden herb, and yet you ignore justice and the love of God; but these are the things you should have done *without neglecting the others*. (Luke 11:42)

> "Neglecting the commandment of God, you hold to the tradition of men." He was also saying to them, "You are experts at setting aside the commandment of God in order to keep your tradition." (Mark 7:8–9)

> If you want to enter life, keep the commandments. (Matt. 19:17)

> For the Son of Man is going to come in the glory of his Father with his angels, and will then repay every person according to his deeds. (Matt. 16:27)

These texts depict a Jesus who requires that the whole Law be kept and who, as the eschatological judge, will recompense people according to their deeds. Furthermore, he circumscribes his earthly ministry to his kinspeople, expecting that his Jewish disciples would be leaders over the regathered tribes of Israel:

> These twelve Jesus sent out after instructing them, saying, "Do not go on a road to Gentiles, and do not enter any city of Samaritans; but rather go to the lost sheep of the house of Israel." (Matt. 10:5–6)

> And you are the ones who have stood by me in my trials, and just as my Father has granted me a kingdom, I grant you that you may eat and drink at my table in my kingdom, and you will sit on thrones judging the twelve tribes of Israel. (Luke 22:28–30)

Such sayings require integration within a framework that does not see Jesus critiquing legalism, the Law, or Jewish nationalism. That framework, I suggest, is what some have aptly named "restoration eschatology":[13]

- God has chosen Israel as his "own possession among all the peoples" (Exod. 19:5) and given them the Law, promising blessings if the covenant

---

may not be annulled squares with approaches arguing that Jesus "made redundant" whole swaths of the Law.

13. For this label and a survey of texts, see E. P. Sanders, *Jesus and Judaism*, 267–69.

is maintained and punitive "curses" (Deut. 28) or "discipline" (Lev. 26 ESV) if the covenant is broken.

- Israel breaches the covenant and so is suffering under the promised punitive discipline, and they await the promised restoration following their endurance of that discipline and repentance.
- The discipline entails exile, subjugation (in or out of the land) to foreign nations and their gods, a relative inability to keep all aspects of the Law given that subjugation, the departure of the divine glory, the temple's destruction, and, assuming a rebuilt temple, a question mark hovering over the acceptability of the sacrifices offered there (either because of the corrupt priesthood or the disqualifying disobedience of the people).
- The restoration of the people entails the obverse: the return of the divine glory, the return of the people to the land, a reunification of the scattered tribes, a glorified temple, the judgment of Israel's opponents (human and divine), and a transformed heart enabling the proper keeping of the Law.

This sequence is present in Deut. 28–32 and Lev. 26, retrieved and amplified in the prophetic literature, and assumed and adapted in much Second Temple literature. In this framework, the restoration of the covenant entails not simply Israel's renewed enjoyment of lost "blessings" but also the expectation and enablement of the proper keeping of the God-given Law. In the restoration, Israel will return to God and obey his commands (Deut. 30:1–2), and God will "circumcise their hearts" so that they "love the Lord [their] God" (Deut. 30:6); God will put his Law "within them and write it on their heart" (Jer. 31:33); and he will replace the heart of stone with one of flesh and place his own spirit in them, and they will be careful to "follow [his] ordinances" (Ezek. 36:26–27).

Though variegated, a stable meaning emerges: when Israel is restored, they will keep the Law as God intended, and the sequence of disobedience, punishment, and restoration won't be cyclical because God will transform their heart to enable this obedience. It is within the unfolding of this framework that the Gospels depict Jesus: he is Israel's promised deliverer who relieves Israel of their punitive discipline, bringing the awaited "consolation of Israel" (Luke 2:25), and he teaches Israel the authoritative interpretation of the Law to aid its full keeping. In this way, this book argues that Jesus's legal teaching, his disputes about the Law's proper keeping, and his calling sinners to repentance are not in opposition to the Law but are an intramural discourse about its keeping in light of the dawning of the eschatological age. Because of the widespread agreement among his Jewish contemporaries that restoration is a desideratum, during which the Law would finally be kept, and because of the impending judgment that would follow the restoration, in which God would judge between "the righteous and the wicked" (e.g., Mal. 3:18; Isa. 1:27–31; cp. Matt. 13:41–42), Jesus argues with other teachers about the Law's proper observance for the age of restoration, tells his disciples to follow him and his interpretation, and "calls sinners to repentance" and conformity to that interpretation.

• • •

But why the confusion among Jesus's contemporaries? Why the need for argument among Jews about the proper characteristics of the restoration community? Wouldn't the proper praxis of those whom God would mercifully vindicate be abundantly clear? Yes and no.

In Deut. 30:1–3, Moses tells the people that while in exile, if they "return" to God and obey him, God will restore them from captivity, have compassion on them, and regather them. These words become the foundational promise upon which the prophetic call to "return to the Lord your God" is based. If Israel returns to God, they will experience his compassion. Numerous texts follow this pattern:

> "Return, faithless Israel," declares the Lord; / "I will not look at you in anger. / For I am gracious," declares the Lord; / "I will not be angry forever." (Jer. 3:12)

> "Return to me," declares the Lord of armies, "that I may return to you." (Zech. 1:3)

> "From the days of your fathers you have turned away from my statutes, and have not kept them. Return to me, and I will return to you," says the Lord of hosts. (Mal. 3:7)

Despite this prophetic call, the Scriptures regularly lament that the people did not listen, continuing instead in rebellion and discipline. Nehemiah 9 states, "But they became rebellious and revolted against you, / And threw your Law behind their backs / And killed your prophets who had admonished them / In order to bring them back to you. . . . However, you remained patient with them for many years, / And admonished them by your Spirit through your prophets, / Yet they would not listen. / Therefore you handed them over to the peoples of the lands" (vv. 26, 30). Thus Nehemiah establishes that their continued subjugation "into the hand of the peoples of the lands" is a consequence not simply of their original covenant violation but of their refusal to "return" at the prophetic summons.

Zechariah and Malachi similarly state that the people heard the call of the prophets but did not "return." Zechariah, written after some Judahites had returned to the land but before the temple was rebuilt, states unambiguously: Do not be like your ancestors who didn't listen to the prophets' summons to return, but return to me now (see Zech. 1:3–4; see also 8:14–23). Malachi, written after the return to the land and the reconstruction of the temple, states that, even still, the desired "return" of the people had not yet occurred (Mal. 3:7). Both Zechariah and Malachi therefore indicate that a return to the land and the rebuilt temple did not signal the fulfillment of the restoration.

Consequently, in the eyes of many Second Temple Jews, what was required was the return of the people.[14] But even if this requirement were agreed upon by the people, the question remains: "How shall we return?" Thus Mal. 3:7 continues: "'Return to me, and I will return to you,' says the LORD of armies. *'But you say, "How shall we return?"'*" Realizing that returning to God is necessary to participate in the impending restoration, they justifiably ask for the next critical piece of information: *How?*

Even if "keeping the Law" were assumed to be a feature of the return, as several texts imply (Deut. 30:2; Jer. 17:19–25; Dan. 9:11–15; Neh. 9:16, 26; Mal. 4:4), it would still be incumbent upon a leader, teacher, or prophet to provide authoritative instruction concerning what it would mean to keep the Law rightly, as the Law always requires interpretation. For example, the command to do no work on the Sabbath (Exod. 20:10) requires defining what constitutes "work." Thus, the Law requires interpretation. *How* to return requires an answer. Therefore, what it means to *return* to *Law-keeping* when the stake is *restoration* is especially significant. Combining these premises concerning the Law and the return yields precisely the kind of legal questions we find in the Gospels amid Jesus's announcement of the restoration: *"How shall we return?"* God's people ask (Mal. 3:7). *"What must I do to inherit eternal life?"* asks the young man (Matt. 19:16).

Thus, the question in Matt. 19:16 is not from a man who egotistically "wanted to be judged by his works."[15] It is not the question of one who has wrongly placed his confidence in the Law or has an ill-conceived notion of "nationalism" or his own self-righteousness. Rather, it is a question from a

14. My point is not that "all Jews everywhere" thought this but simply that this expectation is widely expressed in many Second Temple texts based on a demonstrably common pattern of interpretation of certain biblical passages (explored in chap. 2 below).

15. Carter, "Survey."

member of the people "who were in a state of expectation" (Luke 3:15), who have heard that restoration and God's reign have drawn near. This unnamed man has heard that this teacher announces the way to participation in the life to come, and he is eager to know: How can I ensure that I am among the people who "return" to God? This teacher responds, "Keep the commandments" (Matt. 19:17).

This matrix of "restoration eschatology" provides the sociological and soteriological context for Jesus's teaching, his disputes with other teachers, and his call of sinners to repentance according to the Synoptic Gospels. It is *sociological* because he is calling *a people* to repentance, teaching them the characteristics of those who will experience the restoration. It is *soteriological* because it is this group who will inherit eternal life (Matt. 19:16–17, etc.). Jesus, as the God-sent agent of the restoration, has come to call Israel to repentance in view of the impending restoration and divine judgment. Though Jesus's ministry cannot be reduced to nomistic teaching, a vital aspect of his career was the authoritative teaching of the Law in view of God's imminent faithfulness to show mercy to those who return to him. This agenda contextualizes Jesus's teaching not as an abstract moral code or, worse, an abolition of the God-given Law, but as the answer to the question "How shall we return?" This book is an attempt to describe the Synoptic presentation of Jesus's mission and instruction of the Law within the restorationist framework described above.

Outline of *Jesus and the Law of Moses*

In chapter 1, I will summarize the role of the Law in the covenantal relationship according to the Pentateuch, arguing against frameworks that suggest a supposed "legalism," "externalism," "compassionless exclusivism," or "nationalism" inherent in the OT or early Judaism to which Jesus is supposedly a foil. I will also provide a taxonomy of conditions that affect legal obligations.

Chapter 2 will survey the motif of restoration in the Jewish Scriptures and Second Temple texts, including the Gospels, demonstrating both the widespread belief in a prolonged discipline, the concomitant expectation of restoration, and the inevitable variation of "answers" to the question "How shall we return?"

Chapters 3, 4, and 5 will contextualize various discourses of Jesus within a restorationist framework. Chapter 3 will focus on the interpretation of the Law in Matt. 5:21–48, and chapters 4–5 will address nomistic controversies with Jesus's contemporaries in the Synoptic Gospels.

Chapter 6 will discuss how Jesus's prediction of the temple's destruction and his death cohere with his goal of the restoration of Israel, and how those matters relate to the Law.

I will conclude with reflections on what this picture of Jesus as a legal interpreter means for the nascent generation of the messianic group and consider age-old questions regarding continuity between the OT and Jesus, the Gospels and Acts, and the Gospels and Paul.

A Final Note

Before proceeding, a word on method and the goal of this book. This is not a book on the so-called historical Jesus. Adapting Jeff Winger's opinion on "religion" (from the television show *Community*), "To me, the historical Jesus is like Paul Rudd. I see the appeal, and I would never take it away from anyone. But I would also never stand in line for it."[16] I am grateful for the scholars who have caused me to reflect more deeply on the method of historical inquiry. While the historical contexts of Matthew, Mark, and Luke will contextualize my interpretation, my goal is neither to adjudicate the historicity of the events narrated in the Synoptic Gospels nor to distill the distinct accounts into the "original" and subject that form to inquiry. My goal is to interpret various episodes in the Synoptic Gospels within their literary and historical settings (i.e., their respective narratives and their mid-first-century Jewish context) to present a reading of their "Jesus and the Law" scenes that is different from those often set forth in contemporary scholarship. In this sense, this book is neither a study of exclusively Mark's or Matthew's or Luke's Jesus nor an account of "the historical Jesus." Rather, it is an attempt to describe the Synoptic presentation of Jesus and interpret each episode within its own narrative setting. I intend to describe the Synoptic presentation by looking at distinct events in a given Gospel to create a mosaic whose contributing pieces are themselves whole pictures. In practice, this endeavor will sometimes entail examining a scene that is unique to one Gospel (e.g., Luke 11:38–41) or focusing on one account largely without appeal to its alternate version in another Gospel (e.g., Mark 7:1–19 without much attention to Matt. 15:1–20). My point is not to suggest that the differences between accounts are meaningless; rather, my method is motivated by two concerns. First, to achieve a "Synoptic presentation," it seems fitting to focus on a single Synoptic account lest I create a composite of all the accounts that is itself available in no specific

16. "Comparative Religion," season 1, episode 12, written by Liz Cackowski, directed by Adam Davidson, aired December 10, 2009, on NBC.

Gospel. A full examination of each shared scene would be more thorough,[17] but space does not permit such a treatment, and even if completed, its results would not aid my goal in this book. However, meaningful differences will be briefly engaged in the footnotes.

This brings me to my second concern. One motive for writing is to counter prevalent readings of the material that I think are incomplete or misleading. To that end, it is not necessary to examine each version or to distill what may be the original, but instead we must focus on representative versions, or even the "hardest" version, of the saying from which the misleading readings have flowered. For example, because scholars have occasionally interpreted Jesus's interaction with the *lepros* in Mark 1:40–44 and parallels to indicate Jesus's indifference to purity regulations or even as a challenge to the Jerusalem temple, and because Matthew's and Luke's versions are nearly identical, it is sufficient to focus on Mark's version both to provide a positive interpretation of the event and to counter widespread but misinformed readings of the scene. By focusing on representative examples from distinct accounts, my goal is to present a portrait of Jesus's interpretation of the Law according to the Synoptic Gospels. Because I argue that a restoration-eschatological framework contextualizes the Synoptic accounts, attention will be given to each when establishing this commonality. Likewise, when turning to Jesus's final week in Jerusalem, because of the vast overlap and yet subtle distinctions among the Gospels, more attention will be given to the differences in each, lest I create a portrait distilled from only one Gospel or, worse, a composite available in none of them.

17. For such an account, I highly recommend Oliver, *Torah Praxis*.

1

Israel and the Law of Moses

"Let them build me a sanctuary so I may dwell among them" (Exod. 25:8 AT). So God speaks to Moses atop Mount Sinai after delivering the people from Egypt and their gods. After Israel constructed a tabernacle per God's specifications, "the glory of the Lord filled the tabernacle" (Exod. 40:34). Now dwelling in their midst, God delivers to Moses regulations by which the people should maintain the purity of the sacred space and themselves and express their allegiance to this God and no others.[1] Throughout the Torah more widely, God instructs Israel in how they ought to obey him and live justly toward each other. This sequence of events implies that Israel does not keep these commandments in order to become God's covenantal people; they are already God's covenantal people whom he redeemed from slavery, and so now they express their allegiance to him through this obedience.

The obedience required to maintain the covenant is not depicted as that of "sinless perfection." God is aware of Israel's sinfulness and "stubbornness" (on display since crossing the sea; Deut. 9:6–7), and knowing this, he both commands their obedience and instructs how they can procure the forgiveness and atonement on offer through the divinely prescribed sacrifices. Thus Israel's commission of transgressions is an assumed aspect of the covenantal relationship. As Paula Fredriksen puts it, "God builds a relationship meant to last."[2] Many sins can be atoned for through the purification offering and

1. I refer here to Leviticus, but such regulations are scattered throughout the Pentateuch.
2. Fredriksen, *Paul*, 16.

guilt offering,[3] and in itself an individual Israelite sinning does not remove him or her from the people, nor does it automatically result in a breach of the covenant. Someone sins, and recognizing their guilt, they can make the requisite offering, and "the priest shall make atonement for them, and they will be forgiven" (Lev. 4:20). Moreover, God prescribes an annual ritual ("the Day of Atonement/Purification") by which the entire sacred space and the people receive atonement and cleansing (Lev. 16:30–34) from "all their sins" (Lev. 16:34).

The depiction, therefore, of Israel living under the Law is not that of a people bearing an intolerable burden by which they struggled to "earn" their salvation, or a burden causing despair of ever finding a gracious God. On the contrary, the Law assured them of God's desire to dwell with them, revealed to them God's requirements, and declared to them the divinely prescribed means through which they could regularly commune with God and experience his forgiveness and grace.

So far, so good. Nothing thus far should come as a surprise (though it should forestall attempts to describe this pattern of religion pejoratively as "legalism"). However, numerous misunderstandings pertaining to the Law and its interpretation haunt the field of NT studies, not to mention Christian preaching and teaching. Many of these misunderstandings relate to the language of (im)purity, purification, and eating while pure/impure.[4] Because contemporary readings of Jesus so often falter on these matters, a crash course on these categories as the Law presents them is necessary before turning to an evaluation of some contemporary scholarship.

I'll begin with ritual (im)purity. Ritual purity is a biological-legal state denoting a lack of impurity.[5] Ritual impurity is a biological-legal state resultant

3. On Lev. 4's offering as the "purification" rather than "sin" offering, see Milgrom, *Leviticus 1–16*, 253–58.

4. Matthew Thiessen has recently written (persuasively) on Jesus and impurity in *Jesus and the Forces of Death*. For discussion of (im)purity in the Bible and early Jewish sources, see Klawans, *Impurity and Sin*, 3–42; Wassén, "Jewishness of Jesus"; Feder, *Purity and Pollution*; Adler, *Origins of Judaism*, 50–86; Furstenberg, *Purity and Identity*.

5. "Ritual" impurity is the term advocated by Klawans (*Impurity and Sin*, 3–42) to refer to the category of impurity resulting from natural bodily occurrences. He distinguishes this from "moral" impurity, which refers to impurity resulting from sin. Ritual impurity is not sinful, is shareable by contact or shared airspace in a ceilinged room, and is often ameliorated only by washing and waiting (with the exception of *lepra*, prolonged genital discharge, and childbirth, which require sacrifice for atonement/cleansing but not forgiveness). Moral impurity results from certain sins; may nonmetaphorically defile the sinner, land, and/or sanctuary; and is not sharable in the way that ritual impurity is. That is, one who commits murder does not render another person ritually impure by touching them. On moral impurity, see also Wassén, "Moral Impurity." These categories are to be partially distinguished from animal impurity (e.g., pork being labeled "unclean" in Lev. 11:7). The "uncleanness" of certain animals indexes not their

from contact and, in some cases, shared airspace in an enclosed environment with sources of impurity. The sources of impurity are corpses, human bones and graves, certain animal carcasses, menstrual and postpartum blood, semen, irregular penile/vaginal discharge, and a superficial condition labeled *lepra*.[6] Contact or shared airspace in an enclosed room with corpses and/or contact with the above sources renders one impure. But those contracting such impurities are not thereby considered sinful or morally questionable. The events that likely comprise most cases by which one was rendered impure—handling certain animal carcasses, regular seminal discharge through sex or nocturnal emission, and menstruation—are remedied by washing and the arrival of sundown (Lev. 11:24–40; 15:16–24). Cases with more complicated purification procedures—corpse contamination, a human who has recovered from *lepra*, childbirth, and irregular penile/vaginal discharge—require, in addition to washing and waiting, procedures such as shaving and offering sacrifices.

It is important to note, however, that each of these cases is a by-product of having a body subject to death and decay,[7] and none of them is considered sinful. The most morally scrupulous priest and the most recalcitrant nonpriest are equally susceptible to such impurities, and they are remedied in the same way. That is, impurity is an index of one's mortality, not one's

---

capacity to defile by ingestion or by touch while alive, but their prohibited-for-consumption status. Thus one who eats pig does not need to wash and wait till sundown (as one rendered impure by, say, semen) but instead, assuming the act was unintentional, must give a purification offering. This will be explored more in the section on Mark 7. For additional details, see Furstenberg, "Defilement," esp. 195. See also Balberg, *Purity, Body, and Self*, 1–2. Other scholars have also described "gentile impurity" to refer to a kind of moral and/or genealogical impurity thought to be intrinsic to gentiles. On "gentile impurity," see Hayes, *Gentile Impurities*; Thiessen, *Contesting Conversion*. Because many Jewish texts simply employ "impure" to refer to distinct kinds of impurity that behave and are regulated differently, I occasionally employ the heuristic labels "ritual," "moral," and/or "gentile" impurity to clarify the category.

Roy Gane (*Cult and Character*, 160–62) describes ritual impurity in both biological and legal terms based partially on the regulations concerning items in a house with *lepra*. The priest tells the inhabitants to empty the house prior to his inspection (Lev. 14:36) because pronouncing the house "unclean" would render certain items in it unclean. If ritual impurity acted on a solely biological/contagion basis, removing items before the pronouncement would not protect them.

6. These sources of impurity are described in Lev. 12–15; Num. 19. For arguments that *lepra* does not refer to the disease now called "leprosy," see Thiessen, *Forces of Death*, 43–52. I transliterate rather than translate the Greek terms *lepra* (the defiling condition) and *lepros* (a person with *lepra*) because it is not clear what one term could denote the cluster of described conditions affecting houses, skin, and garments, but the English term "leprosy," which refers only to a skin disease, is inadequate.

7. Milgrom (*Leviticus 1–16*, 766–67) theorizes that impurity symbolizes death. Hyam Maccoby (*Ritual and Morality*, 49) refines Milgrom's theory, arguing that impurity "is an expression of the birth-death cycle that comprises mortality."

morality: those affected by such conditions need purification and in some cases "atonement," but not forgiveness. It is telling that the refrain—"the priest shall make atonement for them, and they will be forgiven" (Lev. 4:20; cp. vv. 26, 31, 35)—punctuating the purification offering occasioned by sin does not occur in any of the procedures prescribed for purification. The man with an irregular penile discharge gives a purification offering, but he does not receive forgiveness (15:15). The woman after childbirth offers a purification offering, and Lev. 12:8 assures that "the priest shall make atonement for her, and she will be clean." But in neither case is forgiveness pronounced, because in neither case is it needed.

Moreover, not only is it not sinful to contract ritual impurity; on some occasions, obedience to positive commandments results in impurity. For example, speaking of a man executed for a capital crime, Deut. 21:23 states: "His body is not to be left overnight on the tree, but you shall certainly bury him on the same day." Obeying this commandment would require at least one person to contract corpse impurity. Additionally, in Num. 19 God "commands" (19:2) the preparation and use of the ashes of a red heifer for the purpose of purifying those who have contracted corpse impurity; the priest who sprinkles the bull's blood and contributes materials to the fire (19:4–7), the one who burns the heifer (19:8), the one who gathers and deposits the ashes for future use (19:10), the one who touches the water for the purifying ritual, and the one who sprinkles it (19:21)—all become unclean in the process. Therefore, rather than impurity necessarily signaling one's immorality or sin, occasionally obedience leads to impurity, and the latter impurity is remedied not by repentance or divine forgiveness but by washing and waiting. As Jacob Milgrom demonstrates, a lay Israelite "might contract impurity with impunity."[8]

What Israel must beware of is transmitting their impurity to holy objects. Holy objects include the sanctuary (e.g., Lev. 15:31), sacrificial meals—that is, food from a festal or sacrificial event, whether a Passover meal (Num. 9:6–13) or a peace offering (Lev. 7:19–21)—and possibly the tithe given to the Levites (Deut. 26:13–14). Such spaces/objects must be handled or approached in a state of purity because they are God's earthly residence and/or objects made sacred by dedication to his domain. However, such festivals and sacred meals constitute relatively few occasions in a given day, week, or year of nonpriestly Israelites, the majority of whom live at a distance from the Jerusalem temple. Purity was likely regarded as an ideal state, and impurity did not govern *only* one's approach to the temple; people evidently purified irrespective of any

8. Milgrom, *Leviticus 1–16*, 43.

plan to travel to Jerusalem or the temple.[9] However, my point is simply that the contracting of impurity by nonpriests was not prohibited. Priests were to avoid contracting corpse impurity (Lev. 21:1–4, 10–11), but if they contracted impurity, they would simply wash and be unclean until evening (22:5–7). Grasping this, one can recognize that "becoming impure" is not an occasion for weeping and gnashing of teeth. It's just life.

Additionally, common food—that is, the regular domestic eating encompassing nearly all food eaten by a nonpriest—did not need to be eaten in a state of purity. This should not be surprising. Consider the implications if one could eat only when pure! Any human affected by *lepra* would starve. Women with regular menstrual cycles, who are considered impure for at least the duration of a given cycle (Lev. 15:19), would miss several days of meals. Any who obeyed God's command to bury a corpse wouldn't eat for at least a week, and the woman in Mark 5 with a twelve-year discharge would have been in quite a pickle. The list goes on.[10] The relevant point, especially when interpreting Jesus's practice of eating with "sinners," is that common food did not need to be eaten in a state of purity, and eating while impure did not threaten the sanctity of Israel or indicate the immorality of the eater. Relatedly, it is worth challenging the assumption that the sinners with whom Jesus ate were ritually impure. It is, of course, possible that their status as sinners was earned by a reputed noncompliance with God's laws, including potentially the purity regulations. But their ritual purity status is never stated, and it is conceivable that they were regarded as sinners for some specific reason, such as their occupation or some known moral failures,[11] in which case their ritual purity may not be of concern.[12] However, even if Jesus were ritually defiled by eating with sinners due to their supposed noncompliance with purity regulations (a debatable supposition), it would be no sin. He would merely wash and be clean by sundown. Thus, Jesus's practice of eating with sinners did

9. See the discussion in Adler, *Origins of Judaism*, 50–86. He employs a useful analogy regarding truth-telling. One should always tell the truth (aspire to purity), but one will pick one's words especially carefully when in court (approaching the temple).

10. On purity and common food, see E. P. Sanders, *Jewish Law*, 134–254. For a brief analysis of purity and Jesus studies, see Fredriksen, "Did Jesus Oppose?"

11. James Crossley and Robert J. Myles (*Jesus*, 117) note that when the so-called sinners' "socio-economic status is mentioned, it is *always* to designate oppressive rich people." For a survey of evidence, see Crossley, *Jesus and the Chaos of History*, 96–111.

12. For a refutation of the supposition that tax collectors were "unusually unclean," see Maccoby, "How Unclean Were Tax-Collectors?" Maccoby shows that they did not transmit impurity in a higher degree than others by virtue of their occupation. Moreover, that they are regarded as unclean in certain circumstances does not indicate that they were always regarded as ritually impure, and their potential to transmit impurity indicates not a gross immorality but merely that they are Jewish humans.

not flout the impurity laws or the food regulations; nor did it threaten the established order of the Law, its interpretation, or the sanctity of Israel. It was simply, but graciously, Jesus's means of rubbing elbows with those he came to call to repentance (see Luke 5:30–32).

To be sure, some degree of purity was a prerequisite for participation in certain communal activities of voluntary associations (e.g., the *haverim*, the Qumran sect, possibly the Pharisees if they are distinct from the *haverim*),[13] but exclusion based on ritual impurity was not soteriologically charged. Impurity may have prevented access to meals with *haverim*, but not being a member did not signal exclusion from Israel or from the life to come. Similarly, the Qumran sect probably considered outsiders impure and not part of the community that would experience salvation; however, this evaluation was based not on outsiders' ritual impurity itself but on their failure to "return" to the Law of Moses (CD-A 15.9; 16.4) and to join "the new covenant" (CD-A 6.19). This is proven in that members of the sect could become impure but not thereby be excluded from "salvation." The impure were temporarily excluded from participation in pure communal meals, but such separation did not signal their exclusion from the community as an outsider.[14]

Returning now to the general public, it was incumbent upon those with an impurity to be aware of their state in order to curb its spread either to food that would be tithed, to someone en route to the temple (lest the traveler need to delay the trip), or to the temple itself by approaching it in an impure state. Apart from these relatively rare events, impurity was a rather quotidian affair. Its seemingly prolonged discussion in Leviticus, Numbers, and Deuteronomy—not to mention its foreignness to many modern, non-Jewish readers—tends to convert this mundane aspect of life (i.e., slipping in and out of purity) into some insurmountable and moralized burden that one could never possibly keep track of. But this reaction merely demonstrates that the customs of a particular group often appear bewildering to outsiders. Simply reverse the situation: imagine the bemused head tilt of an ancient Israelite witnessing the widespread tradition of Christians celebrating Christmas by decorating a dead pine tree (or a fake tree, for the weak of flesh) and stuffing large socks with unwrapped presents. What is commonplace for one group is exotic for others. Such is often the case

13. On the *haverim*, "a voluntary association of fellows who chose to eat their food in a state of ritual purity," see Klawans, *Impurity and Sin*, 108–9. See Furstenberg (*Purity and Identity*, 111–40) for discussion of the distinct purity practices of the Pharisees, rabbinic law, and Qumran sectarian law. See E. P. Sanders (*Jewish Law*, 147–254) for discussion of eating ordinary food in purity (or not) among the voluntary associations.

14. For a detailed study of ritual impurity in Qumran documents, see Werrett, *Ritual Purity*.

with modern, non-Jewish readers encountering Israel's dietary and purity laws. But modern assessments labeling something "exotic" or "burdensome" should not be projected onto the past and imposed on the psyches of the community for whom such laws were second nature, the water in which they swam.

Many readings of Jesus (discussed below) identify his interaction with sinners, and thus people assumed to be impure, as evidence of his own ambivalence or even antagonism toward the purity regulations and the social dynamics they create. But these interpretations trade on misunderstandings of impurity itself, often by moralizing it. In so doing, they depict a Jesus who is for compassion over against purity codes that engender exclusion;[15] or a Jesus opposed to purity because it symbolizes violent, nationalistic aspirations of liberation and separatism;[16] or a Jesus opposed to the *ordo salutis* of Leviticus and its holiness codes and instead offering a "more inclusive" and "loving" view of God.[17] But none of these depictions accurately describes the Law that Jesus interprets or Jesus's interpretation of that Law.

To orient this book's arguments, it will be helpful to evaluate some scholarship from previous decades. How one frames Jesus's interpretation of the Law and his disputes with contemporaries affects how one talks about the Law itself, Jesus's relation to Israel's ancestral customs, their role or function in the restoration, his relation to his kinspeople, and, for some modern interpreters, the distinction between his teaching and that of "Judaism."[18] The positions surveyed are broadly labeled legalism, exclusivism, and nationalism.

Legalism

In scholarly and popular discourse, "legalism" is often used to describe the belief, especially in ancient Judaism, that one can merit salvation by scrupulous Law-keeping. In the previous century, this view was well represented by

15. Borg, *Conflict, Holiness, and Politics*.

16. Wright, *Victory of God*.

17. McKnight, *New Vision*.

18. It is misleading to contrast Jesus with "Judaism" as if the latter refers to a pattern of religion complete with its own soteriology and doctrinal positions from which Jesus distanced himself to start something different—namely, "Christianity." For critical discussion of the latter approach, see Moore, "Christian Writers on Judaism." I refer instead to Jesus's "ancestral customs" and the nation's devotion to the Lord alone. For discussion of *Ioudaismos* ("Judaism") in its ancient context as "the ways of the Judeans," see Mason, "Jews, Judaeans, Judaizing, Judaism." See further discussion in Novenson, *Paul and Judaism*, 36–42.

Rudolf Bultmann. In his *Primitive Christianity in Its Contemporary Setting*, for example, the chapter describing the Judaism contemporary with Jesus is titled "Judaism: Synagogue and Law: Jewish Legalism."[19]

Bultmann claims that in postexilic Judaism, "doing the Law" gave life meaning and order, and because Jews reduced or essentialized the Law to its ritual prescriptions,[20] which were themselves devoid of ethical significance,[21] Bultmann describes the Judaism of Jesus's day as "overscrupulous and pettifogging"[22] legalism that sought to earn God's merit by scrupulously doing the written Law.[23] But the "error of Jewish legalism," Bultmann writes, is that a written commandment can never encompass all ethical requirements.[24] Thus one might keep the written Law but then feel justified in harboring bad intentions or desires. Moreover, in fulfilling the written code, one might presume to have completely done the will of God and that works done in addition to the Law's requirements could earn merit before God.[25]

Within such a system, Jesus arrives to announce and interpret the demand of God: one ought to submit the whole life to God and his demand to love. "As interpretation of the will, the demand, of God, Jesus's message is a great protest against Jewish legalism—i.e., against a form of piety which regards the will of God as expressed in the written Law and in the Tradition which interprets it, a piety which endeavors to win God's favor by the toil of minutely fulfilling the Law's stipulations."[26] Moreover, in centering love, Jesus abrogated the Law's ritual and purity regulations, which he taught were "meaningless."[27] Thus, for Bultmann, "the upshot is that the Old Testament, in so far as it consists of ceremonial and ritual ordinances, is abrogated. Jesus directs a polemic against the legalistic ritualism of the scribes, whose correct external behavior so often went hand in hand with an impure will."[28]

Because Bultmann has judged that Judaism is legalistic, all elements within this "Judaism" are judged with skepticism. But because a different (supposedly ethical, loving) system characterizes Jesus's instruction, those same elements in his teaching are interpreted positively. Thus both Judaism and Jesus prescribe repentance, but because Judaism is legalistic, such repentance is

19. Bultmann, *Primitive Christianity*, 59.
20. Bultmann, *Theology of the New Testament*, 12; Bultmann, *Primitive Christianity*, 62.
21. Bultmann, *Primitive Christianity*, 62, 67–68.
22. Bultmann, *Primitive Christianity*, 67.
23. Bultmann, *Theology of the New Testament*, 12; Bultmann, *Primitive Christianity*, 68–69.
24. Bultmann, *Theology of the New Testament*, 12.
25. Bultmann, *Theology of the New Testament*, 11–12.
26. Bultmann, *Theology of the New Testament*, 11.
27. Bultmann, *Theology of the New Testament*, 18.
28. Bultmann, *Primitive Christianity*, 74.

interpreted as a work that secures merit,[29] whereas the repentance that Jesus demands is authentic.[30] Judaism teaches retributive judgment because it follows a legalistic tooth-for-tooth arrangement;[31] Jesus teaches such judgment because retribution from the loving God is the organic outworking of one's refusal to love one's neighbor.[32] But it is a cruel double standard that interprets the same elements as "legalistic" when "Judaism" teaches it but "organic" when Jesus requires it.

The error of Bultmann's view (and that of others who similarly identify legalism as what Jesus opposed) is demonstrated by a refined understanding of the Law and incorporation of Synoptic material that Bultmann deemed inauthentic. Regarding the latter, Bultmann claims that Matt. 5:17–19 "cannot possibly be genuine."[33] But it is easy to arrive at certain conclusions when one eliminates evidence that opposes it. And regarding legalism, when one assumes a covenantal system in which atonement and forgiveness are offered through a divinely sanctioned sacrificial system, the presence of demands does not require a legalistic view of how one finds God's grace. Jewish literature from Ezra to the Mishnah makes demands of the people but assumes the gracious nature of the God to whom such obedience is directed. Thus a covenantal arrangement in which atonement is divinely offered indicates that the presence of obligations is not contradictory to the belief that salvation comes through God's mercy.[34]

Additionally, Bultmann critiques the written Law by claiming that it does not make demands on a person's desires or intentions and that obedience consists only in the committing or omitting of certain actions.[35] But the Law itself assumes the relevance of intention in its distinction between unintentional sins (e.g., Lev. 4:2), sins that may be intentional but were committed in rashness or fear (5:1, 4), and defiant sins (Num. 15:30). The Law also prohibits both coveting (Exod. 20:17)—referring to an interior intention or desire—and hatred of one's brother "in your heart" (Lev. 19:17). Therefore, Jesus's commands that one ought not hate his brother or commit adultery "in his heart" are not distinct from what the written Law requires but are interpretations of what the Law already says. In short, those who espouse

29. Bultmann, *Primitive Christianity*, 71.

30. Bultmann, *Primitive Christianity*, 76, 78.

31. Bultmann, *Primitive Christianity*, 69.

32. Bultmann, *Primitive Christianity*, 75–79; Bultmann, *Theology of the New Testament*, 20–21.

33. Bultmann, *Theology of the New Testament*, 16.

34. In addition to E. P. Sanders's summary of "covenantal nomism" (*Paul and Palestinian Judaism*, 17), see the response to his critics in Runesson, *Divine Wrath*, 172–79.

35. Bultmann, *Primitive Christianity*, 72; Bultmann, *Theology of the New Testament*, 13.

the above view about Judaism, legalism, Jesus, and the Law often arrive at their conclusions by misinterpreting both Jewish literature and the Gospels to depict a Judaism and a Jesus available in neither.

Compassionless Exclusivism

After numerous scholars throughout the twentieth century amply demonstrated the erroneousness of the portrait of "Jewish legalism" as the foil to Jesus's teaching, a different view arose: sectarian, compassionless exclusivism.

In *Conflict, Holiness, and Politics in the Teachings of Jesus*, Marcus J. Borg ascribes to other sects, especially the Pharisees, a pursuit of holiness understood as separatism that ostracized and devalued those who did not join the Pharisaic pursuit of holiness and purity. Because this holiness was interpreted in terms of purity and impurity, and because this holiness *qua* separateness was demanded by God,[36] the Pharisees became insular and exclusionary and sought for all Israel to join this path. Those who did not join were not considered "true Israel," and the result internal to Israel was that "a large number of people . . . felt profoundly alienated and worthless."[37] Against this backdrop of Pharisaic separatism, demonstrated in the meticulous keeping of purity regulations, Jesus proclaimed an alternative ethic of compassion. After describing Lev. 19 as "the holiness code," Borg presents Jesus's moral instruction as "the compassion code" and as a replacement for the Pharisaic vision of holiness and purity understood as separateness, citing as evidence Luke 6:36, "Be compassionate, just as your Father is compassionate."[38] From this "deliberate" replacement of "terminology," Borg infers, "Where the tradition of the scribes spoke of holiness as the paradigm for the community's life, Jesus spoke of compassion."[39]

Implying that holiness *qua* separateness is socially and heartlessly exclusive, he says, "The compassion of God [which Jesus promotes] is an *inclusive* compassion."[40] Borg then employs this matrix in the Synoptic legal controversies. For example, regarding Jesus's healings on the Sabbath, Borg states, "Moreover, it was in the name of compassion that modes of behavior mandated by holiness as separation were superseded. . . . The

36. I clarify "holiness understood as separateness" because Borg argues that Jesus also pursues holiness but defines it as compassion. So Borg does not pit holiness against compassion, but holiness *qua* separateness (Pharisees) against holiness *qua* compassion (Jesus).

37. Borg, *Conflict, Holiness, and Politics*, 84.

38. Borg, *Conflict, Holiness, and Politics*, 139.

39. Borg, *Conflict, Holiness, and Politics*, 139.

40. Borg, *Conflict, Holiness, and Politics*, 140.

community which would be faithful was, like God, to subordinate the sabbath to compassion."[41]

His interpretation of the handwashing controversy in Mark 7:1–23 is particularly telling. Borg claims that Jesus's instruction that "nothing going into the person can defile him" (7:15) "called into question and negated the whole notion of how holiness was to be achieved. The equation between holiness and separation was denied, for holiness had nothing to do with separation from external sources of defilement."[42] He interprets Mark 7:19 to indicate the nullification of the food laws,[43] though he does not consider it an authentic saying but takes it instead as a narrator's aside. Borg claims that Mark's interpretation was actually "too narrow in the sense that Mark focuses attention on one part of the Mosaic law rather than seeing the issue as related to the earnest quest for an Israel whose behavior and institutions would manifest holiness. Denying the equation of *qadosh* [holiness] and *parush* [separation] constituted an eminently clear opposition to the main thrust of Pharisaic polity and indeed to much of the postexilic development of Judaism."[44] For Borg's Jesus, then, "impurity is a matter of the heart, not of external behavior."[45]

Moreover, because the Jewish "quest for holiness" *qua* separateness sets the program for the nation, and because this program regards outsiders as enemies, "Jesus saw that the most fundamental commitments of his culture [holiness, purity, Sabbath keeping, and temple] were leading to a collision course with Rome."[46] Thus the quest for holiness fragments Israel internally, distinguishing the pure from the impure, "othering" the latter, and separates Israel from the nations in a way that inevitably leads to Jewish violence against Rome.[47] In contrast, Jesus preaches an ethic of compassion and inclusion.

Borg's sketch has numerous problems. Basic to my critique is that Borg's interpretation presents a fundamental misunderstanding of ritual purity, which I have already discussed above. Recall that one's purity or impurity did not indicate one's moral status. Becoming impure was about as common as eating a meal, and it did not measure one's covenantal or communal standing. Impurity does not seem to have precluded access to the synagogue,[48] and for

41. Borg, *Conflict, Holiness, and Politics*, 172.
42. Borg, *Conflict, Holiness, and Politics*, 112.
43. It does not. This passage will be analyzed in chap. 4.
44. Borg, *Conflict, Holiness, and Politics*, 112 (bracketed text mine).
45. Borg, *Conflict, Holiness, and Politics*, 249.
46. Borg, *Conflict, Holiness, and Politics*, 256.
47. Borg, *Conflict, Holiness, and Politics*, 77–83.
48. Persons with *lepra* were permitted in the synagogue. Mishnah Neg. 13.12 legislates (and thus assumes) their inclusion.

virtually all the Jewish population, purity was not a requirement for common meals or table fellowship with others.[49] Only food dedicated to the temple had to be consumed or separated in a state of purity. Impurity does, however, regulate one's access to the Jerusalem temple and to food dedicated to it.

Borg rightly sees some degree of separation as a feature of purity, but he wrongly moralizes all purity language, presenting Jesus as ignoring or denying the value of such purity in favor of compassion. But as Fredriksen aptly quips, "Compassion is to purity as fish is to bicycle."[50] There is nothing about purity or impurity that puts the human capacity to be compassionate at risk. Jesus could, and did, advocate for compassion and purity (both morally and ritually), and there is no conflict between these pursuits.

For Borg, Jesus regards the sanctity of life as more valuable than certain legal demands, and Borg maps this disjunction onto a framework of purity versus compassion, Pharisees versus Jesus. But had Borg compared Jesus's actions to those rulings recorded in, say, m. Yoma 8.5–6 (which permits profaning legally required fasts, dietary laws, and Sabbaths in order to satisfy ravenous hunger or save a life),[51] he might have seen that non-Christian Jewish interpreters equally interpreted Scripture as prioritizing some requirements over others (e.g., temple law over Sabbath law; circumcision over Sabbath; preservation of life over nearly all else), and he might have concluded that Jesus too sees this in the biblical data. Therefore, it is true: preservation of life or satisfying grave needs takes precedence over Sabbath but not in a

49. Many of these criticisms would apply also to Scot McKnight's book *A New Vision for Israel*, in which he claims to be following paths set by Wright, Borg, and Lincoln D. Hurst (McKnight, *New Vision*, x). For example, McKnight claims that "other holiness movements had a different *ordo salutis*, in which repentance leads to holiness, which permits fellowship. Jesus affirmed, rather, that fellowship leads both to repentance and holiness. In so doing, Jesus had to sit lightly with respect to some of the laws pertaining to periods for establishing purity. . . . In true Levitical fashion, the opponents of Jesus believed that God's law taught that people had to be holy or they would defile the meal and the fellowship and then the nation" (*New Vision*, 49). But holiness was not a prerequisite for meals. Nonpriests had to eat holy food in purity but not "holiness" (Lev. 7:20–21), and one did not have to be in a state of purity (much less "holiness") to eat common food. It is unclear what law or meal McKnight is referencing here. And while Jesus did think that impurity could defile food, he taught that such incidental defilement of permissible food did not defile the body because the body purified the foods through digestion and defecation (see chap. 4). Thus, defiled common food did not lead to a defiled fellowship and nation.

50. See Fredriksen, "Compassion Is to Purity."

51. Mishnah Yoma 8.6 states, "If someone is overtaken by ravenous hunger, one may feed him even impure foods. . . . If someone has a pain in his throat, one administers medicine into his mouth on the Sabbath because there is uncertainty as to whether life [is endangered], and any uncertainty as to whether life [is endangered] overrides the Sabbath." Unless otherwise indicated, all Mishnah quotations are from *The Oxford Annotated Mishnah*, edited by Cohen, Goldenberg, and Lapin.

framework of Pharisees versus Jesus or, worse, Judaism versus Christianity. Rather, such prioritization was common among Jewish readers who recognized that the Law itself pressed for this conclusion when a decision must be made.

Thus, rather than pitting Leviticus and/or Pharisaism against Jesus on the basis of compassion, one ought to say that Jesus and the Pharisees agreed that God was compassionate and forgiving. What often distinguished Jesus from the Pharisees in the Synoptic Gospels was Jesus's claim that he was the divinely authorized herald and executor of the restoration that was breaking in *now*. This, and the interpretation of the Law consequent to Jesus's mission, distinguishes Jesus from the Pharisees.

Nationalism

Eschewing "legalism" or other "patterns of religion" as foils to Jesus's agenda, some have argued that what Jesus critiques is a Law-keeping that inscribes and fuels nationalistic pursuits of liberation or separation. The argument claims that, among others, purity, Sabbath keeping, and reverence for the temple functioned as badges of Israel's national identity. Because such badges either became a source of internal pride or fomented violence against gentiles, especially in a zealotic pursuit of liberty, Jesus challenged their validity through his dismissal of the food laws and his subversion or simple nonobservance of purity legislation and Sabbath. Suppositions common to these interpretations are that these laws symbolize and mobilize the pursuit of separation and liberation (following Borg) and that keeping them almost inevitably leads to violence. These suppositions do not withstand scrutiny.

Several scholars have pursued a form of this characterization of the Law and its criticism by Jesus (and Paul), not least James Dunn,[52] Borg,[53] and Joseph Hellerman,[54] but most prominently N. T. Wright. In *Jesus and the Victory of God*, Wright argues that Jesus is best interpreted within an understanding of Israel's history shared by his contemporaries—namely, that Israel had been called to be the light of the world and had received the Law as its national constitution, but that having violated the covenant, they had received the punitive discipline of God's abandonment of the temple and their exile, punishments that perdured into the time of Jesus. Wright presents Jesus as announcing and inaugurating the restoration and summoning of all Israel to

52. E.g., Dunn, *Jesus, Paul, and the Law*, 17–28.
53. Borg, *Conflict, Holiness, and Politics*.
54. Hellerman, *People of God*.

be the people it was called to be, which would result in the nations flocking to Israel's God.

Within this restorationist context, Wright argues, Jesus sees that the Law is being used as a litmus test of loyalty to God and nation, and he interprets the Law's distinctive markers—Sabbath, food laws, purity, and temple—as symbols of Israel's national identity and their violent pursuit of liberation.[55] Because Jesus disagrees with this way of being Israel, a way marked out by violent revolution and insularity, he calls people to repent and trust him for his way of being Israel. To repent, therefore, refers not reductively to forsaking a life of sin but particularly to forsaking a pursuit of liberation through revolution and adopting Jesus's way instead.[56] For example, Wright claims the zealous, "hard-line" Shammaite Pharisees were defining and pursuing the arrival of God's kingdom as "a matter of national liberation and the defeat of the pagans. For Jesus, the kingdom was on offer to those who would repent of just that aspiration."[57] He proceeds:

> To put it simply, the Temple cult, and the observance of sabbaths, of food taboos, and of circumcision were the key things which marked out Jew from Gentile, which (in other words) maintained and reinforced exactly this agenda, both political and religious, of the hard-line Pharisees. . . . Jesus offered a fresh interpretation of the scriptural tradition which he shared with his Jewish contemporaries. . . . And the object of his critique, I suggest, was the "zeal" that was leading Israel to ruin—and which was maintained and reinforced by precisely those aspects of Torah which marked out Israel over against her pagan neighbors.[58]

Because the above markers "identify and reinforce" Israel's violent pursuit of her "national existence and liberation,"[59] they are to be relativized. For these reasons, Jesus "cryptically subvert[s] the Jewish food laws" (referring to Mark 7:1–23),[60] relativizes the importance of Sabbath keeping, challenges alternative interpretations of purity, and confronts the temple because it "had become, in Jesus' day as in Jeremiah's, the talisman of nationalist violence."[61]

In his chapter on Israel's "symbols"—referring to the temple, Sabbath, purity, and food—Wright says, "Jesus implicitly and explicitly attacked what

55. Wright, *Victory of God*, 379, 383–89.
56. Wright, *Victory of God*, 250–53, 317.
57. Wright, *Victory of God*, 384.
58. Wright, *Victory of God*, 384–85.
59. Wright, *Victory of God*, 390.
60. Wright, *Victory of God*, 284, 396–98.
61. Wright, *Victory of God*, 420.

had become the standard symbols of the second-Temple Jewish worldview."[62] However, Jesus's "attack" was not reducible to the proper interpretation of this or that commandment but focused on his "agenda" over against his contemporaries'. Thus, in addressing "purity," Jesus was not engaging in a mundane debate about how or when to wash one's hands; rather, he was addressing the concept of purity on the level of what it pointed to: national liberation. "Purity . . . was not, in this period, an end in itself, if indeed it was ever really that. It was the symbol, all the more important for a people who perceived themselves under threat, of national identity and national liberation."[63]

Because Jesus was announcing the kingdom in which the renewal of the heart would take effect, and because this announcement would inaugurate the nations' flocking to Israel's God, the laws that regulated only external behaviors, which themselves served to exclude the nations, ought to be relativized. And his announcement of the kingdom was issued to all, including the sinners, with whom table fellowship "virtually replaced the food laws."[64] Jesus thus presented his hearers with a disjunctive option: allegiance to the Law or allegiance to himself. "Jesus was replacing adherence or allegiance to Temple and Torah with allegiance to himself."[65]

Wright helpfully frames his interpretation of the Gospels in restoration-eschatological terms, and I agree with his conclusions that Jesus required allegiance to himself and that nomistic conflicts in the Synoptic Gospels are occasionally based on eschatological agendas rather than "pattern of religion" comparisons. My criticism of Wright pertains to his interpretation of (1) the agenda of Jews contemporary with Jesus, (2) his claims about the relativization of Israel's national distinctiveness, (3) his interpretation of purity, and (4) his disjunctive juxtaposition of the Law and Jesus.

First, it is true, at least according to Josephus, that some Jews contemporary with Jesus pursued liberation through violence.[66] As Wright notes, Paul may have pursued such an agenda; however, Paul's pre-call zeal was internally focused, targeting Jews, not Romans, and per Acts, it was through legal, not militaristic, means. Moreover, Josephus, who supplies the bulk of evidence concerning Jewish liberation movements in the period roughly contemporaneous with the life of Jesus, ascribes such violence and its effects to "innovation and reform in ancestral traditions" (*Ant.* 18.9), not to Law keeping itself. In

62. Wright, *Victory of God*, 369.
63. Wright, *Victory of God*, 379.
64. Wright, *Victory of God*, 432.
65. Wright, *Victory of God*, 274, also 302.
66. See, inter alia, Josephus, *Ant.* 17.269–98; 18.1–10.

any case, the mistake in Wright's portrait is singling out such an agenda as the object of Jesus's critique and implicitly equating Law-keeping with that agenda.

For example, he states that Shammaite Pharisees violently pursued national liberation and that the Jewish symbols (i.e., temple, purity, Sabbath, and food laws) "maintained and reinforced exactly this agenda."[67] But this conflates keeping the Jewish symbols—that is, doing the Law—with violent zeal. Surely one could keep the Law without violence toward foreigners. But to assert that keeping such laws automatically reinforced a zealous agenda against the Romans is not only a non sequitur; it also does not comport with the evidence of the Gospels. In Matthew, for example, Jesus requires keeping "the least of these commandments" (5:17–20) and teaches nonretaliation (5:39). Thus Wright may be correct that Jesus targets a perceived violent zeal among some contemporaries, but he is incorrect to equate Law-keeping with such an agenda. One could keep the Law and not be a proto-Zealot. Even if one were to grant Wright's portrait of Jesus's contemporaries (which is debatable), the correction Jesus would need to make would not be to relativize the Law because keeping it engenders violence, but to keep the Law without violence. The latter comports well with the Gospels' portrait of Jesus. "Keep the commandments" (Matt. 19:17; cp. 5:17–48) and "Do not retaliate" (5:39 AT) sit together easily.

Second, keeping commandments that sustain one's "national existence" is not problematic, especially given the Gospels' contextualization of the narrative in terms of Israel's national restoration. From Leviticus to Luke, the restoration of the covenant has the nation of Israel as the central beneficiary. They are the ones to whom the promises of discipline and restoration are made (Lev. 26; Deut. 28–30), and they are the primary beneficiaries of the restoration named in the Gospels: Jesus will save "his people" (Matt. 1:21); "will reign over the house of Jacob forever" (Luke 1:32–33); is God's promised means of "help to his servant Israel" (1:54; cp. 1:68; 2:32); effects "the consolation of Israel" (2:25); asserts, "I was sent only to the lost sheep of the house of Israel" (Matt. 15:24); and instructs his disciples to preach only in Jewish villages (10:6), avoiding "the way of the Gentiles" (10:5).

Wright is certainly no stranger to the centrality of Israel in the covenantal drama. My reading differs, however, in not describing Israel's national distinctiveness, manifest even in a rigorous keeping of distinctive customs, either as a reality now to be relativized or as a problem to be overcome. In this vein, Wright claims,

67. Wright, *Victory of God*, 384.

> Sabbath spoke of the great day of rest still to come; also, both to Israel and to the pagans, it announced Israel's determination to remain separate. Food laws, too, spoke of an Israel separate from the nations, eating different food, anxious to reinforce her ethnic, and ultimately her national, boundaries. Jesus' whole work was aimed at announcing that the day of mourning, of exile, of necessary and god-ordained national separateness, was coming to an end.[68]

If "separateness" means "only Israel is included," then yes: post-resurrection Jesus commissions the disciples to preach to the nations because of his newly possessed "authority in heaven and on earth" (Matt. 28:18). But it seems that it is not just separateness *qua* exclusivity but even Israel's distinctiveness that comes under Wright's scrutiny, who claims "it was time to relativize those god-given markers of Israel's distinctiveness."[69] But the inclusion of the nations would not necessarily entail that Israel ceases to be distinctive as a nation, and continued performance of the Law in maintaining their national identity would not serve as a barrier excluding fellowship with gentiles. Many, if not all, of Israel's distinctives could be kept without excluding the nations. For example, a Jew could keep the Levitical diet and, with necessary precautions, eat at the same table with gentiles.[70] Moreover, when Acts narrates approximately the first thirty years of preaching, it characterizes Jews as maintaining their ancestral customs both before and after the influx of the nations, while obligating gentiles who believe to observe select Levitical customs. This suggests that Wright is incorrect to collapse "exclusive" with "distinctive" and to claim that this "moment of fulfilment" signals the end of Israel's "god-ordained" distinctiveness and the customs that mark it.[71]

Third, related to the above equation of Law-keeping with violent zeal is Wright's interpretation of purity. He states that purity was not "an end in itself" but was the "symbol . . . of national identity and national liberation."[72] And he asserts that Jesus's table fellowship with sinners "virtually replaced the food laws."[73] But this misinterprets purity and the food laws both from the biblical and Second Temple Jewish perspective. Purity may not be an end in itself, but that does not mean it was only a symbol

68. Wright, *Victory of God*, 435.

69. Wright, *Victory of God*, 389.

70. See "The Gospels and Acts" in the concluding chapter.

71. Some legal customs may be relativized, but not for the reasons Wright avers. For example, "marrying and giving in marriage" (and thus laws that legislate such unions) become redundant not because the nations are included, but because of the bodily transformation that occurs "in the resurrection" (e.g., Luke 20:36).

72. Wright, *Victory of God*, 379.

73. Wright, *Victory of God*, 432.

of national liberation. Purity was a divinely prescribed prerequisite for approaching the temple and handling sacred food (Lev. 7:19–21), and archaeological evidence suggests that Jews aspired to purity irrespective of their intent to approach the temple.[74] While these regulations mark Israel out from the nations, that is only one of their effects. Were Israel to be autonomous, purity would still be pursued, not because it signaled a desire for liberation (which they already had) but to obtain the status required for approaching the temple (at the very least). And eating with sinners did not overthrow the food laws. One could eat with sinners and keep the dietary restrictions, and if eating with sinners defiled you, that would be fine![75] Contracting impurity is not a sin, and purity was not required for consuming common food. Moreover, Jesus prescribes the performance of purification rituals (Matt. 8:4; Mark 1:44; Luke 5:14), critiques the Pharisees for a deficient understanding of ritual purity (Matt. 15:10–20; Mark 7:14–20), and endorses doing all the commandments, which would include purification and food laws (Matt. 5:17–20). The pursuit of ritual purity, then, is a state endorsed and commanded, not critiqued or redefined, by Jesus in the Synoptic Gospels.

Finally, fourth, Wright draws an unnecessarily disjunctive contrast between allegiance to Torah and allegiance to Jesus. But the explicit contrast in the Synoptic Gospels is not between Torah and Jesus but between Torah as interpreted by others and Torah as interpreted by Jesus. Jesus contrasts the insufficient righteousness of the scribes and Pharisees with the righteousness he requires (Matt. 5:20, 47). But this "righteousness" is not expressed apart from Law observance but is manifest through keeping Jesus's interpretation of it. Thus the disciples are to avoid not the Law itself, but "the leaven [the teaching] of the Pharisees and Sadducees" (Matt. 16:11–12). Moreover, when asked "What must I do to inherit eternal life?" (Mark 10:17–21; Matt. 19:16–21; Luke 18:18–22), Jesus responds in terms of keeping the commandments. After hearing that this man has kept many commandments, he tells him "One thing you lack: . . . follow me" (Mark 10:21; cp. Luke 18:22; Matt. 19:20–21), implying not an either/or, "Law or me," but a both/and, "the commandments and me."[76] Thus Jesus does require allegiance to himself but not over and against the Law.

74. See the discussion in Adler, *Origins of Judaism*, 50–86.

75. The supposition that "sinners" refers to those who are ritually impure is debatable (see the discussion early in chap. 1 above).

76. See also Ermakov ("Salvific Significance"), who concludes, "It seems that for Jesus doing the Torah or keeping the commandments is a natural answer for what is required for the inheritance of eternal life" (22). See also Van Maaren, *Gospel of Mark's Judaism*.

What Then Shall We Say?

I have tried to provide a brief evaluation as to why the above proposed critiques of legalism, exclusivism, or nationalism fail to explain either Jesus's positive teaching or the basis of his disagreements with contemporaries. But if these frameworks don't capture Jesus's message and occasional criticisms, what does?

Positively, the Gospels depict Jesus as announcing God's promised restoration of Israel and providing the authoritative interpretation of the Law consequent to this restoration. In this way, allegiance to Jesus entails at least believing his announcement about the incoming reign of God and following his legal instruction. And his call to repentance refers not to the noneschatological repentance one might perform after a transgression but to Israel's corporate restoration-eschatological *return* to God after they had turned away from him and his Law throughout their national history.

Negatively, Jesus does not critique legalism, exclusivism, nationalism, or Judaism as a bad pattern of religion. Rather, Jesus critiques transgression, and he does this in at least two ways. The first critique is simply that of transgression of the Law. This is plain from several texts:

> "Rightly did Isaiah prophesy of you hypocrites. . . . Neglecting the commandment of God, you hold to the tradition of men." He was also saying to them, "You are experts at setting aside the commandment of God in order to keep your tradition." (Mark 7:6–9)

> So you [Pharisees] too, outwardly appear righteous to people, but inwardly you are full of hypocrisy and lawlessness. (Matt. 23:28)

> You [Pharisees] pay tithes of mint, rue, and every kind of garden herb, and yet you ignore justice and the love of God; but these are the things you should have done without neglecting the others. (Luke 11:42)

The irony of these passages in the face of attempts to ascribe "meritorious legalism" to Pharisaism or Jews broadly is that Jesus's critique is not that they are keeping the Law too rigorously but that they (the Pharisees) are not properly obeying the Law.[77] Moreover, popular and scholarly presentations

77. See the similar discussion in Runesson, "Purity, Holiness," 151. Luke 18:9 does not compromise this portrait. There Jesus "told this parable to some who were persuaded about themselves that they were righteous, and viewed others with contempt" (AT). The figures in the parable are a Pharisee (18:11) and a tax collector (18:13). But the issue is not the Pharisee's actions mentioned in the prayer (tithing, fasting), which are depicted as righteous and good.

that depict the Pharisees as overly scrupulous and harsh fail to recognize that a commonly attested criticism of Pharisees in the late Second Temple period was transgression and a perceived "leniency," searching for "easy interpretations."[78]

The second category of transgression is a failure to repent. Not recognizing Jesus as the agent of rescue results in their failure to repent and do the Law as he summons.

A key feature operative within these intramural dynamics of Jesus's mission and message concerning the restoration, his Law-keeping and legal instruction, and the mutual critique of "transgression" between Jesus and some contemporaries is this: Jesus's interpretation and practice of the Law are occasionally conditioned by his conviction that the restoration is being realized through his work.[79] This phenomenon may be described as Jesus's "eschatological nomism," a manner of Law-keeping and legal instruction (nomism) informed by the urgency and nature of his eschatological mission.

For example, because he conceives the work of his mission as "greater than" the work done in the temple (Matt. 12:6), and because temple law overrides Sabbath law (12:5), he argues that work done in service of his mission is permissible, and sometimes even required, on the Sabbath.[80] Thus, according to Jesus, just as the priests profane the Sabbath "and are innocent" when they do their commissioned work (offer sacrifices) on the Sabbath (12:5),

---

The critique is that those targeted by the parable "viewed others with contempt" (ἐξουθενοῦντας τοὺς λοιπούς, 18:9). That is, such persons fail to keep the Law's instruction in Lev. 19:17: "You shall not hate your fellow countryman in your heart; you may certainly rebuke your neighbor, but you are not to incur sin because of him." Instead of reproving or guiding his neighbor, the parabolic Pharisee "despised" him, the very thing prohibited in the Law. Thus the figure breaks the Law through such an attitude and act of omission. Moreover, the audience of the parable is Jesus's disciples, not the Pharisees. Though Jesus uses a Pharisee in the parable, it does not indicate that all Pharisees, much less "Pharisaism," are thereby indicted. Moreover, Luke presents other Pharisees as attempting to aid Jesus (13:31), as encouraging caution and patience in dealing with the new movement (Acts 5:34), as believers in Jesus (Acts 15:5) who agreed with the council's decision concerning gentiles (Acts 15:22, 25, 28), and as defenders of Paul (Acts 23:9). Thus, to infer from this parable a stance on "Pharisaism" or all Pharisees is misguided, and to take the parable as a criticism of Law-keeping misunderstands the characterization of those targeted. Moreover, his disciples later remind Jesus of what *they have done* to follow Jesus, which Jesus endorses and rewards (Matt. 19:27–28 and par.). Jesus here criticizes self-exaltation, something the Jewish Scriptures and their interpreters also criticize (e.g., Deut. 17:20; Philo, *Sacrifices* 55–57). That "some" do this should not be extrapolated to indict all the people or even all the Pharisees. See further discussion in A.-J. Levine, "Pharisee."

78. E.g., 4Q169 frags. 3–4, I.2. See also m. Yad. 4.6–8. On sectarian criticisms of certain Pharisaic rulings in the late Second Temple and rabbinic material, see Furstenberg, "Laws of the Pharisees"; Furstenberg, *Purity and Identity*, 68–82. On the lackluster depiction of the Pharisees in Josephus, see Mason, "Narratives"; Mason, "Philosophy."

79. Some nomistic differences are noneschatologically motivated, such as the handwashing controversy (Mark 7).

80. This passage will be interpreted in detail in chap. 5.

so his disciples profane the Sabbath by plucking grains to eat, but they do so innocently because they act while engaged in authorized work (12:6–8). But one can accept Jesus's legal argument and consequent declaration of his disciples' innocence only if one accepts his claim to be the authorized agent of restoration, whose work occasionally overrides the Sabbath because it is "greater than the temple" (12:6). A nonrecognition of his authorized status would result in the rejection of his legal defense. If he's not really the agent of restoration, they are nonpermissibly violating the Sabbath. If he's not really working with God's sacred Spirit, his exorcisms must be wrought by the ruler of demons (12:24–28 and par.). If he's not the Son of Man divinely authorized to forgive sins, he blasphemes (12:3–8 and par.). Thus contemporaries who reject his authorized status would regard him not simply as *wrong* ("restoration isn't coming") but as transgressing ("his defense is unjustified"). And his "transgression" marks him not just as belonging to the lamentable but otherwise mundane class of "sinners"; rather, on their view, given his transgression, popularity, and unfounded assertion of divine authorization, he is "leading the people astray" (Luke 23:2 AT) and must be scrutinized.

• • •

To understand Jesus's interpretation of the Law, it will be helpful to provide a (nonexhaustive) taxonomy of categories that affect legal obligations. Interpretations that utilize a one-size-fits-all framework for the Law fail to recognize how various factors condition what is legally permissible/prohibited and how such factors aid the interpretation of Jesus's praxis and nomistic instruction.

Space

Though "the earth is the Lord's, and all it contains" (Ps. 24:1), not all space is regulated equally, and one's spatial location governs nomistic practice. Activity permissible at home, such as eating in a state of impurity, is prohibited at the temple. One's proximity to the temple affects one's capacity to celebrate Passover. If you are on a distant journey, you are not required to celebrate Passover at the (first) instituted time (Num. 9:10). Such people may observe it in the second month (9:11). Produce grown in the land (18:13) is subject to tithes (whether grown by an Israelite or not), but produce sourced from outside the land (even that grown by Israelites) is not.[81] Location, then,

81. For discussion of tithes and sabbatical-year produce, see Shevi'it, Terumot, Ma'aserot, and Ma'aser Sheni in the Mishnah. On produce from outside the land not being subject to tithes

conditions certain legal obligations, and this category is partially relevant to Jesus's meal with sinners and his interactions with the ritually impure, which take place away from the temple.

Time

As with space, not all time is legislated equally, and not everything permissible on one day is permissible on another. Work permitted on days 1 through 6 becomes transgression if done on the Sabbath (Exod. 20:8–10). Sacrifices not to be offered on a regular day are mandated on a festival day, such as the Day of Atonement. Food such as leaven, which is permitted on a regular day, is prohibited during Passover (Exod. 12:15). Activities permitted throughout the years/seasons (e.g., debt collection, sowing, and pruning) are prohibited in the year of remission (Deut. 15:1–2), the sabbatical year (Lev. 25:1–7), and the Jubilee (Lev. 25:11). Similarly, activities that are permitted in other years (e.g., debt cancellation) become mandated in the year of remission (Deut. 15:1–2).

Given the chronological conditions of certain commandments, matters of ambiguity inevitably arise. The classic example is the potential conflict between performing circumcision, which must be done on the eighth day of a boy's life (Gen. 17:12; Lev. 12:3), and observing the Sabbath. Jewish interpreters widely agreed that you "violate" the Sabbath to keep the chronological requirement of the circumcision commandment. In this case, the legal principle at work is that circumcision overrides Sabbath.[82] Significantly, violation of the Sabbath for this purpose is not construed as breaking the Law but keeping it. Note how Jesus frames the issue in John 7:23: "If a man receives circumcision on the Sabbath so that that the Law of Moses will not be broken [ἵνα μὴ λυθῇ ὁ νόμος Μωϋσέως], are you angry with me because I made an entire man well on the Sabbath?" Significantly, violating the Sabbath to circumcise is construed as ensuring that the Law *isn't* broken. The question is not "Is the one who circumcises really loyal to the Law?" but "Given God's commandments and knowing the time, what is required of me?" This framing, I will argue, more accurately captures the flavor of some of Jesus's healings, his perceived violations of the Sabbath, and his instruction that one ought to turn the other cheek rather than exact an eye for an eye (Matt. 5:38–39).

---

or sabbatical-year prohibitions, see m. Terumot 1.5; m. Shev. 6.1. Such opinions are based, in part, on the geographical factors of the commandments. For example, regarding the tithes, the Law specifies "all that is in their land" (Num. 18:13).

82. See m. Shabb. 18.3; b. Shabb. 132a.

Cultic/Political Office

Different offices or social positions have different legal obligations. Officiating the offerings on the altars is permissible for and required of a priest but is prohibited for nonpriests (Num. 18:1–7). Contracting corpse impurity to bury a nonrelative is permissible for nonpriests but is prohibited for priests, who may contract such impurity only for immediate family (Lev. 21:1–4). What is permitted for priests is prohibited for the high priest, who may not contract corpse impurity for anyone (Lev. 21:11). Work constitutes Sabbath violation for nonpriests, but priests are required to work daily, including on the Sabbath (Num. 28:9–10). These distinctions gain their significance not just as illustrations of different requirements of a given office but in recalling the purposes of these distinct offices: priests serve the temple, and nonpriests do not.

These distinctions, then, should be mapped not onto a moralized social hierarchy ("priests think themselves superior to nonpriests") but onto a hierarchy of official responsibility (priests administer divinely prescribed temple rites; nonpriests do not) and a hierarchy of legal responsibility (temple law overrides Sabbath law). For example, because priests do the work of the temple, they must be ultracautious about their purity. This is not a moral category, as if the Law proclaims priests morally "purer" (superior) to others; rather, purity is a necessity of the office. Similarly, the temple is the earthly residence of Israel's God, and so laws governing its maintenance are of supreme importance. When conflict potentially arises among laws regulating Sabbath and laws regulating the temple, temple law often overrides Sabbath law.

For example, Passover (a festival kept at the temple) must be kept on the fourteenth of Nisan (Num. 9:3). If the fourteenth of the month coincides with the Sabbath, work necessary to observe the Passover at the right time (temple law) is permitted, even though such work would otherwise violate the Sabbath.[83] Numerous examples illustrate and name this principle.[84] Grasping this legal principle will greatly impact our interpretation of what Jesus considers permissible for him to do in pursuit of his work to announce and inaugurate the covenant restoration. If temple law overrides Sabbath law, and his own work/announcement is "greater than the temple" (Matt. 12:6), what would this mean for his capacity to profane the Sabbath when doing the work requisite for the restoration?

83. See m. Pesah. 6.1–6 for opinions on what work completed for Passover does and doesn't override the Sabbath.

84. In addition to Matt. 12:5 and m. Pesah. 6, see m. Shev. 1.4; m. Rosh Hash. 1.4.

Male and Female

The Law legislates many things, one of which is the human bodily condition. The most obvious issue is the distinction in bodily discharges. Discharge of semen or menstrual blood defiles the person, and these sources of impurity will naturally affect men and women differently. The commonality, of course, is that both are required to undergo purification. Differing legal obligations based on gendered realities abound, such as laws pertaining to childbirth (Lev. 12:1–6), circumcision of boys (Lev. 12:3) and adult men (Gen. 17:10–13), and vows and their nullification (Num. 30:2–16).

Ethnic and/or Covenantal Status

Because God is uniquely in covenant with a people genealogically descended from Abraham, Isaac, and Jacob, one is "born into" the covenant, as it were, and becomes obligated to the whole Law. However, even this must be qualified because not every Israelite is obligated to every commandment, as we have already seen. For example, Israelite nonpriests are not obligated to fulfill priestly requirements. Similarly, just as the Law obligates differently based on the categories above (priest, nonpriest, etc.), so also the Law differently obligates people living in the land who are not Israelites. For example, "all the congregation of Israel" are to celebrate the Passover (Exod. 12:47), but a "stranger" or "hired servant" may not (12:45). But a stranger who resides in the land and wishes to keep the festival may eat if he is first circumcised (12:48). Or consider the dietary laws: "unclean" food, such as pork, is "unclean to you [Israelites]" (Lev. 11:4, 5, 6; cp. v. 2), but it is not forbidden for gentiles. And though Israelites may not eat anything they find already dead, they may give it to the foreigner who lives in their town, and they may eat it (Deut. 14:21).[85] In these cases, food prohibited to an Israelite is permitted for a non-Israelite.[86] Thus the Law does not identically obligate Israelites and non-Israelites.[87] Recognizing this will greatly aid the interpretation of the Jerusalem Council in Acts 15 and, arguably, aspects of Paul's letters.

85. Leviticus 17:15 legislates a case in which someone eats a carcass, but this is unrelated to the point at hand concerning Deuteronomy's permitting one thing to a gentile that it forbids for an Israelite.

86. On the nonobligatory status of Israel's food prohibitions for gentiles (except the consumption of blood, which is universally prohibited), see Maccoby, *Ritual and Morality*, viii; Rosenblum, *Food and Identity*, 68; Oliver, *Torah Praxis*, 244. See also Gen. 9:3; Lev. Rab. 13.1–2; b. Sanhedrin 56b, 58b–60a.

87. On the Law's commands for non-Israelites, see van Houten, *The Alien in Israelite Law*; Achenbach, Albertz, and Wöhrle, *The Foreigner and the Law*; Zellentin, *Law beyond Israel*.

Creaturely Status

Not all creatures are equally bound by the Law. At one level, this seems obvious. Fish can't tithe and goats don't pray. But legal obligations and benefits redounding to nonhuman creatures appear more than one might think. Cattle participate in the Sabbath rest (Exod. 20:10). Even more, the people are to rest from labor "*so that* your ox and your donkey may rest" (23:12). An ox responsible for someone's death is executed by stoning (21:28). In some traditions, suprahuman creatures also come under God's legislative control. According to Jubilees, some angels observe the Sabbath (2.21) and are circumcised (15.27). The details of the latter phenomenon are perhaps mercifully muted, but the point is made: the behavior of even nonhuman creatures is regulated by the Law.

The relevance of this taxonomical category is significant. When given the scenario about many brothers married to the same woman and asked by the Sadducees, "In the resurrection, which one's wife does she become?" Jesus responds: "The sons of this age marry and are given in marriage, but those who are considered worthy to attain to that age and the resurrection from the dead, neither marry nor are given in marriage; they cannot even die anymore, for they are like angels, and are sons of God, being sons of the resurrection" (Luke 20:33–36). Significantly, the answer to a legislative question hinges on the ontological nature of the creature potentially legislated. Participants in this age die. For this reason they marry and reproduce and so require laws legislating such realities. But once creatures participate in that age and are resurrected, they can no longer die, being "like angels." The incapacity to die negates the necessity to marry (for reproduction), affecting the applicability of a commandment given to mortal humans.

Divine Discipline

Because aspects of the Law regulate the temple (sacrifices) and Israel's life in the land (tithes and the sabbatical year), circumstances that affect these conditions affect the obligations. For example, one is not obligated to observe the sabbatical year for the land when living outside the land. The land of Israel itself may "have [its] rest" (Lev. 26:35), but a Jew in Babylon is not obligated to forego sowing and reaping the land of Babylon.

This should not be too surprising. What constitutes obedience is always contextual. In the wilderness, God tells Israel to enter the promised land. When they demur, God consigns the disbelieving generation to the wilderness until they perish (Num. 14:30–34). When the sentence is too much to bear, they acknowledge their sin and intend to proceed into the land. Moses responds: "Why then are you violating the command of the LORD, when doing so will not succeed? Do not go up, for the LORD is not among you" (14:41–42). What was before a commandment ("enter the land") would now constitute transgression when their entrance would have circumvented the decreed discipline. This category thus highlights the conditional and contextual nature of legal obligations and acknowledges that being in a state of divine discipline is one such contextualizing factor.

Weighty Matters and Urgent Overrides

Some duties are of such significance or urgency that fulfilling them may require temporarily forfeiting the keeping of other commandments that might hinder completing the weightier matter. At one level, this category is akin to instances already discussed above under "Time" and "Cultic/Political Office" (e.g., temple law and circumcision overriding Sabbath). But some examples are sufficiently distinct to justify a unique taxonomical category, and I discuss it last because it conditions the keeping of the commandments generally. For instance, m. Ber. 3.1 exempts one engaged in burying a dead relative "from the recitation of the Shema, from the Prayer, and from *tefillin*." The Babylonian Talmud adds to these exemptions "and from all the commandments mentioned in the Torah" (b. Ber. 17b). Evidently, the import of burial justifies temporarily forfeiting commandments that might conceivably hinder that task. Similarly, those who witnessed the new moon were permitted to profane the Sabbath to bring their testimony to Jerusalem for verification so that a uniform calendar could be proclaimed. Such witnesses could profane the Sabbath to complete their mission because of the importance of "regulating the sacrifice" (m. Rosh Hash. 1.4). The general principle at work was eventually formulated as such: "One who is engaged in a commandment is exempt from another commandment" (b. Sukkah 26a). Though the latter text considerably postdates the Gospels, the principle was operative already in the Mishnah (m. Sukkah 2.4), and the force of this reasoning is arguably in effect in cases of Sabbath profanation in order to save a life, a halakhic question predating the Gospels by decades, if not centuries.[88] For example, though the Sabbath prohibits work, fighting in self-defense against

88. See CD-A 11.13–14, 16–17. The text states that one may not use a rope or ladder to draw out a human who fell into a reservoir on the Sabbath. That it rules on the issue likely indicates that it was a known practice with which the community disagreed. See Oliver, *Torah Praxis*, 49–53.

gentile attack was regarded as permissible by many.[89] This ruling reasons according to the principle that came to be formulated in the Mishnah as an override for the sake of preservation of life (m. Yoma 8.6). When life is at stake, or even suspected of being at stake, one could profane the Sabbath to administer medicine or remove rubble off potential victims, feed prohibited food to one in dire need, or violate a fast by feeding a pregnant woman who felt sudden hunger (m. Yoma 8.5–7). In the above cases, the importance of one duty—burying a relative, testifying concerning the new moon, saving a life—overrides other duties, including recitation of certain prayers, Sabbath observance, dietary restrictions, and fast days. Such examples and the legal reasoning they employ are the stuff of Jesus's "eschatological nomism"—that is, his practice of the Law in light of his urgent duty to herald and inaugurate the restoration.

Conclusion

Interpretations of Jesus's nomistic discourse that name legalism, exclusivism, or nationalism as the issues Jesus is critiquing do not adequately interpret the Law itself or its interpretation in Jesus's setting or in the Gospels. Moreover, there is no one-size-fits-all category of the Law that explains every instance of Jesus's interpretation of the Law, his legal defenses, or his conflicts with contemporaries. We will have to draw upon several taxonomical categories to offer a fuller portrait. Because I will argue that a restoration-eschatology framework encompasses some of the above taxonomical categories and contextualizes the Synoptic Gospel's depiction of Jesus, the next chapter will briefly describe this restoration framework in Jewish texts.

89. According to 1 Macc. 2:27–41 and Josephus, *Ant.* 12.272–77, this ruling originated in response to the decrees and persecutions of Antiochus. This ruling is possibly contested in Jub. 50.13.

2

Restoration Eschatology in Early Judaism

"May your name be sanctified. May your kingdom come. . . . Release us from our debts. . . . Deliver us from the evil one" (Matt. 6:9–13 AT). Like many prayers that have become traditional, familiarity of expression may numb comprehension. I prayed the Lord's Prayer for years without pausing to ask what it would mean for God's name to be "sanctified," and that was only after I finally asked what it meant for it to be "hallowed" (ἁγιασθήτω τὸ ὄνομά σου, 6:9). God's kingdom arriving was plain enough (though I thought he'd always been in charge), and I think I understood well enough the plea for forgiveness. But it wasn't until my first year of Greek that I heard the translation "Deliver us from the evil one" (i.e., Satan)[1] rather than a general request to avoid bad things happening to me. With these few words, Jesus teaches his disciples to pray that God sanctify his own name;[2] that he bring *his* kingdom, trumping all others; that he release Israel from indebtedness; and that he rescue his people from captivity to Satan. But these translations do not simply render Greek words more plainly; they also imply a situation that requires some explanation. What would it mean for God to sanctify his

1. On Matt. 6:13's τοῦ πονηροῦ as "the evil one" (i.e., Satan), see Lohmeyer, *Lord's Prayer*, 209–16. See supplements to his argument in Ridlehoover, *Lord's Prayer*, 110–12. Matthew refers to the devil as "the evil one" in Matt. 13:19, 38. See comparable phrasing with respect to the devil or some evil spirit in Eph. 6:16.

2. As Davies and Allison (*Matthew*, 93) note, "The passive construction ["May your name be sanctified"] probably has . . . God as the implicit subject: the Father is being called upon to act."

name? And why does Jesus characterize his people's plight in terms of debt and captivity? Why does Jesus single out these predicaments as requiring resolution? And how did such predicaments come about?

An audience familiar with Israel's Scriptures would likely hear in this prayer an implicit naming of the plight experienced because of Israel's breach of the covenant. In this scenario, the violation of God's Law led to the outpouring of the punitive disciplines announced in Deut. 28 and Lev. 26: Israel's sin accrued a debt that was to be paid off by their exilic captivity to foreign nations and their gods,[3] where, in that exile, God's name was "profaned among the nations" (Ezek. 36:23). In light of this intolerable situation, God asserts in Ezek. 36:23 "I will sanctify my name" (AT; ἁγιάσω τὸ ὄνομά μου, LXX) in the sight of the nations by gathering the exiles and bringing them into the land, cleansing Israel, and giving them a new heart and spirit by which they walk in God's statutes.[4] Jesus, then, still under the weight of that condition with his people but heralding its imminent resolution, teaches his disciples to pray that God keep this promise *now*, that he sanctify his profaned name by rescuing them from their punitive exile and giving them hearts to obey him.

Similarly, construing Israel's plight as a penal debt-servitude, he prays for the eschatological Jubilee, a release from the debt that manifests itself in captivity to Satan and foreign nations. Rather than being ruled by other nations and their powers, Jesus prays for God to bring *his* reign and accomplish his will, voicing Isaiah's expectations that in the restoration, God himself would reign (Isa. 52:7–8) and effect an eschatological release of Israel's sin debt (40:2; 61:1). Much of Jesus's prayer, in fact, is informed by the Jewish metaphorization of Israel's plight as indebtedness and her restoration as a release from these debts in an eschatological Jubilee. How this construal came about is not difficult to imagine. Because many Jews interpreted the noneschatological Jubilee (Lev. 25) to require the release of slaves and the forgiveness of debts and expected divine provision of extra food in view of the command to let the land lie fallow,[5] and because many texts envisage Israel's plights in precisely these terms (debt, servitude, hunger), some passages consequently envision the restoration as an eschatological Jubilee, wherein God would forgive their debts (sins), release them from captivity, and satisfy the hungry. Jesus participates in this pattern of interpretation and so prays

3. Lev. 26:43; Isa. 40:2. Gary Anderson (*Sin*) discusses the metaphor of sin as "debt" and its usage in biblical, Second Temple, and rabbinic texts. See also Anderson, "From Israel's Burden."

4. Ezek. 36:23–27. See the discussion in R. Brown, "Pater Noster," 186–87; Davies and Allison, *Matthew*, 93. I'm also grateful to Jason Staples for conversation on the relation of this petition to Ezek. 36.

5. Discussed below and in chaps. 3 and 4.

for their deliverance from their captor, Satan; for the release of their debts (transgressions); and for God to give them today their bread for tomorrow.[6] Though the Lord's Prayer is widely recognized as eschatological,[7] it is more specifically a prayer for the eschatological Jubilee.

Jesus's prayer, therefore, participates in a widely held expectation of restoration and renewal fostered by an interpretation of Israel's history informed by Deut. 28–32 and Lev. 26, in which Israel's violation of the covenant led to the punitive discipline promised in the Law, after which God would restore his chastened people, give them a new heart, return to them, and bring them back to the land. This pattern of interpretation is widely attested in Second Temple literature and is often labeled a "restoration eschatological" reading of Israel's history.[8] To grasp the nature of these plights, their causes, how Jesus could still consider them in effect in the first century CE long after the return of some tribes from Babylon to Judea, and how such expectations shape both the plot of the Synoptic Gospels and Jesus's nomistic teaching in light of their resolution, it will be necessary to survey this pattern as described in the Law, the Prophets, and Second Temple literature.

Restoration Eschatology in the Law

The Law's commandments constitute the stipulations by which Israel maintains the covenant and enjoys its inherent blessings. Violating the covenant results in God's employment of the punitive curses through which Israel is disciplined. Importantly, the covenantal agreement assumes that Israel will commit transgression—hence the divinely prescribed sacrificial system. Thus Israel's commission of certain transgressions does not automatically incur the covenant curses. Rather, Leviticus states that God sends the promised discipline only if "you reject my statutes, and if your soul loathes my ordinances so as . . . to break my covenant" (Lev. 26:15). Similarly, while Deut. 28–32 describes the disobedience that merits the discipline as not keeping all

6. On this petition as "bread for tomorrow," see France (*Matthew*, 248) and the discussion of Matt. 5:38–42 in chap. 3 below.

7. E.g., R. Brown, "Pater Noster"; Davies and Allison, *Matthew*, 91–94; Nolland, *Matthew*, 286–87.

8. For surveys of restoration eschatology in Second Temple texts, see Steck, *Israel und das gewaltsame Geschick*; Ackroyd, *Exile and Restoration*; Knibb, "Exile"; E. P. Sanders, *Jesus and Judaism*, 267–69; Wright, *Climax of the Covenant*, 141–56; Wright, *New Testament and the People of God*, 254, 268–74, 299–307; Wright, *Paul and the Faithfulness of God*, 105–63; Scott, "Restoration"; Evans, "Exile and Restoration"; Halpern-Amaru, "Exile and Return"; Pitre, *Jesus, the Tribulation*, 1–130; Peters, "Dead Sea Scrolls"; Staples, *Paul and the Resurrection*, 52–63.

the Lord's commandments,[9] it more frequently names the abandonment of worshiping the Lord and its complement, the worship of other gods.[10] Deuteronomy 31:16–18 is representative: "This people will arise and play the prostitute with the foreign gods of the land, . . . and they will abandon me and break my covenant which I have made with them. . . . But I will assuredly hide my face on that day because of all the evil that they will have done, for they will turn to other gods" (Deut. 31:16–18). This and other passages identify Israel's illicit corporate worship of other gods as the basis for the outpoured wrath and discipline.[11]

The Discipline

Deuteronomy 28:15–68 and Lev. 26:14–39 make plain the content of this punishment:

- The land and the people will be invaded (Deut. 28:49–52).
- Enemies will take over every facet of life (Lev. 26:17, 25; Deut. 28:25, 29–34).
- Sickness and disease will run amok (Lev. 26:16, 25; Deut. 28:21–22, 27–28, 35, 59–61).
- Drought and famine will pervade (Lev. 26:16, 19, 20, 26; Deut. 28:23–24, 38–40).
- The people will be sent into foreign lands (Lev. 26:33; Deut. 28:36–37, 63–64; 29:28; 30:18).
- In exile, they will serve the nations (Deut. 28:48, 65, 68) and their gods (28:36, 64).
- God will abandon the temple (Lev. 26:31; Deut. 31:17–18; 32:20).
- God will cease to regard the sacrifices (Lev. 26:31).
- Cities and sanctuary will be devastated (Lev. 26:30–32).
- The people will "die" or "perish" (Lev. 26:38; Deut. 28:20, 21, 22, 24, 45, 48, 51, 61).

9. Deut. 28:14, 15, 45, 58, 62; 29:9; 30:17; 32:46.

10. Deut. 28:14, 20; 29:18, 25–26; 30:17; 31:16, 18, 20, 29; 32:15–17, 21.

11. As the references in the preceding note indicate, "worshiping other gods" and "breaking the Lord's commandments" are not mutually exclusive. Worshiping other gods entails that they are not keeping the Lord's requirements. Prophetic indictments additionally name "bloodshed" and mistreatment of the poor as reasons for judgment (e.g., Isa. 1:15–17; Ezek. 22:1–9).

As this short summary shows, exile is undeniably a major component of the punitive discipline, but it would be a mistake to reduce the curses to that.[12] In addition to disease and agricultural catastrophe, the Law also names the divine rejection of sacrifices (Lev. 26:31) and captivity to other gods (Deut. 28:36, 64). Regarding the latter, Deuteronomy states that other "powers" rule the other nations by the Lord's appointment.[13] Numerous texts assume this political cosmology.[14] For Israel to be exiled into foreign lands, then, is to be thrust into the control of the gods who rule in those territories. As God asserts in Jer. 16:13, "So I will hurl you off this land to the land which

12. In numerous publications, Wright has argued that what Israel awaited in Jesus's day was the "real 'return from exile'" (*Victory of God*, 404, 420). For the scheme of prolonged exile and Israel's expectation of restoration, see Wright, *Climax of the Covenant*, 141–56; Wright, *New Testament and the People of God*, 254, 268–74, 299–307; Wright, *Paul and the Faithfulness of God*, 105–63. My distinction from Wright is largely, but not exclusively, terminological. Wright is clear that the plight is not reducible to exile, and he names the divine abandonment of the temple as a major issue. My main concern is that people may hear the label "exile" and, even when Wright and others are careful to describe the other troubles, ignore the serious plights that hover around the temple and the subjugation to enemies, human and nonhuman. While Wright is correct that many Jews considered restoration a *desideratum*, the label "exile" unhelpfully places the emphasis on the geographical location of the people when the plight centers on their captivity to foreign nations and their gods and the questionable effectuality of the priesthood and their offerings. Moreover, many from the Southern Kingdom (Judah) did return; thus, to label their plight "exile" obscures the fact that those returnees still regarded themselves as in *captivity* even in the land. Additionally, it is important to recognize that those from the Northern Kingdom (the "ten tribes") were regarded as still literally in exile. On the latter, see Pitre, *Jesus, the Tribulation*, 35; Staples, *Idea of Israel*; Staples, *Paul and the Resurrection*, 52–63. For discussion critical of the "exile" label along these lines, see Pitre, *Jesus, the Tribulation*, 32–40; Bryan, *Jesus and Israel's Traditions*, 12–20; Staples, *Paul and the Resurrection*, 97–101; and Wright's concession to some of these criticisms, "In Grateful Dialogue," 259–60.

13. Deut. 4:19; 32:8–9. A text-critical issue is present in Deut. 32:8. Does it read "the number of the sons of god" or "the number of the sons of Israel" (per many English translations of the MT)? See the discussion in Tigay, *Deuteronomy*, 513–18. A Hebrew witness of Deut. 32:8 preserved among the Dead Sea Scrolls states "according to the number of the sons of god" (4Q37). Supporting the "divine" version is the Septuagintal translation, which reads: "according to the number of the angels of God" (ἀγγέλων θεοῦ), which evidently translated its Hebrew *Vorlage* in terms of divine beings. See also Targum Pseudo-Jonathan on Deut. 32:8, which preserves both readings: God apportioned "the seventy angels" over the other nations, and the number of the nations (seventy) coincided with the number of the "seventy Israelite persons who went down to Egypt." Numerous Second Temple texts operate with the assumption that the other nations are ruled by other divine beings (see the next note below). The ancient witnesses (4Q37, LXX, and Fragmentary Targum reception) lead me to prefer the "divine" option for Deut. 32:8.

14. See Deut. 4:19–20; Pss. 82; 95:5 LXX (96:5 Eng.); Zeph. 2:11; 1 Cor. 8:5; Jub. 15.31–32. The last of these is instructive: "And he sanctified them [Israel] and gathered them from all the sons of man because (there are) many nations and many peoples, and they all belong to him [the Lord], but over all of them he caused spirits to rule. . . . But over Israel he did not cause any angel or spirit to rule because he alone is their ruler" (Wintermute, *OTP* 2:87).

you have not known, neither you nor your fathers; and there you will serve other gods."[15]

Regarding the punitive rejection of sacrifices, Lev. 26:31 states, "I will turn your cities into ruins as well and make your sanctuaries desolate, and I will not smell your soothing aromas." That God "will not smell" them implies the divine disregard of these gifts. As Baruch Levine notes, "God will refuse to accept the offerings of those who have angered Him by violating his commandments."[16] This comports with the role of the sacrifices themselves: as a benefit of the maintained covenant, they cease to be effectual once the covenant is broken. Even though theoretically good and God-given, the temple and its sacrifices are not equipped to restore the covenant once it is broken, and they do not obviate the divine punishment once it is announced as certain.

"How Long, O Lord?"

The duration of this divine discipline is a vexed question. Deuteronomy does not place a literal chronological limit (seventy years or any other number) as much as a purposive limit ("until you are destroyed," "until you perish")[17] and a hyperbolic chronological description ("continually," "all the days," "forever," or "until the age").[18] "Forever" is clearly hyperbolic, given Deuteronomy's insistence that God will restore the people.[19] However, "until the age" (ἕως τοῦ αἰῶνος, Deut. 28:46 AT, LXX) could have been interpreted literally and so generated the eschatological expectation that the restoration would inaugurate "the age to come."[20]

What Deut. 28 names "curses,"[21] Lev. 26 calls "discipline" intended to turn Israel back to obedience.[22] After describing a handful of hard times (terror, consumption, fever, being ruled by enemies), God says: "If also after these

15. See also Jer. 5:19 and comments by Holladay, *Jeremiah*, 191. This plight of captivity to foreign gods/powers is also acknowledged in several Second Temple texts (1 En. 89.56, 59; 4Q389), not least the Gospels (e.g., Mark 3:22–27; Luke 4:4–7). See the discussion of this theme in Dimant, "Israel's Subjugation." On this theme in Mark, see Shively, *Apocalyptic*, 41–83.

16. B. Levine, *Leviticus*, 189. See also Kiuchi, *Leviticus*, 483. Jacob Milgrom (*Leviticus 23–27*, 2320–21) adds that Lev. 26:31 "implies that YHWH rejects not only the sacrifices but the sacrificer."

17. Deut. 28:20, 21, 22, 24, 45, 48, 51, 61.

18. Deut. 28:29, 33, 46.

19. Deut. 4:30–31; 30:1–6.

20. For terminology such as "age(s) to come," or "this present age" and "that age," see Dan. 7:18; Matt. 12:32; 13:39, 40, 49; 24:3; Mark 10:30; Luke 18:30; 20:34–35; 1 Cor. 10:11; Gal. 1:4; Eph. 1:21; 2:7; 3:21; Heb. 6:5; 9:26.

21. Deut. 28:15, 16, 17, 18, 19, 20, 45.

22. Leviticus 26 LXX employs not the nominal form of "discipline" (παιδεία) but the related verb (παιδεύσω; 26:18, 23, 28).

things you do not obey me, then I will punish you seven times more for your sins."[23] The punishments are remedial, intended to turn Israel back to obedience, and if the people do not listen, the punishment will be increased sevenfold (plausibly referring to intensity or duration).[24]

But exile, subjugation, and an abandoned temple are not God's last word. God promises that the discipline will end, and he will restore his people. The main texts from the Law on this matter are Deut. 4:27–31; 30:1–6; and Lev. 26:40–45. In these passages, Israel is told that in exile, after these blessings and curses have come upon them (Deut. 30:1), they should "seek" God and "return" to him, "listen to" and "obey" him (Deut. 4:30; 30:2), and "confess their wrongdoing" (Lev. 26:40). And they are told that their exile and captivity are how they "pay for" or "accept" (HB רָצָה, *rāṣâ*) the cost of their iniquity (Lev. 26:41, 43). The verb's meaning is context-dependent, but Gary Anderson cogently argues that it can denote payment or acceptance of the payment.[25] For example, one might vow to God an offering if he provides some good. Such vows must be "paid" (Deut. 23:21; Pss. 22:25; 50:14), and the form of "payment" for the benefit provided by God is a "votive" or "vow" offering (Lev. 7:16). When offered properly, God "accepts" it. When offered improperly (e.g., if the offerer eats any of the meat on the third day), "it shall not be acceptable [לֹא יֵרָצֶה]; it shall not be credited to the account of [the one] who offered it" (7:18).[26] Its rejection implies that the Israelite has not "paid off" his vow.[27] Consequently, for Israel to become "acceptable" by enduring exile (26:43) suggests their endurance "pays" the penalty incurred through their sin. Commenting on Lev. 26:43, Anderson says, "Leviticus 26 declares that Israel will remain in her current plight until such time as the Israelites have repa[id] the debt accrued through their iniquity."[28] Similarly, commenting on the same verse, Milgrom writes: "The implication is that Israel, in a state of remorse, must wait *passively* until its punishment is paid in full."[29] Key to these texts, then, is that endurance of the penalty and returning to God are the means through which Israel pays the debt accrued by their sin, exhausting the wrath manifest in various judgments, and arrives at the restoration.

23. Lev. 26:18; see also 26:21, 24, 28.

24. Daniel 9 plausibly interprets Lev. 26's "sevenfold" punishment in terms of duration (discussed below).

25. See the discussion in Anderson, *Sin*, 49–54.

26. Translation by Anderson, *Sin*, 52.

27. Anderson, *Sin*, 52.

28. Anderson, *Sin*, 65.

29. Milgrom, *Leviticus 23–27*, 2333. Of Lev. 26:34 he states that the use of *rāṣâ* implies that "payment is involved" (2323).

From this state of discipline, the people are to return to God. Numerous texts play on the spatial imagery of turning to depict Israel's sin, God's response, and the restoration of the people to God and of God to the people (e.g., Mal. 3:7). As the people turned away from God, so God turned away from the temple and the people, resulting in their exile. But in their captivity, they are to return to God; he will return to them and their temple; they will return to the land; and God will return to blessing them. A foundational text promising Israel's national restoration (Deut. 30:1–3, 8–10) uses terms deriving from שׁוּב (*šûb*) seven times in six verses: in exile, Israel ought to "return" the promised blessings and curses to their mind (30:1) and "return" to God (30:2), after which God will "return" them from captivity (30:3) and "return" to gather them (30:3); Israel will "return" and obey God (30:8); and God will "return" to rejoicing over them (30:9) when they "return" to God (30:10). In their state of punitive exile, then, what is expected of Israel is an eschatological "return."[30] This terminology and the covenant-restoration realities it encodes ought to contextualize the interpretation of the Gospels' presentations of John and Jesus calling Israel to return to God in the last days.

The Restoration

The blessings basic to the restoration naturally resolve the punishments Israel experiences: Though they will be plagued (Lev. 26:21) and diseased (Deut. 28:21, 59, 61), in the restoration God will heal them (Deut. 30:3; Isa. 6:10; Jer. 33:6–7). They will be handed over to their enemies (Lev. 26:25), but God will save them from their enemies (Ps. 106:47; Isa. 35:4); scattered (Lev. 26:33; Deut. 4:27; 28:64), but God will "gather" them from exile (Deut. 30:3–4; Isa. 40:11; 43:5); subject to captivity (Deut. 28:41; 30:3), but God will "redeem" or "release" them from captivity (Isa. 35:9; 52:3; 61:1; Jer. 31:11); and bereft of the divine presence in the temple (Lev. 26:31; Deut. 31:17–18), but God will return to them (Isa. 40:3–5, 9–10; 52:6–12; Ezek. 43:1–5). However, this restoration will not be just a change of address (from Babylon to Judea) or a change of ruler (from foreign gods to the Lord). Explicit in Deuteronomy is a change also of the anthropological condition. The people who were commanded to love the Lord with all their heart (6:5) will have their hearts

30. Lambert (*Repentance*, 72–85) notes that acts of returning do not always entail turning back to the Law or covenant obedience. I am not suggesting that all acts of *šûb* are "returning to the Law" or a "return" in a restoration-eschatological context. Rather, my point is only that several texts employ *šûb* (or related Greek terms) in the latter sense, including several Second Temple texts and the Synoptic Gospels, in their reading of their current situation in light of Deut. 28–30//Lev. 26.

"circumcised" (MT) or "purified" (LXX) so that they "love the LORD your God with all your heart and with all your soul, so that you may live" (30:6).

The Synoptic Gospels operate within this restorationist framework and portray Jesus as its herald and executor, which is suggested by their depiction of him as the one anointed to proclaim "release to captives" and "to heal the broken" (Isa. 61:1 AT).[31] He regularly heals those in need (e.g., Mark 1:30–42) and points to such healing as evidence that restoration is coming through him (Matt. 11:1–5). He eats with sinners, calling them to repentance because "it is not those who are well who need a physician, but those who are sick" (Luke 5:31 AT). As the divinely sent agent of "salvation,"[32] he "redeems" his people[33] and "gathers" the scattered.[34]

The Prophets and Restoration

As is often recognized, Israel's prophetic literature participates in this restorationist framework. A pattern common to several texts is accusing Israel or Judah of transgression—typically the worship of other gods, bloodshed, and economic injustice—followed by a warning to return to fidelity to God or face punishment. Punishment typically includes invasion and exile. Assurances of restoration postpunishment often follow, if not in the immediate passage, at least in the same book.

Isaiah 1 is exemplary and saturated with Lev. 26 and Deut. 28's terminology.[35] The prophet addresses "Judah and Jerusalem" (Isa. 1:1) and accuses them of having "abandoned the LORD" (1:4; cp. Deut. 28:20; 29:25; 31:16). Instead of justice, the city is full of "murderers, . . . rebels, . . . thieves" (Isa. 1:21, 23). As promised in Lev. 26, God is disciplining them with "strikes" from his sword (see Isa. 1:5, 20; cp. Lev. 26:24–25), manifest in a "desolate" land (Isa. 1:7; cp. Lev. 26:33) invaded by enemies (Isa. 1:7; cp. Deut. 28:33, 51). Given that Lev. 26 considers such punishments restorative, intended to turn Israel back to God (26:18, 21, 23, 27), Isaiah asks punished Judah, "Where will you be stricken again?" (1:5). Within this context Isaiah expresses hope and a warning: "If

31. Quoted in Luke 4:18–19; see also Matt. 11:5.

32. Matt. 1:21; Luke 1:69, 71; 2:11, 30; 3:6; 9:56; 19:9, 10.

33. Matt. 20:28; Mark 10:45; Luke 1:68; 2:38; 24:21.

34. Matt. 3:12; 12:30; 13:47–48; 22:10; 23:37; 24:31; Mark 13:27; Luke 3:17; 11:23; 13:34.

35. Though he thinks the language is conventional, Joseph Blenkinsopp (*Isaiah 1–39*, 182) notes the "Deuteronomic resonance" of Isaiah's critique. See comparable indictments in Jer. 3–5; 7; Ezek. 5–8; 16; 20:1–20. Of the latter, Risa Levitt Kohn (*New Heart*, 113) notes, "The punishment of Exile was, in [Ezekiel's] analysis, the direct result of Israel's failure to practice the legal precepts found in both Priestly and Deuteronomic traditions."

you are willing and obedient, / You will eat the best of the land; / But if you refuse and rebel, / You will be devoured by the sword" (1:19–20). The "sword" is Lev. 26's metonymy for the punitive discipline, typically manifest in foreign subjugation (26:25, 33, 36, 37).

In this sinful and punished state, additional sacrifice will not avail (Isa. 1:10–15); rather, Israel must keep God's requirements for justice in the land (1:17). Convinced that they will not repent, God declares, "I will also turn my hand against you" (1:25), after which he will "restore" the city and "redeem" Zion (1:26–27). Those who return will be redeemed (1:27), but those who remain transgressive will be destroyed (1:28). This pattern well represents the shape of restoration eschatology in many prophetic passages, in which rebellion is met with the promise of (additional) punitive discipline, during which the prophets call the people to return.[36] If the people do not respond, they will be further disciplined, but they are nonetheless promised eventual restoration, which benefits those who "return" or "repent" (e.g., Isa. 59:20).[37]

Frequently in prophetic indictments of the people, the prophets denounce the efficacy of sacrifice. Because this is sometimes misunderstood in popular and scholarly representations, and because such indictments bear upon the interpretation of the Synoptic Gospels' depiction of Jesus's temple action and his death, a brief excursus on this phenomenon is necessary.

Discipline and Sacrifice

The prophetic denunciation of sacrifice (e.g., Isa. 1:11–15; Jer. 6:20; 11:15) is not a critique of ritual or sacrifice in general but claims, in keeping with the Law, that sacrifice cannot mend the named breach.[38] Isaiah 1 is once more exemplary. Having accused the people of the grave sins of abandoning the Lord (1:4), murder, bribery, and injustice (1:15–23), Isaiah famously announces the Lord's rejection of offerings:

> "What are your many sacrifices to Me?"
> Says the LORD.
> "I have had enough of burnt offerings of rams
> And the fat of fattened cattle;

36. Isa. 31:6; 44:22; 55:7; Jer. 3:12, 14, 22; 4:1; 15:19; Lam. 3:40; Hosea 6:1; 12:6; 14:1–2; Joel 2:12–13; Zech. 1:3–4; Mal. 3:7.

37. Not every prophetic passage names "returning" as Israel's requisite act. Ezekiel 36–37 simply describes the restoration as a divine act. Early Jewish interpretations of what Israel must do (if anything) are discussed in Lambert, *Repentance*, 121–50.

38. For a distinct but related interpretation of the prophetic denunciations of cult, see Klawans, *Purity, Sacrifice*, 75–100. Closer to my position, see Rillera, *Lamb*, 141–49.

> And I take no pleasure in the blood of bulls, lambs, or goats.
> When you come to appear before Me,
> Who requires of you this trampling of My courtyards?
> Do not go on bringing your worthless offerings,
> Incense is an abomination to Me.
> New moon and Sabbath, the proclamation of an assembly—
> I cannot endure wrongdoing and the festive assembly.
> I hate your new moon festivals and your appointed feasts,
> They have become a burden to Me;
> I am tired of bearing them.
> So when you spread out your hands in prayer,
> I will hide My eyes from you;
> Yes, even though you offer many prayers,
> I will not be listening.
> Your hands are covered with blood." (1:11–15)

This passage and others like it have been seriously misunderstood when interpreted to indicate either God's rejection of ritual or sacrifice in itself, or a supposed moral superiority of prophet over priest, in which prophets are characterized as morally enlightened and priests as concerned only with the correct performance of arcane rites.[39] On the contrary, in announcing God's rejection of offerings in light of the grave defection of the people, the prophets simply announce what the "priestly" literature instructs and predicts. Two points should be made here.

First, even in a maintained covenant, the sacrificial system does not provide forgiveness or atonement for every kind of sin.[40] Numbers 35 explicitly forbids accepting a ransom for one guilty of murder and states, "[The murderer] must be put to death" (35:31). It further asserts that "no atonement can be made for the land for the blood that is shed on it, except by the blood of the one who shed it" (35:33). This does not declare that God cannot forgive a person for such a sin (as David's life shows), but such forgiveness is not a by-product of the prescribed sacrifices.[41] As Andrew Rillera notes, "The entire system of atonement (decontamination) is limited in what it solves, according to the Torah."[42] Similarly, those guilty of sins named in Lev. 18 and 20 are "cut off from among their people" (18:29) and/or "put to death" (e.g., 20:2–3, 27). If

39. Classical versions of these positions are articulated in Wellhausen (*Prolegomena*, 392–401, 422–25) and Weber (*Sociology of Religion*). These positions are summarized and critiqued in Klawans, *Purity, Sacrifice*, 75–77.

40. See the discussion in Rillera (*Lamb*, 84–98, 132–36) concerning the limits of atoning sacrifices.

41. So also Rillera, *Lamb*, 95–96, 132–33.

42. Rillera, *Lamb*, 132.

the people follow such prohibited practices, they will be exiled (20:22). While scholars debate the scope of the remedy provided by the Day of Atonement—whether it atones for all sins, including those of Lev. 18 and 20, or only for unintentional sins, which are expiable[43]—the point is moot in Isa. 1, which announces God's rejection not just of individual sacrifices but also of their "appointed feasts" (מוֹעֵד, τὰς ἑορτάς, 1:14). Given that the Day of Atonement is one of the "appointed feasts" (מוֹעֵד, ἑορταί) that Israel is to keep (Lev. 23:2, 4, 27–32), it follows that whatever the Day of Atonement covers, even this is rejected in Isa. 1. The Greek translation (LXX) of Isa. 1:14 states the point forcefully: "My soul hates your appointed feasts. . . . *I will no longer forgive/bear your sins*" (οὐκέτι ἀνήσω τὰς ἁμαρτίας ὑμῶν).[44]

Second, Lev. 26:31 and Deut. 31:17–18 claim that when the covenant is violated, God will not regard their offerings and will hide his face from them. When the people go astray and do not turn back, God states: "I will not smell your soothing aromas" (Lev. 26:31). The prophetic denunciation of sacrifices exemplifies, then, the instruction and prediction of the priestly/legal literature that (a) not all sins have a sacrificial remedy, and (b) one of the punishments consequent to the violated covenant is the divine disregard of offerings. Therefore, when Isaiah announces God's rejection of sacrifices, it is not a blanket condemnation of offerings in themselves but a rejection of these offerings, given the nature of the accusations against them: murder, bribery, and defection from the Lord.[45]

According to Jeremiah, the sacrifices, though good, will not help Israel avert the decreed punishment. Because sacrifices are a blessing of the maintained covenant, they are no longer efficacious once the covenant is broken. Having failed to repent, the people must now endure the promised discipline, and sacrifice will not change the matter.[46] Jeremiah 11 is clearest here: "'The house

43. See the discussion in Gane, *Cult and Character*, 198–213; Rillera, *Lamb*, 95–96, 132–36. Rillera reminds us that the Day of Atonement purges only the tent and its sancta, not the land. As murder and certain prohibited sexual acts defile the land (Num. 35:33; Lev. 18:25, 27–28), sacrifices that purge the sancta would not atone for these sins. On the significance of this ritual, see Milgrom, *Leviticus 1–16*, 1011–84; L. Feldman, *Story of Sacrifice*, 153–69; Janowski, "Das Geschenk der Versöhnung," 3–31; Rillera, *Lamb*, 127–32. For interpretations of the Day of Atonement in early Judaism, see Hieke and Nicklas, *Day of Atonement*.

44. Unless otherwise indicated, all LXX translations are mine.

45. See also Rillera, *Lamb*, 144–45. He states, "It is not as if the sacrificial system was considered inherently 'ineffective' or 'merely rituals.' It is just that the corruption is so pervasive that the sacrifices themselves are considered invalid *now* due to these *particular reasons*" (145, italics original).

46. See Jer. 6:15–20; 11:10–15. *Pace* Holladay (*Jeremiah*, 223), such "critiques" of sacrifice do not amount to Jeremiah's "rejection of the sacrificial system altogether" due to an increase of "religious bureaucracy." If Jeremiah were against the cult itself, he would not encourage

of Israel and the house of Judah have broken my covenant.' . . . Therefore this is what the LORD says: 'Behold I am bringing disaster [κακά] on them which they will not be able to escape; though they will cry out to me, I will not listen to them" (11:10–11). God then tells Jeremiah: "Do not pray for this people, nor lift up a cry or prayer for them; for I will not listen when they call to me because of their disaster. What right has my beloved in my house / When she has done many vile deeds? / Can the sacrificial flesh take away from you your disaster [κακίας σου], / So that you can rejoice?" (11:14–15). Here Jeremiah is critiquing not "the sacrifices" but the people's misdeeds. Because Jeremiah's command to "return" has gone unheeded, exile and captivity are decreed, and sacrifice will not avert that punishment.

Much of the above is powerfully narrated in 2 Chron. 36. Referring to the temple's destruction by Babylon and the subsequent captivity, the Chronicler states:

> All the officials of the priests and the people were very unfaithful. . . . The LORD, the God of their fathers, sent word to them again and again by his messengers because he had compassion on his people and on his dwelling place; but they continually mocked the messengers of God, despised his words, and scoffed at his prophets, until the wrath of the LORD arose against his people, until there was no remedy. And so he brought up against them the king of the Chaldeans. (2 Chron. 36:14–17)

"Until there was no remedy"; this prognosis is as dire as it is startling. As Ralph Klein summarizes, God's anger "flared up against his people without any chance of avoiding this punishment."[47] All plight, no (sacrificial) solution.[48]

All Plight, One Solution

Given God's promise of punishment and restoration, what is Israel to do once the punishment is decreed and sacrifice and prophetic intercession do not avail? If Israel is subject to the plights, what's the solution? A thread in several texts states that once the offer to repentance has been refused and the

---

the people by saying that in the restoration, all the temple's vessels hauled to Babylon will be brought back (27:21–22) and that "the Levitical priests shall never lack a man in my presence to offer burnt offerings . . . and to make sacrifices forever" (33:18 ESV).

47. Klein, *2 Chronicles*, 541.

48. I do not imply that Judaism as a religion was hopeless, in need of something new (i.e., Christianity). I am referring to the recognition in many texts that the plights occasioned by Israel's breach of the covenant were not remediable by sacrifice; what was needed after they had endured the discipline was the eschatological return, a divine act of rescue.

discipline is set, the only remaining course of action is to endure it.[49] Addressing Zedekiah, who was resisting Babylonian invasion, Jeremiah says: "Thus says the LORD: . . . 'Behold, I will turn back the weapons of war that are in your hands and with which you are fighting against the king of Babylon. . . . And I will bring them together into the midst of this city. I myself will fight against you . . . in anger and in fury and in great wrath" (Jer. 21:4–5 ESV). God will thwart the efforts of Zedekiah and make Babylon the chosen instrument to execute God's covenant vengeance. Or in Isaiah's vocabulary regarding Assyria, they are the "rod of [God's] anger" (Isa. 10:5). Since captivity is the promised punishment for their covenant violation, Judah is to submit to Babylon and go into exile.

Significantly, Jeremiah does not simply give Israel their marching orders; rather, he interprets their submission to the punitive discipline as the way they manifest the obedience required by Deut. 30. Jeremiah speaks to the people: "This is what the LORD says, 'Behold, I am setting before you the way of life and the way of death [ἐγὼ δέδωκα πρὸ προσώπου ὑμῶν τὴν ὁδὸν τῆς ζωῆς καὶ τὴν ὁδὸν τοῦ θανάτου, LXX]. Anyone who dwells in this city will die by the sword, by famine, or by plague; but anyone who leaves and goes over to the Chaldeans who are besieging you will live, and he will have his own life as plunder'" (Jer. 21:8–9). The phrase "I set before you life and death" recalls Moses's language in Deut. 30: "I call heaven and earth to witness against you today, that I have placed before you life and death [τὴν ζωὴν καὶ τὸν θάνατον δέδωκα πρὸ προσώπου ὑμῶν, LXX], the blessing and the curse. So choose life in order that you may live" (30:19).[50] In context, Moses is exhorting obedience to God's commandments and "his voice" (30:15–20). In Jeremiah's context, what God's "voice" has spoken is a temporary discipline: exile to Babylon. Thus Jeremiah announces that the way to Moses's promised "life" is not staying in the city, but surrendering to the Babylonians. The one who wishes to save his life by staying in Jerusalem will lose it, but the one who loses his life to the Babylonians in obedience to the prophet's message will save it.[51]

And Jeremiah is not alone in this regard. For example, after naming the transgression of the people, their refusal to repent, and the decreed outcome

49. This is implied already by Num. 35:33 and Lev. 18:25, 27–28, wherein certain sins defile the land, for which the only remedy is exile. See comparable points in Rillera, *Lamb*, 141–49. See also Anderson (*Sin*), who argues that in many texts sin is metaphorized as "debt" that must be repaid. He so interprets Lev. 26:43 and Isa. 40:2, wherein Israel's sin is conceived as debt that their exile/endurance of the punishment pays (*Sin*, 45–66). Blenkinsopp (*Isaiah 40–55*, 180), commenting on Isa. 40:2's declaration that "Her debt has been paid" (his translation), says that Israel's endurance of exile is how she "satisfied her obligations and paid off her debts."

50. See the discussion in Parke-Taylor, *Book of Jeremiah*, 203; Plant, *Good Figs, Bad Figs*, 64.

51. See further discussion in Plant, *Good Figs, Bad Figs*, 69, 132. See also Jer. 24:1–10.

of warfare, Isaiah says: "Certainly this wrongdoing will not be forgiven you / Until you [plural] die [ἕως ἂν ἀποθάνητε]" (22:14).[52] These and other texts (discussed below) interpret Israel's plight as the wrath of God manifest in their subjection to foreign enemies, poured out as promised in Deut. 28–32 and Lev. 26 because of both Israel's covenant violation and their failure to repent when given the option for decades. This punishment is disciplinary, intended to motivate their reformation, and as such it is temporary. But for those reasons, according to such texts, it is also mandatory: once decreed, it must be endured. This outlook is implied in the covenant codes themselves: the restoration follows after "all of these things have come upon you, the blessing and the curse" (Deut. 30:1). In their exile, the land will enjoy its Sabbath rests, and the people will be making amends for their guilt (Lev. 26:43). Lest one forget that this book is about Jesus, the Law, and the restoration, my point is that the Gospels employ these ideas—not an abstract "Someone must die"—to depict Jesus as the one who calls Israel to repent. And when they do not, Jesus endures the punitive discipline still hanging over the people, being himself "handed over to the nations," while assuring that those who heed his instruction to repent and follow him in his bearing of the affliction will experience the restoration.

Restoration, Kingdom, Jubilee, and Law

Despite the morose context of some of the above material, the prophets remain certain that God will keep his promise to restore his exiled people. Prophetic depictions of the restoration often entail a gathering of the exiles (e.g., Isa. 11:12; 40:11; Jer. 23:3; Ezek. 34:13; 36:24), a return to the land (e.g., Isa. 54:3; Jer. 29:14; Ezek. 36:24), and the return of the divine presence (e.g., Isa. 40:3–9; 60:1–2; Jer. 3:16–17; Ezek. 43:1–5).

Due to their impact on the Synoptic Gospels' presentation of Jesus, three additional depictions of the restoration according to the prophets should be highlighted: the restoration and the kingdom, the eschatological Jubilee, and the Law.

May Your Kingdom Come

God is regularly referred to as Israel's "King."[53] Because he ideally rules over his people, his departure from the temple and their subjection to other

52. See also Lam. 3:28–32, wherein Jerusalem's destruction is described as what the speaker ought to endure as the divinely placed "yoke," confident that the one who laid it upon him "will not reject forever" but will eventually show "compassion" (3:31–32).

53. Frequently in Psalms (e.g., 5:2; 44:4; 45:6; 68:24; 95:3; 145:1). See also Isa. 33:22; 43:15.

nations and their gods suggest that God is no longer "reigning" over them. When lamenting the plight of his people, Jeremiah says: "Behold, listen! The cry of the daughter of my people from a distant land: / 'Is the Lord not in Zion? Is her King not within her?'" (Jer. 8:19). In their subjugated state, the people cry: "We have become like those over whom you have never ruled" (Isa. 63:19). Though biblical authors would not claim that God has been "dethroned," they nonetheless await the return of his reign and the supplanting of their enemies' rule. For these reasons, Isaiah occasionally announces the restoration in terms of God's return to "rule" and "reign" over his people. Isaiah 52:7–8 states, "How delightful on the mountains / Are the feet of one who brings good news, / Who announces peace / And brings good news of happiness, / Who announces salvation, / And says to Zion, 'Your God reigns!' [βασιλεύσει σου ὁ θεός, LXX] / Listen! Your watchmen raise their voices, / They shout joyfully together; / For they will see with their own eyes / When the Lord restores Zion."[54] The Gospel resonances are clear: Jesus announces Isaiah's "good news" and the nearness of God's reign (e.g., Mark 1:14–15) and teaches his disciples to pray, "Your kingdom come" (Matt. 6:10). Since "kingdom" language signals restoration (see also Zech. 14:9), and Jesus's teaching about the kingdom of God is fundamental to his message, his announcement of the impending restoration would be basic to his preaching.

Forgive Us Our Debts

In Lev. 25, God legislates a Jubilee every fiftieth year (vv. 8–10). In this year, land sold or leased (probably due to debt; v. 25) reverts to its original owner (vv. 10, 28), the land remains unsown and unharvested (v. 11), and Israelite slaves captive either to Israelites (vv. 39–41) or non-Israelites (vv. 47, 54) are released. Though these laws legislate noneschatological realities, given that Israel's punishment was expressed in terms of their exile from their ancestral land and captivity to non-Israelites, some restoration texts employ Jubilee terminology and logic to describe God's act of restoration in which Israel will return to its ancestral land and be released from captivity to foreign nations.[55]

These themes rush together in the description of Isa. 61's appointed figure. The passage reads: "The Spirit of the Lord God is upon me, / Because the Lord anointed me / To bring good news to the humble; / He has sent me to bind up the brokenhearted, / To proclaim liberty to captives, / And freedom to prisoners; / To proclaim the favorable year of the Lord, / And the day of vengeance of our God; / To comfort all who mourn" (61:1–2). Several things

54. See also Isa. 40:9–10.
55. See Bergsma, *Jubilee*, 177–304.

should be noted: First, the anointing by God's spirit distinguishes the figure for this role. Second, all that this figure accomplishes pertains to many of the restoration themes already discussed: announcing "the good news" (cp. Isa. 40:9; 52:7–8), healing the wounded (Deut. 30:3, 9; Hosea 6:1; Jer. 33:6–7), freeing the captives (Deut. 30:3; Isa. 51:14; 58:6), and comforting those who mourn (Deut. 32:36; Isa. 40:1). Third, his role to "proclaim liberty" (קָרָא דְרוֹר, Isa. 61:1) likely alludes to the Jubilee legislation in Lev. 25:10,[56] wherein every fiftieth year Israel is to "proclaim liberty" (קָרָא דְרוֹר) throughout the land, permitting any portion of land leased or sold to revert to its original family. Though Lev. 25:10 is not itself a promise about eschatological restoration, Isa. 61 evidently uses the imagery eschatologically to describe it: Israel, captive in foreign lands, will be released from captivity and return to their land. As recognized by many, the Gospels' depiction of Jesus as the one anointed by the Spirit at the beginning of his ministry (Mark 1:10; Matt. 3:16; Luke 3:22) recalls these themes. He is the Spirit-anointed agent of the restoration, who will heal the sick, preach the good news to the afflicted, proclaim release to the captives, and enact Israel's "consolation" (Luke 2:25). Jesus reads Isa. 61 and refers it to himself and his ministry (Luke 4:18–21),[57] and he alludes to it in his answer to John's disciples as proof that he is "the Expected One" (Matt. 11:3–5 NASB [1995]), signifying that Jesus's restoration announcement/activity is coded as an eschatological Jubilee. Mark similarly employs these themes in his implicit description of the restoration as the eschatological Jubilee.[58] Significantly, just as the Jubilee was interpreted to require the forgiveness of debts,[59] so in the eschatological Jubilee, God will enact a release of Israel's debts (i.e., their sins). For this reason, Jesus teaches his disciples to pray, "Release us from our debts!" (καὶ ἄφες ἡμῖν τὰ ὀφειλήματα ἡμῶν, Matt. 6:12 AT), which clearly refers to people's "transgressions" (παραπτώματα, 6:14).[60]

Restoration and the Law

Deuteronomy 30 promises that in the restoration, God will transform Israel's heart so that they will keep the Law's fundamental requirement of loving the Lord with all their heart (30:6, alluding to 6:5). This restoration of the heart to equip it for obedience and fidelity to the LORD alone is attested in

56. Commonly noted. See Motyer, *Isaiah*, 500.

57. On this scene and its Jubilee resonances, see R. Sloan, *Favorable Year of the Lord*.

58. See the discussion in Williams, "Melchizedek."

59. See Josephus, *Ant.* 3.282; Philo, *On the Virtues* 1.99; *Spec. Laws* 2.110–18, 122. Further discussed under "Retaliation" in chap. 3.

60. See also Luke 7:36–50, where debt forgiveness parabolically illustrates forgiveness of sins, and Luke 13:4's sinners as "debtors" (ὀφειλέται). See J. Sanders, "Sins, Debts, and Jubilee Release."

prophetic literature. The new covenant will not be like the old in that the Law will be "within them and [God will] write it on their heart" (Jer. 31:33). After their rescue, God promises, "I will remove the heart of stone . . . and give you a heart of flesh. And I will put my Spirit within you and bring it about that you walk in my statutes, and are careful and follow my ordinances" (Ezek. 36:26–27). This he will do when he sanctifies his own name (36:23). Hence Jesus's disciples should pray, "Sanctify your name!" (Matt. 6:9 AT). Far from abolishing the Law, then, a benefit of the restoration is the transformation of the heart to enable its keeping.

The Prolonged Discipline

While much of the above is relatively straightforward, it is important to grasp that for many, the return to the land of some from the Southern Kingdom did not fulfill the awaited restoration. This conviction is shared by numerous biblical and Second Temple texts, including the Synoptic Gospels. A brief survey will help contextualize the eventual discussion of Jesus's mission and teaching. Readers already familiar with these ideas will forgive, I hope, any perceived tedium of such a survey, which I present for two reasons: (1) to demonstrate that the Synoptic Gospels clearly and thoroughly participate in this restorationist discourse and (2) to avoid the dreaded accusation that I am merely "reading my biblical theology into the texts."

Daniel 9, ostensibly set in the Babylonian exile, opens by Daniel positioning his plea for restoration approximately seventy years after the deportation promised by Jeremiah, who had asserted that Israel's Babylonian captivity would last "seventy years" (Jer. 25:11–12). This prediction by Jeremiah is recounted in Dan. 9:2, after which Daniel prays for restoration. However, Daniel confesses that though God brought the promised curses, Israel still has not repented (9:13–14). The divine response to this prayer is that Israel's desolation will last an additional "seventy sevens" (9:24 AT). This is potentially inferred from Lev. 26's promise of sevenfold punishment if Israel does not turn back (26:18, 24, 28): because Israel did not respond to God's discipline, the punishment that was to last seventy years will now be increased sevenfold, resulting in a desolation that lasts an additional seventy sevens—that is, 490 years.[61]

61. So Gabriele Boccaccini, "Covenantal Theology," 43; Bergsma, *Jubilee*, 225–26; Hartman and Di Lella, *Daniel*, 250. For an alternative basis of calculating Daniel's "seventy sevens," see Anderson, *Sin*, 84. For an example of Second Temple exegesis of Daniel's "490 years," see 4Q390 and its exposition by Eshel, "490-Year Prophecy." Other durations of Israel's discipline were probably calculated. See CD 1.5–6 and 20.15, appealing evidently to Ezek. 4:5–6's "390 years" and "forty years" of iniquity. See the discussion in Knibb, "Exile," 262.

Ezra and Malachi likewise assume that the return to the land by some Judeans did not constitute the restoration. Ezra 9 states: "Since the days of our fathers to this day we have been in great guilt, and because of our wrongful deeds [ἀνομίαις] we, our kings, and our priests have been handed over [παρεδόθημεν] to the kings of the lands, to the sword [חֶרֶב, ῥομφαίᾳ], to captivity [שְׁבִי, αἰχμαλωσίᾳ], to plunder, and to open shame, as it is this day" (9:7). Nearly every descriptor in his claim refers to punishments promised in Lev. 26 and/or Deut. 28.[62] Even those returned from Babylon are still, "to this day," in captivity, "in great guilt," and "handed over" to others. "For we are slaves," he continues (Ezra 9:9). The return of a few tribes to the land, therefore, has not fulfilled what was predicted. The temple is not glorified, captivity persists, guilt remains, the tribes are not united, the people neither know nor obey the Law (9:14–15), and so the restoration remains an event on the horizon.[63] Likewise, Malachi implies that God is not in the temple (3:1), he is not accepting their sacrifices (1:10; 2:13),[64] and both priests and nonpriests transgress the Law (1:6–8; 2:7–11). They are assured, however, that God will return and that he will send a messenger before his arrival (3:1; 4:5 [3:23 MT; 3:22 LXX]) who "will [re]turn the hearts of the fathers back to their children and the hearts of the children to their fathers" (4:6 [3:24 MT; 3:23 LXX]).

Thus Malachi confirms that restoration awaits, yet the Lord is certainly coming. But a somber note resounds: When he comes, who will be ready? The chord struck by Moses and other prophets is hit one last time: "From the days of your fathers you have turned away from my statutes and have not kept them. Return to me, and I will return to you" (3:7). Alongside the regularity of this call to return, often without any accompanying detailed explanation as to what such a "return" would require, the text unsurprisingly articulates this question of the people: "But you say, 'How shall we return?'" (3:7).

"How Shall We Return?"

"How shall we return?" This basic question is at the core of this study. Israel needs to return to participate in the promised restoration, but many

62. Leviticus 26:43 claims that Israel is under the punitive curses for their "lawless" (ἀνομίας) deeds, and Lev. 26 and/or Deut. 28 describe the covenantal punishments in terms used in Ezra 9:7: i.e., being "handed over" (Lev. 26:25; Deut. 32:30), suffering from the "sword" (Lev. 26:25, 33, 36, 37), and "captivity" (Deut. 28:41). See further McConville ("Ezra-Nehemiah," 209), who states, "The language of Deuteronomy is an important factor [in Ezra 9], in providing a standard by which present experience can be measured." He concludes that Ezra-Nehemiah depicts the restoration as unfulfilled.

63. See also Zech. 8:14, 16–17; 10:6–10.

64. So Jacobs, *Haggai and Malachi*, 196–200.

prophetic calls lack a thorough description of what that would entail. Several texts name a few specific commands that suggest how Israel might obey the prophetic summons. Jeremiah 17:21–27 asserts that if the people "keep the Sabbath day holy" (17:24), Jerusalem will be "inhabited forever" (17:25). Zechariah 8:16–17 requires speaking and judging with truth, avoiding perjury, and not scheming against each other. Hosea 12:6 asserts simply: "Return to your God, / Maintain kindness and justice [ἔλεον καὶ κρίμα, 12:7 LXX], / And wait for your God continually." After providing various instructions they ought to obey (Mal. 2:15; 3:5, 10), Malachi concludes: "Remember the Law of Moses my servant, the statutes and ordinances which I commanded" (4:4 [3:22 MT; 3:24 LXX]).

As helpful as these instructions are, basic interpretative questions arise. What does it mean to "observe justice"? What does it mean to keep the Sabbath? The commandments are not self-interpreting. A moment's reflection on the commandment "Do no work on the Sabbath" reveals this,[65] not to mention commandments with temporal components that threaten keeping one or the other. Thus if the requisite "return" entails Law-keeping, and if the restoration benefits those who "obey God's voice according to all that he has commanded" (Deut. 30:2–3 AT), then knowing how to return necessitates knowing what the Law requires. It is these questions—How do we return? and How do we keep this Law rightly?—that govern much of the discourse known in preserved texts of the Second Temple period, including the Synoptic Gospels, to which I now turn.

Second Temple Judaism and the Eschatological Return

As Michael Stone notes, "By the period of the Second Temple, the Deuteronomic pattern had become normative in many circles."[66] Numerous texts of the Second Temple period express dissatisfaction with the events following the return under Cyrus and a concomitant conviction of a restoration yet to come. With such hopes, many of these writings prescribe what they regard as necessary to guarantee participation in that coming age. Jubilees, for example, describes Israel's "history" and future restoration in terms of Moses's warnings in Lev. 26 and Deut. 28–30.[67] Moses is assured that Israel will break

65. For example, see the extensive survey of Second Temple interpretation of Sabbath legislation in Doering, *Schabbat*.

66. Stone, *Ancient Judaism*, 81.

67. James C. VanderKam (*Jubilees 1*, 2–4, 25–38) argues that Jubilees's composition dates to the mid-second century BCE, but see criticisms of his view by Michael Segal (*Book of Jubilees*,

the Law and worship other gods and so receive the promised discipline (Jub. 1.7–14), but in the future, some within Israel will begin to return to the Law (23.26).[68] The text contains nomistic legislation that serves as the interpretation of the Law from which Israel has deviated; obedience to such interpretation characterizes those who return and will experience the promised restoration—still future from the text's perspective (50.5)—which includes the transformation of the heart, the performance of God's commandments, the eschatological sanctuary, deliverance from Satan/Mastema, and renewal of creation (1.15–29; 23.27–30; 50.5). Until then, Israel languishes under the punitive discipline.

Tobit and Baruch similarly characterize Israel as in exile due to their violation of the Law, employing the language of Lev. 26, Deut. 28–30, and Dan. 9 to describe Israel's "current" situation.[69] Tobit 14 claims that the return to the land and rebuilt temple did not constitute the restoration and states that the eschatological temple would not be built "until the period when the times of fulfillment shall come," after which "they all" will return from exile (14:5). As Beate Ego notes, "The author does not regard the Exile as being ended with the return to Jerusalem and the rebuilding of the temple. . . . The Exile encompasses the complete current and future history of Israel, continuing until the fulfilling of the great eschatological day of salvation that the prophets have . . . promised."[70] Assured that restoration will come, Tobit describes who will participate in its blessings: those who "love God" (οἱ ἀγαπῶντες τὸν θεόν) and are "mindful" of God will be saved, gathered, and inherit the land (14:7). Such benefits redounding to those who "love God" likely alludes to Deut. 30's promises that in the restoration, the returnees will be "gathered" (30:3), inherit the land (30:5), and have their hearts divinely transformed to "love the Lord your God . . . so that you may live" (ἀγαπᾶν κύριον τὸν θεόν σου . . . ἵνα ζῇς σύ, 30:6). Moreover, Tobit elsewhere employs "mindful" as a quality of those who keep the Law's commandments (1:10–12; 4:5, 19). Through its protagonist's approved actions and speeches, Tobit endorses the dietary laws (1:10); purity laws (2:5, 9); acts of charity, often manifest in burying corpses (1:16–18; 4:7–11, 16–17); and endogamy (4:12–13; 6:12).[71] Such actions will characterize those who "return" to God in the restoration, for which reason

35–40), who opts for a date (of redaction) after "the formation of the Essene sect or stream" (322), with a terminus ad quem between 125 and 100 BCE (36).

68. On the exile-return theme in Jubilees, see Halpern-Amaru, "Exile and Return."

69. Fitzmyer (*Tobit*, 51–52) argues for a date of composition ca. 225–175 BCE.

70. Beate Ego, "Tobit," 45. For Tobit's reception of Deuteronomic ideas, see Hofmann, "Die Rezeption des Deuteronomiums."

71. On the halakhic practices in Tobit, see Dimant, "Tobit and the Qumran Halakhah."

from his deathbed he exhorts obedience (14:8). Baruch similarly names Israel's transgression as the basis for their punishment, which endures even to "this day" (1:20). From that setting, Baruch exhorts the audience to "return [ἐπιστρέφου] and take hold [of the Law]" (4:2 AT) and to "return with tenfold zeal to seek him" (4:28 NRSV) because the divine "mercy" and "comfort" are soon to be revealed (4:22, 30).

Josephus paraphrases Moses's speech at the end of Deuteronomy, claiming that the temple will be burned and Israel will go into exile for their violation of the laws (*Ant.* 4.302–3, 313–14). During the time of affliction, repentance will not benefit them (4.191, 314). Such discipline will happen "not once, but often" (4.314), and he describes it as still ongoing in his day (4.303).

In 2 Maccabees, the people are suffering under the punitive discipline, manifest in foreign persecution, due to Jewish lawbreaking (4:10–16; 5:17). Such persecution is labeled "discipline" (7:33) and the "wrath of the Almighty that has justly fallen on our whole nation" (7:38) "because of our own sins" (7:32). Through the brothers' endurance of the plight (7:1–42), God's wrath "turned to mercy" (8:5), leading to reclamation of the temple (10:1).[72] However, even with the above events in their past, the letter prefixed to the narrative expresses hope that God will soon reveal his glory, have mercy, and gather the scattered people (2:7–8, 18). Thus, even with partial independence and a reclaimed and functioning temple, the letter indicates that in the late second century BCE,[73] the promises of the restoration are regarded as unfulfilled.

Finally, 2 Baruch, though it may postdate the Gospels, is quite illustrative.[74] Cast as the Babylonian invasion as experienced by "these two tribes which remained" (1.2), it probably reacts to the Roman destruction of the Jerusalem temple.[75] The people's judgment is described as occasioned by their covenant violation, and yet the promised restoration is on the horizon. Considering such catastrophes, the writer of 2 Baruch asks: "Where is all that which you said to Moses about us?" (3.9). He is assured that a messianic figure will judge the nations and comfort his people. Trusting that restoration will come, Baruch asks, "For whom and for how many will these things be? Or who will be worthy to live in that time?" (41.1).

72. Doran, *2 Maccabees*, 163. On the Jewish "martyrs" in 2 Maccabees, see van Henten, *Maccabean Martyrs*.

73. For discussion of composition, see Doran, *2 Maccabees*, 14–17. John J. Collins (*Daniel, First Maccabees*, 262) dates the first letter (2 Macc. 1:1–9), which itself approximates the composition of the epitome, to 124 BCE.

74. Second Baruch was possibly composed in the early second century CE. Daniel Gurtner (*Second Baruch*, 18) dates it to 95 CE. Translations are by Klijn, *OTP* 1:621–52.

75. See the discussion in Gurtner, *Second Baruch*, 1–20.

In other words, 2 Baruch wants to know how people may experience the restoration. In Malachi's idiom, "How shall we return?" The response: "The good that was mentioned before will be to those who have believed [or "been faithful"], and the opposite of these things will be to those who have despised" (42.2). Subsequent material implies that believing/fidelity refers to obeying the Law (esp. 54.5, 21).[76] Thus, 2 Baruch addresses the people: "You, however, do not withdraw from the way of the Law, but guard and admonish the people who are left lest they withdraw from the commandments. . . . For when you endure and persevere in his fear and do not forget his Law, the time again will take a turn for the better for you. And they will participate in the consolation of Zion" (44.2–7). Note that their Law-keeping does not earn their salvation or cause God to act; rather, Law-keeping guarantees that they will participate in the restoration.

After a vision describes their judgment and restoration (2 Bar. 53–74), Baruch is told, "Go, therefore, now during these days and instruct the people as much as you can so that they may learn lest they die in the last times, but may learn so that they live in the last times" (76.5). Consequently, Baruch writes a letter to those in captivity:

> I say to you after you suffered that if you obey the thing which I have said to you, you shall receive from the Mighty One everything which has been prepared. . . . Remember Zion and the Law and the holy land and your brothers and the covenant and your fathers, and do not forget the festivals and the Sabbaths. And give this letter and the traditions of the Law to your children after you as also our fathers handed down to you. And ask always and pray seriously with your whole soul that the Mighty One may accept you in mercy. (84.6–10)

God will act to restore the people. What remains to be seen is how the people "shall receive" what he has prepared. And the answer is that after they suffer the punitive discipline, they ought to "remember the Law" (cp. Mal. 4:4 [3:22 MT; 3:24 LXX]) and keep it in accord with a presumably authoritative interpretation present in their "traditions." Though 2 Baruch does not state the content of those traditions, presumably a known body of teaching was thereby signified.

Additional texts assuming the plight of a prolonged discipline and future (or only "now" inbreaking) restoration could be added, not least the Damascus Document,[77] 1 Enoch's Animal Apocalypse (1 En. 85–90) and

76. Klijn, *OTP* 1:633.

77. In the second century BCE, the community responsible for CD believed that the people were still in the "age of wrath" (CD-A 1.5–6). Those in the group were members of "the new

Apocalypse of Weeks (1 En. 93.1–10; 91.11–17),[78] Pss. Sol. 17, and Philo's *On Reward and Punishments*.[79] But the point is made. With the exception of 2 Baruch, each of these texts is written sometime between the second century BCE and the mid- to late first century CE, implying several things. First, even in those decades, well after the return to the land and the reconstruction of the temple, several texts employ the terminology of Lev. 26 and Deut. 28–30 in describing Israel as under punitive discipline—commonly described in terms of captivity, exile, and the questionable status of the temple—due to Israel's historic and/or present transgression. Restoration remains on the horizon, and what Israel must do is "return." Second, the interpretation of the Law to which they must return is exposited (CD, Jubilees) or implicitly endorsed (1 Enoch, Tobit, 2 Baruch). Consequently, the notion that Israel remains under the punitive discipline and awaits restoration, whose benefits redound to the repentant/obedient, is both a well-established historical expectation and a widely expressed reading of the Law and the Prophets.

Restoration Eschatology in the Gospels

At last, we arrive at the Synoptic Gospels. Matthew, Mark, and Luke each open by characterizing Israel as still enduring the punitive discipline, and each presents the activity of John and Jesus as the divinely appointed heralds and agents of the restoration. Through them, Israel will experience God's mercy or judgment depending on the people's response to their instruction. Recognizing the restoration-eschatological context of their missions will help situate Jesus's announcement and teaching as the answer to the question "How shall we return?" It will also contextualize his legal controversies as intramural debates about his interpretation of the Law conditioned by the irrupting restoration and his role in inaugurating it.

---

covenant" (CD-A 6.19) who had "returned to the Law of Moses" (CD-A 15.9), which they kept in step with the group's teacher(s) (CD-A 1.11; 4.8) while "the curses of the covenant" clung to those who did not "return" (CD-A 1.17). For a study of the Damascus Document, see Hultgren, *Damascus Covenant*.

78. Loren T. Stuckenbruck (*1 Enoch 91–108*, 115) interprets silence about the temple post-return to imply criticism of it.

79. Philo (*Rewards* 126, 138) describes much of Israel in his day (mid-first century CE) as scattered due to their violation of the Law. If they acknowledge their sin and return to obedience (117, 163–65), they will (nonallegorically) return from exile. On Philo's eschatology, see Penner, "Philo's Eschatology." See also E. P. Sanders, *Jesus and Judaism*, 86.

Mark

The Gospel of Mark opens by presenting John as the divinely sent messenger who prepares the people for the Lord's arrival to restore and to judge. Quoting a combination of Exod. 23:20, Mal. 3:1, and Isa. 40:3,[80] Mark describes John as the voice crying in the wilderness who prepares the way of the Lord (Mark 1:2–3). Malachi identifies this messenger as "Elijah" (Mal. 4:5–6), claiming he would "restore" (שׁוּב, *šûb*, 3:24 MT; ἀποκαταστήσει, 3:23 LXX) the people before the Lord's arrival. Jesus identifies John as this "Elijah," who had attempted to restore (ἀποκαθιστάνει) the people (Mark 9:12–13). Consequently, Mark depicts John as the prophet who prepares the people for God's act of national restoration and judgment.

Mark also depicts John as acting in accordance with the implied script of the Mosaic promises (understood in light of Isa. 40:3's directive to "clear the way . . . in the wilderness"), stating that John "appeared in the wilderness, preaching a baptism of repentance [μετανοίας] for the forgiveness of sins [εἰς ἄφεσιν ἁμαρτιῶν]. And all the country of Judea was going out to him, and all the people of Jerusalem; and they were being baptized by him in the Jordan River, confessing their sins [ἐξομολογούμενοι τὰς ἁμαρτίας αὐτῶν]" (Mark 1:4–5).[81] John's activity is probably informed by Moses's assurance that in the restoration, God will forgive Israel's sin (Deut. 30:3 LXX) when the people "confess their sins" (ἐξαγορεύσουσιν τὰς ἁμαρτίας αὐτῶν, Lev. 26:40). Moreover, John's call to "repent" (from μετανοεῖν) likely repeats the prophetic call to "return."

That repentance encompasses the prescribed activity of returning is made plain by the parallel usage of these terms in Jewish texts. Joel 2:14 LXX asks, "Who knows whether God will return and repent [εἰ ἐπιστρέψει καὶ μετανοήσει]?" implying a comparable semantic range for these terms. Similarly, Isa. 46:8 LXX uses the terms somewhat interchangeably: "Repent [μετανοήσατε], you who have gone astray. Return [ἐπιστρέψατε] in your heart." Evidence from Luke-Acts supports this as well. Gabriel says that John will "return" (ἐπιστρέψει) many Israelites back to the Lord (Luke 1:16) and "return" (ἐπιστρέψαι) "the disobedient to the attitude of the righteous" (1:17).

80. On this composite citation, see Watts, *New Exodus*, 61–84; Shively, *Apocalyptic*, 43–49.

81. Second Temple figures occasionally enacted scriptural precedents in restorationist contexts, evidently reading certain Scriptures as directives to imitate. On such figures, see Josephus, *J.W.* 2.261–63; *Ant.* 20.160–68. On this phenomenon, see Horsley, "Popular Prophetic Movements," 15–17; Evans, "Zechariah's Messianic Hope"; Bryan, *Jesus and Israel's Traditions*, 28–33. For example, Isaiah 40's "wilderness" comment informed the Qumran sect's withdrawal to the desert; see Klinzing, *Die Umdeutung des Kultus*, 103–4; Hultgren, *Damascus Covenant*, 315. For a contextualization of John's career within Second Temple Judaism, see Taylor, *Immerser*; Webb, *John the Baptizer*; Marcus, *John the Baptist*; McGrath, *Christmaker*.

When John's actual ministry of returning Israel to God begins, Luke states that John preached "a baptism of repentance [μετανοίας]" (3:3). John's demand of repentance fulfills Gabriel's description of his mission. Similarly, after a public sermon, Peter exhorts his fellow Israelites, "Repent and return" (μετανοήσατε . . . καὶ ἐπιστρέψατε, Acts 3:19; see also Paul in 26:20). John's demand to repent in Mark, then, should be understood as his announcement that Israel ought to return in view of God's imminent act of salvation and judgment.[82]

Matthew

Matthew likewise frames his narrative in national restoration-eschatological terms.[83] A few examples are subtle, but Matthew, regularly keen that everyone get the joke, is often quite plain about it. An obvious instance occurs when an angel states that Jesus "will save his people from their sins" (Matt. 1:21). Jesus's genealogical descent from Abraham and David (1:1) suggests that "his people" refers to the Israelites, as does his claim that he was sent "to the lost sheep of the house of Israel" (15:24). The named purpose of Jesus's mission, then, is to rescue Israel from their sins, referring both to "forgiveness of sins" (26:28) and relief from the punishment that resulted from their prior sins—namely, their exile (1:17) and their scattered state (12:30).

A subtler instance may revolve around Matthew's claim that fourteen generations separate the Babylonian deportation and the Messiah (1:17). If a generation may be tabulated at 40 years,[84] then fourteen generations would amount to 560 years. Matthew may be time-tabling the restoration according to Dan. 9. If Daniel's "seventy sevens" (9:24) refer to an additional period of punishment not included in the original 70 years, then Matthew may interpret Dan. 9 to assert that Israel's punishment will have lasted for Jeremiah's predicted 70 years plus Daniel's 490 years, resulting in a 560-year punishment, or, in Matthew's idiom, fourteen generations. Of course, this cannot be proven, and a tabulation of fourteen generations as 560 years may not work between Abraham and David, though one must allow for some creativity in arranging the genealogy, given its selectivity.

The clearest way Matthew signals the restoration framework is through the characterization of John's preaching. For the many factors already discussed

82. On the Gospel of Mark's focus on Israel's national restoration, see Van Maaren, *Gospel of Mark's Judaism*.

83. On this general theme, see Willitts, *Matthew's Messianic Shepherd-King*.

84. Suggested by Num. 32:13; Ps. 95:10 (94:10 LXX); Josephus, *Ag. Ap.* 1.299. Philo states that 40 years is "the life of a generation" (*Life of Moses* 1.238; *Spec. Laws* 2.199).

in Mark, see the preceding section.[85] But one of the basic components of John's announcement is his claim that "the kingdom of heaven draws near" (Matt. 3:2 AT). Given that God is reckoned as Israel's King and that their exile entails their dispersal to other territories where other powers rule, the restoration of the covenant entails a restoration of the proper rule of God (see Isa. 40:10; 52:7–8). Thus, heralding the nearness of the kingdom heralds the nearness of restoration.

Matthew notes the partial success of John's mission, claiming that "Jerusalem . . . and all Judea and all the region around the Jordan" were going out to him (3:5). When the Pharisees and Sadducees also come, John's preaching sounds a note of judgment: "You offspring of vipers, who warned you to flee from the wrath to come?" (3:7). With the arrival of restoration comes the threat of failing to participate in it and of enduring God's wrath instead. We have already discussed Deut. 30 and Lev. 26: Only those who "confess their wrongdoing" (Lev. 26:40) and "return" to God (Deut. 30:1–3) participate in the divine act of salvation. But other texts make this point as well. Isaiah 1 claims that when God restores Israel, "Zion will be redeemed with justice, / And her repentant ones with righteousness. / But wrongdoers and sinners together will be broken, / And those who abandon the Lord will come to an end" (1:27–28). This passage concludes by saying that those who do not repent will "burn," and "there will be no one to extinguish them" (οὐκ ἔσται ὁ σβέσων, 1:31 LXX). Similarly, Malachi claims that when God returns, he will judge "between the righteous and the wicked" (3:18). This day of judgment "is coming, burning like a furnace; and all the arrogant and every evildoer will be chaff; and the day that is coming will set them ablaze, . . . so that it will leave them neither root [ῥίζα] nor branches" (4:1 [3:19 LXX]). But for those who return, there will be righteousness and healing (4:2 [3:20 LXX]). These images from Isaiah and Malachi likely inform John's warning that God's "axe is already laid at the root [ῥίζαν] of the trees; therefore, every tree that does not bear good fruit is being cut down and thrown into the fire [πῦρ]" (Matt. 3:10) that is "unquenchable" (ἀσβέστῳ, 3:12).[86]

With this announcement of restoration comes the implicit question: "How shall we return?" In case anyone was thinking that Abrahamic descent was sufficient for participation in the restoration, John states: "Therefore produce fruit consistent with repentance; and do not assume that you can say to yourselves, 'We have Abraham as our father'" (Matt. 3:8–9). Significantly, Matthew

85. John is likewise named as "Elijah" sent to "restore" (Matt. 11:14; 17:12–13), alluding to Mal. 4:5–6.

86. On John's saying about the coming "fire," see McManigal (*Baptism*, esp. 13–52), who takes the fire to refer to the day of reckoning for "national Israel."

does not denigrate Abrahamic descent, as if he were dissolving ethnicity of any relevance. God's promises to restore are made to a certain people, hence his emphasis on Jesus's descent from Abraham (1:1) and the claim that Jesus was sent "to the lost sheep of the house of Israel" (15:24). Matthew simply claims that Abrahamic descent does not guarantee participation in the restoration; what is needed is producing "fruit worthy of repentance" (3:8 NRSV).

Luke

Luke opens his account with the depiction of a priestly family, Zechariah and Elizabeth, who "were both righteous in the sight of God, walking blamelessly in all the commandments and requirements of the Lord" (Luke 1:6). This description is instructive in a few ways. First, the Law is not depicted as an impossible burden, and being considered "righteous" in God's sight is possible. Second, their "blameless" doing of the Law is not presented ironically or as "legalism" or "violent nationalism." They are simply members of God's people, walking according to their ancestral customs. Third, though they are blameless and righteous, they are still members of the people over whom God's discipline perdures, and thus, like "sinners," they await the restoration.[87] In this respect, they are like the seven brothers and their mother in 2 Macc. 7, who are keeping the Law and yet are still subject to the "wrath of God" because they are members of the nation over whom God's wrath has "justly fallen" (2 Macc. 7:1, 38). Finally, this description of Zechariah and Elizabeth as righteous precedes the claim that Zechariah received his angelic visitation while performing his priestly duties (Luke 1:8, 11). The temple, then, is clearly functioning, and the latter is not presented negatively. And yet, even with an operational temple, Luke 1–2 presents Israel as awaiting restoration. A functioning temple does not mean that God's glory is there, that God's "mercy" resides over the people, and that Israel has no "plights" that require resolution (cp. 2 Macc. 2:17–18). Equally, however, that Israel awaits restoration does not mean sacrifices are meaningless; it simply means that the temple and its sacrifices do not themselves effect the restoration. The sacrifices are not given for that purpose. But the temple itself will benefit from the restoration, when, having been "rescued from the hand of [their] enemies, [Israel] would serve [λατρεύειν] him without fear" (Luke 1:74). This term for "serve," when used of priests, typically refers to the performance of the sacrificial offerings.[88]

87. Isaac W. Oliver (*Luke's Jewish Eschatology*) persuasively argues that Luke-Acts expects a nonspiritualized, national/political restoration for Israel. See also Kinzer, *Jerusalem Crucified, Jerusalem Risen*; J. Smith, *Luke Was Not a Christian*.

88. See Lev. 18:21 (negatively); Num. 16:9; Josh. 22:27.

Subsequently, Gabriel informs Zechariah that Elizabeth will bear a son, John. In "the spirit and power of Elijah," John "will turn [ἐπιστρέψει] many of the sons of Israel back to the Lord" and "turn [ἐπιστρέψαι] . . . the disobedient to the attitude of the righteous, to make ready a people prepared for the Lord" (1:16–17). Identified as the one appointed to prepare the people for restoration and judgment, John demands repentance and gives specific legal/ethical instructions.

Additionally, Luke depicts Israel as still experiencing the promised discipline. After John is born, his father interprets the arrival of John and Jesus as God's "redemption" of his people (1:68), providing a Davidic ruler who would save Israel (1:69) "as he spoke by the mouth of his holy prophets from ancient times— / Salvation from our enemies [σωτηρίαν ἐξ ἐχθρῶν ἡμῶν], / And from the hand of all who hate us [ἐκ χειρὸς πάντων τῶν μισούντων ἡμᾶς]; / To show mercy [ποιῆσαι ἔλεος] to our fathers, / And to remember his holy covenant [μνησθῆναι διαθήκης], / The oath which he swore to our father Abraham" (1:70–73). Zechariah's language of their current plight and promised deliverance is unsurprisingly expressed with the terminology of Lev. 26 and Deut. 30.

There God promises that if Israel violates the covenant, "those who hate you [οἱ μισοῦντες ὑμᾶς] will rule over you" (Lev. 26:17), and Israel will be "handed over to the enemy" (παραδοθήσεσθε εἰς χεῖρας ἐχθρῶν, 26:25). From their punished state, God assures them that if they confess their sins (26:40), then "I will remember my covenant [μνησθήσομαι τῆς διαθήκης] with Jacob, . . . Isaac, and . . . Abraham" (26:42) and restore them. Deuteronomy names this act of restoration God's "mercy/compassion" (Deut. 30:3). Zechariah thus looks on John and sees the beginning of God's act of remembering his covenant with Abraham to show "mercy" to his people (Luke 1:72–73). As Isaac Oliver notes, here God's act of "mercy" will be a "concrete action that fulfills God's covenantal promises. A (re)new(ed) exodus that will deliver the nation is on the horizon."[89]

Additionally, in Luke 1, Gabriel says of Jesus, "the Lord God will give him the throne of his father David, and he will reign over the house of Jacob forever, and his kingdom will have no end" (1:32–33), probably alluding to 2 Sam. 7:16 and Dan. 7:14. His "reign over the house of Jacob" refers most naturally to the twelve tribes of Israel.[90] After the reign of Solomon, Israel split into two kingdoms, Israel and Judah. But in the restoration, God promises to unite the people and give them one king from the line of David who will rule

89. Oliver, *Luke's Jewish Eschatology*, 33.
90. Oliver, *Luke's Jewish Eschatology*, 29.

over the reunited tribes (Ezek. 37:21–22), a king who would finally "walk in my ordinances" (37:24). This comports with Luke's portrait of Jesus, who as the Davidic king appointed to rule over the regathered tribes, will also serve as their teacher, instructing them in God's Law. For this reason, even as a young boy, Jesus is characterized as one who studied the Law, with seasoned teachers "amazed at his understanding and his answers" (Luke 2:46–47).

After Jesus was circumcised on the eighth day (2:21), Mary completed the Law's required purification rites at the temple (2:22–24; see Lev. 12:8).[91] There a righteous and devout Simeon, who was "awaiting the comfort of Israel" (προσδεχόμενος παράκλησιν τοῦ Ἰσραήλ, Luke 2:25 AT), recognizes Jesus as the executor of this comfort, referring to the promised "comfort" that God would bring after Israel's endurance of the punitive discipline.[92] Awaiting such consolation naturally implies that Israel is still subjected to such discipline.

Turning to John's ministry, Luke 3:3–9 makes many points common to Matthew: John baptized, preached repentance, denounced the sufficiency of Abrahamic descent (without denigrating it), and demanded "fruits that are consistent with repentance" (3:8). But after hearing this demand and the warning that "every tree that does not bear good fruit is cut down and thrown into the fire" (3:9), the crowds justifiably ask: "Then what are we to do?" (3:10). In other words, faced with the prophetic demand to "return," the people ask, "How shall we return?" (Mal. 3:7).

To the general crowds, John gives a general answer: those with sufficient clothing and food ought to share with those who lack (Luke 3:11). Tax collectors should collect only what is required (3:12–13). And soldiers must not rob or falsely accuse (3:14). After such instruction, he heralds the arrival of the one who will judge, stating that he will "gather the wheat into his barn; but he will burn up the chaff with unquenchable fire" (3:17). Thus, according to John, rescue and judgment are coming. To prepare, the people should repent and live righteously. Notably, Luke calls John's message "the gospel" (3:18).

Conclusion

Numerous Second Temple Jewish texts, including the Gospels, interpret Israel's history and their own present moment in light of the discipline and

91. On Luke's reference to "their purification" (2:22) and its implications for the author's familiarity with Jewish halakhah, see Thiessen, *Forces of Death*, 27–41.

92. See, e.g., Deut. 32:36; LXX: Isa. 35:4; 40:1–2, 11; 41:27; 49:10, 13; 51:3, 12, 18–19; Bar. 4:30; 2 Macc. 7:6. On Simeon's prophecy and its relevance to Israel's national restoration, see Oliver, *Luke's Jewish Eschatology*, 36–39.

restoration promised by Moses. Each text surveyed demonstrates that many Jews did not reckon the return to the land under Cyrus as fulfilling the blessings promised in Lev. 26, Deut. 30, and the Prophets. Within this long period of discipline, distinct interpretations of the Law proliferated, and diverse opinions about the current temple's validity grew, but a constant emerged: God promised that restoration would come, and so they believed. But trusting that the promise of restoration would benefit those who "returned" raised a question: "How shall we return?" Answers varied. The group responsible for the Damascus Document answered: Return to the Law as interpreted by our teacher. Baruch said, "Endure with patience the wrath that has come upon you" (Bar. 4:25), and return to the Law with tenfold zeal (4:2, 28). John said, "Repent, and produce fruit worthy of such repentance." But those distinct answers operate within a shared understanding of the situation: We, Israel, transgressed the Law, meriting God's promised punishment. We have endured this punishment for centuries. Many in Israel remain in transgression, but we are on the cusp of restoration, and God's mercy is about to dawn. Return *this way*, and inherit the promised blessings.

The Gospels, too, operate within this framework. The stage is now set to show the ways in which they present Jesus as both the herald of the restoration and the authoritative teacher of the Law basic to its arrival.

3

The Law on the Mount

John the Baptist arrives with a message for all Israel, calling them to repent, confess their sins, and produce fruit worthy of repentance. Jesus undergoes John's baptism, signaling agreement with John's mission, that it is authorized "from heaven" (Matt. 21:25). However, Jesus is not simply one more participant in the restoration that John heralds; he is divinely authorized both to announce that restoration and effect it. Upon emerging from the baptismal waters, Jesus is distinguished by the Spirit descending upon him, naming him as God's "beloved Son" in whom God is "pleased" (Mark 1:10–11; Matt. 3:16–17; Luke 3:21–22).

This divine announcement employs language from Ps. 2:7 and Isa. 42:1. In Isa. 42, exiled Israel is characterized as "blind" (42:16) and "hidden away in prisons" (42:22) because "they were not willing to walk" in God's ways and "did not obey" God's law (42:24). But God authorizes a "servant" "To open blind eyes, / To bring out prisoners from the dungeon / And those who dwell in darkness from the prison" (42:7). This servant is appointed to restore exiled Israel, who "awaits his instruction" (42:4 AT).[1] The divine announcement at Jesus's baptism thus distinguishes him at the outset of his career as God's Son, appointed to restore exiled Israel.

After his baptism he retreats to the wilderness for forty days and nights, where he is tested by Satan (Mark 1:12–13 and par.). Resisting the devil's attempts by obedience to the Law's instruction,[2] Jesus emerges victorious

1. In the LXX, this verse says, "They will hope in his name."
2. In response to Satan, Jesus quotes Deut. 6:13, 16; 8:3.

and returns to Galilee with a message: "The time is up! Repent! God's reign approaches!" (Mark 1:15 AT).[3] This Markan epitome of Jesus's preaching assumes a tightly compressed network of ideas. Israel has long been enduring the covenant discipline, but now that apportioned time is up.[4] The duration of Israel's captivity and punishment is drawing to a close. The reign of God, which will supplant foreign spiritual and human reigns, approaches, and with it comes the promise of restoration for the repentant and judgment for those who refuse. Therefore, Jesus summons Israel to repent, to return their hearts to God and his laws, and to heed his message as the divinely approved herald in whom God's Spirit is at work. Naturally, because the return will entail turning to God's laws, Jesus's teaching also includes what the Gospels present as his authoritative interpretations of the Law by which Israelites express their return and participate in the restoration.

In the next few chapters, I will explore some of Jesus's teaching, interpret some of the legal controversies, and situate his final days in Jerusalem within the restoration-eschatological framework already described. Because the Synoptic Gospels are so alike yet subtly different, and because the logic of the next few chapters will roughly follow the unfolding of the Gospels' plots, a brief synopsis of the plot that is basic to each Synoptic Gospel will orient the discussion.[5]

Jesus preaches and teaches throughout Galilee. His work consists of not only legal instruction but also healing and exorcisms. The latter provide real liberation and serve as signs vindicating his mission and message, demonstrating both that God's reign truly is at hand and that he is the one commissioned to realize it (Mark 3:22–26; 6:7–13; Matt. 11:1–5; 12:28; Luke 11:20).[6] However, he receives a lukewarm reception in his hometown (Mark 6:1–6; Matt. 13:53–58; Luke 4:16–24), and when he commissions his disciples to preach and heal, numerous cities, including his hometown, do not repent (Matt. 11:20–24; Luke 10:13–16). Eventually he gains the attention of scribes and Pharisees by deviating from what they regard as normative or legally permissible practices. For example, he (and/or his disciples) pronounces forgiveness, dines with sinners, violates the Sabbath, does not regularly fast, and does not wash before

3. Matthew 4:17 omits "the time is fulfilled," though Matthew's genealogy and 16:3 frame Jesus's message as the right "time" of God's action. Luke 4:19–21 similarly frames Jesus's activity as "the time" of God's redemption. Luke 4:43 lacks "repent" but preserves "the kingdom of God," and elsewhere Luke makes plain that repentance is integral to Jesus's message (5:32; 10:13).

4. On Mark 1:15's "fulfilled time" as referring to a past time now ending, see Marcus, "'Time.'" See also Williams, "Melchizedek," 127–29.

5. See the brief comments on method in the Introduction.

6. On Jesus's healing and exorcistic powers in Matthew, see Dvořáček, *Son of David*.

eating. These episodes lead to accusations of blasphemy or transgression, in response to which Jesus provides some legal defense. Unconvinced, they express doubts that he is working by the Spirit of God, instead accusing him of working by "the ruler of the demons" (Mark 3:22; Matt. 12:24; Luke 11:15). Tensions heightened, Jesus turns the tables: it is not he but his accusers who blaspheme the Spirit, and they neither know nor keep the Law properly. The mutual critique, then, between the legal experts and Jesus is this: you are transgressing and leading others astray. After John is beheaded, Jesus teaches that he will suffer the same fate of rejection by Israel's leaders (Matt. 17:12; cp. Mark 9:9–13; Luke 9:18–22). But he teaches that this rejection and subsequent vindication by God will be the means through which he restores his people. He travels to Jerusalem, laments that they too have not repented, pronounces judgment on the temple's leadership, and asserts that the temple will be destroyed within a generation (Mark 13:1–2, 30; Matt. 24:1–2, 34; Luke 21:6, 32). Priests commission various groups to present him with legal questions, but he answers the questions well (Mark 12:13–34; Matt. 22:15–46; Luke 20:20–40).[7] However, one of his disciples betrays him, and he is tried and sentenced. Knowing his fate, Jesus goes to the cross willingly, interpreting his death as an endurance of the covenant discipline through which it will be exhausted for those who repent and follow Jesus's instruction. Through his resurrection, the restoration is inaugurated, and (now summarizing just Matthew and Luke) having received authority from his heavenly Father, Jesus commissions his disciples to spread this news to the rest of Israel and the nations, "teaching them to observe all that I have commanded you" (Matt. 28:20; cp. Luke 24:46–47).

Though the above is highly selective, it fairly summarizes the narrative as depicted by Matthew, Mark, and Luke. It is within those plot elements that Jesus's instruction and defenses gain their contextualized significance as, negatively, intramural defense against accusations of transgression and blasphemy and, positively, authoritative instruction of the Law for the impending restoration. Next I turn to the early stages of Jesus's mission in Galilee according to Matthew.

• • •

> Jesus was going about in all Galilee, teaching in their synagogues, proclaiming the good news of the kingdom, and healing every kind of disease and every kind of sickness among the people. And the news about him went out into all Syria. And they brought to him all who were ill, taken with various diseases and pains, demoniacs, epileptics, paralytics, and he healed them. And great

7. The Pharisees seem to act without prompting by the priests in Matt. 22:15.

multitudes followed him from Galilee and Decapolis and Jerusalem and Judea and from beyond the Jordan. (Matt. 4:23–25 AT)

Though he regularly taught in synagogues,[8] on at least the following occasion Jesus opted for a mountain. Matthew 4:25 claims that "great multitudes" followed him, and that "when he saw the multitudes, he ascended the mountain . . . and began to teach them" (5:1–2 AT). On this mountain in Galilee, Jesus presents his interpretation of the Law, incumbent on those who would participate in the restoration. The whole block of teaching spans Matt. 5–7, but the remainder of this chapter will focus on only two sections from Matt. 5: verses 3–12, which are regularly labeled "the Beatitudes," and verses 21–48, which are (unjustly) labeled "the antitheses."

The Beatitudes

The Beatitudes (5:3–12) frame the subsequent legal instruction (5:21–48) by implicitly prescribing the characteristics of those who will participate in the restoration. These sayings function prescriptively in that they assume the desirability of the named benefits (the kingdom, divine comfort, mercy, land inheritance, a vision of God) that redound to such persons.[9] The Beatitudes introduce well the subsequent legal instruction because what the Beatitudes name generically, the legal instructions concretely exemplify. The "merciful" (5:7) turn the other cheek and give to those who ask (5:39–42); the "pure in heart" (5:8) do not harbor anger (5:22) or commit adultery in their heart (5:28); and "peacemakers" (5:9) pursue reconciliation with their brothers and make friends with their legal opponents (5:24–25).

Significantly, each beatitude's promised outcome is one that Israel's Scriptures name as a benefit of the restoration. Nearly every line of the Beatitudes derives from passages that describe Israel's punitive state due to covenant violation and the divine act of restoration that resolves such plights. Once Israel violates the covenant, they are subject to other kings and "become like those

8. Synagogues served as natural locales for such activity. From Philo and Josephus we learn that synagogues served as a venue for hearing the Law read and interpreted on the Sabbath, often for several hours. See Philo, *Hypothetica* 7.11–13; Josephus, *Ag. Ap.* 2.175. Archaeological remains of synagogues suggest that seating lined the circumference of the building, leaving the center as the focal point presumably for the reader and instructor. See Adler, *Origins of Judaism*, 170–88. For a detailed study of synagogues in early Judaism through 200 CE, see Runesson, Binder, and Olsson, *Ancient Synagogue*.

9. See Pennington (*Sermon on the Mount*, 47–54) for a discussion of the relation of the "macarism" (his term) and the named benefit, describing the blessings as an "implicit invitation" (51).

over whom [God has] never ruled,"[10] the land and the people mourn,[11] they are "torn away from the land" and "scatter[ed] among the nations,"[12] the people hunger and thirst[13] and pursue righteousness,[14] God's mercy is withdrawn,[15] God's presence departs,[16] they are called "not his children,"[17] and they are persecuted by the nations.[18] Each of these plights is a punishment named by Lev. 26, Deut. 28, and prophetic literature as discipline resultant from Israel's covenant violation, and each is named by Jesus as a situation to be resolved.

In view of such punishments, God promises in the restoration to reign over Israel once more,[19] to comfort those who mourn,[20] to bring Israel back to inherit the land,[21] to feed the hungry and thirsty of Israel,[22] to return his mercy to them,[23] to return in plain sight,[24] and to call them "sons of God" once more.[25] Each is a promised blessing of the restoration, and each is named by Jesus as what those described in Matt. 5:3–12 will experience: to them belongs "the kingdom of heaven" (5:3), they shall be "comforted" (5:4), "inherit the land" (5:5),[26] be fed (5:6), receive "mercy" (5:7), "see God" (5:8), and "be called sons of God" (5:9). These promised resolutions redound to the "poor in spirit" (5:3), those who "mourn" (5:4), the "gentle" (5:5), those who "hunger and

10. Isa. 63:19; cp. Deut. 28:36, 41, 48–50, 63–65.

11. Isa. 3:26; 61:2–3; 66:10; Jer. 4:28; 6:26; 12:4.

12. Deut. 28:63–64; Lev. 26:33.

13. Deut. 28:31, 33, 38–40, 48, 51–57; cp. Isa. 49:10; Jer. 31:12.

14. Isa. 51:1.

15. Hosea 1:6; 2:4 (2:6 MT/LXX); Zech. 1:12; Isa. 27:11; 59:2 LXX; Jer. 7:16 LXX; Ezek. 5:11. Cp. Deut. 30:3.

16. Deut. 31:17; Lev. 26:31; Ezek. 5:11; 10:18.

17. Deut. 32:5; cp. Hosea 1:9; 1:10 (2:1 MT/LXX).

18. Lev. 26:17, 36; Deut. 30:7; 32:30; Lam. 4:18–19; 5:5.

19. Isa. 52:7–8; Zech. 14:9.

20. Deut. 32:36; Isa. 35:4 LXX; 40:1–2; 40:11 LXX; 41:27; 49:10, 13; 51:3, 12; 57:17–18; 61:1–2; Bar. 4:30; 2 Macc. 7:6.

21. Deut. 30:4–5; Lev. 26:42–44; Isa. 40:11; 43:5–6; 57:13; Jer. 23:4; 31:8; 32:37; Ezek. 36:24; Zech. 10:8–10.

22. Pss. 37:19; 81:16; 107:9; 132:15; Isa. 49:5; 58:14; Jer. 3:15; 31:25; Ezek. 34:14–15, 23.

23. Isa. 12:1–6; 14:1–3; 30:18–19; 33:2; 44:22–23; 45:8; 49:10, 13; 52:8–9; 54:7–8, 10; 55:7; 56:1; 60:10; 63:7, 15; Jer. 12:15; 30:18 (37:18 LXX); 31:20 (38:20 LXX); 33:1–13 (40:1–13 LXX); Lam. 3:32; Ezek. 39:25; Amos 5:15; Mic. 7:18–20; Hosea 2:1, 23; 14:3; Zech. 1:12–17; Ezra 9:9; Dan. 9:9, 18; Tob. 13:5, 10; 14:5; Bar. 3:2; Jdt. 7:30; 1 Macc. 3:44; 2 Macc. 2:18; 7:37; 8:3, 5; 11:10; 3 Macc. 2:19; LXX: Pss. 76:9; 84:8, 11; 97:3; 105:45; 129:7; 135:24; Sir. 35:23–36:1; 50:24; cp. Pss. Sol. 8.27–28; 11.9; 18.5, 9.

24. Isa. 40:5, 9–10; 66:15–18; Ezek. 43:1–5; Mal. 3:1.

25. Hosea 1:10 (2:1 MT/LXX).

26. Though Matt. 5:5 is often translated "inherit the earth" (ESV, NASB, NIV, NRSV) because Jesus is heralding Israel's restoration, in which God promises to bring exiled Israel back to the land, "land" better captures Jesus's meaning. Some texts do "expand" the land promise to entail the (renewed) world (Josephus, *Ant.* 4.116; Jub. 32.19; Rom. 4:13).

thirst for righteousness" (5:6), the "merciful" (5:7), the "pure in heart" (5:8), "peacemakers" (5:9), and those "persecuted" for the sake of righteousness (5:10). These qualities or patterns of behavior are named in Jesus's Scriptures as things God delights in or promises to vindicate, frequently in restoration-eschatological passages.[27]

Thus, in the context of this sermon, the Beatitudes make declarations about the eschatological restoration that implicitly demand the hearer to conform heart and action to the stated norm to participate in the promised realities. In this way, "the beatitudes . . . represent anticipated eschatological verdicts. . . . The pronouncement moreover presents the demand that the person receiving the message takes up in the most serious sense the way of life revealed."[28] Accordingly, far from abstract moral norms, these declarations function as Jesus's positive vision for how one "returns" to God and so participates in the restoration.

The final beatitude (Matt. 5:11) assures divine vindication to those insulted or reproached (ὅταν ὀνειδίσωσιν ὑμᾶς) in the present, but it adds the component "because of me." When reviled for this reason, Jesus tells them to "rejoice and be glad" (χαίρετε καὶ ἀγαλλιᾶσθε). Such insults are seemingly aimed at those who claim Jesus as their teacher and so follow his way of righteousness. This assurance similarly echoes a prophetic restoration promise. In Isa. 51:3–8, God calms the anxious exiles, saying:

> Indeed, the Lord will comfort Zion; / He will comfort all her ruins. . . . Joy and gladness [εὐφροσύνην καὶ ἀγαλλίαμα] will be found in her. . . . Pay attention to me, my people, / And listen to me, my nation, / For a law [or instruction] will go out from me. . . . Listen to me, you who know righteousness, / A people in whose heart is my Law; / Do not fear the taunting of people [μὴ φοβεῖσθε ὀνειδισμὸν ἀνθρώπων], / Nor be terrified of their abuses.

Given the lexical and conceptual congruity between this passage and Matt. 5:11, plus Jesus's pattern of alluding to restoration promises throughout these Beatitudes, here too Jesus instructs based on his conviction that restoration is afoot. His disciples ought to "rejoice" despite the "insults" of the people because the divine comfort is assured, and they will experience it. Comparing his instruction and the activity of his disciples to that of Israel's

27. References for such restoration promises include the following: "the poor in spirit" (Ps. 34:15–18; Isa. 66:2); the comforting of "mourners" (Isa. 57:18; 61:1–2); the "humble" "inheriting the land" (Ps. 37:8–11); the "hungry and thirsty" and the pursuit of "righteousness" (Isa. 51:1; Jer. 31:25); the "merciful" (Hosea 12:6); the "pure in heart" (Deut. 30:6; Ps. 24:4); those who "make peace" (Zech. 8:16–17); and the vindication of "the persecuted" (Deut. 30:7; Ps. 7:1–9).

28. Betz, *Sermon on the Mount*, 94, 96–97.

ancestral prophets—"for so they persecuted the prophets who were before you" (5:12)—suggests that he too is on a mission to Israel, summoning them to repentance in view of the impending restoration and judgment. Those who obey his summons and the teaching particular to it will be granted life in the kingdom of God, and those persecuted for such obedience will receive the reward of divine comfort.

With these pronouncements, Jesus is not requiring sinless perfection. Mercy and forgiveness are assumed aspects of the divine-human relationship both in the Law and in Jesus's instruction.[29] Indeed, one of the named promises at the eschatological judgment is divine "mercy" (Matt. 5:7), implying that no one by doing these practices "earns salvation," if by "earning" interpreters mean "meriting salvation without the need for mercy." But Jesus's instruction does place obligations on his hearers, as he states in the conclusion of his teaching: "Therefore everyone who hears these words of mine, and does them" is like one who builds on a foundation of rock, but everyone who hears "and does not do them" is like one who builds on sand, a house doomed to fall (7:24–27 AT). By "does them" (7:24), Jesus does not mean "keeps my commands perfectly," but "accepts my teaching and lives by it." Such a response is "an expression of a person's complete loyalty to God."[30] It should also be clear that here Jesus is not teaching something called "Christianity" over against his interlocutors who teach "Judaism." Jesus is a Jewish teacher instructing his Jewish disciples about the restoration of Israel from the Law given to Israel. Thus, the "newness" of his teaching is not that of a new pattern of religion—"Christianity now, Judaism before"—but that of *restoration*: Israel was disciplined, but now Israel will be restored. And it is from Jesus's conviction that God has commissioned him to restore Israel that he teaches his people what constitutes the divinely sought "return" to God and his Law. The characteristics named in 5.3–12 are then exemplified in Jesus's subsequent legal instruction (5:21–48), in which he shows how one who would strive to be humble, merciful, pure in heart, and a peacemaker will live in keeping with the Law as Jesus teaches it.

You Have Heard It Said . . . , but I Say to You . . .

After the pronounced blessings, Jesus asserts that he did not come to abolish the Law or the Prophets, but to fulfill them (Matt. 5:17–19). After claiming that even the smallest commandments will perdure until the heavens and

29. On this theme in Matthew, see Runesson, *Divine Wrath*, 84–101.
30. Runesson, *Divine Wrath*, 99.

earth wear out, he delivers several rulings prefixed with the claim "You have heard that it was said . . . , but I say to you . . ." For better or worse (mostly worse), these instructions have been labeled "antitheses": *opposites* or *contradictions*.[31] This label often smuggles in the idea that Jesus is countering the Law in itself, creating a portrait of Jesus "against the Law." And once the Law becomes associated with "Judaism" or a "pattern of religion," such an interpretation communicates Jesus's break with "Judaism."[32] Granted, not everyone who employs the label intentionally implies the latter connotations. But labels are illustrative, and I think it is time to mandate this one's retirement. These are not antitheses. These are Jesus's interpretation of the commandments he references.[33]

Before turning to them, three reasons suggest that Jesus is not contrasting the Law itself with his own commandments. First, the instruction (5:21–48) is introduced by his assertions in 5:17–20, wherein he claims that he came not to abolish the "Law or the Prophets" but to fulfill them. Consequently, Matt. 5:17–20 serves as the hermeneutical key to Jesus's subsequent teaching, which is therefore not the Law's abolition but its fullest keeping.[34]

Second, when coupled with "law" or "commandment(s)," the word "fulfill" effectively means "do."[35] Mentioning "the Prophets" as what Jesus "came to fulfill" (Matt. 5:17) does not require that Jesus is referring to "prophecy fulfillment" in what is regarded as the typical Matthean sense (e.g., 1:22; 2:15, 17). Rather, the prophetic material interprets the Law. Daniel 9:10, for example, states, "We have not obeyed the voice of the Lord our God, to walk in his teachings [i.e., Law] which he set before us through his servants the prophets."[36] In Jer. 17:21–24, the prophet teaches Sabbath legislation. And Sirach 1, before providing commentary on the Law, claims that Israel received instruction "through the Law and the Prophets" (1:1 NRSV). In Matthew, moreover, Jesus states that love of God and neighbor are "two commandments" on which depend "the whole Law and the Prophets" (Matt. 22:40; see also 7:12), implying that Jesus regards the Prophets as instructors of the Law and the divine will. Jesus's point in Matt. 5:17, then, seems to be that he

31. On interpretative options for these verses, see Marcus, "Enigma of the Antitheses."

32. See the discussion of this theme in A.-J. Levine, *Misunderstood Jew*, esp. 47.

33. For overviews of the Sermon on the Mount, see Davies, *Setting*; Allison, *Sermon on the Mount*.

34. So also Davies and Allison, *Matthew*, 72–74.

35. See Philo, *Rewards* 82–83; T. Naph. 8.7; Sib. Or. 3.247; Rom. 8:4. See also the discussion in Sigal, *Halakhah of Jesus*, 19–20.

36. So also 2 Kings 17:13. See also Philo (*Decalogue* 1.175) and Josephus (*Ant.* 15.136), where context suggests that Josephus is referring to prophets as legal instructors.

came to do what the Law and the Prophets require, and such commandments perdure at least until "all is accomplished" (5:18).

Third, the contrasts Jesus makes between his teaching and the Law are not intended to contradict what the Law requires. Rather, the content following "but I say to you" draws from other parts of the Law to rightly interpret the referenced portion. For example, "Do not commit adultery" and "Do not covet/lust" are both commands in the Decalogue (Exod. 20:14, 17). But Jesus does not nullify the adultery prohibition; he employs "Do not covet/lust" (Exod. 20:17) as the control that indexes when the prohibition against adultery (Exod. 20:14) has been violated (Matt. 5:28).[37]

In arguing that Jesus does not contradict the Law, David Daube suggests that the phrase "You have heard that it was said" frames Jesus's discourse not against the Law itself but against erroneous interpretations that his audience may have "heard." He supports this with examples from rabbinic literature, wherein a given legal text is quoted, followed by "I might hear" prefixed to an erroneous interpretation of the quoted text. The passage then provides the correct interpretation.[38] Daube claims that this formally corresponds to Jesus's phrasing "You have heard . . . , but I say to you" through Matt. 5:21–48, arguing that Jesus is not contrasting the Law with his own teaching, but the Law's erroneous interpretation with his correct one. Joel Marcus, however, has justly critiqued this interpretation, stating that "the most crucial step in the argument—the assertion that we are dealing with interpretations rather than quotations or paraphrases of the Bible—is read into the evidence rather than emerging from it."[39] For Marcus, Jesus is not countering erroneous interpretations; rather, "there is absolutely no indication in the Antitheses that Jesus is disputing anything other than the biblical text itself."[40]

Marcus's criticisms of the "rejected interpretation" hypothesis are on target. It appears that Jesus is loosely quoting a given commandment or combination of commandments before providing his instruction. However, I think Marcus is off target to call this "disputing . . . the biblical text itself."

37. Matthew 5:28's infinitive (τὸ ἐπιθυμῆσαι), often translated "lust," repeats Exod. 20:17's prohibition of "coveting" (οὐκ ἐπιθυμήσεις).

38. Daube, *New Testament*, 55–60, citing Mekhilta of R. Ishmael on Exod. 19:20 and 20:12. Kampen (*Matthew within Sectarian Judaism*, 92–111) also reads Matt. 5:21–48 as countering alternative interpretations, comparing Matthew's opinions to those recorded in Qumran documents. However, if another group's interpretation is in focus, Matt. 5:20 suggests that it would be the Pharisees. See the additional criticism of Kampen's view in Marcus, "Enigma of the Antitheses," 130–31.

39. Marcus, "Enigma of the Antitheses," 131.

40. Marcus, "Enigma of the Antitheses," 130.

Marcus interprets Jesus's instruction as exemplifying an attested pattern of "legists" to "revise inherited laws . . . and to insist that they are not changing a thing."[41] He employs the example of Deut. 12:13–14, which revises a sacrificial practice legislated in Exod. 20:24 yet then proceeds to warn against altering the Law at all (Deut. 12:32 [13:1 LXX/MT]). In the same way, the Matthean Jesus "revokes the Pentateuchal edicts on divorce, oaths, and retribution, yet insists that he is not altering a jot or tittle."[42] Consequently, Matthew is "subtly undermining the divine credentials of the Torah passages he wants to relativise ('you have heard that it was said') and at the same time affirming that everything he says is in line with the Torah."[43]

I do not think this summary adequately captures what Jesus is doing. In Matt. 5:21–48, Jesus is not "revoking" legal edicts based on his opinion; rather, his instruction alludes to commandments that either override or condition the keeping of the passage he quotes. For example, as already mentioned, coveting/lusting informs when adultery has taken place, since the Law also prohibits coveting. Murder makes one liable to judgment (5:21), but so does anger (5:22), just as Lev. 19:17–18 implies. As such, Jesus is in line with other "legists" who interpret one commandment in light of another.

The following cases exemplify instances of this kind of interpretation. The Law forbids cutting off the marks of *lepra* (Lev. 13:33), and the Law requires circumcision (Gen. 17:12; Lev. 12:3). But what should one do when a mark of *lepra* is on the foreskin? Rabbi Nehemiah states, "Great is circumcision, for it overrides skin afflictions" (m. Ned. 3.11), meaning one may cut off a mark of *lepra* if it is on the foreskin. Similarly, m. Neg. 7.4 states, "One who plucks out signs of impurity . . . transgresses a negative commandment"—in this case, cutting a sign of *lepra*, which Lev. 13:33 prohibits. However, if the mark or discoloration "was at the tip of the foreskin, he may be circumcised" (m. Neg. 7.5). This ruling is also expressed in b. Shabb. 132b, wherein the legal principle that "a positive commandment comes and overrides a negative commandment" informs the permissibility of cutting off a mark of *lepra* in circumcising. In these cases, the positive command exerts pressure on and "overrides" the prohibition, such that the negative command is violated, but the Law is thereby kept. In other words, one commandment is being interpreted in light of another, and even when one commandment is "broken" to fulfill another, such breaking has as its goal the *keeping* of the Law.

41. Marcus, "Enigma of the Antitheses," 132.
42. Marcus, "Enigma of the Antitheses," 133.
43. Marcus, "Enigma of the Antitheses," 134.

Similarly, harvesting is prohibited in the sabbatical year (Lev. 25:5), and yet the people are regularly to bring "the sheaf" of the harvest to the temple (23:10). In discussing the sabbatical year, Rabbi Ishmael excepts the required sheaf from the sabbatical year's harvest prohibition. That is, one violates the sabbatical year's prohibition of harvesting to bring the requisite sheaf of the harvest (m. Shev. 1.4). One commandment is violated to keep another; in this case, the operative legal principle is that temple rituals override Sabbath/sabbatical year legislation.

What of matters not dependent on overrides? The interpretation of divorce as legislated by Deut. 24:1 is exemplary. There Moses legislates divorce in the case of a man displeased because he "found some indecency [עֶרְוַת דָּבָר] in her." Mishnah Gittin showcases a debate between Pharisaic houses providing interpretations of what constitutes this "indecency" or "matter." The school of Hillel interprets it as relatively any displeasing matter, "even if she ruined his dinner" (m. Git. 9.10). Rabbi Aqiva states, "even if he found another more beautiful than she," taking Deut. 24:1's "if she finds no favor in his eyes" as the controlling phrase and interpreting it with reference to physical appearance (m. Git. 9.10). The school of Shammai interprets Deut. 24:1's "matter" in terms of "indecency" (עֶרְוַת) as the controlling factor and interprets the latter in light of another set of commandments (Lev. 18, 20) that use the same word (from עֶרְוָה) in reference to sexual transgression (m. Git. 9.10; see, e.g., Lev. 18:6, 7, 8, 9). In this case, the words shared by Deut. 24:1 and Lev. 18 suggest that Leviticus should inform Deuteronomy, so that the divorce permitted by Deut. 24:1, according to the school of Shammai, is controlled by cases of sexual transgression as described in another set of commandments.

Jesus's manner of legal reasoning throughout Matt. 5:21–48 is comparable to this example and those containing overrides. That is, the portion quoted/referenced with "You have heard it said . . ." is not relativized or disputed as if Jesus simply disagrees with the Law itself; rather, other portions of the Law exert control either because they are regarded as weightier, exerting an influence on the keeping of the quoted portion, or because the restoration he announces activates accompanying legal overrides. The distinctive aspect of Jesus's prohibiting something the Law permits (voluntary vows and legal retaliation) will be discussed below in the relevant sections.

The table below illustrates how Jesus is not disputing the Law with his own, nonlegally contextualized opinion, but is interpreting one command in light of another.

Matthew	Pentateuchal Law	Jesus's Instruction
5:21–22	No murder (Exod. 20:13)	No anger (Lev. 19:17–18)
5:27–28	No adultery (Exod. 20:14)	No lust/coveting (Exod. 20:17)
5:31–32	Divorce/indecency (Deut. 24:1)	Sexual immorality (Lev. 18:6, etc.)
5:33–37	No false vows / pay vows (Lev. 19:12; Num. 30:2; Deut. 23:21)	No swearing (Deut. 23:22; Eccles. 5:2)
5:38–42	Eye for eye (Exod. 21:24; Lev. 24:20; Deut. 19:21)	Turn the cheek; lend (Deut. 15:1–2, 7–8; Lam. 3:30)
5:43–47	Love your neighbor / hate your enemy (Lev. 19:18)[44]	Love enemies (Exod. 23:4–5; Lev. 19:18; Prov. 25:21)

Finally, I must make two brief comments on Matt. 5:18 and 20 before turning to Matt. 5:21–48. First, in Matt. 5:18 Jesus says, "For truly I say to you, until heaven and earth pass away, not the smallest letter or stroke of a letter shall pass from the Law, until all is accomplished." That "all is accomplished" (or "everything happens") does not refer to his death/resurrection or the destruction of the temple[45]—which would supposedly support the conclusion that the Law *does* pass away after such events—is plain for three reasons. (1) "All is accomplished" is accompanied by the temporal condition "until heaven and earth pass away." As they perdure and are assumed to perdure at least until the coming of the Son of Man (Matt. 24:29–30), if not beyond, their presence and role in the unfolding drama indicates that the Law continues as they do.[46] (2) Matthew's Gospel makes clear that there is much more to happen even after Jesus's death and resurrection, not least his enthronement (26:64); the mission to the nations (28:19–20), where he notes that "the end of the age" has not yet arrived (28:20); his return (24:30–39); and the final judgment (25:31–46). And (3) after his resurrection, Jesus tells his disciples to "make disciples of all the nations, . . . teaching them to observe all that I commanded you" (28:19–20). But as will be argued below, what he has commanded is that they follow the Law (as interpreted by Jesus). If Jesus exposits the Law (5:21–48), then what he has "commanded" (28:20) cannot

44. "Hate your enemy" is not a Pentateuchal command.

45. Davies and Allison (*Matthew*, 1:494) provide some bibliography for such interpretations. See Fletcher-Louis ("Destruction," 145–69) for the view that the passing away of heaven and earth refers to the temple's destruction and possibly Jesus's death.

46. *Pace* Fletcher-Louis ("Destruction"), I do not think the passing away of heaven/earth refers to the destruction of the temple on the alleged grounds that the latter served as a microcosm of heaven and earth. For my interpretation of the relation of the destruction of the temple and the cosmic signs, see P. Sloan, *Mark 13*, 128–35, 190–96. The passing away of heaven/earth would seem to occur (with whatever significance) at the παλιγγενεσίᾳ, "the regeneration" of the world (Matt. 19:28), which occurs when the Son of Man returns to judge (cp. Matt. 25:31).

be disentangled from the Law itself, in which case Matthew's Jesus assumes the Law's commandments perdure after his resurrection. Consequently, Jesus teaches that the Law's commandments obligate his followers—from Israel and the nations—even after his death and resurrection.[47]

Second, Jesus states that one's righteousness must "surpass that of the scribes and Pharisees" to enter the kingdom (Matt. 5:20). Referring to the insufficient righteousness one might attain by following their instruction suggests that what follows in Matt. 5:21–48 is primarily Jesus's instruction juxtaposed predominantly with that of the scribes and Pharisees, not with the Law itself. Probably implied is that Jesus's correlation of the commands is distinct from the Pharisees' and/or scribes' correlation of them.[48] This point is not a return to Daube's argument that Jesus counters only an implied interpretation. Rather, Matt. 5:21–48 implies that Jesus's interpretation and correlation of the quoted commands is superior to the Pharisees' and scribes' interpretations of the commandments. Additionally, surpassing the righteousness of the scribes and Pharisees is not presented as an impossible burden. Such an interpretation assumes that Jesus endorses their legal practice, regarding it as excessively righteous, and then calls his disciples to an impossibly higher one. But this supposition curiously forgets that Matthew's Jesus famously does not approve of (all) their practice, and he consistently criticizes them as "transgressors" who do not in fact keep the Law (cp. 15:3–6, 7, 14; 16:11–12; 23:1–28). Such passages should be regarded as intramural critique in the context of heated debates over the Law and its keeping, but they should also make plain that "surpassing" their righteousness does not refer to an impossible standard, because for Matthew's Jesus, the scribes and Pharisees do not really keep the Law. But the disciple who follows Jesus's instruction will both fulfill the Law's requirements and surpass the righteousness expressed by the scribes and Pharisees. At last, I turn to Matt. 5:21–48 in greater detail.

Murder

> You have heard that the ancients were told, "You shall not commit murder," and "Whoever commits murder shall be answerable to the court." But I say to you that everyone who is angry with his brother shall be answerable to the court. (Matt. 5:21–22)

47. See additional comments on Matt. 28:19–20 under "Teaching the Nations" in chap. 6 below.

48. See also Matt. 7:28–29, where Jesus's authority is contradistinguished not to the Law but to the scribes.

First to note is that Jesus does not counter the murder prohibition. Nor does Jesus prohibit anger only because it is the interior disposition that leads to murder, as if "Do not murder" legislates only observable action but Jesus goes further by making demands of the heart that the Law does not legislate. Jesus is interested in stemming sins from the heart, of course, but in this case, he is not contrasting "an observable action" with "the interior disposition that leads to it," but is instead addressing "what makes one liable to legal judgment." The portion quoted states that whoever murders "is liable to judgment" (ἔνοχος ἔσται τῇ κρίσει, 5:21). Jesus agrees with this, and his subsequent instruction does not alter it. But in Jesus's view, even harboring anger against one's brother makes one "liable to judgment" (ἔνοχος ἔσται τῇ κρίσει, 5:22). Thus, there is no implied contrast between the quoted commandment and Jesus's teaching but only an additional naming of what makes one liable.

And there is precedent for such a ruling. Leviticus 19:18, programmatic for Jesus's interpretation of the Law (Matt. 22:39–40), says not to take vengeance or "bear a grudge against" (לֹא־תִטֹּר, οὐ μηνιεῖς) your people, proscribing prolonged "anger" or "wrath."[49] Additionally, presumably interpreting this commandment (Lev. 19:18), Sir. 28:1 teaches that "the vengeful" will see God's vengeance in the judgment. Consequently, the offended party ought to forgive the other and ought not "harbor anger" (συντηρεῖ ὀργήν) or "wrath" (μῆνιν, 28:2, 3, 5). Instead, Sirach says, "Remember the commandments, and do not be angry with your neighbor" (μὴ μηνίσῃς τῷ πλησίον, 28:7). Not only are these instructions similar to Jesus's, but the fact that Sirach uses μῆνιν and ὀργήν interchangeably (28:3, 5) while interpreting Lev. 19:18 suggests that Jesus's instruction not to be angry (ὁ ὀργιζόμενος) may well be indebted to Lev. 19:18's instruction not to hate/be angry with (οὐ μηνιεῖς) a neighbor.

Additionally, the Damascus Document proscribes bringing accusations "in anger": "Everyone who brings an accusation . . . when he is angry, . . . he is the one who avenges himself and bears resentment" (CD 9.2–4).[50] Thus, bringing an accusation in anger qualifies as a violation of Lev. 19:18's prohibition of vengeance and angry resentment. Furthermore, this section in the Damascus Document states numerous legal decisions and often appends prescribed punishments; though this violation of bringing an accusation in anger does not have a stated punishment, context suggests that the community thought that one who transgressed in this manner would be liable to judgment. Therefore, both CD 9.2–4 and Matt. 5:21–22 instruct that anger against a brother makes

49. See comparable uses of these verbs in reference to God's prolonged anger: Ps. 103:9; Jer. 3:5, 12; Nah. 1:2.

50. So also Keener, *Matthew*, 182.

one liable to judgment. To clarify, I am not suggesting that Jesus's prohibition of anger quotes or directly alludes to the language of Lev. 19:18; rather, Jesus's prohibition of anger may have stemmed from Lev. 19:18's prohibition of grudges and resentment, reflecting an interpretation of Lev. 19:18 attested in Sir. 28 and CD 9.

Reconciliation

Jesus proceeds, "Therefore [οὖν], if you are presenting your offering at the altar, and there you remember that your brother has something against you, leave your offering there before the altar and go; first be reconciled to your brother, and then come and present your offering" (Matt. 5:23–24). Some rightly infer that here Jesus teaches the importance of human-to-human reconciliation prior to performing the requisite rituals. Quite so! But it would be wrong to infer that Jesus was teaching something other than what the Law or its interpreters taught.[51] Rather, Jesus's instruction is likely indebted to Lev. 6:2–7 (5:21–26 MT/LXX), wherein God requires that if anyone wrongs a neighbor, whether through robbery, extortion, a false vow, or basically in any way in which one may sin against another, that person must first go and repay the principle and an added fifth to the one wronged, and then the guilty may make their offering for atonement and forgiveness. Philo interprets this law to teach the same, saying that if anyone sins against someone in such ways,

> [he] shall come and openly confess the sin which he has committed, and implore pardon; then pardon shall be given to such a man, who shows the truth of his repentance, not by promises but by works, by restoring the deposit which he has received, and by giving up the things which he has stolen or found, . . . paying also in addition one-fifth of the value, as an atonement for the evil which he had done. And then, after he has appeased the man who had been injured, the law proceeds to say, "After this let him go also into the temple, to implore remission of the sins which he has committed." (*Spec. Laws* 1.235–37 LCL)[52]

Similarly, the Mishnah records decisions on how/whether the Day of Atonement atones for various kinds of sins. Mishnah Yoma 8.9 states, "Transgressions between a person and God, Yom Kippur atones; transgressions between a person and another, Yom Kippur does not atone until he appeases the other person." One must first reconcile with the other person before the rituals of the Day of Atonement can be effectual. These scenarios are not formally

51. Contra Simon Joseph (*Jesus and the Temple*, 120), who claims that this statement would have shocked hearers by the supposed reversal of an assumed primacy of sacrifice above all else.

52. Unless otherwise indicated, all Philo quotations are from the Loeb Classical Library.

identical to the one stated in Matt. 5:23–24, but there is a comparable principle at work: reconciliation with a brother or sister takes precedence over an offering. Moreover, if Philo and m. Yoma illuminate Matt. 5, the effectuality of the offering in 5:23–24 may depend on whether you have first reconciled with your fellow. "Therefore," Jesus says, "pursue peace with your opponents" (5:25–26 AT)!

Adultery

> You have heard that it was said, "You shall not commit adultery"; but I say to you that everyone who looks at a woman with lust for her has already committed adultery with her in his heart. (Matt. 5:27–28)

The quoted commandment prohibits adultery, and Jesus does not counter that prohibition. Nor does he simply prohibit the activity (lust) that leads to adultery. Rather, he states that one who covets/desires (ἐπιθυμῆσαι) a woman has already (ἤδη) committed adultery (ἐμοίχευσεν) in his heart. Once again, there is no contrast between the quoted portion and Jesus's instruction. Rather, he interprets the prohibition of adultery (οὐ μοιχεύσεις, Exod. 20:14 [20:13 LXX]) by another commandment's prohibition of coveting/lust (οὐκ ἐπιθυμήσεις, Exod. 20:17), stating that once one has violated the commandment against coveting, one has thereby "already" violated the commandment against adultery.[53]

It is not difficult to imagine that the prohibition of adultery led to questions concerning what precisely constituted the act. Some may have considered adultery to have taken place only upon completion of the physical act; others, upon beginning it; and still others, even if it is only intended. Jesus regards the act of coveting/lusting in the heart to have completed the adultery "already," and other Jewish texts teach similarly. As Wim Weren notes, Jewish texts provide "numerous parallels of the opinion expressed in Matthew 5:28 that adultery already begins with someone's desires or intentions."[54]

Jubilees (composed around 200 years before the Gospels) has Abraham command his children "that we should keep ourselves from all fornication and pollution, . . . and let them not fornicate with her [any woman or girl] after their eyes and hearts" (Jub. 20.4).[55] Evidently illicit actions of the eyes and heart constituted fornication. This passage in Jubilees, and possibly Jesus's

53. See also Weren, "Marriage," 146.

54. Weren, "Marriage," 146. He cites Job 31:9–12; Prov. 6:25; Sir. 9:8; 26:21; 41:20–21; T. Reu. 3.10; 4.1; 6.1; T. Iss. 4.1–4; Lev. Rab. 23.12; b. Ber. 16a; 11QT[a] 59.14.

55. Wintermute, *OTP* 2:93–94.

instruction in Matt. 5, may be indebted to Num. 15:39, which states concerning the requisite tassels affixed to Israelite garments, "It shall be a tassel for you to look at and remember all the commandments of the LORD, so that you will do them and not follow your own heart and your own eyes, which led you to prostitute yourselves" (זֹנִים, ἐκπορνεύετε).

The Babylonian Talmud describes a scenario in which a man had ceased having sex with his wife (possibly due to age). The wife then disguised herself as a prostitute, and the man had sex with her, not knowing it was his wife. However, he later expressed his guilt, and his wife explained what had happened. Nonetheless he lamented: "He said to her 'I, in any event, intended to transgress.' All the days of that righteous man he would fast until he died by that death" (b. Qiddushin 81b).[56] The passage gives additional examples wherein intent to transgress makes one just as guilty as the actual acts themselves. This talmudic example is not identical to Jesus's assertion, but such texts demonstrate analogous opinions regarding how/when a given sin may be regarded as having occurred. Jesus teaches, then, that the commandment that proscribes desiring/coveting another's wife (Exod. 20:17) conditions the prohibition of adultery (Exod. 20:14), instructing that one has already transgressed "Do not commit adultery" when one violates "Do not covet/desire."

Divorce

> It was said, "Whoever sends his wife away is to give her a certificate of divorce"; but I say to you that everyone who divorces his wife, except for the reason of sexual immorality, makes her commit adultery; and whoever marries a divorced woman commits adultery. (Matt. 5:31–32)

In this instruction, Jesus quotes a requirement within a casuistic setting. Because one is not required to divorce one's wife, the prescription regarding "a certificate of divorce" is a commandment in the case that another contingency (divorce) arises. Consequently, this reading and employment of Deut. 24:1 entails that Jesus is not countering the Law. This law does not mandate divorce, and thus Jesus's prohibition of divorce in some circumstances does not violate a commandment. If a man kept this teaching of Jesus, he would not violate the Law. Moreover, Jesus in Matthew permits divorce in some circumstances (5:32), indicating that Jesus's instruction here is not against the Law in itself but engages in intramural discourse on the permissible grounds for divorce.

Significantly, a controversy between various schools of interpretation (Hillel, Shammai, and Akiva) as recorded in the Mishnah (m. Gittin) debates the

56. Translations of the Babylonian Talmud are from Steinsaltz, *Babylonian Talmud*.

permissible grounds for divorce. The issue arises from the wording of Deut. 24:1, which states: "When a man takes a wife and marries her, and it happens, if she finds no favor in his eyes because he has found in her an indecent matter [עֶרְוַת דָּבָר], that he writes her a certificate of divorce . . ." (AT). Readers evidently took "indecent matter" as the potential grounds for divorce and then debated what might constitute such a "matter" or "indecency."

Mishnah Git. 9.10 records these decisions: "The House of Shammai say: A man may not divorce his wife unless he finds a matter of unseemliness [sexual transgression] in her, as it says: *Because he found in her an unseemly matter.*"[57] The school of Shammai evidently interprets the "matter" in question as a "matter of unseemliness" (דְּבַר עֶרְוָה), using the term עֶרְוָה (nakedness),[58] which is elsewhere associated with matters of illicit sexual conduct (Lev. 18:6, 7, 8, 9, etc.) to clarify what kinds of "matters" are intended by Deut. 24:1. Another opinion: "But the House of Hillel say: Even if she ruined his dinner, as it says: *Because he found in her an unseemly matter.*"[59] A third opinion: "R. Aqiva says: Even if he found another more beautiful than she, as it says: *And it shall be if she shall not find favor in his eyes.*"

Though Jesus does not cite various opinions and then distinguish his own, his instruction coincides with that of the school of Shammai, teaching that divorce is permissible on the grounds of sexual immorality (Matt. 5:32).[60] Evidently the school of Shammai and Jesus interpreted Deut. 24:1's "some indecency" (עֶרְוַת דָּבָר) in light of Lev. 18's use of that noun (עֶרְוָה, nakedness) in reference to sexual immorality. Thus, in Matt. 5:32 Jesus interprets the permission of one commandment (Deut. 24:1) in light of prohibitions named in other commandments (Lev. 18), stating that the latter inform the permissible grounds legislated in the former.[61]

57. Bracketed text employs the translator's (David Brodsky) vocabulary from the note on m. Git. 9.10 in Cohen, Goldenberg, and Lapin, *Oxford Annotated Mishnah*, vol. 2. Additionally, b. Git. 90a–b discusses Shammai's position as it pertains to "forbidden sexual intercourse."

58. The term for "nakedness" is translated "unseemliness" by David Brodsky.

59. The distinction between Shammai and Hillel may obtain due to their emphasizing different words in the phrase עֶרְוַת דָּבָר ("unseemly matter," AT) from Deut. 24:1, with Shammai taking עֶרְוַת as the controlling idea and Hillel emphasizing דָּבָר ("matter") and interpreting it to refer to basically any matter. The Kaufmann manuscript of m. Git. 9.10 seemingly presents the house of Hillel as referring only to the word "matter" from Deut. 24:1 ("unseemly" appears in the margin). See also Sifre Deut. 269, where the school of Hillel justifies its interpretation with "as it says, *thing* [שנאמר דבר]" (trans. Hammer, *Sifre*, 263). I am grateful to Logan Williams for conversation on the text of m. Git. 9.

60. See also J. Brown and Roberts, *Matthew*, 61–62; Crossley, "Matthew and the Torah," 34–35.

61. Crossley ("Matthew and the Torah"), though, rightly argues that Matt. 5:32's "sexual immorality/unchastity" (πορνείας) would be broader than Lev. 18's prohibition of incest, noting

Oaths

> Again, you have heard that the ancients were told, "You shall not make false vows, but shall fulfill your vows to the Lord." But I say to you, take no oath at all. (Matt. 5:33–34)

Once more, Jesus's teaching does not counter the Law. The command to pay one's vows is embedded within a situation (the making of vows) that Jesus speaks to, but the Law does not require the kinds of vows this commandment legislates.[62] As activity not required by the Law, prohibiting them does not counter the Law, and a disciple keeping Jesus's instruction will not break a commandment.[63] Moreover, Jesus is far from alone in concluding that one simply ought not make vows.

Deuteronomy 23:21–22 states: "When you make a vow to the Lord your God, you shall not delay to pay it, for . . . it will be a sin for you. However, if you refrain from making vows, it will not be a sin for you." Here the Law is explicit: refraining from vowing is no sin. The type of vows in question, then, are not requirements but legal permissions.[64] Interestingly, m. Shevu'ot 3.6 refers to these types as "oaths that concern voluntary actions, these being actions to which one can just as easily say 'no' as 'yes.'" In Matthew, such oaths are a legal permission that Jesus tells his audience not to utilize, instead being satisfied with "yes" or "no." Consequently, Jesus interprets one permission (voluntary vows) in light of another permission (not making vows) and concludes that it is better not to vow at all. Several Jewish texts rule similarly.

Ecclesiastes 5:4–5 (5:3–4 MT/LXX) says, "When you make a vow to God, do not be late in paying it. . . . It is better that you not vow, than vow and not pay." Interpreting this verse, Rabbi Meir (2nd cent. CE) is remembered as teaching: "And it is written: 'It is better that you should not vow, than that you should vow and not pay.' And it is taught: Better than this one [who vows and does not pay] and that one [who vows and pays] is one who does not take a vow at all" (b. Hullin 2a). Further, m. Ned. 1.1 refers to one who makes a vow with the formula "as the vows of the wicked," concluding "he has vowed with respect to a *nazir* vow, to a sacrifice, or to an oath." That these are called "the vows of the wicked" suggests that "the wicked" "are

---

that early Jewish usage of the term denoted activity "perceived to be sexually problematic" besides "incest" (34n10).

62. See Klawans, "Prohibition of Oaths," 43–45, contesting John P. Meier's claim that Jesus's instruction would violate biblical law. See Meier, "Historical Jesus."

63. So also E. P. Sanders, *Question of Uniqueness*, 8.

64. See also Crossley, "Matthew and the Torah," 36.

prone to utter impulsive or frivolous vows."[65] Similarly, m. Ned. 1.1 refers to one who vows with the formula "as the vows of the righteous," concluding, "He has not said anything." That is, "the righteous" do not typically make vows, so to vow "as the vows of the righteous" indicates one has made no vow. The Babylonian Talmud similarly records an opinion of Shmuel, who stated that even one who fulfills his vow "is called wicked" (b. Ned. 22a).[66] Rabbi Abbahu (b. Ned. 22a) clarifies the scriptural basis for this opinion by comparing Deut. 23:22 ("If you refrain [תֶחְדַּל] from making vows, it will not be a sin for you") to Job 3:17 ("There the wicked cease [חָדְלוּ] from raging") on the basis of the catchword "refrain/cease" (from חָדַל) to conclude that vowing is an act of the wicked.

Regarding the Essenes, Josephus states: "Whatever they say also is firmer than an oath [ὅρκου]; but swearing [τὸ δὲ ὀμνύειν] is avoided by them, and they esteem it worse than perjury [τῆς ἐπιορκίας], for they say that he who cannot be believed without [swearing by] God is already condemned" (*J.W.* 2.135). Philo, like the Essenes, comparably advises against oaths and swearing: "Next to not swearing at all, the second best thing is to keep one's oath; for by the mere fact of swearing at all, the swearer shows that there is some suspicion of his not being trustworthy. Let a man, therefore, be dilatory and slow if there is any chance that by delay he may be able to avoid the necessity of taking an oath at all" (*Decalogue* 1.84–85). Even closer to Jesus's instruction—who says, "Let your word be [ἔστω δὲ ὁ λόγος ὑμῶν] 'Yes, yes' or 'No, no'" (Matt. 5:37 NRSV)—is Philo's claim that one's word should be one's oath: "And the first of these other commandments is not to take the name of God in vain; for let the word [λόγος] of the virtuous man, says the law, be his oath [ὅρκος ἔστω], firm, unchangeable, which cannot lie, founded steadfastly on truth" (*Spec. Laws* 2.2).

Once more, then, Jesus's instruction does not contradict the Law; it prohibits a permission. But the sources cited above indicate that this was not regarded as a violation of the Law; on the contrary, many regarded oath-taking as evidence that one could not be trusted. Jesus, agreeing with this insight, commands his hearers to speak truthfully without the aid of oaths.[67]

65. So Robert Goldenberg, translator of m. Nedarim in Cohen, Goldenberg, and Lapin, *Oxford Annotated Mishnah*, 2:131.

66. I'm grateful to Logan Williams for alerting me to m. Ned. 1.1 and b. Ned. 22a.

67. For a contextualization of Matt. 5:21–48 within Second Temple and rabbinic texts and an exploration of the possible link between Lev. 19:17–18 and oaths, see Goldstone, "Structure."

Retaliation

> You have heard that it was said, "Eye for eye, and tooth for tooth." But I say to you, do not show opposition against an evil person. (Matt. 5:38–39)

In this famous instruction, Jesus refers to the principle of legally implemented retaliation as stated in Exod. 21:24, Deut. 19:21, and Lev. 24:20. It is not clear that he is singling out one of these contexts over another, though the prohibition against "resisting" or "opposing" in Matt. 5:39 (μὴ ἀντιστῆναι) may be informed by the context of the principle in Deut. 19:18–19, which prescribes the penalty in question against one who "accused [another] unjustly" (ἄδικα ἀντέστη), using a form of the verb (ἀνθίστημι) that appears in Matt. 5:39. In any case, "eye for eye" appears to be a principle that Jesus demands his hearers not to utilize. From the Pentateuchal context, this penalty is given by "judges" in a judicial setting (Exod. 21:22; Deut. 19:17–21), suggesting that the outcome of "eye for eye" is conditional upon an existing situation (a legal case with witnesses).[68] Jesus's instruction not to oppose the one who wrongs suggests that he is not overturning "eye for eye" as a permissible legal outcome in judicial settings but is instructing his disciples to act in such a way that will obviate such cases in the first place.[69] There will be no need to employ the legal sentence ("eye for eye") if his disciples pursue peace and reconciliation beforehand and thus avoid going to court at all. Consequently, strictly speaking, this instruction does not contradict a legal requirement: prohibiting a permission is not equal to permitting a prohibition (without an override) or nullifying a requirement.

Translating Matt. 5:39's μὴ ἀντιστῆναι is difficult. Generally, the Greek term can simply refer to "opposition." But "opposition" can take many forms: Does Jesus prohibit self-defense, recourse to legal retaliation in a judicial setting, or retaliation in any form, whether judicial or extrajudicial? Translating as "do not retaliate" seemingly covers all the grounds while letting the situation provide the precise significance; however, its use in conjunction with a law legislating a judicial process—and Jesus's examples, half of which concern lawsuits and lending—suggests that the primary nuance is to prohibit recourse to judicial retaliation. The verb ἀνθίστημι is regularly used in judicial settings in reference to legal testimony or opposition (Deut. 19:18; Job 9:19; Wis. 12:12; Isa. 50:8; 59:12; Jer. 14:7; 50:44 [27:44 LXX]; Luke 21:15), and Deut. 19:18–21 names "eye for eye" as the penalty for the one who "unjustly accuses" (ἄδικα ἀντέστη). Jesus's employment of this verb after quoting legislation from Deut.

68. See comparably Konradt, *Christology, Torah*, 86.
69. So also Allison, *Sermon on the Mount*, 93.

19:21 suggests that his instruction refers primarily to refusing legal recourse when wronged or insulted[70] and instead pursuing reconciliation that obviates the need for adjudication. As he states earlier: "Come to good terms with your accuser quickly, while you are with him on the way *to court*, so that your accuser will not hand you over to the judge, and the judge to the officer, and you will not be thrown into prison" (Matt. 5:25). But reducing "Do not oppose" to a refusal to go to court would probably press this point too hard; he appears to encourage peacemaking in all avenues of life, even when a judicial process would likely not apply, as in the example of the conscripted mile.

Peacemaking and reconciliation are emphatic elements of Jesus's teaching. However, such elements are far from unique in the Jewish legal and wisdom traditions. For example, Prov. 24:29 says, "Do not say, 'I shall do the same to him as he has done to me; / I will repay the person according to his work.'" This proverb in the LXX brings out that one should not "pay back the one who has committed injustice against me" (μὴ εἴπῃς . . . τείσομαι δὲ αὐτὸν ἅ με ἠδίκησεν). Proverbs 25:21 says: "If your enemy is hungry, give him food to eat; / And if he is thirsty, give him water to drink." Sirach 28:1–8, supposedly interpreting the Law of Moses (28:6–7), prescribes turning away from anger, forgiving wrongs, and refraining from conflicts: "The vengeful will face the Lord's vengeance, for he keeps a strict account of their sins. Forgive your neighbor the wrong he has done, and then your sins will be pardoned when you pray. . . . Set enmity aside. . . . Do not be angry with your neighbor. . . . Overlook faults. . . . Refrain from strife."

Acknowledging that judgment belongs to God, the speaker in Community Rule claims, "I shall not repay anyone with an evil reward; with goodness I shall pursue man. For to God (belongs) the judgment of every living being, and it is he who pays man his wages" (1QS 10.17–18).[71] Pseudo-Phocylides, a text that provides occasional interpretations of laws, advises: "Practice self-restraint and abstain from shameful deeds. Do not imitate evil [actions]; but leave vengeance to justice [*or* abandon vengeance/self-defense, ἀπόλειψον ἄμυναν]" (1.76–77).[72] In Joseph and Aseneth, Levi says to another who is angry, "Why are you furious with anger with this man? And we are men who worship God, and it does not befit us to repay evil for evil" (23.9). From the Babylonian Talmud, Ber. 17a records the closing sentences of a teacher's

70. See Davies and Allison, *Matthew*, 82.

71. Unless otherwise indicated, all translations of Qumran documents are from García Martínez and Tigchelaar, eds., *Dead Sea Scrolls Study Edition*.

72. Bracketed text is my translation. The word ἄμυνα may refer to self-defense or vengeance. For the former, see Acts 7:24; Sib. Or. 2.97; Ps.-Phoc. 1.32. For the latter, Apocr. Ezek. 1.5; Jos. Asen. 24.7; and possibly Sib. Or. 2.146.

regular prayer: "My God, guard my tongue from evil and my lips from speaking deceit. To those who curse me let my soul be silent and may my soul be like dust to all." In a passage recording various sayings, b. Shabb. 88b states: "And the Sages taught: 'About those who are insulted and do not insult, who hear their shame and do not respond, who act out of love and are joyful in suffering, the verse says: "They that love him are as the sun going forth in its might"'" (Judg. 5:31). Second En. 50.2–4 says, "My children, live in patience and meekness. . . . Every assault and every wound and burn and every evil word, if they happen to you on account of the Lord, endure them; and, being able to pay them back, do not repay them to (your) neighbor."[73]

These examples are quite general, but they communicate the point clearly: how to respond to insult and injury was debated, implying that "eye for eye" retaliation was not automatically assumed to be the required or correct response. And in many cases, other Jewish teachers concluded comparably to Jesus's instruction: do not retaliate, quell your anger, and "do not repay" someone according to their unjust action. Moreover, numerous texts debate how one may implement the "eye for eye" legislation, and extant evidence suggests that many did not take it literally.[74]

Josephus claims that the one maimed has the right to accept money rather than requiring a literal exacting of "eye for eye," saying: "He that maims anyone, let him undergo the like himself and be deprived of the same member of which he has deprived the other, unless he that is maimed will accept money instead of it; for the law makes the sufferer the judge [κύριον] of the value of what he has suffered, and permits him to estimate it, unless he will be more severe" (*Ant.* 4.280).

Philo, on the other hand, considers monetary compensation in exchange for assaults a violation of justice. He says, "And anyone may here fitly blame those who appoint that punishments, in nowise corresponding to the offenses, are to be inflicted on the offenders, imposing pecuniary penalties for assaults, or stigma and infamy for wounds and mutilations" (*Spec. Laws* 3.181). Those who so judge "destroy the laws" (3.182). Philo's objection to regarding "eye for eye" as a legal permission not always to be utilized is evidence that the practice of not implementing it literally was sufficiently widespread for him to comment on it. Moreover, even after claiming that such alternative punishments were tantamount to abolishing the laws, he claims that other factors ought to condition whether one mitigates the punishment: "And when

73. Andersen, *OTP* 1:177. Second Enoch is of uncertain date/provenance. This passage may employ material known from the Gospels.

74. On the *lex talionis* in Second Temple and rabbinic texts, see Davis, *Lex Talionis*. See also Crossley, "Matthew and the Torah," 36–38.

we say this [that it ought to be implemented literally], we mean provided no circumstances occur to give a different complexion to the affair; for it is not the same thing to inflict blows on one's father and on a stranger, nor to speak ill of a ruler and of a private person. . . . And all other things of this kind one must examine with a view to judge of the propriety of increasing or diminishing the punishment" (3.183). Thus, even for one who considers the literal implementation just and required, Philo acknowledges that other factors should shape the judgment and the imposed penalty.

Rabbinic material refers almost exclusively to monetary compensation as the expected penalty for injury.[75] From the Mishnah, Bava Qamma 8.1 lists the principles for monetary compensation of various injuries and consequences (referring in 8.1 to "damage, pain, healing, loss of employment, and shame"). For example, regarding injury, they "view him [the injured] as if he were a slave sold in the marketplace, and they assess his value before the damage and after the damage" (8.1). The Talmud relates comparable conclusions.[76] Josephus and Philo demonstrate that what the Mishnah took for granted (monetary compensation) was also practiced during Jesus's career and the composition of the Gospels.

The astute reader will recognize, however, that accepting monetary compensation for injury is not the same as Jesus's admittedly posture-correcting teaching to turn the other cheek, walk the extra mile, lend without scruples, and give away both cloak and shirt. But such instruction is informed not by a completely unique insight into the Law and ethics but by the conviction both that the promised restoration was afoot and that the restoration would affect the applicability/permissibility of the referenced commandment, "eye for eye."[77] This reading recognizes that the Law is not "one size fits all"; rather, *time* regulates the application of certain commandments.

For example, we know from the Law itself that certain times impose certain legal requirements: the Sabbath obligates rest (Exod. 20:10); every seven years, one must cancel debts (Deut. 15:1–11), liberate Hebrew slaves (15:12–15), and let the land lie fallow (Lev. 25:1–7); and in the Jubilee, families return to their ancestral land (25:8–10), and Israelite slaves are released (25:39–41). In the Gospels, this time of restoration would similarly affect Jesus's interpretation of what the Law permitted and required.

75. See further discussion on "eye for eye" in rabbinic texts in Crossley, *New Testament and Jewish Law*, 67–88.

76. See b. Ketubbot 32a–b.

77. Thus, for reasons discussed below, it is inadequate to claim that this instruction is simply akin to "building a fence" around Torah, as argued by Przybylski, *Righteousness in Matthew*, 81–83.

Pertinent for our purposes is the fact that some texts and groups envisaged the restoration as an eschatological Jubilee: just as God during the Jubilee required a "release" of impoverished families to their ancestral land (Lev. 25:10, 25–28) and the liberation of Israelites enslaved even to non-Israelites (25:47–54), so the restoration would be an eschatological Jubilee, in which the exiles enslaved in foreign lands would be "released" from their foreign captors and enabled to return to their ancestral land. Isaiah 61 exemplifies this eschatological employment of Jubilee, depicting the restoration as a "release" from captivity and exile. Just as Lev. 25:10 describes the Jubilee as a time to "proclaim a release" (וּקְרָאתֶם דְּרוֹר), so Isa. 61 refers to one anointed by the Spirit "to proclaim release" (לִקְרֹא . . . דְּרוֹר). What is a noneschatological legal requirement in Lev. 25 becomes an eschatological reality announced and effected by the anointed servant of Isa. 61, who is sent "to bring good news [εὐαγγελίσασθαι] to the oppressed, to bind up the brokenhearted, to proclaim liberty [לִקְרֹא . . . דְּרוֹר, κηρύξαι . . . ἄφεσιν] to the captives" (Isa. 61:1 NRSV). Isaiah 61:1–2's employment of other terms basic to Israel's promised restoration (good news, healing, liberation, comfort) indicates that this "proclamation of release" employs Jubilee motifs to describe the effects wrought during the national restoration.

Similarly, 11QMelch comparably envisages the restoration of Israel and God's salvation and judgment in "the latter days" as an eschatological Jubilee. What remains implicit in Isa. 61, detected by an allusion to Lev. 25:10, is explicit in 11QMelch, which introduces its depiction of the restoration by first citing Lev. 25:10 and then providing its interpretation "for the end of days" (2.1–4). Moreover, the envisaged restoration is wrought by the anointed servant of Isa. 61 (2.18–20). Notably, without explanatory argument this text combines Lev. 25:10, which promises "release," with Deut. 15:1–11, which requires "release" of debts every seven years, and it interprets them eschatologically to promise liberation from spiritual and international oppression (2.13) and the "release" of spiritual debts—that is, the forgiveness of sins (2.6).

Evidently, numerous texts in the late Second Temple period interpreted Lev. 25 and Deut. 15 together, and for somewhat understandable reasons. Leviticus itself may envisage a cancellation of some debts, given the required "release" to one's ancestral land, which may imply a cancellation of the debt that bound the one released.[78] Moreover, the LXX employs the same term (ἄφεσις) to refer both to the cancellation of debt (Deut. 15:1–2) and to the release to one's ancestral land (Lev. 25:10) and indicates that both "releases" are "proclaimed" (Deut. 15:2: ἐπικέκληται; Lev. 25:10: διαβοήσετε), factors

78. For details, see Bartos and Levinson, "'Manner of Remission,'" esp. 363.

that may have suggested to readers the need, or at least permission, to interpret them together. That both events occur in seven-year increments, suggesting that a Jubilee (Lev. 25) could coincide with a year of debt cancellation (Deut. 15:1–2),[79] may also have encouraged mutual interpretation. However the textual combination was suggested, we have evidence that even in noneschatological contexts, the Jubilee was understood to require debt cancellation and liberation of slaves, implying that the events prescribed in Lev. 25 and Deut. 15 were interpreted to coincide. Josephus, for example, explains, "That fiftieth year is called by the Hebrews the Jubilee, wherein debtors are freed from their debts, and slaves are set at liberty" (*Ant.* 3.282). Philo too interprets the Jubilee as liberating slaves and canceling debts: "For, in this fiftieth year, all the ordinances which are given relating to the seventh year are repeated, and some of greater magnitude are likewise added" (*On the Virtues* 1.99). And again, "For this year [Jubilee] both is and is looked upon as a year of remission [ἄφεσις]" (*Spec. Laws* 2.122; see also 2.110–18). Evidently, then, Isa. 61, 11QMelch, and possibly others[80] demonstrate that restoration could be envisaged as an eschatological Jubilee, and such a depiction was informed by combining Lev. 25 and Deut. 15 in ways consonant with late Second Temple exegesis of those requirements.

Significantly, the Synoptic Gospels depict the restoration in just these terms: Jesus is the one anointed by the Spirit to proclaim the good news and actualize the promises of comfort, healing, and liberation proclaimed in Isa. 61. In Luke 4:18–21, the identification is explicit: he reads from Isa. 61:1–2 and applies it to himself. In Matt. 11:5, Jesus answers affirmatively John's question of whether he is "the Coming One" (Matt. 11:3) by referring to his work as a fulfillment of Isa. 61:1–2 and 35:5. Moreover, as we have already seen, some of the Matthean Beatitudes allude to the restoration promises of Isa. 61. Mark also depicts the restoration by employing Jubilee motifs indebted to Isa. 61 and Lev. 25. Jesus is the one anointed by the Spirit (Mark 1:10; Isa. 61:1), who has authority to "forgive sins in the land" (ἀφιέναι ἁμαρτίας ἐπὶ τῆς γῆς, Mark 2:10 AT), corresponding to the expectation in Lev. 25:10 to "proclaim release/forgiveness in the land" (διαβοήσετε ἄφεσιν ἐπὶ τῆς γῆς).[81] With such allusions and quotations, the Gospels participate in an established pattern of depicting the restoration as an eschatological Jubilee. Given the Second

79. Ariel Feldman ("New Light," 178–84) notes that some ancient interpreters translated Deut. 15:1 "at the end of seven years," implying that the year of remission and Jubilee would coincide.

80. See also Dan. 9:24–27. Bartos and Levinson ("'Manner of Remission,'" 360–61) note the 490-year cycle, amounting to ten Jubilees.

81. See detailed discussion in Williams, "Melchizedek," 129–32.

Temple practice of combining Lev. 25's Jubilee with Deut. 15's cancellation of debts in both eschatological (11QMelch) and noneschatological contexts (Josephus, *Ant.* 3.282; Philo, *On the Virtues* 1.99–100), the Gospels unsurprisingly depict the restoration *qua* Jubilee to include not just the return to the land but also the cancellation of debts (as will be shown).

This brings us back to our interpretation of Matt. 5. Instead of pursuing retaliation in legal and monetary matters, Jesus commands his hearers to walk the extra mile, turn the other cheek, and give to one who asks. Given that Jesus regards his moment as the time of eschatological "release/forgiveness" (Matt. 6:12; 9:2–6; 18:21–22; 26:28), he evidently regarded the legislation for the year of release and Jubilee as governing his legal and ethical instruction. This is clear from several shared instructions in Deut. 15/Lev. 25 and Matt. 5–6.[82]

For example, in the year of release, Deut. 15:2 requires that everyone release debts that a neighbor owes (ἀφήσεις . . . ὃ ὀφείλει σοι). Likewise, given that the restoration *qua* Jubilee is the time of "release," Jesus instructs his disciples to pray "release our debts [ἄφες ἡμῖν τὰ ὀφειλήματα ἡμῶν], as we also have released our debtors [ὡς καὶ ἡμεῖς ἀφήκαμεν τοῖς ὀφειλέταις ἡμῶν]" (Matt. 6:12 AT).

Deuteronomy 15, warning the one tempted not to give, states: "Beware, lest there is a base thought in your heart, saying, 'The seventh year, the year of remission, is near,' and your eye is hostile/evil [πονηρεύσηται ὁ ὀφθαλμός σου] toward your poor brother, and you give him nothing [καὶ οὐ δώσεις αὐτῷ]" (15:9 AT). After instructing his disciples to give to the poor (Matt. 6:2–4) and not to hoard wealth (6:19), and before telling them that they cannot serve God and Mammon/riches (6:24), Jesus similarly warns them not to have "an evil eye" (ἐὰν δὲ ὁ ὀφθαλμός σου πονηρὸς ᾖ, 6:23).

Additionally, in Lev. 25's Jubilee legislation, Israel is to forgo sowing (25:11). Anticipating their anxiety, God says, "But if you say [ἐὰν δὲ λέγητε], 'What are we going to eat [τί φαγόμεθα] in the seventh year if we do not sow or gather [ἐὰν μὴ σπείρωμεν μηδὲ συναγάγωμεν] in our produce?'" (25:20). God then assures them he will increase the yield of the sixth year so that they can eat from it for the next three years (25:21). Similarly, in Matt. 6, in instructing his disciples to trust God, Jesus teaches them to pray, "Give us today our bread for tomorrow [τὸν ἐπιούσιον]" (6:11 AT),[83] drawing on the similar motif of God providing "now" what Israel will need in the future. Further, trusting in God's provision, Jesus says, "Do not worry then, saying [λέγοντες], 'What

82. On the interconnectedness of Matt. 5:38–42 with Jesus's broader use of "debt" imagery in Matt. 5–7 and its connection to Deut. 15, see Ridlehoover, *Lord's Prayer*, 156–72.

83. See Acts 7:26; 16:11; 20:15; and 21:18, where the related phrase ἐπιούσῃ ἡμέρᾳ signifies the next day. See France, *Matthew*, 248.

are we to eat [τί φάγωμεν]?" (6:31), exhorting, "Look at the birds: . . . they do not sow [οὐ σπείρουσιν], nor reap, nor gather [συνάγουσιν] crops into barns, and yet your heavenly Father feeds them" (6:26). Such instruction is indebted thematically and lexically to the instructions and assurances given in Lev. 25's Jubilee legislation regarding the certainty of provision given the requirement not to "sow or reap."

Significantly, Deut. 15 warns against withholding money from people in need due to the approach of the year of release. Deuteronomy 15:8–10 asserts to the one tempted not to give: "You shall generously give [διδοὺς δώσεις αὐτῷ], and you shall generously lend [δάνειον δανιεῖς αὐτῷ]" (AT).[84] In Matt. 5:42, *exemplifying his instruction not to exact eye for eye*, Jesus says: "Give to him who asks of you [τῷ αἰτοῦντί σε δός], and do not turn away from him who wants to borrow from you [καὶ τὸν θέλοντα ἀπὸ σοῦ δανίσασθαι μὴ ἀποστραφῇς]." Here Deut. 15's legislation for the year of remission conditions Jesus's requirement of giving to those who ask *in an example of what to do instead of eye for eye.*

Finally, Deut. 15:2 claims that whatever debt a neighbor owes (ὃ ὀφείλει σοι ὁ πλησίον), the one owed may not exact it (οὐκ ἀπαιτήσεις) because the year of release has been announced (ὅτι ἐπικέκληται ἄφεσις). In other words, debt exaction is forbidden in the year of remission. Given that Deut. 15 informs Jesus's instruction both in this particular instance (Matt. 5:38–42) and in Matt. 5–6 more broadly, and given that Jesus in Matthew metaphorizes sin and forgiveness as debt and cancellation (6:12; 18:21–35), Deut. 15:2's prohibition of debt collecting suggests the prohibition of retaliating when wronged. Consequently, one may not pursue judicial retaliation when wronged, and one cannot pursue "what is owed"; instead, one must turn the other cheek. Moreover, commuting the eye-for-eye punishment *to monetary fines* was an attested practice in the first century, commented on by Josephus (*Ant.* 4.280) and Philo (*Spec. Laws* 3.181–83) and broadly assumed in the Mishnah (Bava Qamma 8.1). So if the literary and original audience of Jesus's instruction assumed this practice, his interpreting eye for eye in terms of *debt forgiveness* may have been readily comprehensible.

Interestingly, Philo (*Migration* 1.91) similarly prohibited exacting debts and pursuing legal retaliation on the Sabbath or "festival" days, claiming it unlawful on such days "to bring accusations [ἐγκαλεῖν], or conduct suits at law [δικάζειν], or demand a restoration of a deposit [παρακαταθήκας ἀπαιτεῖν], or exact the repayment of a debt [δάνεια ἀναπράττειν]," actions "usually

84. The quoted portion is Deut. 15:10 LXX, but Deut. 15:8–10 says multiple times in various ways to give and lend freely.

permitted at times which are not days of festival." He elsewhere claims that the Sabbath day "comprehends" the legal requirements named in other "sabbatical" festivals—namely, the year of release and the Jubilee (*Spec. Laws* 2.39), implying that he would regard debt exaction and possibly even legal retaliation as prohibited in the Jubilee. If participating in this tradition of legal opinion, Matthew's Jesus, who likens the restoration to the Jubilee, might similarly prohibit legal retaliation in the (eschatological) Jubilee on such grounds.

Matthew 5:38–42, then, like much of Jesus's teaching, is conditioned by his conviction that the time of restoration is at hand. As God's time of release/forgiveness has been announced, those who wish to participate in that forgiveness must likewise forgive. Or as he states in 6:14–15: "If you forgive [ἀφῆτε] them for their transgressions, your heavenly Father will also forgive [ἀφήσει] you. But if you do not forgive them, then your Father will not forgive your transgressions" (AT). Because they must forgive, his disciples may not use the permission of "eye for eye." Significantly, then, Jesus is not haphazardly revoking a command; rather, his instruction is legally informed. Just as what is permissible in some years (debt collecting) becomes prohibited in the year of release, so "do not retaliate" (i.e., do not exact moral debts) is a legally informed decision based on his conviction about the eschatological time (Jubilee), which is governed by certain legal requirements. Consequently, he is teaching that the restoration *qua* Jubilee overrides the permission to exact debts and requires generosity (materially and spiritually), as Deut. 15 and Lev. 25 mandate.

Enemy Love

> You have heard that it was said, "You shall love your neighbor and hate your enemy." But I say to you, love your enemies and pray for those who persecute you. (Matt. 5:43–44)

In this final instruction, Jesus famously teaches to love one's enemies. As is often noted, "Hate your enemy" is not a commandment in the Law. In Matt. 5:43, Jesus quotes from Lev. 19:18: "Love your neighbor as yourself." A command to "hate your enemy" does not appear in the vicinity or in any other Pentateuchal legislation. Evidently, Jesus is contrasting his requirement to "love your enemies" not with the Law but with a potential corollary one could draw from it. Jesus's words, then, contradict not the Law but some (implied) contemporary interpretation. This latter interpretation is potentially espoused by a Jewish group contemporary with Jesus.

Josephus provides a prolonged description of practices of the Essenes (*J.W.* 2.119–61). Of new initiates to their sect, he says: "And before he is allowed to touch their common food, he is obliged to take tremendous oaths; . . . that he will observe justice toward men; and that he will do no harm to anyone, either of his own accord, or by the command of others; that he will always hate the wicked and assist the righteous" (2.139). Given that the Essenes were scattered throughout the region (2.124) and lived contemporaneously with Jesus by practices sufficiently well known to warrant comment from Josephus,[85] it is plausible that Matthew/Jesus knew of their instruction and commented on it or something like it here. Moreover, if the Community Rule (1QS) represents views of this same group, we have internal evidence of such a view.[86] The text states that "the instructor" and those who "volunteer to carry out God's decrees" ought to "love all the sons of light . . . and to hate all the sons of darkness" (1QS 1.7–11; see also 1QS 9.21–22).[87] Even if Jesus's teaching does not oppose Essene practice specifically, to "hate one's enemy" would seemingly be a common intuition that many humans held (and hold).[88] Thus, Jesus's teaching not to hate one's enemies may simply be combating a tendency of many across time and space.

Additionally, other commands may have encouraged the conclusion that one ought to love one's enemy. Leviticus 19:18 itself states, "You shall not take vengeance, nor hold any grudge against the sons of your people, but you shall love your neighbor as yourself." That the Law must instruct "love" rather than "vengeance" against a neighbor implies that one's "neighbor" might include one against whom vengeance is desired (i.e., an enemy). But Israel is commanded to love them rather than pursue vengeance. Exodus 23:4–5 teaches: "If you meet your enemy's [τοῦ ἐχθροῦ σου] ox or his donkey wandering away, you must return it to him. If you see the donkey of one who hates you lying helpless under its load, you shall not leave it helpless for its owner; you must arrange the load with him."[89] And Prov. 25:21 states, "If your enemy is hungry, give him food to eat; / And if he is thirsty, give him water to drink."

85. In *Ant.* 18.20, Josephus numbers the "men who live this way" at 4,000. It is unclear whether he refers to the Essenes generally or specifically to the Essenes who live in a communitarian environment. Context suggests the latter; elsewhere he refers to another "order" of the Essenes who do not abide by the otherwise accepted practice of nonmarriage (*J.W.* 2.160–61).

86. My conclusion does not depend on this hypothesis. If they're different groups, it would simply show that two groups held this view.

87. Translation modified from García Martínez and Tigchelaar, changing "detest" to "hate."

88. See also Pss. Sol. 12.5.

89. Regarding the requisite help, see m. Bava Metzi'a 2.10: "If he loosened and loaded, loosened and loaded, even four or five times—he is obligated, as it is said: *You shall indeed help* [Exod. 23:5]."

Rather than hatred of one's enemy, Jesus tells his hearers to "pray for those who persecute you." But his instruction is not confined to moments of crisis; he also critiques those who greet only their "brothers" (Matt. 5:47). In all moments of life, his disciples ought to love those hostile to them. And he grounds his instruction in the divine qualities of the heavenly Father, to whose behavior his hearers are to conform, "for [ὅτι] he causes his sun to rise on the evil and the good" (Matt. 5:45).

Jesus then compares the typical behavior (loving only those who love you) not with what the Law requires but with the behavior of tax collectors and gentiles (Matt. 5:46–47). Following Jesus's interpretation on this matter, then, elevates a disciple not above what the Law teaches but above the practices of those widely considered "sinners." Moreover, his question "What more [περισσόν] are you doing [than gentiles and tax collectors]?" (5:47) echoes his opening instruction that one's righteousness must "exceed" (περισσεύσῃ) that of the scribes and Pharisees (5:20). Consequently, living according to the norms Jesus opposes, one might live like a gentile or a tax collector at worst, or the scribes and Pharisees at best, but one would not thereby become like the heavenly Father, suggesting that Jesus's instruction opposes not the Law but a practice of it that he regards as deficient for entering the kingdom. But in keeping Jesus's interpretation of the Law, one imitates God and thereby exudes the abundant righteousness requisite to enter the kingdom.

Jesus concludes this section by saying, "Therefore you shall be perfect [τέλειοι], as your heavenly Father is perfect [τέλειος]" (Matt. 5:48). Jesus is not stating that "sinless perfection" is necessary for salvation. In this body of teaching (Matt. 5–7), he assumes that interpersonal conflicts will persist (5:23–26), stumbling will occur (5:29–30), and ongoing forgiveness (divine and human) will be necessary (6:12, 14–15; cp. 18:15–35). His command to be "perfect" likely intends to promote complete conformity to the divine character in treating the just and the wicked with similar benefits.[90] Even Philo, who plausibly has a more optimistic view of human capacity than Jesus, states that "there is no one born, however perfect [τέλειος] he may be, who can wholly avoid the commission of sin" (*Spec. Laws* 1.252). Consequently, Jesus's summons to "perfection" does not establish an impossibly high standard to make one realize the need for

90. See the discussion of τέλειος in Pennington, *Sermon on the Mount*, 69–85, 203–7. Though (*pace* Pennington, *Sermon on the Mount*, 205) Jesus did not choose "to restate" Lev. 20:26's requirement for holiness "in terms of *teleios*-ity because 'holiness' in the Pharisees' world had come to mean primarily *external* matters of purity and behavior." Evidence for such a claim is lacking. Rather, Matthew's Jesus is likely echoing Deut. 18:13: "You are to be blameless [τέλειος] before the Lord your God." See the discussion in Runesson, "Purity, Holiness," 162; Runesson, *Divine Wrath*, 96–101. Noah was also called τέλειος (Gen. 6:9).

grace—a problem Paul's letters then supposedly answer. He teaches, rather, that humans should pursue the complete character of God, who loves even the unrighteous, and in so doing grow into the completeness basic to God.

Why These Commands?

Why did Jesus speak on specifically these issues/commands in Matt. 5:21–48? If he was working through the so-called Ten Commandments, why no mention of the oneness of God or of Sabbath or theft? And it is not as if he was speaking only on highly debated issues. If he had been, Sabbath and purity legislation would certainly have been discussed.

I suggest that these issues/commands were grouped due to Jesus's conviction (shared by many contemporary teachers) that "love of neighbor" was of utmost importance. When asked about the greatest commandment, he couples love of God with love of neighbor, claiming that the entirety of the Law and the Prophets hangs "upon these two commandments" (Matt. 22:37–40). When a man asks what he must do to have eternal life, Jesus responds by quoting from the Decalogue and adds the Levitical command to love one's neighbor (Matt. 19:18–19). Notably, in the original legislation, each of the commands interpreted in Matt. 5:21–48 explicitly relates the matter to how one treats a neighbor.

Jesus quotes laws on murder, adultery and divorce, false vows, retaliation, and love of neighbor. Respectively, Jesus interprets these matters with additional reference to anger, coveting (lust), not vowing, nonretaliation, and loving neighbors and enemies. The Pentateuchal legislation pertaining to each of these issues (listed below in the order quoted in Matt. 5:21–48) explicitly governs treatment of one's "neighbor."

- Leviticus 19:18 prohibits vengeance and anger against a fellow Israelite, instead prescribing that one ought to "love your neighbor" (τὸν πλησίον σου).
- After prohibiting adultery (Exod. 20:14), the Decalogue prohibits coveting/lusting after the wife of "your neighbor" (τοῦ πλησίον σου, 20:17).
- Leviticus prohibits false/unjust vows contiguously with its prohibition of wronging a neighbor: "And you shall not swear falsely by my name. . . .You shall not oppress your neighbor" (τὸν πλησίον, 19:12–13).
- In Lev. 24, the eye-for-eye principle governs the permissible "payment" for injuries against one's "neighbor" (πλησίον, 24:19).[91]

91. Interestingly, the wound-for-wound examples (Lev. 24:20) are prefaced in 24:19 by the principle: "just as he has done, so it shall be done to him" (ὡς ἐποίησεν αὐτῷ ὡσαύτως

It makes sense, then, that Jesus's interpretation of "love your neighbor" (Matt. 5:43) would conclude this body of teaching about commandments explicitly related in the Pentateuch to neighbor treatment.[92] Loving one's neighbor does not permit hatred of one's enemy; rather, loving one's neighbor, as Lev. 19:18 implies, requires loving one's enemies, pursuing reconciliation with opponents, and treating them in a way that precludes or stems conflicts in the first place. Thus Jesus's command "Love your enemies" both concludes and summarizes his body of teaching that instructs his hearers how they ought to treat neighbors and pursue the abundant righteousness basic to life in God's kingdom.

Conclusion

In Matt. 5, Jesus instructs his hearers in the practices and characteristics they should pursue to participate in the restoration. In the Beatitudes, Jesus proleptically pronounces the blessings of the promised restoration on those who live according to his interpretation of the Scriptures. Matthew 5:21–48 showcases Jesus's interpretation of commandments with reference to other commandments. His interpretation was shown to be occasionally informed by his conviction concerning the inbreaking restoration, an event that exerts pressure on certain commands not haphazardly but due to the legal precedent of events/seasons overriding actions permitted outside such seasons, akin to the year of remission prohibiting debt collection.

Having surveyed Jesus's positive vision of Law-keeping in Matt. 5, the following chapters will survey various nomistic controversies between Jesus and his contemporaries.

ἀντιποιηθήσεται αὐτῷ). Given that Jesus summarizes "the Law and the Prophets" with the Golden Rule ("Whatever you want others to do to you, thus do to them," ὅσα ἐὰν θέλητε ἵνα ποιῶσιν ὑμῖν οἱ ἄνθρωποι, οὕτως καὶ ὑμεῖς ποιεῖτε αὐτοῖς, Matt. 7:12 AT), the latter principle probably governs his interpretation of the legislation concerning treatment of one who has injured a neighbor. One who unintentionally injured someone would likely want the injured party not to retaliate. Therefore, when injured or insulted, "do not retaliate" (Matt. 5:39 AT).

92. For a reception history of Lev. 19:18 in early Judaism, see Akiyama, *Love of Neighbor*. See also Goldstone, "Structure," on the gravitational effect of Lev. 19:17–18 on other commandments.

4

Conflict and Controversy

Jesus came into conflict with his contemporaries over numerous issues: purity, Sabbath keeping, family dynamics, and more. Because conflicts by nature reveal the fault lines in interpretation, the following chapters will delve into representative examples of these interactions and demonstrate the logic of Jesus's alternative practices and, when applicable, how Jesus's mission of restoration affected his activity and his legal defense when confronted. How one interprets these confrontations reveals a great deal about how one positions Jesus in relation to the Law and its practice. Many scholars infer from these interactions that Jesus disregarded the food laws and purity to show that only love and faith matter (Dunn); "redefined" the nation's practices, swapping "allegiance to Torah" with "allegiance to himself" (Wright); or replaced "purity" with "mercy" (Borg). But a refined understanding of purity, Sabbath halakhah, and other contemporary legal debates will show that Jesus does none of these things.

Not every controversy will be covered; instead, nomistic discourse from which scholars have inferred a dramatic break from Judaism or the Law will garner special attention. If the chapter feels haphazard, jumping from topic to topic and text to text, it is because I am examining scenes from which scholars have unjustifiably deduced that Jesus breaks with his ancestral customs, not necessarily because each passage leads organically to the next. The next chapter will focus on controversial practices partially motivated by his eschatological agenda: dining with sinners, claims about family, and a case of Sabbath profanation. The present chapter focuses predominantly on cases wherein Jesus's distinct legal practices hinge not on his eschatological convictions but simply on his alternative interpretation of the commands in question: purity regulations, healing on the Sabbath, and the temple tax.

Purity

According to the Synoptic Gospels, Jesus kept the purity regulations and taught others to do the same. Contemporary claims to the contrary typically reveal modern confusion over basic issues from Leviticus and Deuteronomy rather than well-founded conclusions about either the Law or the Gospels. In numerous studies, one finds the claim that Jesus violated the Law by touching the man with *lepra*,[1] or that Jesus's prioritizing interior purity (or its redefinition as "compassion") signified a dismissal of ritual purity,[2] or that the Law only prescribed purifications for priests,[3] and thus Jesus's dismissal of external purity was a dismissal of the (supposed) Pharisaic concern to imitate the priests. But these views are mistaken: the Law does not prohibit touching a *lepros*; Jesus does prioritize "moral" over ritual purity,[4] but so do Leviticus, the Prophets, and just about any Jewish text from the period. And far from dismissing the need for ritual purity, he commands the healed man to make the requisite sacrifices for purification (Matt. 8:4; Mark 1:44; Luke 5:14). And the Law did not prescribe purification only for the priests, which Lev. 11–15 and Num. 19 make abundantly plain.

The Gospels do, however, occasionally present Jesus and the Pharisees clashing over matters of purity. A recent work by Matthew Thiessen has thoroughly dealt with many of these issues.[5] For this reason, I will focus on Jesus's statements regarding the washing of cups, washing hands before eating, and his interaction with the *lepros*.

First Clean the Inside of the Cup!

In Luke 11, a Pharisee invites Jesus to dine at his house. The scene in question begins:

> When the Pharisee saw this, he was surprised that he had not first washed[6] before the meal. But the Lord said to him, "Now you Pharisees clean the outside

1. Green, *Luke*, 237; Keener, *Matthew*, 261; France, *Matthew*, 306.

2. Borg, *Conflict, Holiness, and Politics*, esp. 112, 139, 173, 249–56; Wright, *Victory of God*, 380, 396–98; Loader, *Jesus' Attitude*, 79; Garland, *Luke*, 495, 498.

3. Garland (*Luke*, 493) claims that "only priests . . . were commanded to wash hands," citing Exod. 30:19–21; 40:12. But these texts address washing hands and feet before sacrificing. And Garland does not cite Lev. 15:11, from which one might infer the need for the man with a seminal emission to wash his hands. François Bovon (*Luke 2*, 158) claims that the Hebrew Bible prescribed "ritual ablutions" only for priests, which is deeply mistaken.

4. These labels are heuristic. See the notes early in chap. 1.

5. Thiessen, *Forces of Death*.

6. The NASB has "ceremonially washed."

> of the cup and of the dish; but your inside [τὸ δὲ ἔσωθεν ὑμῶν] is full of greed and wickedness. You foolish ones, did he who made the outside not make the inside also? But give that which is within as a charitable gift, and then all things are clean for you [πάντα καθαρὰ ὑμῖν ἐστιν]." (11:38–41)

From this passage, scholars have concluded that "Jesus therefore changes the paradigm of what really counts for holiness," replacing a concern for external purity with "love" and "justice."[7] Consequently, "what is important is . . . moral purity and not ritual cleanliness."[8] While this passage is not simple, assumptions about purity as inscribing compassionless exclusivism or an unnecessary concern for external ritual have skewed interpretations. So convinced is Bovon, for example, of his interpretation that when he arrives at Jesus's very next statement—"For you pay tithes of mint, rue, and every kind of garden herb, and yet you ignore justice and the love of God; *but these are the things you should have done without neglecting the others*"—he asserts, "The end of the verse [italicized above] . . . is a gloss attributable to Q, which in my opinion betrays Luke's, even more than Q's, conception of Jesus' intention. This gloss piles on requirements, whereas Jesus advocated what was essential."[9] But setting aside verses that trouble one's interpretation is surely a sign that one is off track in the first place. Was Luke so confused? Did Jesus not realize his inconsistency in supposedly negating ritual purity and yet insisting on tithes? Or is it possible that the error is the interpreter's?

Ultimately, the question is whether Jesus's statement "Give that which is within as a charitable gift, and then all things are clean for you" amounts to a dismissal of ritual purity altogether. It does not for several reasons. First, the public teaching that occasioned the Pharisee's inviting Jesus to the meal insisted that the inward light not be cloudy in order to allow the brightness of the outward illumination to enter (Luke 11:34–36). The interior light does not negate or diminish the outward illumination; rather, the brightness of the exterior illumination depends on the clarity of the interior. The literary context suggests that the Pharisee heard just this instruction before inviting Jesus to eat (11:37). The contiguous placement of these episodes suggests that Jesus's first words in the Pharisee's house function as a continuation of the point he made in public: the inner affects the outer. The implied sense, then, would not be to diminish the outer but to care for the inner because it affects the outer.

7. Garland, *Luke*, 495. Garland cites Borg, *Conflict, Holiness, and Politics*, as support.

8. Bovon, *Luke 2*, 169. Craig L. Blomberg ("Law in Luke-Acts," 60, 65) also claims that this statement may imply the abrogation of ritual impurity and even dietary laws, at least as these statements develop in Acts 10.

9. Bovon, *Luke 2*, 162.

Second, Jesus criticizes the Pharisees for neglecting justice and God's love as they carefully tithe garden herbs, concluding, "But these are the things you should have done [ταῦτα δὲ ἔδει] without neglecting the others" (Luke 11:42). If Jesus were dismissing supposed external trivialities in favor of interior purity, it is odd that he commends the Pharisees' scrupulous tithing. But this statement perfectly illustrates that prioritizing justice and love does not negate the need (ἔδει) to pay tithes; both are necessary. This verse ought to function as a hermeneutical key for other sayings concerning priority of "morals" over external rituals. Priority is just that: a hierarchical evaluation. Prioritizing something does not negate items lower on the list. The saying on tithes may be easily applied to purity: Woe to you Pharisees, for you wash the outside of cups but fail to give alms, but these things you ought to have done without neglecting the others.[10]

Third, after critiquing the Pharisees' neglect of justice and their pursuit of honor (Luke 11:42–43), Jesus characterizes them in a way that depends on his acceptance of the purity system. He says, "Woe to you! For you are like unseen tombs, and the people who walk over them are unaware of it" (11:44). Quite the insult! An unmarked grave would transmit impurity to the walker (Num. 19:16), but they would not know it, and so they risk entering the temple or handling sacred food in impurity and so becoming liable to an offering at best or incurring God's wrath at worst. In either case, the insult depends on Jesus assuming the relevance of such impurity. Otherwise, it would not matter that the grave is unmarked since it conveys a defilement that Jesus has purportedly dismissed as unimportant.

Fourth, in the saying in question (Luke 11:39–41), the situation transitions from being about vessels to humans by metaphorically comparing humans to cups. Jesus asks, "Did he who made the outside not make the inside also?" The form of the question (beginning with οὐχ) expects a positive answer. It depicts God as a potter (so Isa. 29:16; 45:9) who has created humans (cups) with interiors and exteriors. In this image, God has created both the inside and outside of a person, implying that care should be taken for both. If Jesus's intent were to denigrate external purity, a question implying that care should be taken for both interior and exterior would be odd. What, then, is he saying?

To understand this complex passage, we must grasp the contours of contemporary debates about purifying vessels.[11] Leviticus 11:31–32 states that if

10. So also Oliver, *Torah Praxis*, 303.

11. For a short survey of the debate among the Pharisaic schools, see Neusner, "'First Cleanse the Inside.'" *Pace* Neusner (487), the form of the saying in Matthew and Luke does not lead to "irrational results" or "destroy" the form of the supposed "original." See criticisms of Neusner's argument in Maccoby, "Washing of Cups."

a carcass of a "swarming thing" falls onto "any wooden article, or clothing, or a hide, or a sack—any article of which use is made," that thing becomes unclean. To purify it, "it shall be put in the water and be unclean until evening, then it becomes clean." Leviticus 11:33 describes a related but distinct scenario: "As for any earthenware vessel into which one of them may fall, whatever is in it becomes unclean and you shall break the vessel." Here the vessel is pottery, not wood, and it must be broken rather than washed. For the situation of Lev. 11:32, the purification required is presumably immersion ("It shall be put in the water"), presumably cleansing the interior and exterior of the vessel. But cleansing only the exterior of an earthenware vessel into which a carcass had fallen would be insufficient; such a vessel must simply be broken (Lev. 11:33).

Numerous tractates in the Mishnah discuss the impurity of vessels, but none as specifically as m. Kelim. About wooden utensils m. Kelim 2.1 states, "Their flat surfaces are insusceptible to impurity, but their receptacles [interiors] are susceptible to impurity."[12] This principle divides the vessel into interior and exterior parts, rendering its exterior insusceptible to impurity unless first defiled from the interior. This principle is more clearly enunciated regarding earthenware vessels: "They [the vessels, exterior and interior] contract impurity and convey impurity through their interior space; they convey impurity from their outsides, but they do not become impure from their exteriors" (2.1). In other words, once defiled from the interior, the exterior of a vessel is unclean and can convey that impurity, but a whole vessel does not become defiled through its exterior surfaces. If a vessel becomes impure from its exterior, only the exterior is unclean (25.6). Mishnah Kelim 25 discusses this scenario (the defilement of the exterior by impure liquids and its relation to the whole vessel and its contents):[13] "All vessels have an exterior and interior" (25.1). The divisions between exterior and interior are defined based on the product in question: "Bases, rims, handle sockets, or handles of vessels that have a receptacle upon which [impure] liquid fell—one dries them, and they are pure. [Regarding] other vessels lacking an exterior and interior: if liquids fall on part of it, all of it is impure. A vessel whose exterior was rendered impure by liquid—its exterior is impure. . . . But if its inner part becomes impure the whole is impure" (25.6, brackets original to the translation). This passage rules that if the exterior components of the vessels described contact impure liquid, its exterior should be wiped, but its interior and its contents

12. The translations are those of Michael Chernick in *The Oxford Annotated Mishnah*, ed. Cohen, Goldenberg, and Lapin.

13. See also m. Tohorot 8.7.

remain pure. One need only wipe the exterior components, "and they are pure." Such a scenario seems to be the context for Jesus's statement in Luke 11:39: "Now you Pharisees clean the outside of the cup and of the dish."

A few things could be happening here. First, it should be noted that m. Kelim 25.6's purification of the exterior when the exterior is defiled by impure liquids is regarded in the Talmud (b. Bekhorot 38a) as a decree of the rabbis, not the Law.[14] Of the ruling in m. Kelim 25.6, it states: "Here we are dealing with ritual impurity of liquids by rabbinic law" (b. Bekhorot 38a.9). It continues: "By Torah law, food does not transmit impurity to a vessel, and a liquid does not transmit impurity to a vessel. And it was the Sages who decreed it because of the liquid of a *zav* and a *zava*" (b. Bekhorot 38a.10).[15] Regarding the latter situation, Lev. 15:12 states, "An earthenware vessel which the person with the discharge touches shall be broken, and every wooden vessel shall be rinsed in water." Because liquids from a *zav* or *zava* transmit impurity, and because such impurity might defile a vessel and its contents, evidently the sages wished to protect against leniency regarding their "liquids." To do so, they ruled that any impure liquids defile the vessels, an extralegal caution ensuring a higher probability that one will protect against liquids that do in fact defile. In any case, returning to m. Kelim 25, impure liquids that contact the exterior of a vessel affect only the exterior. One need only wipe the exterior, and it is, or remains, pure.

At least two possibilities with respect to Luke 11 result.[16] One, Jesus could simply reject this kind of "divisibility" of the object and consequently reject the Pharisaic practice of wiping its exterior. Yair Furstenberg has argued for this position,[17] claiming that the Pharisees were content to wipe the exterior while the priests held the more stringent view of washing the whole vessel.[18] Furstenberg (who is primarily dealing with the parallel saying in Matt. 23)

14. Logan Williams alerted me to this passage.

15. *Zav* (male) and *zava* (female) refer to persons with irregular penile/vaginal discharges (see Lev. 15:2–15, 19–30). Their "liquids" may refer to their urine or saliva (Lev. 15:8, 11).

16. More than two interpretations are possible, of course. For one that denies the applicability of ritual purity of vessels, see Maccoby, "Washing of Cups." He argues instead that the saying reflects the commonsensical observation that simply polishing the exterior of things while leaving their interiors dirty is bad practice and reflects the hypocrisy of the Pharisees (according to Jesus in Luke 11/Matt. 23). This is possible, though ritual purity seems relevant due to (1) the occasion that elicited Jesus's saying (i.e., the Pharisees' observation that he had not washed before eating, a tradition related to ritual purity rather than hygiene reductively) and (2) his comparison of Pharisees to concealed tombs, which when walked over would transmit only ritual impurity (Num. 19:18).

17. Furstenberg, "Controlling Impurity." Furstenberg (190, 192) argues that Jesus denounces the Pharisaic mechanism of dividing objects into discrete parts.

18. See Furstenberg, "Laws of the Pharisees," esp. 779–82.

argues that Jesus's view coincides with the more stringent view of the priests, and for this reason Jesus complains against the Pharisaic practice of washing only the vessel's exterior. On this reading, Furstenberg concludes, "Jesus was not deriding the Pharisees for their focus on ritual purity. To the contrary, this Jesus tradition aligns with the stringent position taken by the priests."[19] Applied to Luke 11, Jesus would be critiquing their purification of only the outside of the cup and urging them to purify the whole cup, which Jesus then applies metaphorically to the Pharisees themselves. However, if Jesus rejected the division between exterior and interior, his rhetorical question, "Did the one who made the outside not make the inside also?" (11:40), would seem out of place. That question assumes and highlights the division, implying that one ought to care for both interior and exterior. This view is strengthened by Jesus's statement in Matt. 23 (Furstenberg's focus), in that he says, "You blind Pharisee, first [πρῶτον] clean the inside of the cup and of the dish, so that the outside of it may also become clean" (23:26). This sentence likewise assumes the division of interior and exterior, claiming that the Pharisees ought to purify the interior first because it/they are interiorly defiled.

A second possibility is that Jesus does not reject the divisibility of the object, and he accepts wiping the exterior when it alone is defiled. What he—or any Pharisee for that matter—would reject is wiping only the exterior when the interior is defiled. If the vessel is defiled from its interior, the whole vessel is defiled (see Lev. 11:33; m. Kelim 25.6), and wiping only its exterior would be insufficient. A vessel interiorly defiled would need to be rinsed inside first, removing both the source and the resultant impurity, and then its exterior rinsed so that the whole vessel might be pure (so Matt. 23:26).

For example, imagine that two Pharisees sit at a table. A dead gecko falls into a cup, and one Pharisee notices, but the other does not. The one who does not see the carcass comes to believe the exterior of the cup has become impure by impure liquid and so he wipes it. What might the other Pharisee say? "You fool! You wiped the exterior, but inwardly it contains a carcass! Purify the inside and then its exterior!" The mistake at hand is not that one Pharisee believed in the divisibility of the cup and the other did not. It is that one knew it was inwardly defiled and the other did not. What is required is that the one inform the other of the inward defilement. So it is, I suggest, with Luke 11.

In Luke 11, Jesus transitions from talking about cups to metaphorizing humans as cups, saying that the Pharisees are interiorly full of greed and iniquity (11:39). Just as with a cup, the Pharisees need to purify their interior. Because

19. Furstenberg, "Laws of the Pharisees," 782.

the named issue is related to financial iniquity ("greed"), the "purification ritual" is giving alms: "Give what is inside as alms and behold, all is pure for you [πάντα καθαρὰ ὑμῖν ἐστιν]" (11:41 AT). In the declaration "All is pure for you," Jesus transitions from cups to sins "inside" the Pharisees, and his claim "all is pure for you" functions metaphorically to include the "purification" of sin. "All" being pure for them would not mean that giving alms absolves them of the need to continue with ritual purification. That interpretation erroneously transfers his claim that encompasses both the moral and the ritual ("inward and outward") to one that excludes the ritual/exterior practice, which would be a non sequitur. That is, extrapolating from his cup example, he assumes that the Pharisees wash its exterior. Urging them to wash the cup's interior would not mean that they don't need to wash its exterior. It simply means that washing its interior (assuming that they also wash its exterior, as they already do) would render "all" the cup pure. Similarly, the Pharisees are inwardly defiled by greed, and thus solving (purifying) that inward problem by giving alms will entail that "all is pure to you"—that is, their interior and exterior selves will be pure, because he assumes they already attend to "exterior" matters.[20]

His assertion that almsgiving cleanses would have likely been accepted as a noncontroversial statement about the purifying effect of charity. For example, Prov. 15:27a LXX states, "By alms [ἐλεημοσύναις] and acts of faithfulness, sins are purified [ἀποκαθαίρονται]" (AT). Or Sir. 29:12: "Almsgiving . . . will rescue from every disaster" (ἐλεημοσύνην . . . ἐξελεῖταί σε ἐκ πάσης κακώσεως). And Tob. 12:9 is quite telling: "Those who give alms purify all sin" (ἀποκαθαριεῖ πᾶσαν ἁμαρτίαν οἱ ποιοῦντες ἐλεημοσύνας).[21] Nothing from Tobit suggests that purifying all sin through almsgiving replaces the need to practice ritual purity or other components of the Law; on the contrary, the book highlights the fact that Tobit washed after burying corpses (2:4–9) and meticulously kept the festivals and rules regarding tithing (1:6–8). Consequently, Jesus saying that "almsgiving" renders "all pure to you" would be well received, and the "all" includes, but is not limited to, the category he's discussing (i.e., their "inward" sins).[22] Likewise, after this statement about alms in Luke 11, Jesus commends the Pharisaic practice of tithing, calling it necessary, demonstrating that almsgiving rendering "all things pure" does not negate the need for continual practice of "ritual."

20. See a comparable conclusion in Oliver, *Torah Praxis*, 302–3.

21. See also Tob. 4:10–16; Sir. 3:30; 29:12; Dan. 4:27.

22. For a survey of such evaluations of almsgiving in rabbinic literature, see Gray, "Redemptive Almsgiving." See also Anderson, "Almsgiving."

Therefore, Jesus does not reject the practice of exterior purification. His critique is that the Pharisees wipe the exterior without recognizing the interior defilement. In this case, however, the inward defilement transitions from the scenario of the cup to the Pharisees themselves, but the point is the same. Thus, as with the imagined scenario between two Pharisees above, what Jesus needs to do is to object not to exterior purification itself but to exterior purification when the cup/human is inwardly defiled. Taking care of the latter, and assuming they practice exterior purification, all would be pure to them. Therefore, "all" includes the sin of plunder/iniquity that he just described. And just as Proverbs, Daniel, Sirach, and Tobit claim the capacity of alms to purify sin (even "all" sin), so Jesus claims that such charity totally purifies the Pharisees of their plunder and iniquity. Having purified all their sin, everything will be pure for them given that Jesus can assume that they, being Pharisees, continue to practice bodily purification.[23]

Washing Hands and Eating Pure

In Mark 7, scribes and Pharisees note "that some of his disciples were eating their bread with impure hands, that is, unwashed" (7:2 AT). Consequently, they ask Jesus, "Why do your disciples not walk according to the tradition of the elders, but eat their bread with impure hands?" (7:5 AT).[24] After critiquing them for upholding tradition to the detriment of keeping God's commandments (7:8–13), Jesus says, "Listen to me, all of you, and understand: there is nothing outside the person which can defile him if it goes into him; but the things which come out of the person are what defile the person" (7:14–15). When questioned about the meaning of "the parable" (7:17), Jesus states, and here I quote the NASB: "'Do you not understand that whatever goes into the person from outside cannot defile him, because it does not go into his heart, but into his stomach, and is eliminated?' (Thereby he declared all foods clean.)" (7:18–19).

23. Logan Williams suggested the potential significance of "all is pure *for you*"—that is, for the Pharisees.

24. In his section on Mark 7, Kent L. Yinger (*Pharisees*, 115) states, "The Pharisees would have viewed the lax purity practice of Jesus . . . as a danger to the nation (Israel polluting the land via impurity)." But the land is not polluted by a lack of handwashing, which is not required by the Law before eating (hence, it is named "a tradition"). Moreover, Jesus's purity practice is not lax. Because contracting impurity is not forbidden, an evaluation of Jesus as "lax" would apply only if he avoided purifying or advised against it. However, in Mark he directs the healed *lepros* to purify (1:44), and in Mark 7 his ruling concerning eating with unwashed hands is governed not by an indifference to purity but by a confidence that the body will purify all foods (7:19).

I quote this translation, though incorrect, because it typifies the error in both translation and interpretation common to most interpreters.[25] So rendered, Jesus is understood to be nullifying the food laws of Lev. 11/Deut. 14, erasing the distinction between foods permissible (labeled "clean" by Lev. 11/Deut. 14) and prohibited (labeled "unclean" by Lev. 11/Deut. 14). On this reading, the reason Jesus does not bother about handwashing is because the foods that were formerly named "unclean" by the Law are now declared "clean" by Jesus and thus have no capacity to defile a person.

The hermeneutical significance of this erroneous interpretation is difficult to overstate. From it, scholars in the so-called New Perspective or adjacent schools (famously, Dunn, Borg, Wright, and Hellerman) have inferred that the Markan Jesus sets aside a major swath of legal requirements,[26] especially those that divided Jew from gentile, and in so doing lays the groundwork for, or expresses an opinion operative in, the apostolic mission to gentiles,[27] especially Paul's. Thus, not only do these scholars conclude that Jesus set aside or "redefined" the Law (in this case, food laws) because of its redundancy and/or exclusionary role, but they also employ this view in their reading of Acts and Paul's letters to the effect that the food laws were deemed a matter of indifference by these biblical authors.[28] Because these scholars regard food laws as a major symbol of the people and their Law, the nullification of these laws began the domino effect of both the distancing from many of the Law's distinctly Jewish elements (circumcision and Sabbath) among nascent Jesus believers and the consequent "redefinition" of "the people of God" supposedly on display in the NT.

But as Logan Williams has convincingly argued, this interpretation of Mark 7:19 cannot be maintained.[29] This scene and Jesus's saying are not about food laws but about purity. More accurately, this scene is not about the permissible menu, but about ingesting permissible food that has become impure. Readers often err in their interpretation of Mark 7 by collapsing these matters, but this confuses two separate legal categories (ritual purity and menu), since

25. See Williams ("Stomach," 371–79) for a review of scholarship on this issue. For other revisionist readings that do not see Jesus abrogating Torah here, see Crossley, "Mark 7.1–23"; Furstenberg, "Defilement"; Van Maaren, "Mark's Jesus"; Boyarin, "Mark 7:1–23"; Thiessen, *Forces of Death*, 187–95.

26. Dunn, *Jesus, Paul, and the Law*, 37–53; Borg, *Conflict, Holiness, and Politics*, 112; Wright, *Victory of God*, 284, 396–98; Hellerman, *People of God*, 227–33.

27. E.g., Dunn, *Jesus, Paul, and the Law*, 37–47; Wright, *Victory of God*, 397; Hellerman, *People of God*, 230–33. See also Loader, *Jesus' Attitude*, 77; Joseph, *Jesus and the Temple*, 57–59.

28. Dunn, *Jesus, Paul, and the Law*, 39–41; Wright, *Victory of God*, 381–82; Wright, "Letter to the Romans," 740.

29. Williams, "Stomach."

ingesting "illicit" food, which is labeled "unclean," did not ritually defile the eater.[30] Admittedly, the complexity of the issue is compounded due to sources of ritual impurity and forbidden food both being labeled "unclean," but these "unclean" items operate and are legislated differently.[31] As Peter Tomson notes, "Ever since the Church Fathers, . . . New Testament exegesis typically confuses laws belonging to different halakhic areas, especially diet and purity laws. . . . Thus while . . . Mark 7:2–23 is about *purity*, Christian commentators ancient and modern highlight verse 19 to the effect that '(Jesus) declared all foods clean'—*dietary* laws being implicated."[32]

But Jesus does not here nullify the food laws. Rather, in Mark 7 Jesus argues that his disciples do not need to wash their hands before eating because, even if their impure hands were to defile permissible food, the body—through the digestion process, culminating in defecation—"purifies all foods," indicating that the body was not defiled in the process. To begin, note that the scribes and Pharisees ask not whether Jesus and his disciples eat only from the permissible menu as outlined in the Law but why they do not wash their hands before eating. It is assumed that they are eating permissible food (what Mark 7:5 calls "bread"). Additionally, the Pharisees and Jesus name handwashing before eating common food as a "tradition [of the elders]" (7:3, 5, 8, 9, 13). Therefore, what is in question is not Jesus's and the disciples' Law-keeping but their adherence to tradition.

Secondary literature on the origin of handwashing is vast, but this issue need not detain us here.[33] This matter aside, a few things should be noted. First, consuming prohibited foods, which are labeled "unclean" in Lev. 11, does not ritually defile the eater.[34] As Furstenberg notes, no purification procedure is prescribed for the consumption of "unclean" (illicit) food.[35] Logan Williams explains: "The evidence indicates that many ancient Jews distinguished between the domains of *tohorah* (ritual purity) and kashrut from very early on; . . . the early distinction between kashrut and ritual impurity is indicated by the fact that the topic of prohibited animals—let alone any ostensible capacity to contract impurity from prohibited animals—does not appear at all

30. Discussed further below.

31. See the discussion in Boyarin, *Jewish Gospels*, 113; Oliver, *Torah Praxis*, 241–51; Thiessen, *Forces of Death*, 187–88.

32. Tomson, "Jewish Food Laws," 198, italics original.

33. See Booth, *Laws of Purity*, 155–203; Poirier, "Why Did the Pharisees?"; Harrington, "Did Pharisees?"; Furstenberg, "Defilement"; Kazen, "Concern, Custom"; Kazen, "Jesus and the *Zavah*"; Oliver, *Torah Praxis*, 257–64.

34. See the discussion in Furstenberg, "Defilement," 195; Boyarin, "Mark 7:1–23"; Williams, "Stomach," 374–77.

35. Furstenberg, "Defilement," 195.

in Seder Tohorot, the order of the Mishnah that deals with ritual impurity."[36] Second, Lev. 11 does not state that one is defiled by eating permissible food that had become defiled. While Lev. 17:15 claims that one who eats the carcass of a permitted animal that is found dead must purify, 11:39–40 states that simply *touching* such a carcass requires the same purification procedure. Because touching the carcass and eating the carcass defile in the same way and require the same purification procedure, Lev. 17:15 apparently implies that one who eats the carcass is defiled because he has touched it, not because he has eaten it.[37] Williams nuances this point by reminding us that though the latter is probable and supported by rabbinic commentary, the supposition that Lev. 17:15 refers to defilement of the eater only through touching the carcass is not inevitable.[38] He concludes, "Thus, instead of saying 'no biblical source actually suggests that contamination can spread through ingestion,' it is perhaps better to say that these Pentateuchal texts afford differential conclusions regarding the relationship between ingestion and defilement."[39] This nuance is relevant for Mark 7 since it provides the context for why the Pharisees might inquire about the disciples not washing their hands: in their view it might lead to defilement by consuming ritually defiled food, which would suggest to the Pharisees that Jesus does not care about impurity. It also shows how Jesus could come to the legally justified alternative opinion that ingesting defiled food was permissible. We turn now to Jesus's response.

"Listen to me, all of you, and understand: there is nothing outside the person [τοῦ ἀνθρώπου] which can defile him if it goes into him; but the things which come out of the person [ἐκ τοῦ ἀνθρώπου] are what defile the person" (Mark 7:14–15). Here, in keeping with the above interpretation of Lev. 11:39–40 and 17:15 in which the person is defiled not by eating the carcass but by touching it, Jesus states something aligning with the principle that defilement occurs not through ingestion but through things that exit the body. The latter refers to sources of impurity named in Leviticus (seminal, menstrual, and postpartum discharges) that defile the body by "proceeding out of it."[40]

When asked about the meaning of his "parable" (Mark 7:17), Jesus responds with the following. For comparison, I provide the NASB and an alternative translation of 7:18–19.

36. Williams, "Stomach," 374. In context, Williams refers to discussion from Klawans, *Impurity and Sin*, 32.

37. Furstenberg, "Defilement," 195.

38. Williams, "Stomach," 376.

39. Williams, "Stomach," 377. See also Oliver, *Torah Praxis*, 242–43.

40. So Furstenberg, "Defilement," 194–95; Boyarin, "Mark 7:1–23," 26; Williams, "Stomach," 374n25.

> "Do you not understand that whatever goes into the person from outside cannot defile him, because it does not go into his heart, but into his stomach, and is eliminated?" (Thereby he declared all foods clean). (NASB)

> "Do you not understand that whatever goes into the person from outside cannot defile him because it does not go into his heart, but into his stomach, and is eliminated, purifying all the foods [καθαρίζων πάντα τὰ βρώματα]?" (AT)[41]

The NASB takes the participial phrase "cleansing all foods" not as a part of Jesus's speech but as the narrator's aside explaining the import of Jesus's statement to the effect that Jesus has "declared" that prohibited ("unclean") food is now permissible ("clean"). But this makes nonsense of the passage for at least two reasons. First, the initial question is not about the permissible menu but about why his disciples do not wash their hands before eating bread. These are distinct legal categories that overlap terminologically but not procedurally. Prohibited food is "unclean" but does not ritually defile by ingestion, whereas handling food with unwashed hands is a matter of ritual purity. Because eating prohibited food does not ritually defile the eater by ingestion, answering a question about eating with defiled hands by declaring the permissibility of prohibited food would be like answering a question about how best to avoid contracting impurity from a menstruant by answering that sex with a menstruant is now permissible. They are simply different legal categories, and the traditional interpretation of Jesus's answer would be a non sequitur. Second, Jesus has just critiqued the Pharisees for setting aside commandments in favor of their tradition, for which he named them hypocrites, whose hearts are far from God (Mark 7:6–8). It would be very odd for him then to set aside God's commandments about permissible food in favor of his instruction, making himself susceptible to the same charge of "hypocrisy."

What then is Jesus's point? As Williams has argued, it is best to interpret "cleansing all foods" not as a narrator's aside but as part of Jesus's speech, referring not to an interpretative statement ("thus he declared . . .") but to an activity of the person who digests and eliminates the food, "cleansing all foods" in the process.[42] This indicates that "cleansing all foods" is not something that Jesus is doing by fiat but instead is the transformative and purifying work of the digestion process, as attested by Greek medical texts and Jewish

41. This translation follows that argued by Williams, "Stomach," 389.

42. See Williams ("Stomach," 379–84) for his argument about the syntax and examples. He argues that the masculine participle "cleansing" (καθαρίζων) modifies the activity (entering and exiting) done by the subject of those activities, the (masculine) "person" (ἄνθρωπος) of 7:18–19.

halakhic texts.[43] In this vein, it is significant to recognize that in a commonly attested Jewish understanding of ritual purity, excrement was considered ritually pure. The sources of impurity are semen, irregular penile/vaginal discharge, menstrual and postpartum blood, *lepra*, human corpses, and certain animal carcasses. Thus, as paradoxical as it seems to many non-Jewish modern readers, human excrement is not ritually impure. But it is understandable how the point has been missed by many: once "unclean" is collapsed to "dirty," then one could mistakenly consider many things "impure" that the Law simply does not (excrement, mucus, urine, etc.). But according to Jewish sources, such substances are not ritually impure in themselves. For example, m. Makhshirin 6.6 states, "These render impure and convey susceptibility to impurity: the flow of the *zav* [a man with an irregular penile discharge], and his saliva, and his semen, and his urine, and a quarter[-*log*] of blood from a corpse, and menstrual blood." This is followed in m. Makhshirin 6.7 by a list of substances that are not impure: "These do not render impure or convey susceptibility to impurity: sweat, and stinking pus, and excrement, and blood that issues with them."[44]

Thus, because excrement is pure, Jesus reasons that even if one were to eat permissible food defiled by a secondary source, the fact that it exits the body as pure excrement implies that the body has purified the food in the process of digestion. Therefore, the logic of Jesus's response to a question about handwashing is that his disciples do not need to wash their hands because even if their impure hands defiled permissible food, the body would not become defiled through its ingestion because the food is digested and expelled, purifying the food in the process.

And far from an idiosyncratic view of Jesus, such reasoning about the digestive process is attested in Jewish legal sources. For example, t. Miqva'ot 7.8–9 states:

> If someone swallowed an olive's bulk of a corpse and entered a house, the house is pure, for everything swallowed by a human or cattle or beast or birds is pure. If it decomposed or exited from below [as excrement], it is pure. If someone drank impure water and vomited it up, it is impure, because it was defiled when it went out. If one immersed, or if it decomposed, or it came out below, it is pure. If one drank other [impure] liquids even though he immersed and vomited them out, they are unclean, because they are not purified in the

43. See, e.g., Galen (*Natural Faculties* 3.4) and Aristotle (*Parts of Animals* 674a.10–20), both of whom refer to the "transforming" work done by the stomach in digestion. See Williams ("Stomach," 384–89) for discussion and additional texts.

44. See Williams ("Stomach," 384–88) for discussion of Jewish sources concerning the ritual purity of excrement.

> body. If they decomposed or exited, they are pure. If a cow which drank impure water vomited it up, it is impure, because it is not made pure in the body. If it decomposed or went out below [as excrement], it is pure.[45]

Significantly, this and other passages name excrement as pure and the body as the agent of purification. In line with such reasoning, Jesus states that the body purifies the food, and for this reason handwashing is unnecessary since eating permissible food that has become contaminated will not defile the body. Not only does this interpretation make good sense of Mark's Greek in 7:19, but it actually responds to the legal issue posed in 7:3 and 7:5, does not make Jesus subject to the very accusation he just leveled at the Pharisees (hypocrisy), and aligns with Matthew's account. Instead of the potentially confusing "cleansing all foods," Matthew simply states: "but to eat with unwashed hands does not defile the person" (15:20). Moreover, Mark labels the saying about the defiling things that exit the body a "parable" (7:17). Parables are teachings with occasionally allegorical referents that Jesus has already instructed will reward closer hearing (Mark 4:10–25). As a parable, it permits Jesus the occasion to amplify the referent of "things that exit" with his point about the morally defiling activities that exit "out of the heart" (7:20–23). Like Jeremiah before him, who announced, "Wash your heart [τὴν καρδίαν σου] from evil [ἀπὸ κακίας], Jerusalem, / So that you may be saved. / How long will your wicked thoughts [διαλογισμοὶ πόνων] / Lodge within you?" (Jer. 4:14), so Jesus warns his disciples that "from within the heart [ἐκ τῆς καρδίας] proceed evil thoughts [οἱ διαλογισμοὶ οἱ κακοί]" (Mark 7:21 AT). Such activities defile the person, yet those who desire to participate in the restoration must have their hearts purified (cp. Deut. 30:6; Matt. 5:8; Acts 15:8–9).

In this passage, then, Jesus does not nullify Israel's dietary laws. Rather, he answers the Pharisees' question about the disciples' practice of not washing their hands before eating permissible food by reasoning for its redundancy due to the body's capacity to purify potentially defiled permissible food through digestion and defecation.[46]

45. This and additional references are discussed in Williams ("Stomach"), who credits Shlomo Naeh for many of the citations.

46. For a discussion of Matt. 15:1–20 that similarly concludes that it does not nullify the dietary laws but has limited import regarding ritual impurity, see Oliver, *Torah Praxis*, 255–75. Unfortunately, even with Matt. 15:20's claim that "to eat with unwashed hands does not defile the man" instead of what is taken to be Mark's nullification of the food laws (Mark 7:19), scholars interpret Matt. 15:11—"It is not what enters the mouth that defiles the person, but what comes out of the mouth; this defiles the person" (AT)—as all the proof necessary for concluding that Jesus nullifies the food laws. See, e.g., France, *Matthew*, 575–77, 583–84. But this interpretation of Matt. 15:11 makes the same mistake as those who interpret Mark 7:15 to imply the nullification of the food laws. Such interpretations err in that they wrongly assume that eating prohibited

Cleansing Lepra

Jesus regularly heals the blind, deaf, dead, and people with *lepra*. Such healings are signs that restoration is irrupting into the present through Jesus (Matt. 11:1–5; Luke 7:18–23).[47] Consequently, Jesus comes into contact with people affected by conditions that transmit impurity, especially men with *lepra* (Mark 1:40 and par.), the woman with a prolonged discharge (Mark 5:25 and par.),[48] and the dead (Luke 7:12).[49] In healing these people afflicted with defiling conditions, Jesus does not thereby signal a disdain for impurity regulations, thinking them a snobbish expression of compassionless exclusion. Rather, as Thiessen argues, Jesus affirms the defiling effect of their condition and its social effects (e.g., exclusion from the temple), and he heals them of such conditions. If he were simply to deny their defiling effects, having swapped purity for compassion, he could simply teach them to flagrantly violate the requirements to purify. But he does not: after healing the *lepros*, he commands him (Mark 1:44; Matt. 8:4; Luke 5:14) to make the requisite sacrifices (Lev. 14:1–32) to complete his purification.

However, even when accepting the above, confusion pertaining to Jesus's relation to the Law abounds. One aspect that typically elicits this confusion is Jesus touching the *lepros*. Mark's account reads: "Moved with compassion, Jesus reached out with his hand and touched him" (Mark 1:41; also Matt. 8:3; Luke 5:13). Commentators regularly claim that in touching him, Jesus transgressed the Law. For example, Craig Keener states, "Jewish law forbade touching lepers (Lev. 5:3). . . . It is thus no small matter for Jesus compassionately to touch the man . . . as he likewise touches some others who are

food necessarily ritually defiles you. From that assumption, they take Jesus's claim that "it is not what enters into the mouth that defiles the person" (Matt. 15:11 AT) to deny the putative capacity of pork to ritually defile a person and thus to deny the food laws generally. But once more: to eat prohibited food did not ritually defile (see discussion above). One who ate pork would not need to wash and wait until sundown but would need only to give an offering for sin, assuming the act was unintentional. Thus Jesus's claim that what enters the person/mouth does not defile (Mark 7:15; Matt. 15:11) is not a denial of the food laws but a truism basic to the Law's purity regulations: sources of impurity *exit* the body (menstrual blood, semen, etc.); defilement does not occur through ingestion. Therefore, Mark 7:15 and Matt. 15:11 do not in themselves support a claim that Jesus abrogates the dietary laws or the mechanisms of ritual impurity, and their conclusions (Matt. 15:20; Mark 7:19) demonstrate that Jesus's point throughout consistently pertains to the incapacity of eating with unwashed hands to defile the person.

47. So Wright, *Victory of God*, 193–94. For a study of Jesus's healings in Matthew, see Novakovic, *Healer of the Sick*. On God's kingdom and Jesus's healings in Mark, see Shively, "Purification."

48. See Moss, "Man with the Flow"; Thiessen, *Forces of Death*, 69–93.

49. Regarding *lepra* and its capacity to transmit impurity, see Lev. 14:36, 46–47; Num. 5:2–3. Regarding a woman with an irregular discharge, see Lev. 15:25–27. Regarding corpses, see Num. 19:11–16.

unclean."[50] Or Joel Green: "In his interaction with the leper, Jesus' actions express an ambiguity vis-à-vis the law. . . . On the one hand, he is in violation of the law. Luke describes Jesus' action as deliberate ('stretched out his hand' + 'touched'), human contact that violated the law (since uncleanness was communicable) but also communicated acceptance and reentry into the community."[51] Or R. T. France, who states that Jesus "breaks the biblical taboo by touching the unclean man" and that he did so "in the interests of human compassion."[52]

Two things should be noted. First, the Law does not prohibit touching people with *lepra*. Leviticus 5:3, wrongly cited as evidence that it does, states: "Or if he touches human uncleanness, of whatever sort his uncleanness may be with which he becomes unclean, and it is hidden from him, and then he comes to know it, he will be guilty." The guilt involved in Lev. 5:3 is not that he touched a source of impurity; it is that he did not know that he had and so failed to be purified. Having been impure unknowingly, he might have committed a variety of transgressions, such as eating meat of offerings (Lev. 7:20–21), which is prohibited while impure. The regulations concerning *lepra* in Lev. 13–14 imply that *lepra* communicates impurity,[53] but contracting impurity is not prohibited.[54] Impurity happens. That's life. Moreover, as argued above, the keeping of some positive commandments renders a person impure.[55] Naming "contracting impurity" as transgression is simply incorrect; thus, Jesus does not transgress the Law in touching the *lepros*.

Second, many state that Jesus touches the man out of compassion. True enough! But when combining the erroneous notion that the Law prohibits touching *leproi* with the true claim that Jesus acts out of mercy, one ends up reinscribing the falsehood prevalent in many Christian interpretations of the Law and the Gospels that purity and compassion are mutually exclusive. Within the latter framework, one easily lapses into the harmful and false position that the Law and/or early Judaism was a compassionless block of ice that only thawed with the "defiance" of Jesus.[56] This is especially pronounced in

50. Keener, *Matthew*, 261.

51. Green, *Luke*, 237.

52. France, *Matthew*, 306. See also Borg (*Conflict, Holiness, and Politics*, 148n45), who, employing the work of Franz Mussner (*Miracles of Jesus*), suggests that because Jesus touched him, this miracle should be understood to contain an "anti-Pharisaic front."

53. E.g., Lev. 14:46–47.

54. The exception is the priest, who is prohibited from contracting corpse impurity in some cases (Lev. 21:1), with exceptions (21:2–3). The high priest is not granted these exceptions (21:11). See also regulations for the Nazirite (Num. 6:6–7).

55. See the introduction to chap. 1 on burying corpses and Num. 19's purification rites.

56. France (*Matthew*, 307) calls Jesus's act of touching the leper a "defiant mark of acceptance."

the work of Borg, who suggests that Jesus touching the leper had an "anti-Pharisaic front."[57] But to risk a speculative hypothesis: if a Pharisee believed he could heal a *lepros* by touch, I doubt that he would shy away from the prospect. Even if defiled by the event, he would merely need to immerse, and he would be clean by sundown.[58] The notion that touching one with *lepra* to heal him would horrify the Pharisee is a bit preposterous and reveals more about the ignorance of the interpreter than what might be justly said of the Pharisee. Moreover, though an argument from silence, it is surely noteworthy that though the Gospels present various accounts of the Pharisees opposing Jesus's activity on the Sabbath, dining with sinners, or failing to wash before eating, none record their disdain for his having touched someone with *lepra*.[59] But returning to Jesus, it is fair to say that his compassion is directed toward the plight the person is experiencing, but such compassion is not flexed defiantly against the Law that would otherwise preclude mercy; rather, Jesus's action is an expression of the divine will to have "compassion" on the people in the restoration (Deut. 30:3), the manifestation of which is the healing of those in need (e.g., Isa. 35:5–6).

Another matter often misunderstood pertains to Mark describing this healing as a "cleansing." The man says to Jesus, "If you are willing, you can make me clean [δύνασαί με καθαρίσαι]" (1:40), to which Jesus responds, "I am willing; be cleansed [καθαρίσθητι]" (1:41; so also Matt. 8:3; Luke 5:13). Mark then states that the *lepra* left him, "and he was cleansed [ἐκαθαρίσθη]" (1:42; so also Matt. 8:3). Some claim that in satisfying the man's request to be "cleansed" or "purified," Jesus performed what was otherwise only available at the temple. For example, Wright says that the scandalous aspect of Jesus's healing the *lepros* "was not . . . that Jews of Jesus' day were opposed to forgiveness, love, grace, and so forth, but that they were not expecting these gifts to be available outside the context of Temple and cult."[60] Or more forcefully, Nicholas Perrin: "When it came to divine healing, . . . there was no better place to find it than in the temple."[61] Combining the fact that Jesus was famous for healing "with the fact that the temple was the primary venue for healing within Judaism"[62] (no texts are cited for this claim) suggests to

57. Borg, *Conflict, Holiness, and Politics*, 148n45.

58. Leviticus 14:46–47 states that whoever enters a house under quarantine is unclean until evening. Mishnah Zavim 5.6 states that whoever touches one with *lepra* (צָרַעַת) is rendered impure. He or she washes and is clean by sundown.

59. My thanks to Cody Hinkle for pointing this out.

60. Wright, *Victory of God*, 257.

61. Perrin, *Jesus the Temple*, 153.

62. Perrin, *Jesus the Temple*, 153.

Perrin that through his healings, Jesus and "not Zion" was the temple.[63] But these claims assume that healing a man with *lepra* was on offer at the temple. The latter is derived from a common but incorrect set of assumptions: first, that priests were healers (they were not) and, second, that "purifying" always refers to priestly work (it does not).

First, priests are not healers. They diagnose. If one suspects that they have *lepra*, they are inspected, and the priest determines whether it is so. The priest does not heal or prescribe medication. If one thinks that they have been healed of *lepra*, the priest then examines them. If he confirms the healing (ἴαται, Lev. 14:3), then the priest proceeds with the rituals for purification (καθαρισθῇ, 14:2). Therefore, when Jesus heals the man in Mark 1 (and par.) and then sends him to be purified, he is simply acting according to Lev. 14.[64] The man has been healed, and now he will be inspected by the priest, who, after affirming his healing, will complete the purification process.

Regarding the second matter, "purifying" does not always refer to priestly work. In Lev. 15, for example, a man with an irregular discharge is impure while he has the discharge. However, when the discharge ceases, the text refers to this as his discharge being "purified": "Now when the man with the discharge becomes cleansed from his discharge [καθαρισθῇ . . . ἐκ τῆς ῥύσεως αὐτοῦ] . . ." (15:13). This "cleansing" does not refer to his purification by sacrifice post-cessation of his discharge but to the cessation itself. How this happens is not stated. Presumably it "healed" somehow. Once that discharge stops, however, he must complete further steps for his "purification." The text proceeds: "Then he shall count off for himself seven days for his cleansing [τὸν καθαρισμόν]; he shall then wash his clothes and bathe his body in running water and will become clean [καθαρὸς ἔσται]" (15:13). Following this, on the eighth day, he presents offerings for further atonement/purification (15:14). In other words, he had an irregular discharge, which was rendering him impure; this discharge ceased, or in the language of Lev. 15:13, it was "purified"; once this ceased, he then counted seven days, washed, and made offerings for his purification.[65]

Such terminology is similarly employed in m. Nega'im, wherein the marks of *lepra* leaving the body are referred to as the person's having been "purified from it" (וְיִטְהַר מִמֶּנּוּ, 7.4, 5). Such "purification" refers not to the effect of the sacrificial procedures but to the marks of *lepra* having left him. For this

63. Perrin, *Jesus the Temple*, 181–82.

64. See also Rillera, *Lamb*, 153–55.

65. Comparable terminology is used with reference to the woman with a prolonged discharge. The cessation of her discharge is called its "cleansing" (Lev. 15:28), after which she must still perform cleansing rituals for her perduring impurity (15:28–30).

reason, m. Nega'im occasionally differentiates "purifying" in terms of healing (7.4, 5) from "purifying with birds" (13.1), referring to the purification wrought by Lev. 14's sacrificial procedure, which requires birds (14:4–7).

These distinctions are perfectly captured in the Gospel scenario: the man had a condition (*lepra*) that was rendering him impure; Jesus healed, or "purified," it. Just as with the man with the discharge in Lev. 15 or m. Nega'im's "healed" person, the man's "purification" by Jesus does not mean he is ritually clean by Jesus's act of healing.[66] Rather, he has been healed, and he now needs to complete purification procedures per Lev. 14:1–20. For this reason, Jesus then commanded the man to complete the steps for his purification before the priests (Mark 1:44). By "purifying" (healing) the man, Jesus does not do the work of the temple or priest in their stead;[67] rather, Jesus does what the priests cannot do (heal) and then sends the man to the priests for what Jesus cannot do (act as Levitical priest). Curiously, of the latter command to present himself to the priest, R. T. France states, "This should not be pressed as an indication of Jesus' principled observance of the purity laws."[68] It strikes me that only larger assumptions (and misconceptions) about purity would lead one to make such a statement. On the contrary, Jesus's principled observance seems precisely what the text indicates.

The significance of sending the healed man as "testimony to them [the priests]" (Mark 1:44; Matt. 8:4; Luke 5:14) will be discussed below, in chapter 6. In my opinion, the healed man's appearance before the priests can testify to them about his healing, attesting that the kingdom is coming and Jesus is "the expected one." Having received this testimony, the priests, theoretically, ought to be prepared for Jesus's arrival. Grasping that Jesus expects the priests' readiness helps explain why, upon his entry into Jerusalem, their lack of reception of him is met with condemnation.

Healing on the Sabbath

Jesus heals the sick on the Sabbath on numerous occasions: the man with the withered hand (Mark 3:1–5; Matt. 12:10–13; Luke 6:6–11), Peter's

66. *Pace* Blomberg (*Jesus the Purifier*, 342), who states: "Rather, Jesus cleanses the 'leprosy' of the diseased man. He is now both ritually clean and physically healed." Given Blomberg's mistaken collapsing of "purification" as "healing" to "purification" as "purification post-healing," it is unsurprising that he proceeds, "Jesus then issues a pair of somewhat cryptic commands," referring to his requirement to purify with offerings. Such a command is only cryptic if one has mistakenly taken Mark 1:42's "cleansing" to refer to what Lev. 14:1–20 accomplishes.

67. *Pace* Joseph (*Jesus and the Temple*, 119), who claims that Jesus's action is "issuing a challenge to priestly authority."

68. France, *Matthew*, 309.

mother-in-law (Mark 1:30), the woman bent double (Luke 13:10–16), the man with "dropsy" (14:1–6), and if it is still the Sabbath, unnamed crowds (Mark 6:5; Matt. 12:15).[69] Such actions lead to controversy in that healing on the Sabbath was regarded by many as prohibited "work," opening Jesus to an accusation of Sabbath violation. Such will be the focus of the following sections, where I will focus only on the healing of the woman bent double and the man with dropsy.

The Woman Bent Double

In Luke 13:10–16, while teaching in the synagogue on the Sabbath, "there was a woman who for eighteen years had had a sickness caused by a spirit; and she was bent over double, and could not straighten up at all" (13:11). Jesus called her, spoke to her—"You are freed from your sickness"—laid hands on her, and she was healed (13:12). The synagogue official then expressed indignation that Jesus had healed on the Sabbath: "There are six days in which work should be done [ἓξ ἡμέραι εἰσὶν ἐν αἷς δεῖ ἐργάζεσθαι]; so come during them and get healed, and not on the Sabbath day" (13:14).

The synagogue official expresses an opinion widely attested in the Mishnah and further rabbinic literature: lifesaving intervention overrides the Sabbath, but generally, the healing of non-life-threatening predicaments does not. For example, m. Shabbat states that on the Sabbath one may not "set a fracture. One whose hand or foot is dislocated may not stir them in cold water, but he may wash in his usual manner, and if he is healed, he is healed" (22.6; see also 14.4). However, there seem to be exceptions even in non-life-threatening matters. Mishnah Shabb. 19.3 records the opinion of Rabbi Eleazar b. Azariah, stating: "One may wash the child on the third day [post-circumcision] if it falls on a Sabbath. As it is said: *And it came to pass on the third day when they were in pain* [Gen. 34:25]." In this case, doubt about the child's life is not the issue, or at least it is not the named basis for Eleazar's opinion. But generally it appears that only life-threatening cases overrode the Sabbath. Tractate Yoma states this opinion and the general principle: "If someone has a pain in his throat, one administers medicine into his mouth on the Sabbath because there is uncertainty as to whether life [is endangered], and any uncertainty as to whether life [is endangered] overrides the Sabbath" (8.6).

The sticky issue in Luke, of course, is that the woman's ailment was presumably not life-threatening, since she had suffered with the condition for eighteen years (Luke 13:11). Being a non-life-threatening matter, one may

69. On many of these scenes, see Oliver, *Torah Praxis*, 114–46. For Jesus's healing of the man with the withered hand, see Thiessen, *Forces of Death*, 162–71.

infer that the rabbis who voiced the opinions above would agree with the synagogue official that Jesus ought to have healed her any other day. Even if Jesus believed the issue could have been life-threatening, he notably does not defend his action with such reasoning. Rather, he employs legal reasoning typical of the rabbis—namely, a *qal wahomer* (lesser to greater) argument.

In Luke 13:15–16, Jesus responds to the official's indignation: "You hypocrites, does each of you on the Sabbath not untie [λύει] his ox [τὸν βοῦν] or donkey from the stall and lead it away to water it? And this woman, a daughter of Abraham as she is, whom Satan has bound for eighteen long years, should she not have been released [λυθῆναι] from this restraint on the Sabbath day?" Jesus reasons from a known and evidently accepted practice on the Sabbath—releasing an ox or donkey to meet its needs—to defend his practice of releasing the woman from her bondage to Satan.[70] Such reasoning possibly (but not necessarily) derives from the Sabbath legislation itself, which states that Israelites ought to rest on the seventh day, along with their "ox" and "donkey."[71] Exodus 23:12 states it more strongly: Israelites ought to rest "so that [ἵνα] your ox [ὁ βοῦς] and your donkey may rest." In Jesus's reasoning, if the Sabbath requires that one's ox and donkey rest and that an Israelite "release" them and lead them to water to ensure their rest, then he (and anyone else) is all the more permitted to work on the Sabbath to "release" this "daughter of Abraham" (θυγατέρα Ἀβραάμ) from bondage/sickness.[72] Additionally, two of the Sabbath laws (Exod. 20:10; Deut. 5:14) name "your daughter" (ἡ θυγάτηρ σου) as a required recipient of this rest. If Jesus's argument takes into account that the legislation also requires the "daughter" to rest, his argument is *a pari* (for a similar reason). Just as the Sabbath requires "your daughter" to rest, so Jesus permissibly works to bring rest to this "daughter of Abraham."

Though Luke 13's conclusion regarding the permissibility of healing such cases on the Sabbath is not expressed in the Mishnah or other Second Temple sources, one should not forget that halakhah in the NT is itself a witness to late Second Temple Jewish practice and debate. Naturally, not all Jesus's

70. Oliver (*Torah Praxis*, 134–35) rightly notes that no verse from the Pentateuch permits "untying" an animal to provide for it on the Sabbath; rather, Jesus "establishes an analogy arguing that one accepted practice (i.e., untying domestic animals . . .) justifies the application of a similar yet different . . . 'untying,' freeing humans from sickness."

71. See also Exod. 20:8–11 LXX; 23:12; Deut. 5:12–14. Exodus 20:10 MT refers to "cattle" (בְּהֶמְה), but 20:10 LXX refers more specifically to the "ox and donkey" (ὁ βοῦς σου καὶ τὸ ὑποζύγιόν σου).

72. So also Oliver, *Torah Praxis*, 135. John Nolland (*Luke 9:21–18:34*, 724) highlights the duration of the affliction: "The animal is not left tethered for *one day*; the woman has been restricted in this way for *eighteen years!*" (italics original).

interlocutors would or did agree, but such is legal debate, especially over matters as underdetermined as the Sabbath legislation itself. Luke unsurprisingly states that Jesus's reasoning won the day (13:17).

Additionally, Jesus's defense may include an eschatological component.[73] We have discussed already that Luke presents Jesus as the herald of the restoration, which Luke 4:18–19 codes as an eschatological Jubilee via Jesus's reading from Isa. 61:1–2.[74] Isaiah 61 itself alludes to the instruction of Lev. 25, which legislates the noneschatological Jubilee, the "year of release" (ἔτος τῆς ἀφέσεως), in which land is returned to its ancestral owner (25:10), and Israelite servants are released (25:40–41). In Isa. 61, the figure is anointed by God's Spirit to herald the "release [ἄφεσιν] to captives," employing Lev. 25's Jubilee vocabulary to describe the eschatological time of release. Given that Israel's plight in Isaiah is captivity to foreign nations in foreign lands, the Levitical Jubilee, wherein slaves are freed and may return to their native lands, suitably served as a metaphor for the restoration.

Further, we have already discussed that both Josephus and Philo attest that the legislation of Lev. 25 and Deut. 15 were combined, indicating that in the Year of Jubilee (Lev. 25), the requirements for the sabbatical year of release (Deut. 15) were also performed.[75] Moreover, 11QMelch combines all of the above (Deut. 15, Lev. 25, and Isa. 61) to code the restoration as an eschatological Jubilee.[76] After quoting Lev. 25:13 and interpreting its requirement in light of Deut. 15:2, it proceeds, "Its interpretation for the last days refers to the captives" (2.4). As Williams has noted, the scroll concedes that Lev. 25 legislates a mundane, regular calendar event and yet interprets it eschatologically.[77] In its explication, it claims that a commissioned figure (Melchizedek) will cause the captives to "return," proclaim to them "liberty," and "free them from the debt of all their iniquities" (2.4–6). It interprets Israel's plight as a debt-slavery caused by their sins against God, who has handed them over to captors, "Belial and . . . all the spirits of his lot" (2.13). In this narrative frame, Melchizedek is the agent of the captives' debt release and liberation

73. Oliver (*Torah Praxis*, 135–36) also argues for a related eschatological component to the healing, though without emphasizing the Jubilee as such.

74. See also the discussion in Green, *Luke*, 209–13. The connection between the programmatic mission of Jesus in Luke 4:18–19 and his act in 13:10–17 is widely recognized. See Plummer, *Luke*, 343; Hays, *Echoes*, 258.

75. Josephus, *Ant.* 3.281–85; Philo, *Spec. Laws* 2.39; *Decalogue* 1.164; *On the Virtues* 1.99–100.

76. For a recent summary of 11QMelch and a study of the comparable eschatological employment of the biblical texts in Mark, see Williams, "Melchizedek." See also Milik, "Milkisedeq"; Puech, "11QMelkisedeq."

77. Williams, "Melchizedek," 118.

from spiritual powers. Significantly, the text characterizes Melchizedek as the agent named in Isa. 61:1–3, stating that he will "proclaim liberty" to the "captives" (2.4, 6), execute God's "vengeance" (2.13) because it is "the year of grace" (2.9), and "comfort the afflicted" (2.20). This exegetical combination of Deut. 15 and Lev. 25 in 11QMelch is unsurprising, attested as it is in other Second Temple sources. Similarly unsurprising is its characterization of the executor of this eschatological Jubilee as that of Isa. 61, given that the latter text employed Jubilee terminology to describe the eschatological restoration and its herald. These ingredients yield, then, a scenario in which Israel is captive to spiritual powers, but in the restoration, coded as an eschatological Jubilee, the figure promised in Isa. 61 will release the captives.

In the light of these witnesses, it is also unsurprising that Luke 4:18–19 similarly depicts the restoration as an eschatological Jubilee and characterizes the agent of restoration, Jesus, as Isa. 61's herald of that restoration. Consequently, it is Jesus's role to "liberate the captives" (Isa. 61:1; Luke 4:18). In this regard, Luke is not innovating as much as participating in an established interpretative tradition, in which Israel remains in captivity and in need of God's eschatological deliverance, for which the figure of Isa. 61 is sent. With these pieces in place, we return to Jesus's defense of healing the woman on the Sabbath.

The woman is characterized as having a "spirit of sickness" (πνεῦμα . . . ἀσθενείας), probably indicating that this ailment was caused by a spirit (Luke 13:11). This conclusion is strengthened by Jesus's subsequent statement that "Satan" had "bound" this woman for eighteen years (13:16). First to note, then, is that she is characterized not simply as sick, but as bound in a "fetter" (δεσμοῦ, 13:16). Consequently, her healing is characterized as liberation or "release" (λυθῆναι, 13:12, 16) from Satan or the imprisoning spirit. As the Jubilee herald in Isa. 61 announces "release to captives," and as 11QMelch portrays this figure as freeing captives from Belial and his spirits, so Jesus, as the agent of Isa. 61 in Luke, works to "release" those held captive by Satan.[78] Notably, Jesus employs this language of release in his defense, saying, "Was it not necessary [οὐκ ἔδει] that she be released from this bondage on the Sabbath?" (Luke 13:16 AT). Thus Jesus thinks it not merely permissible

78. Luke 13 does not employ ἄφεσις—the term in Deut. 15, Lev. 25, and Isa. 61—for "releasing" debts and slaves. However, he uses forms of ἀπολύω and λύω, which are sometimes used interchangeably or in conjunction with ἄφεσις or ἀφίημι. For example, Job 39:5 asks, "Who is the one who let the donkey go free [ὁ ἀφεὶς ὄνον ἄγριον ἐλεύθερον], who loosed its bonds [δεσμοὺς δὲ αὐτοῦ τίς ἔλυσεν]?" Sirach 27:19 says, "And as you released [ἀπέλυσας] a bird from your hand, thus have you let go [ἀφῆκας] your neighbor" (see also Sir. 28:2). First Maccabees 10:29 states, "I now free you [ἀπολύω ὑμᾶς] and release [ἀφίημι] all the Jews from payment of tribute." See also Ps. 105:20 (104:20 LXX); Isa. 58:6; Matt. 18:27; John 11:44.

but necessary that he heal this woman on the Sabbath. In this, Jesus is apparently taking the Sabbath as a miniature representation of the sabbatical festival (Jubilee) that he inaugurates. This too is attested in biblical and Jewish sources.

Exodus 23:10–12 legislates the sabbatical year and the Sabbath day side by side. Josephus (*Ant.* 3.282) compares the sabbatical years to the rest commanded on the Sabbath itself. Philo claims that the "sacred seventh day" "comprehends an infinite number of most important festivals," referring to the year of release and the Jubilee (*Spec. Laws* 2.39). Furthermore, actions prohibited in the sabbatical year and Jubilee (demanding deposits and exacting debts) are named by Philo as prohibited on the Sabbath itself (*Migration* 1.91). Mishnah Shev. 1.4 quotes a Sabbath-day prohibition and applies it to the sabbatical year. Given the mutual association of "resting" and the events happening in multiples of sevens (seventh day, seventh year, seven cycles of sabbatical years), it is not difficult to see how these requirements were mutually interpreted.

Comparably, then, it seems that Jesus treats the Sabbath as a microcosm of the Jubilee he heralds, and thus he claims that it is not just permissible but necessary that on the Sabbath he do what the Sabbath *qua* Jubilee requires—namely, release the woman from her bondage to Satan.[79] As Oliver notes, "The depth of Luke's argumentation is underappreciated."[80] Jesus's first argument from an accepted practice "stands independently from the question of recognizing his messianic credentials," while "the christological argument is the final argumentation composed of several additional ingredients brought to the table."[81] While the noneschatological halakhic reasoning stands on its own, acknowledging the Jubilee component helps account for Jesus's characterization of her sickness as "bondage" requiring "release" and for his claim that it was necessary (rather than simply permissible) to free her that day.

The Man with Dropsy

We now turn to Luke 14.[82] On the Sabbath, Jesus is in the home of a Pharisee, and a man with "dropsy" (edema) is present. His condition refers to the body's swelling due to excess fluid. Though ancient evidence suggests

79. Similarly, when he reads Isa. 61's Jubilee announcement on the Sabbath, Jesus signifies that the eschatological Jubilee begins on a Sabbath. See Green, *Luke*, 214.

80. Oliver, *Torah Praxis*, 137n86.

81. Oliver, *Torah Praxis*, 137. By "christological," Oliver (136) refers to Jesus's messianic authority to perform eschatological deliverance.

82. On this healing, see also N. Collins, *Jesus*, 108–22; Oliver, *Torah Praxis*, 138–46.

that it can be fatal in certain conditions,[83] the life-threatening nature of this man's condition is not accentuated here. The scene opens by noting that the Pharisees "were watching [Jesus] closely" (Luke 14:1). Jesus then addresses them: "Is it lawful to heal [θεραπεῦσαι] on the Sabbath, or not?" (14:3). The silence of these "lawyers and Pharisees" suggests that they would concur with the synagogue official of Luke 13:14: Jesus should not heal the man on the Sabbath. After he heals the man, he asks, "Which one of you will have a son or an ox fall into a well, and will not immediately pull him out on a Sabbath day?" (14:5). Once again, his legal reasoning operates partially as a lesser to greater, partially as a simple analogy. He may reason from lesser to greater regarding the ox: If you would help an animal, how much more should I help a human? Or he may be reasoning from simple analogy regarding the fallen son: If you would help one human (the fallen son), why cannot I help this human? Additionally, though speculative, I have wondered if Jesus's choice of "well" (φρέαρ), a pit or structure holding water, was selected to suggest parity with the man's condition (dropsy/edema), if the latter was understood by Luke to refer to the body's trapping of fluid/water. "If one might rescue a son from a water pit, why may I not rescue this man from his water-logged condition (ὑδρωπικός)?" As support, recall that in Luke 13 he also employed a case analogous to the one healed: "untying" (λύει) an ox or donkey in comparison to "releasing" (λυθῆναι) the woman from her fetter (13:15, 16). Speculation aside, the phrasing of his question—"Who of you wouldn't?"—suggests that he expects a positive answer. And if they permissibly act on the Sabbath in one instance, Jesus reasons that he is justified in doing so here.[84]

Once more, he may be reasoning from the Sabbath legislation itself. As in the case of the woman in Luke 13, so here: the Sabbath legislation requires animals—specifically "your ox" (ὁ βοῦς σου)—and "your son" (ὁ υἱός σου) to rest on the Sabbath (Exod. 20:10; 23:12; Deut. 5:14). Moreover, Exod. 23:12 says that Israelites ought to rest *so that* the ox, donkey, and son *may refresh* (ἵνα ἀναψύξῃ) themselves. While it is possible to do no work while lying in a well, it is hard to imagine this is a refreshing rest. Thus, to secure their promised rest and refreshment, one must draw them out. It is also possible that Luke's phrasing puns on the word "rest" from these laws (ἀνάπαυσις; ἀναπαύω). For a fallen son or bull to rest (ἀναπαύσηται, Exod. 23:12), it

83. Hippocrates, *On Air, Places, and Waters* 7; *Aphorisms* 6.27. In *Aphorisms* 7.47, Hippocrates states that if one with dropsy coughs frequently, "there is no hope."

84. Oliver (*Torah Praxis*, 143–45) justifiably argues that falling into a "well" would be potentially life-threatening and thus not analogous to the non-life-threatening nature of this man's condition. Consequently, Oliver (145) argues that Jesus's healing may be an extension of the principle of "preservation of life" to non-life-threatening cases. But see the next note below.

is necessary for you to "draw him out" (ἀνασπάσει, 14:5). Analogously, in order to secure rest for this man with dropsy, Jesus must heal him.[85] Jesus's reasoning may be analogous to that on display in b. Shabb. 132b, in which the legal principle "A positive commandment comes and overrides a negative commandment" informs the permissibility of cutting off a mark of *lepra* in circumcising.[86] In Luke 14, the positive requirement to secure the animal's rest (Exod. 23:12) "comes and overrides the negative commandment" to do no work, thus requiring the animal's removal from the well. Analogously, to secure Sabbath refreshment for the man with dropsy (the positive commandment), Jesus must violate the negative commandment (do no work). But in so doing, his action is keeping the Law, not breaking it.

While Jesus may expect a positive answer to his question—"Who of you wouldn't?" (Luke 14:5)—the Damascus Document rules in the negative concerning the animal:[87] "No-one should help an animal give birth on the sabbath day. And if it falls into a well or a pit, he should not take it out on the sabbath. . . . And any living man who falls into a place of water or into a reservoir, no-one should take him out with a ladder or a rope or a utensil" (CD-A 11.13–14, 16–17).[88] Such difference of opinion attests to the varied interpretation of Sabbath observance in the period. That Jesus would disagree with this Damascus Document ruling is plain, but from the manner of his question in Luke 14:5, one may infer that the Pharisees would have agreed with Jesus against the Damascus Document. If so, the intention of Jesus's question is to expose an inconsistency in the practice of the Pharisees. If they would extract an ox or a son on the Sabbath, and if extracting the ox or son is permissible even when life may not be at stake, then Jesus innocently acts on the Sabbath in healing the non-life-threatening condition of this man.

85. In this case, Jesus's healing would not necessarily be an extension of the exception to preserve life, but a corollary drawn from the Sabbath legislation itself. But these conclusions need not be exclusive. If Jesus's reasoning draws an inference from the Sabbath legislation itself, his analogy is not as "weak" as Loader (*Jesus' Attitude*, 335) suggests. Nor is it the case that "the Jewish objections are not taken seriously, but trivialised" by Luke's Jesus (Loader, *Jesus' Attitude*, 335). As Oliver (*Torah Praxis*, 137) notes concerning Luke 13's comparable case, "All of this shows that Luke is not content in simply rehearsing Jesus' christological portfolio as the sole means of justifying his lord's behavior on the Sabbath. Even the messiah must account for his comportment when it deviates from normal conventions."

86. See the discussion in chap. 3 under "You Have Heard It Said . . . , but I Say to You . . ."

87. Crossley ("Matthew and the Torah," 42) suggests that Jesus's question may have even functioned "as an appeal to common difference" between the kind of opinion stated in CD and that potentially held by Jesus and the Pharisees.

88. But one may draw the human out without instruments; see also 4Q265, frag. 7, I.6–8. Discussed also in Oliver, *Torah Praxis*, 145.

The Temple Tax

In Matt. 17:24–27, a collector asks Peter if Jesus pays the temple tax. Peter affirms, and when Jesus sees him, he asks, "'What do you think, Simon? From whom do the kings of the earth collect customs or poll-tax, from their sons [υἱῶν] or from strangers [ἀλλοτρίων]?' When Peter said, 'From strangers,' Jesus said to him, 'Then the sons are exempt'" (17:24–25). Some infer from Jesus's response in this story that he and, by inference, his disciples are "sons" and the rest of the Jewish people are "the strangers."[89] Additionally, if one were (erroneously) to assume that such taxation were a commandment, it would suggest that Jesus here simply asserts his freedom from the Law based on his authority as a "son." However, these inferences are misguided for the simple reason that the annual payment to the temple of "two drachmas," or a half-shekel, is in fact *not* a commandment.

In Exod. 30:13, God tells Moses, "This is what everyone who is counted shall give: half a shekel according to the shekel of the sanctuary, . . . half a shekel as a contribution to the Lord." This is not an annual tax but a payment occasioned by a census. The verse that precedes the requirement states, "When you take a census of the sons of Israel to count them, then each one of them shall give a ransom for himself to the Lord, when you count them, so that there will be no plague among them when you count them." Nehemiah 10, on the other hand, does refer to an annual payment to the temple, but it is named a self-imposed obligation and amounted not to the half-shekel, as in Exod. 30, but a third of a shekel. Nehemiah 10:32 states, "We also imposed on ourselves the obligation to contribute yearly a third of a shekel for the service of the house of our God."

This difference between a Mosaic commandment and a custom seems to be maintained by Josephus, who describes the half-shekel occasioned by a census as something Moses commanded (προσέταξεν, *Ant.* 3.194) and as among "the commands of Moses [τῶν Μωυσέος ἐντολῶν], who told them beforehand, that if the multitude were numbered, they should pay half a shekel" (*Ant.* 7.318). He describes the annual payment of a half-shekel, on the other hand, as "a custom [πάτριον] of our country" (*Ant.* 18.312). Though not stated, Josephus possibly infers the annual custom from the improvised intervention of Jehoash, king of Judah, who declared that "all the money of the sacred offerings which is brought into the house of the Lord, in current money, both the money of each man's assessment and all the money which anyone's heart prompts him to bring into the house of the Lord," ought to be used for temple

89. France, *Matthew*, 669.

repair (2 Kings 12:4–5). Josephus summarizes this account: "Now Jehoash, king of Jerusalem, had an inclination to repair the temple of God; so he called Jehoiada, and bade him send the Levites and priests through all the country, to require half a shekel of silver for every head, toward the rebuilding and repairing of the temple" (*Ant.* 9.161). His description of the contribution as collected throughout the country coincides with his description of the annual half-shekel contribution in *Ant.* 18.312. Also, his alteration from spontaneous gifts of any amount (2 Kings 12:4) to a half-shekel (*Ant.* 9.161), the amount customary for the annual gift to the temple, suggests that the current custom may have resulted from an interpretation of the royal imposition of Jehoash.

Whatever the historical circumstances that led to the annual contribution, Jesus apparently did not regard it as legally binding. And here he was not alone. A document from Qumran (4Q159) states, "The money of valuation which one gives as ransom for his own person will be half [a shekel,] only on[ce] will he give it in all his days" (frag. 1, II.6–7). If this ordinance comments on the half-shekel that others give regularly, which is supported by the fact that it comments on the only law that requires a half-shekel, its express limitation to "only once . . . in all his days" implies that they did not accept the imposition of a required annual taxation of that amount. If this is the case, it shows that Jesus's view is not unique and cannot be interpreted as a violation of, or an assertion of his freedom from, the Law. This conclusion has implications for his statement about "sons" and "foreigners." Jesus reasons from an analogy about sons and foreigners as follows: "Kings annually tax their foreign subjects, not their sons. We (being Jews) are sons,[90] so we (Jews) should not have to pay this annual tax. But because it is their (the Jews' or, more specifically, the collectors') practice, we will do it in order not to offend." On such reasoning, the distinction is not between Jesus and his disciples as sons over against Israel/Jews as foreigners/non-sons. Rather, Israel/Jews are sons, and so the annual taxation (which is not a commandment) is not obligatory and violates the logic of their (Israel's) being God's sons, which is why God never commanded this. Because God never commanded it, "we" (Jews, and thus Jesus and his disciples) are exempt.[91] In this brief passage, then, Jesus does estrange Jewish nondisciples as "foreigners" in contrast to himself and his disciples as "sons," and he does not set aside a commandment in favor of his own opinion. What's more, even if it were a commandment that he supposedly questioned, Matthew presents him as nonetheless keeping it! Thus even then no violation takes place.

90. As Deut. 14:1 explicitly says of Israelites. See also m. Avot 3.14.

91. See a comparable discussion in Flusser, "Half-Shekel"; Evans, *Matthew*, 327.

Conclusion

In these passages, Jesus's distinct practices are based on alternative readings of commands, and the difference of opinion is typically not governed by an alternative eschatological agenda but simply an alternative interpretation of the command in question (with the partial exception of Luke 13's "necessary" healing on the Sabbath). In the next chapter, we will focus on distinct practices largely informed by Jesus's distinct eschatological agenda—that is, his eschatological nomism.

5

Eschatological Nomism

Jesus's alternative practice of the Law is sometimes occasioned by his conviction that the kingdom is irrupting into the present through his own work. This chapter will focus on controversies caused by his distinct practices that are themselves governed by his eschatological agenda, specifically dining with sinners, his claims about family, and a case of Sabbath profanation.

Dining with Sinners

Each Synoptic Gospel records Jesus's habit of eating with sinners and the resultant questioning by the Pharisees and scribes: "Why is he eating with tax collectors and sinners?"[1] Dunn's interpretation represents a common construal: "The issue here [Mark 2:15–17] is what the Pharisees would have seen as Jesus' disregard for the law, in this case the laws governing table-fellowship—particularly clean and unclean food, tithes, and ritual purity. It was just these laws which preserved Israel's holiness as the people of God in the eye of the Pharisees. . . . And it was disregard for these laws in

1. Mark 2:16, with minor, insubstantial differences in Matt. 9:11 and Luke 5:30. Aside from syntax and the precise subject of the speaker, each account moves from the observation that Jesus dines with sinners to his response concerning "the sick," the question about fasting, Jesus's response concerning the bridegroom, and two parables concerning the shrunken cloth and wineskins (Mark 2:15–22; Matt. 9:10–17; Luke 5:29–39). Major differences include Matthew's quotation of Hosea 6:6 and Luke's notion that the old wine is better. The former will be interpreted in the section on Matt. 12, and I will address the latter in this section.

particular which merited the . . . condemnatory epithet 'sinner' from the Pharisees. Jesus in eating with such 'sinners' would be seen by the Pharisees to show the same disregard for these laws."[2] Similarly, Wright states that the controversy "was about the scandalous implied redefinition of the kingdom itself. Jesus was replacing adherence or allegiance to Temple and Torah with allegiance to himself. Restoration and purity were to be had, not through the usual channels, but through Jesus."[3] But such interpretations err in a few ways.[4] While Wright is correct in viewing the meals in the context of restoration eschatology, suggesting that they symbolize and mediate Jesus's announcement of the kingdom of God,[5] he unnecessarily describes a disjunctive relationship between "allegiance to Torah" and "allegiance to himself," especially given the Gospels' insistence that following Jesus means following his interpretation of the Torah. Responding more thoroughly to Dunn's position will sufficiently answer comparable issues present in other interpretations.

Dunn claims that in eating with sinners, Jesus disregarded the laws pertaining to "clean and unclean food, tithes, and ritual purity."[6] But one need not assume that when Jesus or his guests were eating with sinners, they were eating food forbidden in Lev. 11 or Deut. 14. The Pharisees do not make this accusation, Jesus's defense does not respond to it, and notably, it does not come up in his trial in which accusers name Jesus's supposed transgressions. If they made a point about his eating permissible food with unwashed hands (Mark 7; Matt. 15), one would have expected an uproar had he eaten forbidden food. And if Jesus had balked at the food laws, it is unlikely he would have hyperbolically criticized Pharisees as those who "swallow a camel" (Matt. 23:24), an "unclean" animal forbidden for consumption (Lev. 11:4),[7] since such an insult depends on acceptance of their forbidden status. Moreover, it bears repeating: one need not be concerned about ritual purity when eating common meals. Not only does the Law require eating only sacred meals in purity (Lev. 7:20–21), but it explicitly states that one may eat common food while impure (Deut. 12:15). If the Pharisees were to question Jesus for having eaten while ritually impure, Jesus could easily appeal to the permission in Deuteronomy that the unclean may eat permissible food. And if Jesus were to contract impurity while eating, it would be no sin. Though purity is a desirable

2. Dunn, *Jesus, Paul, and the Law*, 17.
3. Wright, *Victory of God*, 274. See comparably McKnight, *New Vision*, 48.
4. For a helpful discussion of these scenes, see Wassén, "Jesus' Table Fellowship."
5. Wright, *Victory of God*, 274.
6. Dunn, *Jesus, Paul, and the Law*, 17.
7. See Oliver, *Torah Praxis*, 286–87.

state, contracting impurity is not prohibited.[8] Rabbinic texts do exhibit concern that one not eat untithed food,[9] but two things should be noted. First, the notion that Jesus ate untithed food is neither specified by the Pharisees nor defended against by Jesus. Second, Matthew and Luke elsewhere signal Jesus's agreement with the Pharisaic concern for tithing (Matt. 23:23–24; Luke 11:42). The notion that he disregarded tithing is either unstated (Mark) or improbable (Matthew and Luke) and is therefore likely not the operative issue. Moreover, it must be recognized that the Pharisees do not here accuse Jesus or his disciples of transgressing the Law as they do when they observe their practices on the Sabbath (Matt. 12:2; Luke 13:14). Something other than lawbreaking is the issue here.

What, then, is at stake in this meal practice of Jesus? The most basic concern is that in eating with sinners, Jesus conceivably implies acceptance of their behavior and/or their status *as sinners*. If table fellowship implies a degree of camaraderie, an onlooker may wonder: Is this so-called herald of the restoration who claims divine authorization actually a sinner?

Not only does this interpretation avoid the mistakes basic to those who see dietary laws or ritual purity at stake,[10] but this interpretation of the query best fits the contours of Jesus's defense: "It is not those who are healthy who need a physician, but those who are sick; I did not come to call the righteous, but sinners" (Mark 2:17; cp. Matt. 9:13; Luke 5:31–32). In each account, Jesus accepts the Pharisaic conclusion that these people are sinners. But it is precisely because his mission is to "return" Israel to God and his Law that he dines with those especially in need of this ministry: sinners or "the sick." Consequently, even if dining with sinners required sitting loosely with respect to purity regulations others highly prized (but which the Law did not require), it would be not because Jesus did not equally prize them but because he weighed his mission to sinners as overriding the concerns that might preclude contact with them.[11] A physician who visits the sick does

8. Exceptions not applicable to this scene exist, such as the high priest and corpse impurity (Lev. 21:11). See "Cultic/Political Office" in chap. 1 above.

9. E.g., m. Demai 4.1.

10. If ritual purity were at stake, the criticism would operate not at the level of transgression of the Law but as a violation of one in-group's practice. But his defense does not lead me to conclude that ritual purity was the issue.

11. *Pace* Yinger (*Pharisees*, 107), who claims that the difference in Jesus's dining habits obtains because the Pharisees "saw impurity as transmissible by contact, as contagious," whereas Jesus "seemed to view holiness, or rather his holiness and the holiness of the inbreaking divine rule, as more powerful. Instead of impurity, it was the purity of the kingdom of God that was contagious." Yinger describes the difference disjunctively rather than in terms of priority, stating that Pharisees viewed impurity as spreadable while Jesus didn't. But the transmissibility of impurity isn't a reductively Pharisaic view. Impurity is spreadable according to the Law. If

not thereby endorse the ailment; on the contrary, it is precisely the desire to cure that leads the physician to treat the patient. So it is with Jesus's dining with sinners: it does not signal a disregard for general Law-keeping, purity regulations, or dietary laws. On the contrary, Jesus risks his reputation, being willing to be known as a "friend of . . . sinners" (Matt. 11:19; Luke 7:34), to lead people he regards as sinners back to what the Law requires of them. Or as Luke states: "I have not come to call the righteous to repentance, but sinners" (5:32).[12]

In each Synoptic Gospel, this episode gives way to a question about the disciples' lack of fasting: "Why do John's disciples and the disciples of the Pharisees fast, but your disciples do not fast?" (Mark 2:18; cp. Matt. 9:14; Luke 5:33). Here a distinction in practice (regular eating versus fasting) raises eyebrows, but as with the question of dining with sinners, no outright accusation of transgression is levied. Here I quote Jesus's response from Mark:

> And Jesus said to them, "While the groom is with them, the attendants of the groom cannot fast, can they? As long as they have the groom with them, they cannot fast. But the days will come when the groom is taken away from them, and then they will fast, on that day. No one sews a patch of unshrunk cloth on an old garment; otherwise, the patch pulls away from it, the new from the old, and a worse tear results. And no one puts new wine into old wineskins; otherwise the wine will burst the skins, and the wine is lost and the skins as well; but one puts new wine into fresh wineskins." (Mark 2:19–22)[13]

Of this episode and the subsequent parables about the cloth and the wineskins, France (interpreting Matthew) states that discipleship under Jesus is not "as it was experienced in other pious circles at the time. It is characterized . . . by joy rather than solemnity, by feasting rather than fasting, and the two graphic sayings of [Matt. 9] verses 16–17 [regarding the cloths and wineskins] indicate a fundamental incompatibility between the dry formality of existing religious traditions and an exuberant vitality in the Jesus circle

---

Jesus were to disagree with this, it would not simply be a disagreement with a Pharisaic view. Moreover, Jesus could agree with the Law and the Pharisees' interpretation that impurity is "contagious" and still eat with sinners, since becoming defiled (theoretically) through such association is not prohibited/sinful. Thus, a difference in opinion regarding the transmissibility of impurity does not explain the nature of the difference/conflict.

12. Matthew and Mark's omission of Luke's "to repentance" (Mark 2:17; Matt. 9:13) does not obscure their concession that Jesus regards them as sinners. All accounts describe them as "the sick" who require the attention of the "physician," Jesus.

13. On Mark's differences with Matthew and Luke, see the first note of the present chapter.

which cannot be confined within conventional forms."[14] He further describes these parables as picking up "the theme of a new and joyful pattern of religion which is incompatible with the old traditions represented by the fasting regimes of the Pharisees and the followers of John."[15] Here France draws the distinction between Jesus and his contemporaries in terms of a noneschatological difference in "patterns of religion": Jesus is joyful, and the Pharisees are formalistic and somber. It is hard not to see here an undesirable return to a caricature of Jews and Judaism over against Jesus and Christianity. But as Wright emphasizes, the controversy "had everything to do with eschatology . . . and little to do with (what we call) 'religion.'"[16]

Wright is correct. Against France and interpretations that primarily see a distinction in customs of piety,[17] the distinct practices of the Pharisees and John regarding fasting, on the one hand, and Jesus feasting, on the other, map onto not two distinct "patterns of religion" but two distinct interpretations of the time on the eschatological clock. Fasting is a practice for those in mourning (2 Sam. 1:12; Neh. 1:4; Esther 4:3). John's disciples (and possibly Pharisees?) may fast due to their recognition that Israel remains in need of restoration.[18] Numerous prophetic texts link fasting with the mourning that accompanies the divine punishments and exile (Joel 1:14; 2:12–15; Zech. 7:5; Isa. 58:1–6; Jer. 14:12; 36:6–9; Dan. 9:3). In fasting, they express sorrow for sin and petition God to restore them.

Conversely, the restoration signals the transition from fasting to feasting. Of the time when God rescues Israel, Zechariah says: "The Lord of armies says this: 'The fast of the fourth, the fast of the fifth, the fast of the seventh, and the fast of the tenth months will become joy, jubilation, and cheerful festivals for the house of Judah'" (8:19). Similarly, Jer. 31:11–13 states that when God rescues Israel, "They will come and shout for joy . . . , / And they will be radiant over the bounty of the Lord— / Over the grain, the new wine, the oil, / And over the young of the flock and the herd. / And their life will be like a watered garden, / And they will never hunger[19] again. . . . / For I will turn their mourning into joy / And comfort them." In the restoration, hunger gives way to abundance.

14. France, *Matthew*, 351. France (*Mark*, 140–42) makes comparable comments regarding the Markan version, but I engage his comments on Matthew to interact with his interpretation of Hosea later in this chapter.

15. France, *Matthew*, 356.

16. Wright, *Victory of God*, 272. See also Yinger, *Pharisees*, 77–78.

17. See Borg, *Conflict, Holiness, and Politics*, 173; McKnight, *New Vision*, 46–49.

18. Lambert (*Repentance*, 13–31) discusses the various goals and contexts of "fasting" within the Hebrew Bible.

19. NASB: "languish."

Consequently, because Jesus understands himself to be the agent of restoration, he feasts. In his meals with his disciples, and possibly with sinners, with whom he acts as the "physician" (Mark 2:17; Matt. 9:12; Luke 5:31) who calls them to repentance (Luke 5:32), he is imaging the prospective eschatological banquet. Fasting versus feasting, then, codes not two patterns of religion—one dry and the other vivacious—but two convictions about restoration: not here yet (John and the Pharisees) versus breaking in now (Jesus and his disciples).[20]

Because the subsequent parables (Mark 2:21–22; Matt. 9:15–17; Luke 5:36–39) illustrate Jesus's answer to the question about fasting, the interpretation of one naturally affects the other. Because France (interpreting Matthew) takes the eating to signal a joyful pattern of religion, he takes the following parables to illustrate that Jesus's teaching (the new wine) cannot fit into the old "religious structures" (the old wineskins).[21] He concludes that "the history of the church ever since [the time of Jesus and "hostility from the rabbinic establishment"] has been punctuated by the bursting of old wineskins and the need to find suitable new containers for the new wine."[22] But if my interpretation is correct, the materials in the parables do not correspond reductively to different practices of piety or as objects to be allegorized; instead, they illustrate Jesus's point about the eschatological time. As Suzanne Watts Henderson notes, "Rather than subverting torah, the sayings in Mark 2:21–22 mainly concern allegiance to Jesus's messianic vision."[23] These parables, then, do not present allegories for decoding but illustrate that certain practices befit certain seasons.

In this framework, fasting during feast time offends the host of the party; likewise, mending a cloth before the patch is shrunk tears the garment, and filling an old wineskin with new wine tears the skin and wastes the wine. In each, a practice not befitting the time is criticized. Significantly, the wineskins parable does not even seem to emphasize the obvious superiority of the new over the old, as one would infer from France's interpretation, in which the new wine and skin are identified with Jesus and the church. Such a conclusion pays too much attention to only the parable of the wine/skins and ignores the fact that older wine is typically superior.[24] But in the parable of the clothing, it is the old garment that the tailor intends to repair. The tragedy is that the

20. Moreover, if fasting did index dry formalism, Jesus would be "guilty" of invoking such a travesty on his disciples as well, since he says they will fast when he is gone (Mark 2:20; Matt. 9:15; Luke 5:35). See similar comments regarding Jesus's "eating and drinking" in Henderson, "Was Mark a Supersessionist?," 154.

21. France, *Matthew*, 357.

22. France, *Matthew*, 357.

23. Henderson, "Was Mark a Supersessionist?," 163.

24. So Luke 5:39: "And no one, after drinking old wine wants new."

old garment is ruined by the new patch. If the new is superior to the old, then illustrating the lamentable loss of something old due to the ill use of something new was surely confusing. But such confusion is avoided if one does not attempt to allegorize one or all of the parable's components, mapping them onto Jesus or Judaism or a practice of religion. They function much better as parables about appropriate actions given the season, illustrating that Jesus's practice of eating with sinners and not fasting is based on his understanding that "the time is fulfilled" (Mark 1:15; cp. Matt. 16:3; Luke 12:56). Fasting is appropriate when in mourning, but in Jesus's announcement, teaching, and healing, the kingdom is irrupting, and restoration is afoot. It is time to celebrate!

Jesus and the Family

In Mark 3, having been informed of the presence of his family awaiting him "outside" (3:31), Jesus responds, "'Who are my mother and my brothers?' And looking about on those who were sitting around him, he said, 'Here are my mother and my brothers! For whoever does the will of God, this is my brother, and sister, and mother'" (3:33–35). This and comparable sayings about family have led to theories that Jesus set aside a major symbol (the family) enshrined and legislated in the Law.

For example, Wright states that Israel's laws "formed the boundary fence around the people of Israel, the nation of the Jews."[25] According to Wright, "the rigorous application of the law in the way we have observed, as a defence against the Gentiles and hence as a reinforcement of national boundaries and aspirations had become, in Jesus' view, a symptom of the problem rather than part of the solution."[26] Yet, according to Wright, Jesus's teaching constituted not "an attack on Torah as such but a radically different interpretation of Israel's ancestral tradition."[27] Within the latter context, Wright suggests that "national solidarity" itself became a "major symbol and boundary-marker"[28] and that "the election of Israel generated the symbol of nation or family,"[29] beside which "Jesus, to put it mildly, set a time-bomb."[30] This is of no small hermeneutical significance for Wright's reading not just of a few sayings but indeed of the NT itself, not least Paul's letters, for whom Jesus's statements

25. Wright, *Victory of God*, 388.
26. Wright, *Victory of God*, 388.
27. Wright, *Victory of God*, 388.
28. Wright, *Victory of God*, 399.
29. Wright, *Victory of God*, 400.
30. Wright, *Victory of God*, 400.

about family lie "at the root of that multi-ethnicity which came, quite quickly, to be advocated by Paul and others."[31] In support of such statements, he asks, "What else can we conclude, from a passage like this?" after which he quotes the above statement from Mark 3 and the saying in Luke 9:60 to "leave the dead to bury their dead" (AT).

To understand these statements in Mark 3:33–35 and Luke 9:60, it is necessary to recall a component basic to Jewish legal reasoning—namely, overrides. Israel's law theoretically legislates all facets of Israel's life, but inevitably conflicts between laws will arise. Mentioning again the example discussed earlier, when the time for circumcision coincides with the Sabbath, a decision must be made regarding which command takes precedence. In this scenario, the Mishnah consistently rules that one should circumcise on the eighth day, thereby profaning the Sabbath. Or in the rabbinic idiom: circumcision overrides Sabbath (m. Shabb. 19.2). Examples abound, and significantly they do not all pertain to temporal facets of the Law. Some examples also suggest that certain loyalties override others.

The priesthood is one such example. Because of their duty, which is of utmost priority for maintaining the temple and its sacrifices, priests are not just permitted but praised for their concern for the temple or the honor of God over their family. After the golden-calf incident in Exod. 32, Moses shouts, "'Whoever is for the Lord, come to me!' And all the sons of Levi gathered together to him" (32:26). He tells them to put to death those who have committed idolatry. Once they complete the task, Moses says, "Dedicate yourselves today to the Lord—for every man has been against his son and against his brother—in order that he may bestow a blessing upon you today" (32:29). Evidently their zeal for God justifiably overrode their loyalty to their families. While pronouncing blessings upon his death, Moses says over Levi, "Let your [God's] Thummim and your Urim belong to your godly man [Levi], . . . / Who said of his father and his mother, / 'I did not consider them.' / And he did not acknowledge his brothers, / Nor did he regard his own sons, / For they observed your word, / And complied with your covenant" (Deut. 33:8–9).[32] Here the Levites are praised for "not considering" or "acknowledging" their family when faced with the choice between loyalty to God ("observ[ing] your word") and family relationships. Generally these loyalties do not compete, but when they do, the Law praises those who prioritize God over family.[33]

31. Wright, *Victory of God*, 400.
32. See also Fletcher-Louis, "'Leave the Dead,'" 46.
33. See also Deut. 13:6–11 and Philo's interpretation of it in *Spec. Laws* 1.315–16.

Similarly, because the duties of the temple are of utmost importance, for which the high priest must be in a state of purity, the high priest is prohibited from defiling himself "even for his father or his mother" (Lev. 21:11). In this case, his temple duties override those of honoring his parents by participating in their burial. This understanding of the priest's duties was recognized by Philo as well, who states, "The man who has been assigned to God, and who has become the leader of his sacred band of worshippers, ought to be disconnected with, and alienated from, all things of creation, not being so much the slave of the love of either parents, or children, or brothers, as either to omit or to delay any one of those holy actions, which it is by all means better should be done at once" (*Spec. Laws* 1.114). Similarly, reflecting on Exod. 32, wherein the Levites killed the idolaters, Philo states, "Those who have applied themselves to prayers and sacrifices, and the whole body of ceremonies connected with the temple, are, what seems a most paradoxical thing, homicides, fratricides, murderers of those persons who are nearest and dearest to them" (*On Drunkenness* 1.66). Even of the Nazirites, who are under a voluntary vow, Philo states, "They are commanded to keep their body pure and undefiled, so as not even to approach their parents if they are dead, nor their brothers; piety overcoming the natural good will and affection towards their relations and dearest friends, and it is both honorable and expedient that piety should at all times prevail [over natural affections]" (*Spec. Laws* 1.250).

My point is not to argue that these situations are identical to Mark 3 but to show that loyalties overriding natural kinship have precedent in the Law and its contemporary interpretations. Moreover, these texts go further than the purported snub of Mark 3:33–35 in that they highlight the negative component—not considering or acknowledging one's family—whereas Jesus does not. Rather, he employs the familial terms only positively to characterize those who do the will of God (3:35). If he had said "I do not consider them my family because they do not do the word of God," he would then only be saying something analogous to sentiments expressed in the Law itself. Consequently, using this scene to demonstrate that Jesus nullifies the significance of genealogical kinship (and thus redefines the Law in the process) misses the point.

Additionally, Mark indicates elsewhere (as do Matthew and Luke) that Jesus implies or positively teaches the good of honoring one's father and mother. When critiquing the Pharisees for upholding tradition to the detriment of God's Law, he cites their tradition about "Corban," by which materials that could have been used to aid their parents are instead claimed as "given to God" (Mark 7:10–11), such that they "no longer allow him to do anything for his father or his mother" (7:12). Here Jesus names the failure to provide materially for one's parents as "invalidating the word of

God" (7:13), constituting the Pharisees as "hypocrites" with disobedient hearts (7:6). Moreover, he names the honoring of father and mother as one of the commandments whose keeping is necessary to "inherit eternal life" (Mark 10:17–19; Matt. 19:19; Luke 18:20). It would be strange to conclude, then, that Mark 3:35's statement about family should be interpreted as a redefinition that entails negative inferences about one's biological family or the Law.

But why does Jesus use family terminology to describe the restoration community? Jesus may use such terminology descriptively due to its positive, covenantal valence. God is the father of the nation, and its citizens are family/kin toward one another. In the context of restoration, participating in covenant renewal entails reinforcing, or forging anew, those familial ties.[34] Moreover, prophetic texts use familial language to characterize those who experience the restoration.[35] Thus, those who obey God's will (repenting, heeding Jesus's message) are family in the covenantal sense: they acknowledge God as "the father" who saves them, and they become family to one another. Additionally, naming each other as "brother and sister" fosters familial affection toward one another and makes plain the obligations members have toward one another. That seems in Mark to be how Jesus characterizes the community of followers who have left their families to follow him, as in his announcement: "There is no one who has left house or brothers or sisters or mother or father or children or farms, for my sake and for the gospel's sake, but that he will receive a hundred times as much now in the present age, houses and brothers and sisters and mothers and children and farms, along with persecutions; and in the age to come, eternal life" (Mark 10:29–30).[36] Or as he says in Matthew, "You are all brothers and sisters. And do not call anyone on earth your father; for only one is your Father, he who is in heaven" (23:8–9).[37] As "family" to one another, followers of Jesus owe each other, and enjoy together, material support (Mark 10:29–30; Luke 18:29–30; cp. Acts 2:44–45) and forgiveness (Matt. 18:15–22).

But this all raises a significant question. Does describing the community as "family" efface the perduring validity of family who do not join the movement? I think not. In fact, to view this practice as a redefinition of the election

34. See Isa. 49:18–21; 60:4; Mal. 4:6; Sir. 48:10. See Marcus, *Mark 1–8*, 286.

35. Isa. 66:20; Ezek. 16:55–61; Hosea 1:11–2:1 (2:2–3 MT); Mic. 5:1–3. Moreover, the Law promises restoration to Abraham's descendants (Lev. 26:40–45; Deut. 30:5–6).

36. Marcus, *Mark 1–8*, 286.

37. As noted by France (*Matthew*, 863), "father" here does not refer to one's biological father but is "a term of respect, usually applied to someone older and/or socially superior to the speaker (e.g., 1 Sam 24:11; 2 Kings 2:12; 5:13; 6:21)."

of Israel and its symbols is dangerously wrong. Genealogical descent from Abraham, Isaac, and Jacob was regularly regarded as a normal feature of being reckoned among God's covenantal people, but such descent was not a sufficient condition for being in good standing within the covenant according to numerous Second Temple interpretations of biblical material. One could be genealogically descended from Jacob, circumcised on the eighth day, and still grow up to commit the sins for which the punishment was being "cut off" from the people (Exod. 31:14; Lev. 7:27; 17:4; 18:29); or one could be a member of the generation that was exiled to Babylon. In neither case would genealogical descent guarantee protection from divine punishment. Similarly, genealogical descent from Abraham was no guarantee that one would participate in the restoration and avoid "the wrath to come" (Matt. 3:7). On the contrary, one needed to "return" to God (Deut. 30:1–6; Lev. 26:40–42) or "repent" (Mark 1:15). Or in John's instruction: "Therefore produce fruit consistent with repentance; and do not assume that you can say to yourselves, 'We have Abraham as our father'" (Matt. 3:8–9). John is denying not the goodness of Abrahamic descent but its sufficiency to secure participation in the restoration. In the same way, Jesus in Mark 3, especially in view of his requirements to honor one's genealogical parents (Mark 7:8–13) as an obligation for inheriting eternal life (10:17, 19), is not denying the goodness of family as traditionally defined. Rather, he is employing familial terminology positively to characterize those who participate in the restoration by "do[ing] the will of God" (3:35).

Therefore, it is unnecessary to conclude that employing familial terminology toward those who are not biological kin either nullifies the significance of one's biological kin or suggests that the latter are replaced, and it certainly does not imply a redefinition of the Law. Were it to challenge the latter conceptions, Jesus's expressed intent to feed "the children [Israelites] . . . first" (Mark 7:27) and to pursue "the lost sheep of the house of Israel" (Matt. 15:24), and to commission the summoning of the non-Israelite nations only after his resurrection and enthronement (Mark 13:10; cp. Matt. 28:19; Luke 24:47) would surely sit as odd features of the Gospels, not to mention Acts and Paul's letters. Discrete entities such as the house of Israel and the non-Israelite nations simply would not exist if a "redefinition" of Israel and the nations occurred.[38] These statements about the family do, however, suggest a hierarchy in view of an implied eschatology.[39]

38. On the problems that redefinition creates when an author continues to use "Jew" and/or "gentile" in otherwise stable senses, see Thiessen, *Gentile Problem*, 69–71.

39. See Davies and Allison, *Matthew*, 168–69.

The hierarchy in question seems to be that of loyalty to Jesus overriding the loyalty typically due to the family. While implicit in Mark 10:29–30, this conclusion is best represented in the following teaching from Matthew: "Do not think that I came to bring peace on the earth; I did not come to bring peace, but a sword. For I came to turn a man against his father, and a daughter against her mother, and a daughter-in-law against her mother-in-law; and a person's enemies will be the members of his household. The one who loves father or mother more than me [ὑπὲρ ἐμέ] is not worthy of me; and the one who loves son or daughter more than me [ὑπὲρ ἐμέ] is not worthy of me" (Matt. 10:34–37). The loyalty demanded by Jesus is not necessarily competitive, either Jesus or family, but comparative, Jesus above one's family. When there is no competition between these loyalties, there is no need to leave one's family and/or disregard obligations owed to them.[40]

To be sure, Jesus is saying something astounding in Mark 3:33–35 and elsewhere. But astounding is not the same as unprecedented, and the known precedent of the temple's duties overriding familial obligations for the priests aids comprehension of Jesus's claims. That is, priestly duties to God and the temple override obligations to the family. Analogously, due to the urgency of Jesus's mission, in which the life of Israel is at stake due to the impending judgment, loyalty to his message takes utmost priority in the way the temple did for the priests. That is, Jesus's mission makes halakhic demands on Israel analogous to the demands that temple duties make on priests; both activities (fidelity to Jesus's message and maintaining the temple) are accompanied by demands that override other obligations, even to the family, due to their relative importance.[41]

In what way Jesus's mission is "greater than the temple" (Matt. 12:6) will be explored below. But before turning to Matt. 12, it is necessary to attend to one more saying about the family.

Luke 9:60: "Let the Dead Bury Their Dead"

Luke's Gospel records the following exchange: "And he said to another, 'Follow me.' But he said, 'Lord, permit me first to go and bury my father.' But he said to him, 'Allow the dead to bury their own dead; but as for you,

40. See the discussion in Luz, *Matthew 8–20*, 112–13.

41. Thus I disagree with Fletcher-Louis ("'Leave the Dead,'" 46) that such statements are evidence that "Jesus enlisted followers to a new Levitical or priestly community." It is not that they are becoming priests but that he is calling them to work that is as important as that of the priests, which grants them comparable permissions.

go and proclaim everywhere the kingdom of God" (9:59–60). Of this statement, Martin Hengel writes, "There is hardly one logion of Jesus which more sharply runs counter to law, piety, and custom than does this,"[42] by which Jesus expresses "his sovereign freedom in respect of the Law of Moses and of custom in general among Jews and Greeks."[43] Following Hengel, E. P. Sanders regards this saying as "the most revealing passage in the synoptics for penetrating to Jesus' view of the law,"[44] suggesting that "Jesus *consciously* requires disobedience of a commandment understood by all Jews to have been given by God,"[45] meaning that Jesus required "disobedience to God."[46] Wright follows the work of Hengel and Sanders, employing them in support of his paradigm that through such statements, the "symbols of Israel's worldview had now become . . . redundant."[47] However, Luke 9:60 is best understood when situated within the legal category of overrides, as described above.

Jesus's mission to herald God's kingdom is his highest priority, "because for this reason I was sent" (Luke 4:43 AT). Moreover, this mission is Jesus's divinely commissioned task: "The Spirit of the Lord is upon me, / Because he anointed me to bring good news to the poor" (4:18). Because this divine commission requires that he herald the kingdom, and because the approaching kingdom promises restoration to the repentant and judgment for those who do not repent (3:9; 13:1–9), his mission takes precedence over otherwise good rituals and commandments when a conflict obtains. Such priority is analogous to the requirement that the high priest not endure the loss of his capacity to perform his required rituals by participating in funereal rites or being defiled by the dead "even for his father or mother" (Lev. 21:11). Because the high priest was commissioned by God to perform duties necessary for the maintenance of the temple and consequently the life of Israel, which received atonement and purification through rituals only he could perform (Lev. 16; see also Philo, *Spec. Laws* 1.113), the high priest needed to be in a constant state of readiness, which required that others bury his parents. In the same manner, Jesus is implying that his divinely authorized mission takes a similar precedence. If one wants to participate in this mission of "preaching the kingdom of God" (Luke 9:60), one must be prepared to leave others to bury one's dead when a conflict in one's duties arises.

42. Hengel, *Charismatic*, 14.
43. Hengel, *Charismatic*, 11.
44. E. P. Sanders, *Jesus and Judaism*, 252.
45. E. P. Sanders, *Jesus and Judaism*, 254, italics original.
46. E. P. Sanders, *Jesus and Judaism*, 253.
47. Wright, *Victory of God*, 400.

Within this framework, it is inaccurate to conclude, as Sanders does, that Jesus thereby requires "disobedience to God."[48] The Law does not require a son to bury his father. Deuteronomy 21:23 implies that burial of corpses is required, but Jesus does not say that the corpse of the man's father should be left unburied. Rather, Jesus says that if the man wishes to participate in the mission of announcing the kingdom (Luke 9:60), he should leave others to bury the dead. "Honor your father and mother" may have been interpreted to entail the requirement to bury them, but again, Jesus does not express a disdain for the requirement to bury the dead or one's father. Rather, he implies that the importance of his mission requires the same single-minded devotion that the high priest shows toward his duties.

Though Lev. 21's requirement that a high priest not participate in the burial of even his parents so that he may fulfill his duty presents a fruitful analogy for the import of Jesus's mission likewise requiring abstention from such duties,[49] many scholars, in their characterization of Luke 9:60 as an unprecedented "break" from Jewish custom, either mispresent Jewish sources employed toward such a characterization or (perhaps unintentionally) apply a double standard when comparing Luke 9:60 to other legal decisions. For example, Hengel argues against such an analogy with Lev. 21 due to a supposed dearth in early Judaism of following this commandment. For support, he states that Philo's exegesis of Lev. 21:11 "clearly shows an anti-ritual bias."[50] I do not follow this conclusion nor quite understand how Hengel gets there. Philo names the prohibition as coming from Moses and then justifies it on the basis of the need for the high priest to be kept from defilement since "there is no one besides the high priest himself who is permitted to perform his duties instead of him; for which reason [παρ' ἣν αἰτίαν] he must always be kept free from defilement in order that [ὅπως], being always ready to offer up prayers and sacrifices, . . . he may continue to fulfill the duties of his office without hindrance" (*Spec. Laws* 1.113). Describing this as evincing an "anti-ritual bias" makes one suspect a degree of anti-ritual projection on the part of Hengel. Philo, then, interprets Lev. 21 to imply that the import of the high priest's duties requires him to abstain from such funereal duties.[51] If Jesus believed his divinely commissioned mission to herald the kingdom were as or more important than the work of the temple (as he states explicitly in Matt. 12:6), then he would be justified in operating with the same halakhic principle

48. E. P. Sanders, *Jesus and Judaism*, 253.
49. The analogy is noted approvingly even in Milgrom, *Leviticus 17–22*, 1817.
50. Hengel, *Charismatic*, 11.
51. See also Josephus, *Ant.* 3.277.

that those who herald the kingdom with him ought to leave the burial, even of parents, to others if necessary.[52]

Similarly, Sanders (uncharacteristically) misrepresents a rabbinic text in service of his characterization of Jesus's saying as one that "counters . . . the Mosaic legislation."[53] Sanders states, "It thus becomes clear that the requirement to care for dead relatives, especially one's parents, was held very strictly among Jews at the time of Jesus. In addition to the obligation to bury one's parents, the general obligation to care for the dead was very strong. According to later rabbinic opinion, even the High Priest and a Nazirite, ordinarily forbidden to contract corpse-uncleanness, should do so in the case of a neglected corpse (Nazir 7.1)."[54] However, the scenario in Luke 9 is not a neglected corpse but that of one's parents. When the issue of a neglected (potential) corpse is at play, Jesus would seemingly agree with the rabbinic opinion stated above, per an implicit critique in the so-called parable of the good Samaritan, wherein a priest and a Levite fail to tend for one who could

52. See Bockmuehl ("'Let the Dead'") for comparable critiques of Hengel and Sanders. He suggests that the Nazirite legislation provides a context in which Jesus's saying "can be understood by way of analogy" (577). I differ from Bockmuehl only in that he sets aside the priestly tradition because this saying does not depict Jesus "in high priestly categories" (565). But the logic depends on Jesus being presented not *as* a high priest but with a duty *as important* as theirs. Crispin H. T. Fletcher-Louis ("'Leave the Dead'") disagrees with Bockmuehl, claiming that Jesus was not calling for followers to enter a Nazirite vow (46–47). However, this misrepresents Bockmuehl's point, as Bockmuehl is arguing not that they become Nazirites but that Jesus's requirement is analogous to the piety expressed by one taking such a vow. Bockmuehl responds to Fletcher-Louis in "A Brief Clarification." However, on a different note, Fletcher-Louis ("'Leave the Dead,'" 51–56) justifiably argues that "dead" in the phrase "leave the dead" refers to those who are spiritually dead (see also Kister, "Leave the Dead"). Fletcher-Louis ("'Leave the Dead,'" 50–51) thus argues that Jesus's call in Luke 9:60 implies not a redefinition of Torah but a redefinition of the family to whom Torah applies. However, in light of Jesus's positive references to one's biological family as owed honor (Mark 7:8–13; 10:17–19; Matt. 19:19; Luke 18:20), Jesus does not redefine family disjunctively but subordinately. That is, Jesus still agrees that Torah requires honor toward one's biological parents. Thus, while allegiance to one's spiritual family may override what one owes to one's biological family when requirements compete, the deadness of the nonspiritual family does not negate the requirement to support them. Therefore, Jesus's instruction is not strictly a redefinition of family but a definition of the discipleship community as family that is prioritized over—but does not negate—the biological family when requirements compete. A relative can be dead spiritually (per Fletcher-Louis's reading of Luke 9:60) and still belong to one's biological family to whom one owes honor. Therefore, an argument explaining why the summons to follow Jesus is prioritized above the requirement to bury is still needed. Byron McCane's theory ("'Let the Dead'") that Luke 9:60/Matt. 8:21–22 may refer to "second burial" does not affect my argument. If "second burial," the transfer of the bones to an ossuary, were regarded as obligatory for honoring one's father, the shock of Jesus's claim still requires explanation. Indeed, McCane ("'Let the Dead,'" 42) offers his argument as further support of Hengel's position.

53. E. P. Sanders, *Jesus and Judaism*, 252.

54. E. P. Sanders, *Jesus and Judaism*, 253.

be dead (Luke 10:30–32).[55] Additionally, Sanders omits the very first line of the source he quotes (m. Nazir 7.1), which states, "A high priest and a Nazirite may not become impure for their relatives." Thus m. Nazir 7.1 maintains the opinion stated in Lev. 21:11, and so the potential analogy between Lev. 21:11 and Luke 9:60 is not affected by this text. If Jesus's statement operates within the analogous requirement of Lev. 21:11, it is a simple case of overrides. Just as the priest's duty in the temple overrides the obligation to bury his parents, so Jesus's duty, which is as important or more so, operates with the same override. At the level of legal reasoning, then, this is no different from any other case of an override. Yet in juxtaposing rabbinic statements to Jesus's, Sanders employs a double standard, leading to a misrepresentation of Jesus's relation to the Law.

Concerning the importance of burying the dead, for example, Sanders cites m. Ber. 3.1, which claims that burying the dead overrides the requirement to recite the Shema. Here Sanders concedes that one commandment overrides another, but he does not interpret this pejoratively as the rabbis "*consciously* requiring disobedience to God" as he does when describing Jesus's statement.[56] Rather, the rabbis are weighing the import of commandments when a conflict arises and claiming that one overrides the other. As a thorough student of Jewish legal literature, Sanders knows well that occasions arise when one commandment (deemed less important) will "consciously" be broken so that another commandment (deemed more important) can be kept, all in order to keep the Law. This point is exemplified in John 7: "Even on a Sabbath you circumcise a man. If a man receives circumcision on a Sabbath so that the Law of Moses will not be broken, are you angry at me because I made an entire man well on a Sabbath?" (7:22–23). Such "conscious" violations of a command are depicted more accurately as decisions made "so that the Law of Moses may not be broken" (7:23), and yet when interpreting the same legal reasoning in Luke 9:60, Sanders wrongly presents it as Jesus cavalierly requiring disobedience to God.[57]

Instead, when Jesus proclaims that heralding the kingdom of God is accompanied by the same rigors of the high priesthood, Jesus is weighing the importance of two conflicting duties and choosing the more urgent one so that God's will is done. Because the fate of the individual/nation depends on their response to Jesus's message, proclaiming it overrides the importance of other duties when they conflict. Importantly, following Jesus on this mission should

55. Admittedly, this point is debatable, as the victim is left "half dead" (Luke 10:30).
56. E. P. Sanders, *Jesus and Judaism*, 253.
57. E. P. Sanders, *Jesus and Judaism*, 253–54.

not be interpreted disjunctively with the Law or keeping the commandments. Like Matthew and Mark, Luke describes Jesus's mission as calling sinners "to repentance" (Luke 5:32), and he includes Law-keeping as the means to "life" (10:27–28; 18:18–22). Moreover, in the transfiguration (9:28–36), which immediately precedes this saying (9:60), God calls Jesus his "Son" and says, "Listen to him!" (9:35), alluding to Deut. 18:15,[58] where the people are told to listen to the prophet whom God would appoint. Consequently, listening to and obeying his requirements is itself obeying a commandment (Deut. 18:15). In the case of Luke 9:60, then, Jesus calls for the man to suspend one requirement, that of honoring/burying one's father, in order to keep another: listening to God's appointed prophet who summons him to another duty of higher import, that of proclaiming the kingdom. In this, Jesus's point is not unlike an opinion in Sifre Deuteronomy. Interpreting Deut. 18:15's command to "listen" to God's prophet, Sifre Deut. 175 states, "*Unto him shall you hearken*: Even if he tells you to disobey one of the commandments of the Torah in order to meet the needs of the hour, as did Elijah on Mount Carmel, hearken unto him."[59]

Jesus's mission, then, comes with at least the same prioritization as the work of the temple, and thus with the requirement to leave the burial of parents to others because his work of restoration is of a higher importance than the temple's work. This will be explored further below, but such a hierarchy does not reflect disdain for the temple. Rather, it is because the temple is subject to the same discipline as the people. When the people are under divine judgment, the temple is also under judgment and so cannot be the means of escaping that judgment and effecting restoration. Referring to the discipline resulting from nationwide transgression (2 Macc. 4:10–16; 7:32–38), 2 Macc. 5 illustrates the point: "But the Lord did not choose the nation for the sake of the holy place [the temple] but the place for the sake of the nation. Therefore the place itself shared in the misfortunes that befell the nation and afterward participated in its benefits" (5:19–20).

This passage summarizes a viewpoint expressed widely in the prophetic literature: the sacrifices presented in the temple are good, but they do not in themselves effect the restoration. To participate in the restoration, the people, including the priests, must repent, and if they do not, the people and the temple will be subject to judgment. For this reason, Jesus's preaching of the kingdom of God is of equal if not greater import than the work of the temple, and as such, it is authorized with a priority granted previously only

58. Fitzmyer, *Luke I–IX*, 803.

59. Translation by Hammer, *Sifre*, 202. My thanks to Isaac Paley for this reference.

to the high priest, whose duties were of such importance that he could not participate in the funeral rites even of his parents lest he be rendered incapable of completing his own commissioned office. With an import and urgency analogous to the work of the high priest, the preaching of the kingdom by Jesus and his followers requires the same devotion, and those who wish to follow him to herald the kingdom must leave the burying of the dead, even one's father, to others.

Importantly, the granting of such overrides/permissions to "violate" commandments in view of an important mission finds precedent in m. Rosh Hash. 1. The topic in this passage is establishing the calendar to regulate the proper timing of the offerings at the new moon (Num. 28:11–15) and the festivals. Because the Law dictates when festivals are to be held, the priests and the rest of Israel necessarily set a uniform calendar. Because the calendar followed the lunar cycles, the calendar and its festivals were set by observing the new moon. If one witnessed the new moon, one could travel to Jerusalem to testify regarding the observation, and approved messengers were sent to proclaim the festivals "in their times" (Lev. 23:4 AT) to Israel. Because of the importance of this mission, by which the sacrifices are regulated, those traveling to Jerusalem to testify were granted permission to "profane the Sabbath" to complete the mission of establishing the calendar. Mishnah Rosh Hash. 1.3–4 states:

> With respect to six New Moons messengers go forth: with respect to Nisan because of Passover; with respect to Av because of the Fast; with respect to Elul because of Rosh Hashanah; with respect to Tishre because of regulating the Festivals; with respect to Kislev because of Hanukkah; and with respect to Adar because of Purim. And when the Temple existed, one would go forth also with respect to Iyyar because of [the need to set] the Second Passover. With respect to two New Moons one may profane the Sabbath: with respect to Nisan and with respect to Tishre. Because on them messengers go forth to Syria and on them the festivals were regulated. And when the Temple existed, one would profane [the Sabbath] with respect to all of them, because of regulating the sacrifice.

The permitted profanations are then detailed: "If one saw the New Moon but cannot walk, they [may] bring him [on the Sabbath] on a donkey, even on a bed. If any lie in ambush for them, they [may] carry staves. And if it was a long way, they [may] carry food. For with respect to a journey of a night and a day one [may] profane the Sabbath and go forth to bring evidence of the New Moon, as it is said [Lev. 23:4] 'These are the set times of the Lord . . . which you shall declare each at its appointed time'" (m. Rosh Hash. 1.9). Thus the permission to profane the Sabbath is granted to those who travel to Jerusalem to testify concerning the new moon; those traveling from Jerusalem to proclaim the calendar to those distant from Jerusalem may also be granted this permission.[60] Three aspects should be noted.

First, accounting for common translations of Hebrew by Jewish Greek speakers, m. Rosh Hash. 1 corresponds lexicographically with related descriptions in Luke. In m. Rosh Hashanah, some travel to Jerusalem to "give testimony" (לְעֵדוּת), and then "messengers" are sent "to proclaim" (תִּקְרְאוּ) the calendar.[61] "Messengers" (הַשְּׁלוּחִין) derives from a term regularly translated by the LXX with forms of ἀποστέλλω[62] or ἀποστολή.[63] The related Hebrew terms for "testimony" and "proclaim" are often translated in the LXX by forms of μαρτύριον[64] and κηρύσσω,[65] respectively. Comparably, in Luke 9–10, Jesus "sent" (ἀπέστειλεν) the twelve apostles "to proclaim" (κηρύσσειν) "the kingdom of God" (9:2), and their actions serve as a "testimony" (μαρτύριον, 9:5; cp. Matt. 10:18). Moreover, m. Rosh Hash. 1.6 implies that the witnesses traveling to Jerusalem to give testimony travel in pairs, just as the apostles travel in Luke 10:1. My point is neither that Luke is dependent on m. Rosh Hashanah nor that these legal issues are identical. I am simply noting the legal logic of granting an override because of the importance of the mission itself and the (incidental?) overlap in terminology.

Second, somewhat exceptionally in the Mishnah, the passage twice distinguishes post-temple practice from that "when the temple was standing" (m. Rosh Hash. 1.3–4), suggesting that this was a known practice in the time of Jesus and the composition of the Gospels. Consequently, Jews familiar

60. Mishnah Rosh Hash. 1.3 states that for "six New Moons messengers go forth," referring to the approved messengers traveling from Jerusalem to proclaim the calendar. Then 1.4 begins, "On two months they may profane the Sabbath" (AT). Grammatically, the antecedent of "they" is the messengers of 1.3, but a new halakhic situation may be in view, in which case the referent of "they" may not be the "messengers" but those traveling to Jerusalem to give testimony However, 1.4 proceeds, "On Nisan and on Tishri because in these [months] messengers go forth to Syria" (AT), which is possibly read as granting the permission to the messengers leaving Jerusalem to proclaim the calendar. Rosh Hash. 21b in the Babylonian Talmud supports this interpretation, stating, "So too [Sabbath] may be desecrated [by the messengers] so that [the Festivals] may be observed. The verse states, 'Which you shall declare.' For the declaration [of the New Moon] you may desecrate [Sabbath]." (I am grateful to Oren Hayon for this reference.) However, t. Rosh Hash. 1.17 claims that R. Eleazar b. Ṣadoq said that "messengers go forth to Syria only when they have heard instructions from the court on the next day" (trans. Neusner, *Tosefta*). If they arrive on the Sabbath, this would mean they do not go out until the next day. It is not clear what would happen if they arrive on a Friday.

61. But see the preceding note.

62. E.g., Gen. 8:7; 19:13; Exod. 2:5; 3:10; Lev. 14:7; 16:10; Num. 13:2, 27; Deut. 1:22; 7:20.

63. Ps. 78:49 (77:49 LXX); Eccles. 8:8; Song 4:13; 1 Kings 5:14 (5:28 LXX).

64. Exod. 16:34; Lev. 16:13; 2 Kings 11:12; Pss. 78:5; 81:5 (77:5; 80:6 LXX); Isa. 8:2.

65. Gen. 41:43; Exod. 32:5; 2 Kings 10:20; 2 Chron. 20:3; Prov. 8:1; Mic. 3:5; Joel 1:14; Isa. 61:1.

with the practices and the legal permissions granted to those traveling to Jerusalem (and possibly to the messengers sent thereafter) may have recognized the halakhic reasoning operative in Luke 9:60: that Jesus's mission and demand to proclaim the kingdom is of such import that it overrides other duties.

Third, in m. Rosh Hashanah, nonpriests travel to Jerusalem to give testimony. The exemption allowing them to work on the Sabbath is predominantly granted only to priests. Because God requires priests to offer sacrifices daily, they must work on the Sabbath (e.g., Num. 28:9–10; Lev. 24:8). So the priests profane the Sabbath to do their commissioned duty. Significantly, m. Rosh Hashanah grants the permission to profane the Sabbath to nonpriests who give testimony regarding the new moon because of the overriding importance of establishing the calendar to regulate the sacrifice. Analogously, in Luke nonpriests—people who follow Jesus to give testimony regarding the kingdom and proclaim its arrival—are granted a permission/burden that was formerly held only by a priest: they leave the burial of their family to others. If one were to object, "But the nonpriests in m. Rosh Hashanah were granted this authority by Jerusalem!" or, "The high priest was granted this authority by God! By what authority does Jesus do these things?" then we may have stumbled upon the precise point of conflict narrated in the Gospels between Jesus and those who do not believe his claim to being God's divinely commissioned agent of an authorized mission.

So the argument that Jesus's point in Luke 9:60 is without precedent either in terms of the specific exemption (Lev. 21) or the halakhic reasoning (m. Rosh Hashanah) is contradicted by the evidence. When Jesus does express freedom from a commandment/custom, it should not be presented as Jesus provocatively demonstrating his freedom from the Law, abolishing the Law, or making redundant Israel's symbols. Rather, it is a matter of one duty overriding another one due to urgency and divine commissioning. And importantly, Jesus's requirement in Luke 9:60 is built not on the supposition that Jesus or his followers are high priests but on the claim that their responsibilities are equally urgent. Commissioned by God to herald God's reign, on the basis of which one either participates in the restoration or perishes, Jesus understands the import and urgency of his mission to grant him and his followers exemptions formerly given only to the high priest.

In keeping with my goal to address passages from which interpreters have routinely inferred Jesus's break from the Law, I now turn to a comparable legal argument in Matt. 12.

Matthew 12:1–8: "The Son of Man Is Lord of the Sabbath"

While traveling to a synagogue on the Sabbath, the disciples pluck grain, and Pharisees accuse them of transgression. In Matthew, this scene occurs immediately after Jesus's declaration that he will "give rest" (ἀναπαύσω) to all the burdened who come to him (11:28).[66] As Oliver notes, "Matthew also ascribes an eschatological dimension to the notion of rest mentioned in 11:25–30. This should come as no surprise since several Second Temple sources express a yearning for collective eschatological restoration couched in primordial language stemming from the establishment of the Sabbath at creation."[67] With Matt. 11:25–30 likely serving as an introduction to the Sabbath controversies of 12:1–14,[68] the subsequent Sabbath disputes "exemplify in concrete circumstances how the notion of eschatological rest plays out in the daily lives of Jesus and his followers."[69] As this section will show, on the basis of his status as the Son of Man authorized to inaugurate this eschatological "rest," Jesus argues that he and his coworkers enjoy overrides that permit them to profane the Sabbath when engaged in their mission, not because the Sabbath is abrogated but because, for Jesus and his disciples, keeping it is subordinated to their duty to preach the kingdom of God and perform the signs of its inbreaking (i.e., healing).[70] The controversy of my present focus (Matt. 12:1–8) unfolds as follows:

> At that time Jesus went through the grainfields on the Sabbath, and his disciples became hungry and began to pick the heads of grain and eat. Now when the Pharisees saw this, they said to him, "Look, your disciples do what is not lawful to do on a Sabbath!" But he said to them, "Have you not read what David did when he became hungry, he and his companions—how he entered the house of God, and they ate the consecrated bread, which was not lawful for him to eat, nor for those with him, but for the priests alone? Or have you not read in the Law that on the Sabbath the priests in the temple profane the Sabbath, and yet are innocent? But I say to you that something greater than the temple is here. But if you had known what this means: 'I desire mercy and not sacrifice,' you would not have condemned the innocent. For the Son of Man is Lord of the Sabbath."[71]

66. For a detailed study of the "rest" motif in the NT, see Laansma, *I Will Give You Rest*. Matthias Konradt ("'Nehmt auf euch mein Joch,'" 24) does not deny that coming to Jesus entails following his legal instruction, but he highlights Jesus's "yoke" as his benevolent messianic rule.

67. Oliver, *Torah Praxis*, 86, citing 2 En. 33.1–2; LAE 51.2; Heb. 4; Isa. 66:23.

68. See Yang, *Jesus and the Sabbath*, 141–61; Oliver, *Torah Praxis*, 81.

69. Oliver, *Torah Praxis*, 86.

70. See also Sigal, *Halakhah of Jesus*, 122.

71. NASB with modifications.

France exemplifies a "pattern of religions" interpretation of this dispute, in which Jesus disagrees with the Pharisaic interpretation of the Law generally and the Sabbath particularly, and thus denies that he and his disciples have broken it at all. Because Jesus quotes Hosea 6:6 in his defense (Matt. 12:7), and because it is the second use of this verse by Jesus (cp. Matt. 9:13), France justifiably interprets Matt. 12's scenario in conjunction with the former conflict in Matt. 9. There Jesus defends his practice of dining with sinners by quoting Hosea 6:6 ("I desire mercy and not sacrifice," AT) because they, as the "sick," are in need of a physician. France comments, "The principle [of mercy over sacrifice] is applied here not to sacrifice as such . . . but to the Pharisees' preoccupation with ritual purity, which overrides concern for those in need."[72] Ignoring for the moment that this conflict is not about ritual purity but the Pharisaic concern that Jesus endorses the sinners as sinners,[73] France proceeds to relate Jesus's dining with sinners to the subsequent question about Jesus and his disciples not fasting like the disciples of John and the Pharisees (Matt. 9:14–15). For France, recall, Jesus's feasting indicates "a fundamental incompatibility between the dry formality of existing religious traditions and an exuberant vitality in the Jesus circle."[74] Taking Matt. 9:10–17 to contextualize 12:1–8, France says of the latter: "The basic prophetic principle . . . justifies Jesus' less formal approach to Sabbath observance. Hosea 6:6 has already been quoted against the Pharisees in 9:13 when they objected to Jesus' loose attitude to the purity laws. . . . Here the specific issue is different, but the principle is the same: in God's scale of priorities a positive concern for the good of others ('mercy') takes precedence over formal compliance with ritual regulations."[75] Thus, France's interpretations characterize the difference between Jesus and the Pharisees in noneschatological, "pattern of religion" distinctions. The Pharisees are formalistic and dry; Jesus is new, lively, and joyous.

Jesus's dining with sinners, not fasting, and the parable of the wineskins have already been discussed. Turning, then, to France's interpretation of Matt. 12, it is vital to note that Jesus does not think the Pharisees' interpretation of the Sabbath is wrong. Jesus concedes that his disciples have broken the Sabbath. His examples demonstrate cases where someone broke the Law in permissible ways. David broke temple law. The priests profane the Sabbath and yet are innocent. These examples require grasping that David and the

72. France, *Matthew*, 354.
73. So also Oliver, *Torah Praxis*, 97n61.
74. France, *Matthew*, 351.
75. France, *Matthew*, 461.

priests have in fact "violated" the Law, but they show that in some cases violations are permitted.

The juxtaposition of Matt. 12 to Matt. 9's conflict is relevant. There Jesus's distinct practices evince not an alternative "pattern of religion" but a conviction that the time of God's restoration is now, warranting dining with sinners. Here too the disciples' profanation of the Sabbath expresses not an alternative interpretation of the Sabbath law in a noneschatological sense, but Jesus's conviction that their work of heralding the kingdom is "greater than the temple"; consequently, they are permitted to violate temple law and Sabbath law when doing the work necessary for its proclamation. In this case, they are permitted to satisfy hunger while en route to the synagogue to "proclaim the kingdom of God" and heal. Conceding that his disciples have violated the Sabbath, he defends their actions by referring to examples in which commissioned figures were permitted to violate temple and Sabbath law to fulfill needs or obligations experienced during their time of duty. Because Jesus is the Son of Man, commissioned to inaugurate God's restored mercy, he and his disciples may violate the Sabbath innocently when doing their required work. Now back to Matt. 12.

While journeying on the Sabbath to the synagogue, a customary site of Jesus's teaching about the reign of God (Matt. 4:23; 9:35), the disciples pluck heads of grain, and Pharisees call it out: they are doing what is not permitted on the Sabbath.[76] In this case, the plucking is the prohibited action, possibly viewed as harvesting.[77] Jesus does not think the Pharisees' accusation is wrong. Rather, he employs defenses that highlight someone having broken a commandment to show that overriding situations exist.

Significantly, Matthew highlights the disciples' hunger (12:1), which probably refers not to a hobbit-like hunger for "second breakfast" but to being famished. Matthew employs the same term referring to Jesus's hunger after his forty-day fast (4:2).[78] That their hunger is not incidental to the narrative is

76. Scholars debate whether this or some other act (e.g., transgressing the limits of permissible travel on the Sabbath) constituted the transgression. For discussion of the latter, see Doering, "'Much Ado about Nothing?'"; Doering, "Sabbath Laws." For reasons discussed in, e.g., Banks, *Jesus and the Law*, 114; Doering, "Sabbath Laws," 214; and Oliver, *Torah Praxis*, 87–91, and in view of Matthew's exposition and Jesus's defense revolving around hunger/eating, the infringement was probably plucking grain.

77. Eating is not only permissible on Sabbath but widely regarded as best practice. Fasting is what some regard as prohibited (Jub. 2.21, 29; 50.9–10, 13; Jdt. 8:6; 10:2; 2 Macc. 8:27; implicitly: Josephus, *Life* 279; see also CD 2.4). Though the biblical law does not itself proscribe "plucking," it implies one ought not "harvest" (Exod. 34:21) or "gather food" (Exod. 16:23–29; 20:8–11; cp. Philo, *Life of Moses* 2.22).

78. The LXX uses the term to describe severe hunger (Gen. 41:55; Deut. 25:18; Ps. 107:5; Isa. 8:21).

suggested by Jesus referring to an event wherein he names hunger as justification for breaking a command:[79] "Have you not read what David did, when he became hungry, he and his companions . . . ?" (12:3).

Jesus here recalls 1 Sam. 21. David's "hunger" is not mentioned there, but it is evidently assumed by Jesus. This interpretation was possibly traditional, as it is recorded also in the Jerusalem Talmud, which states that David was so hungry that he ate all twelve loaves.[80] Moreover, this talmudic passage is based on a ruling in the Mishnah, which claims that one may feed impure (*qua* prohibited) food to a person who is "ravenous" (m. Yoma 8.6). Jesus appeals to David and his men's extreme hunger and their eating bread permitted only to the priests to justify an action otherwise prohibited by law. David broke temple law to satisfy hunger, but this example applies to Matt. 12's accusation of Sabbath violation only if a hierarchy in legal observance exists. At best, this Davidic episode shows that one may violate some prohibitions in case of extreme hunger, but it does not yet clarify that Sabbath law is one such case. Consequently, Jesus needs to prove the hierarchy of temple over Sabbath, which would prove that their hunger overrode Sabbath. Hence his next example.

"Or have you not read in the Law that on the Sabbath the priests in the temple profane the Sabbath, and yet are innocent?" (Matt. 12:5 AT). According to Num. 28:9–10 and Lev. 24:8, priests are commanded to present various offerings on the Sabbath. Therefore, priests work in the temple on the Sabbath and profane it innocently, temple law thus overriding Sabbath law.[81] If David's hunger overrides temple law, and temple law overrides Sabbath law, then extreme hunger that overrides temple law also overrides Sabbath law, and Jesus's disciples can pluck grain to satisfy extreme hunger. It seems like the case should be closed![82]

However, if Jesus were simply arguing that hunger overrides temple law and thus also Sabbath law, then at this juncture the Pharisees could reasonably object that the Davidic and priestly examples do not serve his argument, because David and the priests were doing work necessary for their responsibility. David claims that he was "commanded" (ἐντέταλται) by the king (1 Sam. 21:2 [21:3 LXX]), and the priests were "commanded" (ἔντειλαι) by God (Lev. 24:2). Because Jesus and his disciples are not doing commissioned work, the

79. So also Oliver, *Torah Praxis*, 93n50. But with Oliver (94n52), and contra Luz (*Matthew 8–20*, 181), their hunger need not be regarded as "life-threatening."

80. See y. Yoma 8.5 (2). This reference is cited in Kister, "Plucking."

81. Sigal, *Halakhah of Jesus*, 132.

82. Up to this point, I basically follow Kister ("Plucking") and Thiessen (*Forces of Death*, 155–62).

Pharisees could contend that they should have stayed at home and procured food another way. Jesus must therefore argue that his work is commissioned and that such commissioned work is at least on par with the temple. Hence his following statement.

"But I say to you that something greater [μεῖζον] than the temple is here" (Matt. 12:6). The word "greater" is neuter here, indicating that it does not refer directly to Jesus, but relevance for his argument requires that it involve him and his disciples. The "greater" thing may be "mercy" (also neuter), but this obfuscates the logic of his argument since the mercy in question would then be the need of the Pharisees to show mercy, whereas Jesus concludes the argument logically with reference to himself as "the Son of Man" (12:8). I think that what is "greater than the temple" refers to the activity of Jesus and the disciples, specifically their ministry of heralding the restoration. This and the work necessary for it are greater than the temple. Effort necessary to complete this work, even if it results in Sabbath violation, is permissible in the same way that priests who work in the temple may profane the Sabbath and yet be innocent. That is, Jesus argues from lesser to greater: if priests can profane the Sabbath to do commanded work in the temple, and if Jesus's commanded work is greater than the temple, then Jesus's work and the effort necessary to complete it likewise permit Sabbath profanation. Therefore, they are profaning the Sabbath, but innocently.[83]

The idea that what is "greater" refers to Jesus's heralding the kingdom is supported by a proximate comparable saying. When asked for a sign that he is commissioned by God, Jesus responds: "The men of Nineveh . . . will condemn [this generation] because they repented at the preaching [τὸ κήρυγμα] of Jonah; and behold, something greater than Jonah is here" (Matt. 12:41). Here too the adjective "greater" is neuter and thus likely refers not to Jonah but to his "preaching" (κήρυγμα), a neuter noun, such that Jesus says, in effect: "Something greater than the message of Jonah is here." Given the adjacent, comparable context, Jesus is likely referring to his work of "preaching" (κηρύσσων) the approach of God's kingdom as greater than the temple.[84] This

83. Oliver (*Torah Praxis*, 96–97) comes close to this interpretation by tying the mercy to "the message and mission of Jesus." However, he then aligns this mercy with "a more gracious disposition" in one's Sabbath halakhah (99). I do not want to rule out the latter, but because "mercy" is logically connected to the Son of Man's mission and based on the majority of Matthew's other usages of "mercy" (see below), I align "mercy" with Christ's eschatological activity. But Oliver is right to conclude that "Matthew's effort in multiplying justifications for this 'transgressive' act . . . reveals his ongoing concern for Sabbath keeping" (99).

84. Alternatively, it may be that 12:6's elided neuter is ἔργον (labor)—i.e., a labor greater than that done in the temple is here. Jesus is referring to labor forbidden on the Sabbath, which Exod. 23:12 names τὰ ἔργα, and the Law describes the Levites' tabernacle labor as their "working"

is supported by two Matthean editorial claims: that Jesus frequented the synagogues, to which he is en route in this episode (12:9), to "preach [κηρύσσων] the gospel of the kingdom [of God]" (4:23; 9:35). While the "kingdom" or "restoration" may be greater than the temple, in context Jesus refers more specifically to his work of proclaiming it, because for that reason he was sent.[85] Because that responsibility is greater than work done in the temple, proving that work necessary to the temple permits Sabbath violation likewise absolves Jesus and his disciples when they expend effort necessary for their divinely commissioned task on the Sabbath.[86]

Jesus proceeds, "But if you had known what this means, 'I desire mercy and not sacrifice,' you would not have condemned the innocent" (Matt. 12:7 AT). I suggest that "mercy and not sacrifice" signifies not just in general that meeting human needs takes precedence over ritual (true as that may be) but more specifically that the work of heralding Israel's restoration ("mercy") overrides the work done in the temple and therefore the Sabbath as well. Three points support this.

First, in Matt. 9:13 Jesus employs Hosea 6:6 not to justify welfare deeds overriding Sabbath/temple/ritual but to justify his ministry as Israel's "healer," calling sinners to repentance. There "mercy and not sacrifice" justifies his meeting not general human need (these sinners were not starving) but their eschatological need (calling them to repent). Significantly, Matt. 9's use of Hosea 6 is presented as hermeneutically determinative for the second occurrence: in Matt. 9:13 Jesus says, "Go and learn what this means," and in Matt. 12:7 he says, "If you had learned what this means . . ." (AT). The restoration-eschatological context of Matt. 9 should therefore inform our reading of Matt. 12.

Second, the next verse states, "For [γάρ] the Son of Man is Lord of the Sabbath" (Matt. 12:8), describing his declaration about the Son of Man as the logical basis of his claim regarding mercy and sacrifice. If Jesus's point is simply that human need overrides ritual, and if this is derivable from Hosea 6 itself, it is unclear how this is supported by Jesus's concluding assertion. Some circumvent this criticism by saying that here "son of man" is euphemistic for "humans" and that Jesus is saying, "Human needs take precedence over the

---

its "works" (ἐργάζεσθαι τὰ ἔργα, Num. 3:7). Jesus could therefore be referring to his "labor" of preaching as greater than the "labor" of the temple.

85. Matt. 4:17; 9:13; 10:1–14 in conjunction with 10:40; 15:24; cp. Luke 4:43; Mark 1:38.

86. *Pace* Yang (*Jesus and the Sabbath*, 180), who denies the lesser-to-greater nature of Jesus's legal reasoning because "the disciples were neither engaged in any religious practice nor in direct service to Jesus by plucking the grain." Such "religious" activity—in my view, proclaiming the kingdom of God—is precisely what Jesus and the disciples are en route to do. See the discussion of the related parallel in m. Rosh Hashanah below.

Sabbath."[87] But in Matthew, Jesus uses the title "Son of Man" some twenty-seven times apart from 12:8, and arguably all of these are self-identification.[88] Moreover, each arguably refers to his authority *qua* Son of Man to act as God's commissioned agent of the restoration. The Son of Man effects the eschatological gathering (13:41); came to give his life as a ransom (20:28); will be enthroned at God's right hand (26:64); and will judge and reign in the kingdom (16:28; 19:28; 25:31). Likewise in Matt. 12, he is the Son of Man commissioned to herald the kingdom, and work he completes in pursuit of this mission takes precedence over the Sabbath.[89]

Third, if Jesus's point is simply that "human need" overrides Sabbath, the priest example does not help, as the priests are not satisfying human need. They are, however, doing work necessary for their commissioning. Granted, if the argument is only about human need overriding the Sabbath, then the reference to the priests could simply prove that temple overrides Sabbath; however, he claims that the priests are "innocent" in their Sabbath profanation (Matt. 12:5), and he aligns the priestly innocence with that of Jesus and the disciples (12:7), suggesting that the disciples' innocence is based on the same legitimating factor: they are also doing commissioned work. In this sense, Jesus's reasoning is analogous to an opinion expressed in rabbinic literature that one engaged in a mission/commandment is exempt from other commandments that might interfere with that mission. Though it is considerably later, Num. Rab. 16.1 succinctly expresses the logic: "However, one who sets out for a matter of commandment/duty [mitzva], it is permitted for him to set out any day that he wishes. Why? It is because he set out for a matter of mitzva; one who sets out for a matter of mitzva overrides Shabbat."[90]

Notably, if "I desire mercy and not sacrifice" justifies Jesus's claim that heralding the restoration is of greater import than temple work, this entails

87. E.g., Sigal, *Halakhah of Jesus*, 132; see also 234n74 for additional bibliography.

88. Matt. 8:20; 9:6; 10:23; 11:19; 12:32, 40; 13:37, 41; 16:13, 28; 17:12, 22; 19:28; 20:18, 28; 24:27, 30, 37, 39, 44; 25:31; 26:2, 24, 45, 64. That Matt. 9:6, "The Son of Man has authority . . . to forgive sins," refers specifically to Jesus is not negated by Matt. 9:8, "They marveled that God gave such authority to humans." When someone jumps high and people say, "I didn't know humans could jump so high," they're not naming something that all humans can do but something that this member of the class of "humans" can do (analogy original to Logan Williams).

89. For a related argument that Jesus's messianic authority conditions his reasoning, see Boyarin, *Jewish Gospels*, 59–70.

90. Noted by Sigal (*Halakhah of Jesus*, 133) as reasoning that Matt. 12 could have employed but did not. Though Numbers Rabbah is considerably later, a comparable opinion relating to the (non)obligation to sleep in a sukkah (booth) for one engaged in a required duty is recorded in m. Sukkah 2.4. See also b. Sukkah 26a, reporting the dictum of Rabbi Yose haGelili (2nd cent. CE): "One who is engaged in a mitzva is exempt from another mitzva." See also discussion of m. Rosh Hashanah above and below, which claims to describe pre-70 CE practice.

taking "mercy" to signify "restoration" and the work necessary for it. This is easily supported. Dozens of texts use "mercy" metonymically to refer to God's act of restoration.[91] For example, Deut. 30:3 claims that when Israel returns, "God will restore you from captivity, and have mercy on you [ἐλεήσει σε]." Hosea characteristically describes God's restorative act as the return of his mercy. In Hosea 1:6, God tells Hosea to name the child "No Mercy" (Οὐκ-ἠλεημένη) because God will not have mercy (οὐ μὴ προσθήσω ἔτι ἐλεῆσαι) on Israel; but in the restoration, God says, "I will also have mercy [ἐλεήσω] on her who had not obtained mercy" (2:23 [2:25 LXX]).

In each reference listed in the notes below, the word "mercy" signals the return of God's mercy after Israel's punishment.[92] But most refer to God's act of mercy, not the human acts of doing mercy, which makes the use of Hosea in Matthew especially telling. As far as I know, Hosea is unique in claiming that Israel experiences the withdrawal of divine "mercy" for not doing "mercy" and, conversely, that Israel participates in the restoration of divine "mercy" by doing "mercy."

Hosea laments that there is no mercy in the land (4:1) and that Israel's mercy fades (6:4 LXX). In the latter context, God desires "mercy and not sacrifice" (6:6 AT). And Hosea 12 urges the people to "return to your God," thereby participating in the restoration, by doing mercy: "Return to your God: do mercy and justice" (12:6 AT [12:7 LXX]). Thus, according to Hosea, one participates in the future bestowal of God's mercy by "doing mercy." Or in Jesus's idiom in Matt. 5:7, "Blessed are the merciful [οἱ ἐλεήμονες], for they will receive mercy [ἐλεηθήσονται]."

Additionally, Matt. 9:13's use of Hosea 6:6 justifies his calling sinners and acting as Israel's physician (Matt. 9:12–13), suggesting that "mercy" refers to God's eschatological expectation that mercy be enacted toward those in need. After this scene, in which Jesus tells them to "learn what this [Hosea 6:6] means," Matthew most frequently uses "mercy" to refer to Jesus's healing, exorcising, and forgiving—actions testifying that the restoration is inbreaking and that Jesus is "the expected one" who effects it (Matt. 11:3–5). For example, on two occasions blind men cry out, "Have mercy on us," and he heals them (9:27; 20:30–31). A man calls, "Have mercy on my son," and Jesus

91. Deut. 30:3; Pss. 77:8; 85:7, 10; 98:3; 106:45; 130:7; 136:25 (76:9; 84:8, 11; 97:3; 105:45; 129:7; 135:24 LXX); Isa. 12:1–6; 14:1–3; 30:18–19; 33:2; 44:22–23; 45:8; 49:10, 13; 52:8–9; 54:7–8, 10; 55:7; 56:1; 60:10; 63:7, 15; [negatively: 59:2]; Jer. 12:15; 30:18 (37:18 LXX); 31:20 (38:20 LXX); 33:1–13 (40:1–13 LXX); Lam. 3:32; Ezek. 39:25; Dan. 9:9, 18; Amos 5:15; Hosea 1:6–7; 1:10 (2:1 MT/LXX); 2:23 (2:25 MT/LXX); Mic. 7:18–20; Ezra 9:9; Zech. 1:12–17; Bar. 3:2; Tob. 13:5, 10; 14:5; Jdt. 7:30; 1 Macc. 3:44; 2 Macc. 2:18; 7:37; 8:3, 5; 11:10; 3 Macc. 2:19; Sir. 35:23–36:1; 50:24; Pss. Sol. 8.27–28; 11.9; 18.5, 9; Matt. 5:7; Luke 1:54, 72, 78.

92. Some are negative examples claiming punishment is the divine withdrawal of mercy.

exorcises and heals the son (17:15). In a parable, forgiveness of sins is labeled as "mercy" (18:33). Most significantly, in Matt. 15 a non-Jewish woman cries for mercy on behalf of her daughter (15:22), but Jesus responds by saying that he was sent "to the lost sheep of the house of Israel" (15:24). This strongly suggests that Matthew presents Jesus's acts of mercy as acts of restoring Israel, since responding to a request for mercy by claiming "I was sent for Israel" would be a non sequitur unless Matthew depicts such mercy as Jesus's acts of restoring the nation. Therefore, it accords with Matthew's wider usage to interpret the claim that God wants "mercy and not sacrifice" to indicate that the eschatological need for the work of mercy overrides otherwise good and God-given commands ("sacrifice").

Thus, in both Hosea and Matthew, "mercy" refers to (a) God's act of restoration and (b) the human acts of mercy required to participate in that restoration. Because Jesus and his disciples perform this mercy in heralding the arrival of God's mercy, they are permitted to profane the Sabbath because they are doing the ministry of restoration, whose work overrides the temple and thus the Sabbath. Therefore, they do profane the Sabbath, but because they are doing the commissioned work of heralding God's mercy, they do so innocently.

Once more, the halakhic reasoning on display in Matt. 12 is analogous to that of m. Rosh Hash. 1.[93] There, witnesses traveling to Jerusalem to regulate the sacrifice were permitted to profane the Sabbath due to the overriding import of sacrifice. In that regard, because sacrifice is greater than Sabbath, nonpriestly witnesses were authorized to profane the Sabbath to complete their commissioned task, ultimately assisting in the proclamation of the calendar. The Sabbath profanations permitted were carrying a witness who could not walk, carrying weapons for self-defense, and carrying food in case their journey was long. Thus, according to m. Rosh Hash. 1.9, hunger experienced during the execution of their commissioned task permitted Sabbath profanation due to the overriding import of their mission. Likewise, in the episode preceding this Sabbath controversy in Matt. 12, Jesus commissioned his messengers and sent them to announce the arrival of God's reign (10:1–7). Moreover, they were told not to carry food because they were to eat from the tables of those who received them (10:8–11). Matthew 11:20–24 then indicates that many cities had not accepted Jesus's message (so the disciples may be quite hungry!). Now, reunited with their master, the disciples are still on their mission, abroad, and en route to a synagogue to herald the kingdom.[94]

93. Once again, I am not claiming intertextual dependence. Rather, I am highlighting the congruity of legal reasoning shared by these passages.

94. Note that Matt. 12:1 begins with "at that time," connecting this episode with the instructions and fulfillment of the mission to herald the kingdom in Matt. 10–11, noted also by

Hungry from all this travel, they pluck grains to eat, and Jesus permits their Sabbath profanation so they can eat to satisfy hunger. The legal logic may be presented so:

- Mishnah Rosh Hash. 1.3–5, 9: Sacrifice is greater than Sabbath. Thus, witnesses commissioned to testify for the calendar to regulate sacrifice may profane the Sabbath to eat when traveling for their duty.
- Matthew 12:1–8: Temple law is greater than Sabbath, permitting commissioned priests to profane the Sabbath. The mission of Jesus and the disciples is even greater than the temple/sacrifice. Thus, as heralds commissioned to announce the kingdom of God, they may profane the Sabbath to eat when traveling for their duty.

This interpretation has numerous benefits. First, it explains why Jesus proceeds beyond the Davidic example, which would suffice were he simply arguing that human need overrides other concerns. Second, it aligns his innocence with that of the priests. If Jesus simply argues for the permissibility of satisfying hunger, this priest example is less relevant, since the priests are not satisfying hunger but performing obligatory work. But since Jesus and his disciples are doing commissioned work, their innocence aligns with that of the priests, who profane the Sabbath innocently while doing their work. Third, this kind of legal defense clarifies subsequent questions about Jesus's authority, because his legal logic depends on his claim that something greater than the temple is present. If one doubted that, one could question his innocence, which explains why subsequent episodes heighten disputes about Jesus's identity. *By whom does he exorcise demons? Show us a sign! By what authority do you do these things?* Fourth, it interprets "mercy" in ways that resonate with both Hosea and Matthew to refer, not generically to noneschatological human needs, but specifically to the restoration and the work necessary to inaugurate and participate in it. Finally, it suggests that the halakhic difference between the Pharisees and Jesus does not map onto a "patterns of religion" frame of "rigid Pharisees" versus "lax Jesus" but is rather a distinction in recognizing the eschatological time: Pharisees do not accept his eschatological claims and so do not accept his halakhic practices,

---

Sigal, *Halakhah of Jesus*, 122: "The mission is the act of bringing the Kingdom and is parallel to the Temple, and even greater. . . . Therefore, in the service of the Kingdom (the Temple) the Sabbath is a secondary consideration. . . . 'At that time' reverts to the mission (Mt. 10–11). When Jesus defends his disciples he is alluding to more halakhah than is evident in the text, all of which is designed to argue for a sabbath exemption."

while Jesus asserts that God's reign is at hand and thereby adjusts his halakhic barometer accordingly.

Jesus's Authority and Eschatological Nomism

In some of the above examples—requiring the man to neglect burial of his father, defending the disciples' Sabbath profanation—the legitimacy of Jesus's legal arguments depends on the truthfulness of his claim to be the commissioned Son of Man who proclaims God's kingdom. If he truly is authorized by God, then his legal practice is acceptable, given the overriding import of his mission. However, if he is an impostor, acting not on God's authority but on his own, then he is transgressing and, worse, is leading others to transgress. Because crowds are following him in droves, his actions—if not divinely authorized—may well be leading the nation astray (Luke 23:2), causing a great deception of the people (Matt. 27:64). But according to the Gospels, Jesus keeps the Law, provides its authoritative interpretation, and "breaks" a given commandment only when the import of another duty—proclaiming the kingdom of God—competes with his duty to keep a given commandment, in which case his mission overrides the commandment. In the latter event, a given "violation" is not actual transgression but is akin to a priest "profaning" the Sabbath to keep his commissioned duty of offering sacrifices daily. But one would only concede the acceptability of Jesus's legal practice if one granted his authorized status as the herald/executor of the restoration. And how is such authority to be proved? The priests have the benefit of a publicly recognized office and written laws proving their "innocence" when they "profane the Sabbath" to offer sacrifices. Jesus, in many ways, does not. He can apply written texts to himself (see, e.g., Luke 4:21), but such is mere assertion. He can perform works of power, but how does one know they are from God and not from some other being?

Consider a modern analogy. Running a red light is normally a violation of law. But if one is driving an ambulance en route to the hospital, such action is legally permissible because of the urgency of the situation. However, the ambulance has the advantage of being visibly recognized as an ambulance. When an unmarked car runs a red light, its claim for urgency must be defended, and a driver who cannot prove that the situation is urgent would likely receive a ticket. Thus the same action—running a red light—is permissible for a driver whose authority is recognized but transgressive for another who is unauthorized.

The legitimacy of Jesus's practice depending on the truthfulness of his eschatological claims provides a meaningful framework for the many controversies that ensue, many of which revolve around his identity. Take, for example, his exorcisms: rather than deny the efficacy of his actions, the question becomes whether he performs these actions by the power of demons or of God (Matt. 12:22–45). Having exorcised one possessed, the crowds murmur, "This man cannot be the Son of David, can he?" (12:23). They took his power to indicate a royal or messianic status. But the Pharisees said, "This man casts out demons only by Beelzebul the ruler of the demons" (12:24). Jesus's answer is telling: Satan would not cast out Satan, for then his own kingdom would fall (12:25–26), "but if I cast out demons by the Spirit of God, then the kingdom of God has come upon you" (12:28). If Jesus's authority comes from the divine Spirit, it vindicates his message that God's kingdom is truly irrupting through his works. Recognizing what is at stake, the scribes and Pharisees ask for a sign to verify his status as one commissioned by God (12:38). Jesus then flips the implicit accusation, naming them as members of "an evil and adulterous generation" (12:39) who seek a sign. Notably, when his legal or exorcistic practice relies on claims about his identity and mission, explosive controversy ensues. Because the crowds hang on his words and deeds, what is at stake is not simply whether he is a transgressor but whether he is divinely commissioned: Does he work by the power of Satan or of God? Is he leading the nation toward restoration or away from God's paths?

Within this framework, an interesting pattern emerges. In several instances, Jesus's legal practices do not hinge on his eschatological identity. For example, his defense of healing the man with "dropsy" is not based on his eschatological authority. Rather, it hinges on an analogy with the presumably accepted practice of extracting one's ox or son from a well (Luke 14:1–6), and it results in no plot to kill Jesus or questioning of his authority. His defense of his disciples' not washing their hands (Mark 7:1–23; Matt. 15:1–20) is based not on his identity but on his purity halakhah, and it results in the Pharisees being "offended" (Matt. 15:12), but they neither question his authority nor plot to kill him. Jesus's saying about cup washing similarly does not depend on his divine authority, nor does it result in the desire to arrest or kill him.[95] Similarly, after his opponents have already decided that he must be arrested due to his actions in the temple, they pepper him with nomistic questions regarding taxes, marriage in the resurrection, and the greatest commandment (Mark 12:13–34 and par.). None of his answers depend on his eschatological identity, and no one responds with an outcry.

95. Luke's account eventually says that they became hostile to him (11:53), but that results from his accusation that they reject God's prophets (11:47–51), not their cup-washing practices.

However, when his or his disciples' practices of dining with sinners, forgiving sins, not fasting, and plucking on the Sabbath depend on Jesus's claim to be Israel's healer, the authorized Son of Man, and the bridegroom, then controversy ensues, and subsequent nomistic debates sometimes function as controversies occasioned by doubts concerning such identity claims. The sequence in Mark 2:1–3:6 is telling: scribes accuse him of blaspheming because he forgave sins, which he justifies by claiming that he is the authorized Son of Man (2:10);[96] scribes and Pharisees question him about eating with sinners, which he justifies by claiming to be Israel's healer (2:17); they question him about his disciples not fasting, which he justifies by claiming that he is the bridegroom (2:19); they question him about plucking on the Sabbath, which he justifies by asserting that the Son of Man is Lord of the Sabbath (2:28). Immediately following this sequence, they watch Jesus to see whether he will heal the man with the withered hand on the Sabbath (3:1–6). This sequence of precisely these controversies followed by that Sabbath healing is preserved in Luke 5:17–6:11 and in Matt. 9:1–17 and 12:1–14. In each, the questionable practices are justified by asserting a divine authorization; only after such claims do the scribes and Pharisees "watch him closely" to "see if he would heal . . . on the Sabbath, so that they might accuse him" (Mark 3:2; see Luke 6:7; Matt. 12:10). The latter healing controversy, then, is seemingly generated due to preexisting doubt about Jesus's eschatological identity claims raised in the immediately preceding episodes. Though his healing of the man with the withered hand (Mark 3:1; Luke 6:6; Matt. 12:10) is based on his interpretation of the Sabbath legislation itself and does not necessarily depend on any eschatological claims, it serves to confirm their doubts that were occasioned on other grounds. We see, then, three categories of controversy:

96. Space precludes thorough examination of Jesus "forgiving sins" (Mark 2:10 and par.), but in short, Jesus's claim that the Son of Man has authority "to forgive sins on the land" (ἀφιέναι ἁμαρτίας ἐπὶ τῆς γῆς, Mark 2:10 AT) alludes to Lev. 25:10, which states that in the Jubilee they ought to proclaim "release [= forgiveness] in the land" (ἄφεσιν ἐπὶ τῆς γῆς, Lev. 25:10 AT). As Dan. 7's Son of Man, who has received authority (7:13, 14), and as the one anointed by the Spirit (Mark 1:10) to do the work of Isa. 61:1, who is to "proclaim release/forgiveness to the captives" (AT, κηρύξαι αἰχμαλώτοις ἄφεσιν), Jesus is characterized as someone divinely authorized to enact the eschatological Jubilee, an enactment that employs Lev. 25:10's announcement of "release" eschatologically to refer to the release/forgiveness of sins. Notably, he pronounces such forgiveness only upon "seeing their faith" (Mark 2:5). When such faith is lacking, which transpires as the narrative continues, Jesus utilizes a different method from the Jubilee legislation to effect the same release—namely, paying the "ransom" (Lev. 25:51–52; cp. Mark 10:45). On the relation of Jesus's announcement of forgiveness early in the narrative to his subsequent death as ransom, see "Ransoming the Captives" in chap. 6 below and the notes there. On the above interpretation of Mark and the Jubilee, see Williams, "Melchizedek."

1. Noneschatological nomistic disputes: legal practices based simply on Jesus's alternative interpretation of legal texts (e.g., healing the man with dropsy, handwashing, cup washing, taxes to Caesar, the temple tax, the question about divorce, marriage in the resurrection, the greatest commandment). Opponents are offended, but no plot to arrest/kill/accuse results.
2. Eschatological nomism: practices based on his eschatological identity, which become occasions to question his authority (self-identifying as the herald of Isa. 61, forgiving sins, dining with sinners, not fasting, plucking grain on the Sabbath, exorcising demons, his action in the temple).
3. Nomistic suspicions: nomistic controversies that themselves may not involve eschatological claims but arise because of preexisting doubts about his identity claims (healing on the Sabbath).

Viewing the material in this light, we see what E. P. Sanders made plain so many years ago: Jesus was not arrested simply for disagreeing with legal experts. As Sanders comments, often the Pharisees could vehemently disagree with one another, but they did not kill each other over such matters.[97] This view has been reinforced by Chris Keith, who argues that while nomistic debates themselves could get heated, they would typically not result in a secret arrest and execution. What particularly frustrated Jesus's opponents, according to Keith, was his lack of educational/scribal authority.[98] While Keith accentuates the scribal frustration caused by Jesus's lack of education, I am emphasizing the complementary factor of Jesus's assertion of divine authorization.[99]

It is Jesus's self-presentation as one divinely authorized that leads to his eschatologically motivated distinct practices. The legitimacy of such practices depends on his claim to be the divinely commissioned and empowered healer of Israel sent by God to gather Israel and return them to God's Law. If that claim is false, then his practices do in fact deviate from the commandments, and he ought not forgive sins, defend Sabbath profanation, and demand abnegation of one's family out of allegiance to him. But questions remain: Why not just ignore him? Why would such actions lead to a trial and execution? The answer is not obvious.

Sanders helpfully surveys several twentieth-century attempts to answer this question in which Christian authors frequently identify a Jewish opposition to

97. E. P. Sanders, *Historical Figure*, 222–23.

98. Keith, *Jesus against the Scribal Elite*, esp. 6.

99. Keith (*Jesus against the Scribal Elite*, 112, 126) also acknowledges this component.

Jesus's show of grace, his offer of forgiveness, or his supposed opposition to Jewish legalism and the Law itself.[100] At this point it is unnecessary to refute such positions. Sanders himself doubted that Jesus truly came into conflict with the Pharisees over matters of food, purity laws, or the Sabbath,[101] and he argued that the true offense was his temple action and his offer of the kingdom without requiring repentance. I will turn to the temple action in the next chapter, but here I simply note Sanders's correct observation that (noneschatological) nomistic debates in themselves cannot account for Jesus's last week in Jerusalem. Keith likewise acknowledges that the scribes' frustration at the perceived threat to their own social position caused by Jesus's lauded teaching does not sufficiently explain Jesus's arrest and execution, but he rightly argues that it was a contributing factor to the beginning of the controversy.[102] What, then, might account for transition from controversy over the Law to his action in the temple to his eventual arrest?

The lynchpin uniting some controversies over the Law, his action in the temple, and his eventual trial, I suggest, is Jesus's claim to being not just the herald but the executor of the restoration, divinely authorized as the Son of God to teach the Law and to serve as Israel's authoritative prophet endowed with the authority to summon Israel to God through himself. If he is wrong about such claims, *and if large groups are following his teaching*, then rather than leading the people into the restoration, he would be leading them into further transgression, for which the wrath of God may fall on the nation. Like Nehemiah before them, Jesus's opponents might accuse: "What is this evil thing that you are doing, by profaning the Sabbath day? Did not your fathers do the same, so that our God brought on us and on this city all this trouble? Yet you are adding wrath against Israel [προστίθετε ὀργὴν ἐπὶ Ισραηλ] by profaning the Sabbath" (Neh. 13:17–18 [= 2 Esd. 23:17–18 LXX]). Or as in the days of Antiochus, they might fear that a mass migration away from Law-keeping would result in "great wrath upon Israel" (1 Macc. 1:64). Because of Jesus's claims of divine authorization and his popularity, his opponents fear and accuse Jesus of "misleading our nation [διαστρέφοντα τὸ ἔθνος ἡμῶν]" (Luke 23:2). Such action might "add to the guilt of Israel" (Ezra 10:10) and would transform Israel into the people of Deut. 32:5—a "crooked and led-astray [διεστραμμένη] generation"—subjecting them to (further) judgment, hindering their prospects of restoration, and prolonging the endurance of God's wrath. As in previous generations, God's "wrath" (i.e., his covenantal

100. E. P. Sanders, *Jesus and Judaism*, esp. 23–44.
101. E. P. Sanders, *Jesus and Judaism*, 265.
102. Keith, *Jesus against the Scribal Elite*, 140–51.

discipline) is expressed through Israel being handed over to their enemies—in this case, the Romans. Rather than risk additional punitive attention from God at the hands of foreign enemies, the expedient and justified action (from the covenantal and legal perspective of Jesus's opponents) would be to put him on trial for transgression and blasphemy. This is captured well in John 11:48: "If we let him go on like this, all the people will believe in him, and the Romans will come and take over both our place and our nation." Hence Caiaphas's conclusion: "It is in your best interest that one man die for the people, and that the whole nation not perish instead" (11:50).

While controversies over Jesus's actions and identity claims contributed to the suspicion of his opponents, the Gospels name his action in the temple as the tipping point. Too often investigations of Jesus's handling of the Law are divorced from his temple action, but his temple action is not something separate from his eschatologically motivated practice of the Law, for the temple itself and its rituals are legal realities. The tabernacle's sacrificial rites are practices commanded and legislated in Israel's Law. This point is made forcefully by E. P. Sanders:

> It is one of the curiosities of research on the question of Jesus and Judaism that Jesus' sayings and actions with regard to the temple are often separated from his attitude toward the law. . . . It seems not to have occurred to . . . numerous others, that Jesus' attitude towards the temple cannot be dissociated from his attitude towards the Torah, nor can his attitude towards law be studied without dealing with the traditions on the temple; for *the temple rites were based on the Torah*. It is hard to conceive that Jesus could have had fundamentally different attitudes toward the temple and towards other points of the Mosaic legislation.[103]

Sanders is right. Recognizing that temple and law are inextricably bound, we turn now to Jesus's action in the temple.

103. E. P. Sanders, *Jesus and Judaism*, 251, italics original.

6

The Temple and the Cross

Having arrived at Jerusalem for Passover, Jesus enters the temple, turns over the tables of the money changers, drives out the buyers and sellers, forbids anyone from carrying a vessel through the temple, and shouts, "Is it not written: 'My house will be called a house of prayer for all the nations'? But you have made it a den of robbers."[1] What is justifiably striking to many is the apparent suddenness and lack of obvious warrant for Jesus's action. Is it a "cleansing" of the temple, implying intent to reform? Is he protesting a supposed commercialism or economic exploitation? Is it a prophetic, parabolic sign-act by which he intimates its destruction?

Each of the above interpretations has been offered in previous studies, and they are not mutually exclusive.[2] These options will be explored below, but I suggest that the action is not as sudden as a myopic reading of the scene might suggest. If the Synoptic accounts had depicted Jesus before his arrival to the temple as preaching a message already well received by his

1. Mark 11:15–17; cp. Matt. 21:12–13; Luke 19:45–46. Matthew and Luke lack "for all the nations" from Jesus's quotation of Isa. 56:7. Matthew makes no mention of Jesus forbidding people to carry vessels through the temple, while Luke refers only to his expulsion of "those who were selling."

2. These listed options are not exhaustive. For various interpretations of the temple action, see Roth, "Cleansing of the Temple"; N. Hamilton, "Temple Cleansing"; Trocmé, "L'expulsion"; Telford, *Barren Temple*; Bauckham, "Jesus' Demonstration"; Evans, "Jesus' Action"; Tan, *Zion Traditions*, 158–96; Ådna, *Jesu Stellung zum Tempel*; Ådna, "Jesus and the Temple," 2635–68; A. Collins, "Jesus' Action"; Bryan, *Jesus and Israel's Traditions*, 206–29; Jonge, "Cleansing"; Reinhartz, "Temple Cleansing"; Marcus, "No More Zealots." For a thorough history of interpretation, see Ådna, *Jesu Stellung zum Tempel*, 334–86; Ådna, "Temple Act," 949–51.

contemporaries, then the compressed nature of his action would indeed seem sudden and out of joint with the preceding narrative, and one would be forced to infer from only the event itself what it might mean. But this is not the account we have before Jesus's arrival, and if the preceding narrative is duly considered when interpreting the temple action, the latter becomes more comprehensible.

A brief survey of interpretative options will orient the discussion. E. P. Sanders famously argues that the action in the temple is a parabolic act portending its destruction.[3] The destruction is a prerequisite for the new, eschatological temple,[4] a motif commonly attested in Jewish restoration-eschatological expectations.[5] He argues that the expulsion of the money changers and sellers of sacrificial animals would not in itself indicate a protest of commercialism. The temple authorities accepted (or preferred) coinage bereft of images of emperors, and thus coins in circulation had to be changed, presumably for payment of the temple tax.[6] Similarly, sacrificial animals had to be unblemished; therefore, procuring one near the temple protected one from the risk of transporting one from afar only to arrive with an animal blemished during transit. These commercial operations provided a service for the necessary activities of the temple. Thus, according to Sanders, Jesus's actions did not critique financial corruption or the sacrificial system; nor did they imply judgment. Rather, Jesus parabolically enacted the temple's future destruction to make way for the renewed temple.[7]

Others accept Sanders's point that Jesus is not protesting the sacrificial system itself, but they still see financial corruption or exploitation as at least part of the reason behind Jesus's action.[8] On this reading, Jesus confronts some economic malfeasance—whether the financial corruption of the priests,[9] the "oppressive" temple tax,[10] or the "exorbitant" prices of doves, which were for the poor[11]—and his action "cleanses"[12] the temple or

3. E. P. Sanders, *Jesus and Judaism*, 75.

4. E. P. Sanders, *Jesus and Judaism*, 66, 71, 75.

5. E. P. Sanders, *Jesus and Judaism*, 77–90.

6. E. P. Sanders, *Jesus and Judaism*, 64.

7. See the whole discussion in E. P. Sanders, *Jesus and Judaism*, 61–76. See also Fredriksen, *Jesus of Nazareth*, 207–12.

8. E.g., Evans, "Jesus' Action"; Tan, *Zion Traditions*, 177–85.

9. Evans, "Jesus' Action," 270. To supply a plausible construct to interpret Jesus's act, Evans draws on several Second Temple texts that criticize the Jerusalem priesthood for corruption or greed. However, he concedes that, except for the Testament of Moses, none of the texts adduced "necessarily apply to the late 20s and early 30s C.E." (263).

10. Tan, *Zion Traditions*, 177.

11. Tan, *Zion Traditions*, 178.

12. Evans, "Jesus' Action," 270.

"protests" its corruption.[13] Still others see an eschatological basis for Jesus's action, wherein he critiques the leadership and/or the worshipers not for some deficient halakhic practice or economic corruption but for failing to realize the goal of the eschatological temple, which would be "a house of prayer for all the nations."[14]

Borg characteristically interprets the event to refer to Jesus's inclusivity and compassion over against the "temple ideology" that defined holiness in terms of separateness. Borg rightly argues that the word translated "thieves" (λῃσταί, Mark 11:17, quoting Jer. 7:11) is best translated as "violent ones" or "brigands," highlighting the violent aspect of the "thievery" in question. Consequently, "'robbers' almost certainly cannot refer to economic dishonesty on the part of the merchants, or to the inappropriateness of commercial activity in the Temple precincts."[15] However, after noting that the term comes from Jer. 7 and was there employed to characterize the people as having "violated the covenant,"[16] Borg remarkably concludes that the use of the term in Mark 11 "points decisively to the role of the Temple in resistance toward Rome."[17] He states that Jesus's action targets "the role of the Temple ideology in the quest for holiness with its corollary of resistance to foreign rule."[18] Intent on separateness, the leaders made Jerusalem and the temple into "a fountain of resistance" rather than "the city set on a hill whose light was to reach the nations."[19] Consequently, the temple was "a pillar of chauvinism."[20] Borg claims that this explains Jesus's expulsion of the merchants, as "the reason for their presence" was "to protect the holiness of the Temple. They did this by exchanging profane coinage for 'holy' coinage, by providing sacrificial doves . . . guaranteed free from blemish. Manifesting the clear-cut distinction between holy/profane, holy nation/profane nations, their activity served and symbolized the quest for holiness understood as separation, a quest at the root of resistance to Rome."[21]

13. Tan, *Zion Traditions*, 181, 185. Tan (181) states, "Jesus was protesting against the temple establishment for turning the sacrificial system into an oppressive profit-making industry."

14. Pitre, *Jesus, the Tribulation*, 375; Ådna, *Jesu Stellung zum Tempel*, 276–87; Bryan, *Jesus and Israel's Traditions*, 222–23; S. Smith, *Jerusalem Temple*, 71–72. Tan (*Zion Traditions*, 188–92) combines his view of economic protest with the temple's failure to be the eschatological temple. Dunn (*Partings*, 64) argues Jesus's action was a symbolic cleansing "necessary if [the temple] was to serve its intended eschatological function."

15. Borg, *Conflict, Holiness, and Politics*, 185.

16. Borg, *Conflict, Holiness, and Politics*, 185.

17. Borg, *Conflict, Holiness, and Politics*, 186.

18. Borg, *Conflict, Holiness, and Politics*, 186.

19. Borg, *Conflict, Holiness, and Politics*, 187.

20. Borg, *Conflict, Holiness, and Politics*, 188.

21. Borg, *Conflict, Holiness, and Politics*, 188.

But on this reading, Borg would have Jesus simply denounce things required by the Law, which states that priests should distinguish between the holy and the profane (Lev. 10:10), that the people are to be holy, set apart from the nations (20:26), and that offerings ought to be without blemish (22:20–24). For Jesus to criticize such practices would not simply be a critique of contemporary practice or their supposed "resistance to Rome," but a critique of God's requirements themselves. And as already noted, it is possible to be a holy nation, with practices distinct from the nations, and maintain purity laws, all while arguing against nationalistic violence. To correlate the temple in itself with separatist violence is simply a non sequitur. In other words, to return to Fredriksen's analogy, "unblemished animals" is to "resistance to Rome" as fish is to bicycle.

So Borg's reading fails dramatically. Jesus did not oppose the legal requirements regarding the distinction between the holy and the profane, the pure and impure. And other aspects of Jesus's teaching in the temple do not suggest a critique of nationalist violence or liberation. This is not to say he would affirm such activity. Rather, the Gospels simply do not make that the object of his critique in these chapters. Moreover, rather than critiquing the Jewish insistence on distinguishing holy from profane, Matt. 23 has Jesus critiquing the Pharisees for swearing by the temple's gold or the offering rather than by the temple or the altar themselves: "You fools and blind men! Which is more important, the gold or the temple that sanctified the gold? . . . You blind men, which is more important, the offering or the altar that sanctifies the offering?" (Matt. 23:17, 19). This critique requires maintaining the distinction between holy and profane and acknowledging the higher sanctity of the temple.[22] Such teaching does not square with a supposed critique of a "Temple ideology" for distinguishing such matters.

What then shall we say? As often, much of Sanders's position is right: Jesus is not protesting the sacrificial system itself. Elsewhere Jesus prescribes offerings (Matt. 8:4; Mark 1:44; Luke 5:14), and his instruction assumes the good of the practice (Matt. 5:23–24). Additionally, with Sanders, it is not clear that Jesus is protesting economic exploitation. If the buyers in Mark 11:15 are worshipers purchasing sacrificial goods, why would he drive them out? They're the ones supposedly getting fleeced! But even if those "buying" refers to other vendors rather than to worshipers, it is telling that none of his teaching after the event singles out financial corruption among priests or temple leadership as a contributing factor to the temple's future destruction/judgment.[23] How-

22. Runesson, "Purity, Holiness," 151; Furstenberg, "Laws of the Pharisees," 774–77.

23. Discussed further below, along with the citation of Jer. 7:11. For criticism of the "financial corruption" hypothesis, see Bryan, *Jesus and Israel's Traditions*, 219–20.

ever, Sanders argues that Jesus's action is a parabolic sign-act symbolizing the temple's future destruction without notes of judgment, positing instead that the destruction is merely a prelude to its rebuilding. I do not think these points are correct. Though not impossible, it is far from obvious that his action symbolizes its destruction.[24] And the Synoptic evidence does not permit dissociating the temple's destruction from judgment. It seems more likely that Jesus's action is an act of judgment for some perceived failure that guarantees the temple's destruction as an act of divine judgment by the hands of foreign enemies (in this case, Rome). In context, Jesus evidently judges the temple's failure to be the eschatological temple announced in Isa. 56 as it ought to have been if Jerusalem and its leaders had heeded the messages of John and Jesus (discussed below). Because it's the time for restoration, it's time for the temple to become, or begin to become, the eschatological temple as envisaged in Isa. 56.[25]

Additionally, while the details of the temple incident are not insignificant, attempting to interpret the event without attention to the preceding narrative excludes vital information. As I will argue, Jesus's action is an act of judgment that is not based exclusively on what he sees when he arrives but also reflects his realization of Israel's, including Jerusalem's, unrepentance *prior to* his entry into Jerusalem and the temple. Knowing, as he approaches, that Jerusalem has not repented, he weeps over their fate (Luke 19:41–44), parabolically curses the fig tree (Mark 11:12–14), performs an act of judgment that temporarily halts sacrificial practices, and then explains the meaning of his actions with parables and predictions pertaining to the temple's destruction for unrepentance.

This argument stands on four theses:

1. The command to "repent" indicates that Israel is in crisis, during which the sacrificial system itself does not avert the disaster. If Israel does not repent, the nation and the temple may be subject to judgment.
2. According to the Gospels, Israel is in such a crisis, and because the people are, by and large, not repenting, Jesus warns of judgment.
3. Even Jerusalem has not repented, and Jesus knows this prior to his arrival. For this reason, he regards the temple's judgment as an assured fate even before his arrival.

24. See criticisms in Dunn, *Partings*, 63; Tan, *Zion Traditions*, 166–68; Ådna, *Jesu Stellung zum Tempel*, 354–57.

25. And possibly Zech. 14:21, which plausibly prohibits traders in the eschatological temple. See, e.g., Roth, "Cleansing of the Temple." I focus on Isa. 56 due to its quotation.

4. His action judges the temple for its failure to be the eschatological temple, which serves as evidence of the people's unrepentance. Because of this, it will be destroyed as an act of judgment, indicated by the Scriptures quoted, the spoken parables, and the explicit predictions.

I begin with thesis 1: The command to "repent" indicates that Israel is in crisis, during which the sacrificial system itself does not avert the disaster. If Israel does not repent, the nation and the temple may be subject to judgment.[26] Numerous prophetic passages suggest that the temple comes under judgment during moments of national crisis. Regularly, the prophets call Israel to repent and inform them that their sacrifices are meaningless in such a context. The latter message has nothing to do with a so-called prophetic critique of ritual, temple ideology, or sacrifice in general. On the contrary, the priestly texts themselves do not claim that sacrifice may avert any and all punishment; several texts even state that once the divine punishment is decreed, sacrifice (and even repentance) is of no avail.[27] The only recourse is repentance before reaching this point and doing what God requires. Failing that, the temple will be judged along with the nation. This pattern is evident in numerous passages.

For example, in Num. 14, due to their lack of trust in God's capacity to deliver (14:6–11), the people are sentenced to wander in the wilderness until that generation dies (14:22–35). Having heard this decree, "the people mourned greatly" (14:39), and the next morning they repent: "Here we are; and we will go up to the place which the Lord has promised, for we have sinned" (14:40). Because the people have repented *after the decreed punishment*, Moses responds: "Why then are you violating the commandment of the Lord, when it will not succeed?" (14:41). They ignore his warning, proceed to the land, and are badly beaten (14:44–45). This episode illustrates the legal logic employed in the description of the punitive curses and much prophetic discourse: repentance and/or obedience is necessary when the opportunity is given, but once the punishment is decreed, neither repentance nor sacrifice can avert the disaster.

In Lev. 26 God promises that failure to maintain the covenant will result in punitive discipline intended to turn Israel back to obedience. If they do not repent, one of the promised punishments is that God will make the sanctuaries "desolate" (ἐξερημώσω) and ignore their sacrifices: "I will turn your cities into ruins as well and make your sanctuaries desolate, and I will not smell your soothing aromas" (26:31). The term "soothing aromas" refers to the burnt

26. Runesson, *Divine Wrath*, 114. On Jewish texts that envisage certain sins as leading to national catastrophe, see Klawans, *Impurity and Sin*, 118–31.

27. See also Rillera, *Lamb*, 84–98, 132–36, 141–49.

offerings and sin offerings (e.g., 1:9; 4:31). Consequently, God is stating that he will not regard their means of atonement once the punishment has been decreed.[28] Sacrifices may theoretically still be offered, but they will not avert the coming wrath.

This pattern of indictment, a call to repent and do what God requires, and a lament for unrepentance coupled with a declaration of punishment that sacrifice cannot avert is a pattern that appears often in prophetic literature.[29] Isaiah 1 and Jer. 11, for example, denounce the efficacy of sacrifice given the accused sins. Sacrifices in themselves are not critiqued; rather, sacrifices do not avert the promised disaster once the people have rejected the prophetic message of repentance.

This view is also articulated in numerous early Jewish texts. For example, in his description of the high priest's garments, Josephus states, "For he [Moses] . . . left it to God to be present at his sacrifices when he pleased, and when he pleased, to be absent. . . . For as to those stones [on the high priest's breastplate] the one of them shone out when God was present at their sacrifices" (*Ant.* 3.214–15). He then states, "Now this breastplate, and this sardonyx, stopped shining two hundred years before I composed this book, God having been displeased at the transgressions of his laws" (*Ant.* 3.218). Whether he refers to a momentary or perduring nonacceptance, Josephus states that transgression of the laws so displeased God that he disregarded their sacrifices. This is consonant with Josephus's explication of the situation when Israel violates the covenant and experiences the punitive discipline, during which even repentance will not benefit them (*Ant.* 4.191, 312–13). And if repentance will not help, a fortiori, sacrifice would not avail. Once more, examples could be multiplied.[30] But the point is made: in a state of rebellion, with punishment on the horizon, sacrifice is of no avail. The only recourse is to heed the prophet's message. Failure to do so results in punishment, typically culminating in invasion or the destruction of the temple, war, and exile.

Turning to the Gospels and thesis 2, Israel is in such a crisis: restoration and judgment are imminent, and they must heed the divinely commissioned

28. B. Levine, *Leviticus*, 189; Kiuchi, *Leviticus*, 483; Milgrom, *Leviticus 23–27*, 2320–21.

29. Jer. 7:1–24; 14:9–10; Hosea 3:4; 5:5–6, 15; 8:13; 9:5; Amos 5:21–24; Mal. 1:9–14; 2:12–14; Lam. 2:1–7. See Bryan, *Jesus and Israel's Traditions*, 146–47. Concerning limits of sacrifice, see Rillera, *Lamb*, 84–98, 132–36, 141–49. See also the discussion under "The Discipline" and "Discipline and Sacrifice" in chap. 2 above.

30. Josephus, *J.W.* 5.411–12; *Ant.* 10.60; Philo, *That the Worse Attacks the Better* 1.20–21; Pss. Sol. 2.3–4; Jub. 21.4–5; 33.18–20; Bar. 4:9–20. Though he disagrees with the view, Irenaeus, writing in the late second century CE, quotes Isa. 1's criticism of sacrifice and refers to some who say that God rejected sacrifices due to his anger (*Against Heresies* 4.17.1–2).

prophets sent to elicit their obedience. However, by and large, they are not repenting. The Synoptic Gospels open with a depiction of John the Baptist as one appointed by God (Luke 1:11–17) and whose message is foretold in the Prophets (Mark 1:2–3; Matt. 3:1–3; Luke 3:1–6) and accepted and employed by Jesus (Mark 1:9, 15; Matt. 3:13–16; 4:17; Luke 3:21; 13:3, 5). John's teaching that God's judgment is approaching (Matt. 3:7; Luke 3:7), that "the axe is already laid at the root of the trees" (Matt. 3:10; cp. Luke 3:9), and that all Israel must "repent" is a message that Jesus also accepts (Luke 13:3–9). Jesus too calls Israel to repent (Mark 1:15; 6:12; Matt. 4:17; Luke 5:32; 13:1–5),[31] warning that failure to do so will result in judgment, death, and the temple's destruction. This is made plain in many sayings.[32]

> And whoever does not receive you nor listen to your words, as you leave that house or city, shake the dust off your feet. Truly I say to you, it will be more tolerable for the land of Sodom and Gomorrah on the day of judgment, than for that city. (Matt. 10:14–15; cp. Luke 10:10–12)

> Then he began to reprimand the cities in which most of his miracles were done, because they did not repent. "Woe to you, Chorazin! Woe to you, Bethsaida! . . . I say to you, it will be more tolerable for Tyre and Sidon on the day of judgment than for you." (Matt. 11:20–24; cp. Luke 10:13–16)

> The men of Nineveh will stand up with this generation at the judgment and condemn it, because they repented at the preaching of Jonah; and behold, something greater than Jonah is here. (Luke 11:32; cp. Matt. 12:38–42; see also Luke 11:31)

> Woe to you [Pharisees and lawyers]! For you build the tombs of the prophets, and it was your fathers who killed them. . . . For this reason also, the wisdom of God said, "I will send them prophets and apostles, and some of them they will kill, and some they will persecute, so that the blood of all the prophets, shed since the foundation of the world, may be charged against this generation, from the blood of Abel to the blood of Zechariah, who was killed between the altar and the house of God; yes, I tell you, it shall be charged against this generation." (Luke 11:47–51)

> "No, I tell you, [these Galileans were not greater sinners (ὀφειλέται),] but unless you repent, you will all likewise perish. Or do you think that those eighteen on

31. On John's and Jesus's call to repentance relative to Israel's national restoration, see Oliver, *Luke's Jewish Eschatology*, 34.

32. These quotations derive from Matthew and Luke, but the theme of national judgment for failure to heed John's and Jesus's message is also present in Mark (discussed below).

> whom the tower in Siloam fell and killed them were worse offenders than all the other people who live in Jerusalem? No, I tell you, but unless you repent, you will all likewise perish."
>
> And he began telling this parable: "A man had a fig tree which had been planted in his vineyard; and he came looking for fruit on it and did not find any. And he said to the vineyard-keeper, 'Look! For three years I have come looking for fruit on this fig tree without finding any. Cut it down! Why does it even use up the ground?' But he answered and said to him, 'Sir, leave it alone for this year too, until I dig around it and put in fertilizer; and if it bears fruit next year, fine; but if not, cut it down.'" (Luke 13:3–9)

> Jerusalem, Jerusalem, the city that kills the prophets and stones those who have been sent to her! How often I wanted to gather your children together, just as a hen gathers her young under her wings, and you were unwilling! Behold, your house is left to you desolate. (Luke 13:34–35)

In light of such data, Steven Bryan concludes, "The following propositions are firm: (1) Jesus preached the arrival or imminent arrival of the time of fulfilment; (2) Jesus' ministry stirred broad interest but his message did not finally gain wide acceptance; (3) Jesus believed that the rejection of his message was morally culpable."[33] The common denominator in the texts above is that failure to repent and heed Jesus's message results in judgment. Several texts lament that many cities have not repented, and each pronouncement occurs prior to Jesus's arrival in Jerusalem. Several warn that the judgment will fall on "this generation," implying the inclusion of Jerusalem, and one pronouncement made prior to his arrival (Luke 13:31–35) explicitly names Jerusalem's failure to repent, because of which the temple is "desolate," bereft of God's protective presence, and so will experience punitive destruction (Luke 19:43–44).[34]

This point deserves expanding, which brings us to thesis 3: even Jerusalem has not repented, and Jesus knows this prior to his arrival, because of which he regards its judgment as assured. This thesis is most plain in the Gospel of Luke. Luke 13:34–35 has already been quoted, but additionally, as Jesus rides from the slope of the Mount of Olives into Jerusalem just before his entry into the temple, he laments the city's unrepentance:

> When he approached Jerusalem, he saw the city and wept over it, saying, "If you had known on this day, even you, the conditions for peace! But now they have been hidden from your eyes. For the days will come upon you when your

33. Bryan, *Jesus and Israel's Traditions*, 21.
34. S. Smith, *Jerusalem Temple*, 67.

> enemies will put up a barricade before you, and surround you and hem you in on every side, and they will level you to the ground, and throw down your children within you, and they will not leave in you one stone upon another, because you did not recognize the time of your visitation." (19:41–44)

First, Jesus claims that they did not learn/know (ἔγνως) "the conditions for peace" (τὰ πρὸς εἰρήνην, 19:42), and they did not recognize "the time of [their] visitation" (19:44). This lament signals Jesus's awareness that Jerusalem did not heed John's message, of which Zechariah prophesied: "For you [John] will go on before the Lord to prepare his ways, / To give his people the knowledge [γνῶσιν] of salvation / By the forgiveness of their sins, / Because of the tender mercy of our God, / With which the Sunrise from on high will visit us [ἐπισκέψεται ἡμᾶς], . . . / To guide our feet into the way of peace [εἰς ὁδὸν εἰρήνης]" (1:76–79). John offered "knowledge" for "the ways of peace," but Jerusalem did not learn it (19:42), and his ministry represented a "visitation" of God's mercy, but Jerusalem did not recognize it (19:44).[35]

Second, Jesus characterizes both his and John's ministry as "the time of your visitation" (τὸν καιρὸν τῆς ἐπισκοπῆς σου, 19:44). A "visitation" (ἐπισκοπή) generally refers to being "attended" to, but in context, it refers either to punishment (Isa. 10:3; 24:22) or rescue/restoration (Exod. 3:16; Luke 1:68, 78; 7:16). Psalms of Solomon 11.1 employs the term in reference to God's restorative action toward Israel: "Proclaim [κηρύξατε] in Jerusalem the voice of him who brings good news, for God has had mercy on Israel in their visitation [ἐν τῇ ἐπισκοπῇ αὐτῶν]" (AT). Similarly, in Luke 1 Zechariah claims that with the birth of John, God "has visited us [ἐπεσκέψατο] and accomplished redemption for his people" (1:68; cp. 1:78). So also in Luke 19, Jesus's ministry heralds "the time of [Jerusalem's] visitation," which must refer to their restoration,[36] but they "did not recognize" it (19:44). Thus, "now [the conditions for peace] have been hidden from your eyes" (19:42), and the fate of Jerusalem has reached "a point of no return."[37] Because of their rejection of John's and Jesus's message, Jerusalem and the temple will be destroyed (19:43–44). After uttering this lament and prediction, Jesus enters the temple and begins "to drive out those who were selling" (19:45). According to Luke, then, Jesus's driving out the sellers is not based exclusively on what he sees when he arrives. Rather, he is motivated by his prior conviction of Jerusalem's assured destruction because of their unrepentance.

35. Bryan, *Jesus and Israel's Traditions*, 22; Kinzer, *Jerusalem Crucified, Jerusalem Risen*, 32.
36. Johnson, *Luke*, 299; S. Smith, *Jerusalem Temple*, 62.
37. S. Smith, *Jerusalem Temple*, 60.

This pattern is also evident in Mark and Matthew. In Mark 11, prior to his action in the temple, Jesus curses the fig tree for its lack of fruit (11:13–14), after which he performs his temple action (11:15–16). Upon passing by the tree once more, Peter points out that it has withered (11:20–21). Many regularly note the Markan pattern of intercalation, a pattern suggesting that the temple action should be understood in light of the fig-tree actions that "sandwich" it. Just as the fig tree was fruitless and so was cursed and withered, so the temple is not yielding its fruit, and Jesus enacts and predicts its destruction.[38] Interpreting the temple action as a result of Jesus's prior knowledge of its "fruitlessness" is supported by the parable he tells "the chief priests, the scribes, and the elders" (11:27) in the temple courts (12:1–8), which predicts the destruction of "the vine-growers" (12:9) for their rejection of the prophets, including Jesus, the "beloved son," and their consequent failure to deliver the fruit of the vineyard (12:2–8). Moreover, when the priests ask about the origin of Jesus's authority (11:28), he responds by asking them whether John's baptism was "from heaven, or from men" (11:30). They will not answer, and presumably Jesus knows this, implying that he knew beforehand of their rejection of John's divinely commissioned "baptism of repentance" (1:4). Thus, before his arrival in Jerusalem, Jesus knew of their unrepentance, which leads him to curse the fig tree as a parable of the temple's destruction (see 13:28–29).[39]

In Matthew 21, after Jesus's action and instruction in the temple, he is approached by "the chief priests and the elders of the people" (21:23), who ask about the origin of his authority (21:23). Jesus in turn asks them about the authority of John's baptism. They reason, "If we say, 'From heaven,' he will say to us, 'Then why did you not believe him?'" (21:25). They rejected John's baptism, and Jesus knows it, and they know that Jesus knows it! So they claim ignorance (21:27). Jesus then tells them a parable about a son who agreed to work in the vineyard but then did not, and a son who refused but then worked

38. Mark 11:13 adds "It was not the season for figs," which could make Jesus's expectation and consequent pronouncement of judgment seem unreasonable. However, Bryan (*Jesus and Israel's Traditions*, 224–25) notes that some restoration or divine-blessing texts characterize the eschaton as a time of boundless agricultural yield year-round. He cites Lev. 26:4–5; Ezek. 47:12; Joel 2:22; Hag. 2:19; Mic. 4:4; Zech. 3:10; 1 En. 10.18–19; 2 Bar. 29.5; Sib. Or. 2.320; 3.744–51; Philo, *Rewards* 100–104. In other words, it wasn't the regular season for figs, but because it should have been the time of restoration—in which "will grow all kinds of trees for food. Their leaves will not wither and their fruit will not fail. They will bear fruit every month because their water flows from the sanctuary" (Ezek. 47:12)—Jesus looks for fruit and finds none. The people have not repented, and the restoration has failed to materialize. Consequently, he curses (judges) the tree. This dovetails with his expectation that because it should be the time of restoration, the temple ought to be the eschatological temple of Isa. 56. Because it is not, he judges it. See discussion below.

39. On relating the fig tree incident to Mark 13:28–29, see P. Sloan, *Mark 13*, 205–11.

(21:28–30). He asks, "Which of the two did the will of his father?" (21:31). When the priests answer that it is the son who eventually goes to work in his father's vineyard, Jesus responds: "Truly I say to you that the tax collectors and prostitutes will get into the kingdom of God before you. For John came to you in the way of righteousness and you did not believe him; but the tax collectors and prostitutes did believe him; and you, seeing this, did not even have second thoughts afterward so as to believe him" (21:31–32). He then tells the parable of the vine growers who do not yield the fruit of the vineyard (21:33–39), because of which the owner "will bring those wretches to a wretched end" (21:41). Thus, Jesus knows of Jerusalem's rejection of John's (and his own) message of repentance prior to his arrival,[40] because of which they will be subject to divine judgment in the form of the temple's destruction.

This leads to thesis 4: given Jesus's teaching that unrepentance results in punishment, the temple act should be construed as an act of judgment ahead of the temple's impending punitive destruction.[41] Jesus's action is followed by parabolic teaching about (Matt. 21:33–44; Mark 12:1–9; Luke 20:9–18), and plain prediction of, the temple's destruction (Matt. 24:2; Mark 13:2; Luke 19:43–44), suggesting that his teaching informs us about the significance of the action. Because his parables/predictions pertain to the temple's destruction due to unrepentance, his action is likely associated with his announcement of judgment.

Additionally, the passages he quotes after his act suggest that restoration and punitive destruction are the focal points of his act. After his action, Jesus says, "It is written: 'My house will be called a house of prayer'; but you are making it a den of robbers" (Matt. 21:13).[42] The first portion quotes Isa. 56:7, and the second, Jer. 7:11. Occasionally, interpreters collapse the restoration-eschatological context of Isa. 56 to reduce Jesus's point to one of distinct patterns of religion. Green, for instance, claims that Jesus sees what the temple could be in a steady-state, noneschatological context—an inclusive

40. Bryan, *Jesus and Israel's Traditions*, 73.

41. Prophets regularly performed outlandish sign-acts to serve as graphic symbols of their message: e.g., Ezek. 4:1–8; 5:1–17; Isa. 20:1–6; Hosea 1:1–11. Kelvin Friebel (*Jeremiah's and Ezekiel's Sign-Acts*, 12) defines such acts as "prophetic gestures and actions" wherein "nonverbal elements were laden with message content." However, it is not clear that Jesus's act is intended to function as a *symbol* of its future destruction. If his act has symbolic meaning, I think it relates to the temporary cessation of temple activity as an act of judgment on that activity because of the temple's failure to be the eschatological temple, but this is slightly different from the overturning of the tables symbolizing, or visually representing, its future destruction. For criticism of Sanders's interpretation of a symbolic destruction, see Ådna, *Jesu Stellung zum Tempel*, 354–57.

42. Mark includes "for all the nations," which Luke lacks, but this difference is not relevant to the case at hand.

space for outcasts—but he laments that instead it had become a house of power brokers harnessing "temple ideology" to exclude people.[43] While it is true that the temple was to be a space where "the foreigner" could come and "pray toward this house" (1 Kings 8:41–43), the text from which Jesus quotes refers not to what the temple is already, but what it will be in the restoration.[44] The context of Isa. 56 makes this clear:

> "Guard justice and do righteousness, / For my salvation is about to come / And my righteousness to be revealed. . . . / Also the foreigners who join themselves to the Lord, / To attend to his service and to love the name of the Lord, / To be his servants, every one who keeps the Sabbath so as not to profane it, / And holds firmly to my covenant; / Even those I will bring to my holy mountain, / And make them joyful in my house of prayer. / Their burnt offerings and their sacrifices will be acceptable on my altar; / For my house will be called a house of prayer for all the peoples." / The Lord God, who gathers the dispersed of Israel, declares, / "I will yet gather others to them, to those already gathered." / All you wild animals, / All you animals in the forest, / Come to eat. (56:1, 6–9)

When God gathers the dispersed of Israel, when he reveals his coming salvation in the restoration, then God's house will be a house of prayer for all the nations.[45] Jesus's quotation of Isa. 56, then, is not a description of what the temple always had been or should have been; it is a declaration that this was to be the time of restoration, which would have resulted in his temple being the promised "house of prayer for all nations."[46] Instead, it is "a den of robbers," characterized as the temple of the transgressive generation, who

43. Green, *Luke*, 690–93. See also Joseph (*Jesus and the Temple*, 115), who claims that Mark criticizes "Israel's particularity."

44. Tan, *Zion Traditions*, 188–92; Bryan, *Jesus and Israel's Traditions*, 189, 217; S. Smith, *Jerusalem Temple*, 71; Ådna, *Jesu Stellung zum Tempel*, 276–87.

45. The Babylonian Talmud also interprets Isa. 56 to refer to the temple during the time of redemption (b. Shabb. 118b [3–4]), when the Messiah comes (b. Megillah 17b [20]–18a [1]). The latter states: "And once Jerusalem is rebuilt, David will come, as it is stated: 'Afterward the children of Israel shall return, and seek the Lord their God and David their king' [Hosea 3:5]. And once David comes, prayer will come, as it is stated: 'I will bring them to my sacred mountain and make them joyful in my house of prayer [Isa. 56:7].'" The omission of "all the nations" from Luke 19:46 and Matt. 21:13 does not alter this point: they are still referring to the eschatological temple of Isa. 56. Luke 19:46 refers to what the temple "will be" (ἔσται), and Mark 11:17//Matt. 21:13 to what "it will be called" (κληθήσεται), signaling what it would/should become in the eschaton.

46. Bryan, *Jesus and Israel's Traditions*, 189; S. Smith, *Jerusalem Temple*, 71, with a slight nuance of Bryan's conclusion; Ådna, *Jesu Stellung zum Tempel*, 276–87. However, Ådna ("Jesus and the Temple," 2671) suggests that the temple act also offered a final chance of repentance. Possibly, but given Ådna's focus on Mark, this seems improbable; the fig tree incident suggests that the temple's fate is already sealed.

failed to uphold God's law and heed the prophet's message of repentance.[47] The phrase "den of robbers" is from Jer. 7:11, which is Jeremiah's description of the people not because of financial corruption in the temple courts but because of the people's general transgression and unrepentance.[48]

In Jer. 7, the prophet, in the temple's gates, indicts the people for theft, murder, adultery, swearing falsely, walking after other gods (7:8), and yet treating the temple as a guarantee of protection despite their transgression (7:10). Consequently, he characterizes the temple as "a den of robbers" (7:11). The passage continues: "'Because you have done all these things,' declares the LORD, 'and I spoke to you, speaking again and again, but you did not listen, and I called you, but you did not answer'" (7:13), God promises to destroy the temple and send the people into exile (7:14–15). Similarly, reacting to the unrepentance of Jerusalem and its leaders, Jesus sees the writing on the wall: Jerusalem's fate is sealed, and it will be destroyed. So Jesus's quotation of Isa. 56:7 combined with Jer. 7:11's description "den of robbers" likely refers not to some frustration about financial corruption in the temple's courts but to Israel's failure to achieve the goal that was to take place in the restoration. Because they do not repent, the goal of Isaiah's eschatological temple is unrealized, and the leaders are depicted instead as in a state of transgression that will result, as in the days of Jeremiah and Ezekiel, in the destruction of the temple.[49]

However, if, according to the Synoptic Gospels, Jesus had not yet preached in Jerusalem, how could the people be on the hook for a failure to repent? Two things should be said here. First, the Gospels depict John as active in Judea, summoning all of Israel to repent, and it names "Jerusalem" as having come out to him (Mark 1:5; Matt. 3:5).[50] Evidently, while many did heed John's

47. See also Bryan, *Jesus and Israel's Traditions*, 217. An opinion in b. Sanhedrin 98a is somewhat related and quite suggestive given Jesus's entry into Jerusalem on a donkey. In discussing the manner of the Messiah's arrival, Rabbi Alexandri states, "If [the people] merit [redemption, the Messiah will come] with the clouds of heaven [Dan. 7:13]. If they do not merit [redemption, the Messiah will come] lowly and riding on a donkey [Zech. 9:9]."

48. Perrin (*Jesus the Temple*, 92–93) argues that in Targum Jeremiah, Jer. 7 was interpreted with an accentuation on thievery. But see criticisms in S. Smith (*Jerusalem Temple*, 75), who helpfully notes what should have been obvious to Perrin: that Jeremiah names several transgressions unrelated to financial corruption (7:8) and that Tg. Jer. 7:11 translates the Hebrew "den of robbers" as "a synagogue of the wicked."

49. Moreover, as Amy-Jill Levine ("Matthew and Anti-Judaism," 414) notes, "a den" of robbers refers not to the location of the robbery but to the hideout after the fact, suggesting not that the "thievery" (= transgression) is happening in the temple but that the temple is being used as a safehouse after and despite transgression/nonrepentance.

50. Luke does not mention "Jerusalem" but says that John preached in "all" the regions surrounding the Jordan. And Luke 20:1–8 assumes awareness by the "chief priests" of John's preaching (hence their culpability).

message, the priests, elders, and Pharisees did not (Mark 11:27–33; Matt. 21:25–32; Luke 20:1–8). As already discussed, the religious leaders concede this, and Jesus is aware of it. Similarly, people "from Jerusalem" evidently had heard of the work of Jesus prior to his arrival (Matt. 4:25; Mark 3:8; Luke 5:17; 6:17). Moreover, in Matthew and Mark, Jesus evidently interpreted the fate of John as portending his own:

> And he answered and said, "Elijah is coming and will restore all things; but I say to you that Elijah already came, and they did not recognize him, but did to him whatever they wanted. So also [οὕτως καί] the Son of Man is going to suffer at their hands." Then the disciples understood that he had spoken to them about John the Baptist. (Matt. 17:11–13; cp. Mark 9:11–13)

In other words, the people did not accept John, and because Jesus preaches a comparable message of repentance, he perceives that they will not accept him either.[51]

Second, Jesus did in fact send testimony to the temple about the inbreaking restoration. In each Synoptic Gospel (Matt. 8:1–4; Mark 1:40–44; Luke 5:12–15), Jesus is approached by a *lepros* for healing. Having healed him, Jesus says, "But go and show yourself to the priest, and make an offering for your cleansing, just as Moses commanded, as a testimony to them [εἰς μαρτύριον αὐτοῖς]" (Luke 5:14; cp. Matt. 8:4; Mark 1:44). In each Synoptic Gospel, "testimony" occurs in evangelistic contexts, either as an occasion of positive witness to Jesus's message (Matt. 10:18; 24:14; Mark 13:9–10; Luke 21:13; 24:47–48) or a sign of judgment after unrepentance (Mark 6:11; Luke 9:5). Given the nonjudgmental context of this healed man's theoretical offering, his healing and offering are likely meant as evidence both that restoration is irrupting and that the one who healed him is its agent. This is strengthened by the observation that in Matthew and Luke, Jesus submits his healings, including the healing of *lepra*, as evidence that he is "the expected one." In response to John's inquiring whether Jesus is "the expected/coming one," Jesus responds, "Go and report to John what you hear and see: those who are blind receive sight and those who limp walk, those with *lepra* are cleansed and those who are deaf hear, the dead are raised, and the poor have the gospel preached to them" (Matt. 11:3–5; cp. Luke 7:19–23). Jesus's acts of healing vindicate his divine authorization as "the coming one" who heralds and effects the restoration.[52] Consequently, his sending the healed

51. For a brief discussion of the relation of John's fate and Jesus's (but not necessarily within the matrix I've suggested), see Shedd, *Dangerous Parting*, 92–99.

52. See further discussion in Bryan, *Jesus and Israel's Traditions*, 24–26.

man as testimony to the priests is likely to serve as a message to the temple that restoration is at hand and Jesus is its authorized agent.

This supposition, combined with the data presented throughout this chapter, suggests that according to the Synoptic accounts' distinct though common depictions, Jesus summoned even Jerusalem to repent before his fateful arrival. However, knowing their rejection of John (Mark 9:13; 11:28–33; Matt. 17:12; 21:23–32; Luke 20:4–8) and that they had not recognized the "time of [their] visitation" (Luke 19:44; cp. 13:34), he, with great sadness, predicts its destruction. His action in the temple, then, is based not exclusively on what he sees upon arriving at its courts but on his realization that because the people have not accepted John's message or his as divinely commissioned, Jerusalem has not repented and so is subject to judgment. What he sees in the temple—namely, that it is neither the eschatological temple nor even prepared to be—confirms their unrepentance. After his action of judgment, he warns of the temple's fate.

How does this relate to the topic of Jesus and the Law? First, how Jesus interacts with the temple is related to how he treats the Law, given that the temple's maintenance is legislated by the Law. Second, failure to recognize the restoration-eschatological context of the narrative and how it conditions the temple action (mis)leads interpreters to attempt to find something wrong with the temple practice itself rather than its failure to be the eschatological temple. Inevitably, this move often reduces Jesus's temple action to a pattern-of-religions critique, wherein caricatures of Judaism as a religion of externals fostered by chauvinistic "temple ideology" are presented as the foils to Jesus's mission of inclusion and compassion.

But referring to the way God required the temple to function as unjust "temple ideology"[53] would suggest that the fault is not with priests or Pharisees or any Jewish group but with God himself. How could Jesus critique the priests or Pharisees for maintaining this system when it is simply what God commanded? The answer is that he does not critique these parties for such a system; this is not the nature of his critique. His conviction is not that the temple is inherently unjust or that the priests are wrong for exercising their God-given authority. Nor is Jesus opposed to blood sacrifice or external rituals.[54] Jesus's criticism is of the failure of Israel, generally, and Jerusalem

53. Green, *Luke*, 691, also 693–94.

54. Contra Joseph (*Jesus and the Temple*, 161), who remarkably claims that "the Temple cult trafficked in violence; the sacrificial system required an incessant supply of blood from the marketplace to the altar. Jesus' radical imperative [of enemy love] collided with and undermined the most obvious site of violence in his world." This view mistakenly collapses sacrifice to violence, downplays or ignores evidence that Jesus commands the man healed of *lepra* to make blood sacrifice (Mark 1:44, requiring the sacrifices prescribed in Lev. 14:1–20), and unnecessarily interprets hierarchical evaluations concerning love of neighbor exceeding sacrifice (Mark

and their leaders, representatively, to heed his message of repentance and listen to him as the divinely commissioned agent of the restoration. Instead of repenting, the Pharisees (a group intent on instructing fellow Jews in the proper keeping of the Law) and Israel's leaders (represented by the priests and elders) transgress the Law and ignore the prophets sent to them. Consequently, the temple is not the eschatological "house of prayer" that it should be. For these reasons, and these alone, Jesus predicts with sadness the punitive destruction of the temple.

The Cross and the Restoration

An examination of restoration eschatology in the Gospels would not be complete without an analysis of Jesus's death, though in truth, it requires an entire book. What follows will sketch not everything that could be said but what I think must be said about Jesus's death, given the nature of his mission.

Jesus is determined to save his people from their sins, proclaim release to the prisoners, and rescue captive Israel as he inaugurates the promised restoration. However, what hangs over Israel at the beginning of the Gospel narratives—punitive discipline occasioned by their historic covenant violation—remains operative due to their ongoing unrepentance. However, Jesus will not let his people's unrepentance deter his determination to restore them. To that end, Jesus gives himself up as a ransom for the people, entering into solidarity with their predicament—subjugation to foreign enemies and their powers—to bear its weight for Israel's benefit. This he does on the cross, enduring the precise content of Israel's covenant discipline: being handed over to the nations to be put to death. In so doing, he "drains the cup" of God's discipline of Israel so that those who subsequently repent and are baptized in his name may receive the forgiveness of sins on offer in the renewed covenant, which is effected and embodied through his death and resurrection. This is the position for which I will sketch a brief defense.

Israel's Covenant Discipline

Each Gospel presents Israel as awaiting redemption, the promised comfort, salvation from sins, the eschatological gathering, and the realization of the good news of God's return and restoration. This implies that they remain under the prolonged punitive discipline prior to the mission of John and Jesus.

12:33) to indicate a rejection of temple sacrifices (see Joseph, *Jesus and the Temple*, 119). For the dissociation of sacrifice from "violence," see Rillera, *Lamb*, 9–22.

Recall also that the Law and prophetic literature regularly state that Israel's covenant obligation during the period of punishment is to endure it. Moses declares that Israel's punishment for their covenant violation is "death" and "perishing."[55] They are sentenced to exile for their covenant violation, and thus in their exile they "die" (Ezek. 37:1–11). Echoing Moses's claim that through the Law God sets before Israel "life" and "death" (Deut. 30:15), Jeremiah declares that the way to "life" is voluntary subjection to Babylon, and the way of "death" is to attempt to stay in Jerusalem (Jer. 21:8–9). Thus, voluntary submission to the punitive discipline—in this case, exile to Babylon—is the path of obedience that leads to life. A comparable interpretation is expressed in Bar. 4 and 2 Macc. 7.

In Bar. 4, Judah is sent into exile for transgression. A personified Jerusalem, who "saw the wrath that came upon you [Jews] from God" (4:9), speaks, "I was left desolate because of the sins of my children, / because they turned away from the law of God. . . . / But I, how can I help you? / For he who brought these calamities upon you / will deliver you from the hand of your enemies. / Go, my children, go; for I have been left desolate. . . . My children, endure with patience the wrath that has come upon you from God" (4:12, 17–19, 25). Jerusalem concedes that she can do nothing to help "deliver" her children—a claim indebted to the legal and prophetic assertion that sacrifice will not avert a disaster occasioned by inexpiable sin and unrepentance. The directive, then, is to go into exile and endure God's judgment, here termed God's "wrath."

In 2 Maccabees, Israel is characterized as enduring God's wrath, expressed through foreign persecution, due to Israel's past and current disobedience. In 2 Macc. 7, seven brothers are compelled to eat food forbidden by the Law. Each brother abstains and so is tortured and executed (e.g., 7:3–5). The sixth brother says such affliction is due to their own sin (7:18). He adds, "Therefore astounding things [ἄξια θαυμασμοῦ] have happened" (7:18), echoing the claim in Deut. 28:59 and Lev. 26:32 that such punishments will be "astounding" (θαυμαστάς and θαυμάσονται respectively). The seventh brother likewise states that they "are suffering because of [their] own sins," which he characterizes as the Lord's "discipline" (7:30, 32–33).[56] He concludes: "I, like my brothers, give up [προδίδωμι] body and life for the laws of our ancestors, appealing to God to show mercy soon to our nation . . . and through me and my brothers to bring to an end the wrath of the Almighty [τὴν τοῦ παντοκράτορος ὀργήν]

55. Lev. 26:38–39; Deut. 28:20, 22, 24, 45, 48, 51, 61, 63; 30:15, 18–19; 32:36.

56. J. Collins (*Daniel, First Maccabees*, 312) rightly notes that the sins in question are those "of the Jewish people" and "not so much the personal sins of the brothers."

that has justly fallen [δικαίως ἐπηγμένην] on our whole nation" (7:37–38). Both Deuteronomy and Lev. 26 describe the covenant curses as "discipline" (Lev. 26:18, 23, 28; cp. Isa. 53:5) and "wrath" (Deut. 29:22, 23, 26, 27; 31:17) that God "brings upon" (ἐπάγω: Lev. 26:25, 26; Deut. 28:49, 61; 29:27 [29:26 LXX]) the people "justly" (Lev. 26:45; Deut. 32:4; cp. Neh. 9:33; Dan. 9:14; Bar. 1:15), typically in the form of foreign domination. The seventh brother interprets their plight accordingly: they are under God's wrath, manifest in foreign persecution, and he interprets it as temporary discipline resulting from the nation's transgressions. He sees this suffering as necessary because it is Israel's justly given plight but also finite because it is the promised wrath that, once endured, will lead to Israel's restoration. To that end, he prays for their suffering to still the divine wrath and lead to the revelation of Deut. 30:3's promised "mercy to the whole nation" (2 Macc. 7:37). Thus, they willingly "give up" their bodies to endure Israel's punitive discipline in the hope that the rest of Israel will be freed from it.[57]

Importantly, such "wrath" in Baruch and 2 Maccabees (and the Law and the Prophets) is an interpretative evaluation of the plight the people experience. Not all subjugation is the manifestation of covenant wrath; sometimes it is only the zealous violence of wicked leaders. But when framed in the Deuteronomic matrix of Israel's covenantal relationship with God, foreign invasion is interpreted as the expression of God's wrath against Israel for their covenant violation. Occasionally interpreters (for and against "penal" views of Jesus's death) caricature the wrath of God as a burst of uncontrolled, angry passion at the first sign of disobedience. But realizing that the wrath of God is the promised punitive discipline occasioned by Israel's covenant breach expressed in foreign invasion contextualizes it, not as that of an abusive father who cannot control his temper or, abstractly, as lava falling from the sky, but as the promised and divinely enabled eventuality (exile, invasion, etc.) resulting from forsaking God. Though divinely wrought by Israel's God, the punishment expresses a kind of poetic justice: if Israel wants to submit to other gods and rely on other nations, God will give his people what they want, which is subjection to those gods and exile into their territories. And as is clear from the texts above, the endurance of this plight—subjugation to the nations occasioned by Israel's sins—is identified as an endurance of the covenantal wrath of God, who employs the nations to execute his judgments (discussed further below).

In the Gospels, the discipline is still operative; yet restoration is on the horizon. Therefore, God has sent the promised prophet, "Elijah," and his own Son, Jesus, to call for their repentance and to rescue Israel (Matt. 1:21; Mark

57. See also Moffitt, "Isaiah 53," 55–62.

1:1–15; Luke 1:54–55, 71). John and Jesus call the people to repent, but by and large they do not. This unrepentance culminates in Israel's leadership's mistreatment of John and Jesus, because of which Israel remains under God's discipline. Within this context, Jesus announces that he will be rejected in Jerusalem. Four distinct sayings suggest that Jesus is interpreting his death as a participation in Israel's punitive discipline in faith that, by enduring it, he will cause a key aspect of that discipline to pass away for those who follow him.[58] I will focus on Jesus's being "handed over to the nations," giving his life as a "ransom," the Last Supper, and the cup prayer in Gethsemane.

Handed Over to the Nations

Traveling to Jerusalem in his final days, Jesus tells his disciples: "Behold, we are going up to Jerusalem, and the Son of Man will be handed over [παραδοθήσεται] to the chief priests and the scribes; and they will condemn him to death and will hand him over [παραδώσουσιν] to the Gentiles" (Mark 10:33).[59] In this prediction, we must not miss that what Jesus will endure is the precise content, thematically and lexically, of Israel's covenant discipline: being handed over to the nations who put Israel to death. Numerous Pentateuchal and prophetic passages predict and/or lament this fate. In Lev. 26:25, God promises that "you will be handed over to the enemy" (παραδοθήσεσθε εἰς χεῖρας ἐχθρῶν). Ezra (= 2 Esd.) 9:7 states, "Since the days of our fathers to this day we have been in great guilt, and because of our wrongful deeds we, our kings, and our priests have been handed over to the kings of the lands [παρεδόθημεν ἡμεῖς . . . ἐν χειρὶ βασιλέων τῶν ἐθνῶν], to the sword, to captivity, to plunder, and to open shame, as it is this day." Lamenting Israel's state, Isaiah cries, "You have hidden your face from us / And have surrendered us [παρέδωκας ἡμᾶς] to the power of our wrongdoings" (64:7 [64:6 LXX]). Additional examples could be given,[60] but especially telling is Isa. 53.

58. To clarify, Jesus's death does not liberate them from persecution or cross-bearing, nor does it prevent the temple's destruction. As discussed below, the Gospels (along with other Second Temple texts) envisage God's discipline as meted out by other spiritual powers. Subjugation to these powers is one manifestation of God's punitive wrath, and Jesus's death, resurrection, and enthronement liberate followers from captivity to those powers, specifically Satan. In that way, he liberates them from punitive discipline.

59. See also Mark 8:31; 9:9–13, 31; 10:33; Matt. 16:21; 17:9–13, 22–23; 20:17–19; Luke 9:21–22, 43–45; 17:25; 18:31–34.

60. See also Deut. 32:30; 2 Chron. 36:17; Judg. 2:14; Mic. 6:16; Isa. 37:10; Ezek. 7:21; 11:9; LXX: Jer. 15:4; 21:10; 32:28, 36, 43; 34:2; Bar. 4:6; Jub. 1.13.

In Isa. 53 LXX, the people remain under the punitive discipline, but an unnamed figure is said to be wounded "because of our lawless deeds, . . . because of our sins," so that "the discipline that leads to our peace fell upon him" (παιδεία εἰρήνης ἡμῶν ἐπ' αὐτόν, 53:5). The term translated as "discipline" (παιδεία) plausibly derives from Lev. 26's use of a related verb form to refer to Israel's punitive discipline (Lev. 26:18, 23, 28). If so, Isa. 53:5 claims that a figure endures the content of the covenant curses, bringing Israel "peace" and "healing."[61] Though all Israel has strayed, the Lord "handed him over because of our sins" (παρέδωκεν αὐτὸν ταῖς ἁμαρτίαις ἡμῶν, 53:6), and "because of the lawless deeds of my people, he was led to death" (ἀπὸ τῶν ἀνομιῶν τοῦ λαοῦ μου ἤχθη εἰς θάνατον, 53:8). Bearing the sins of "many," he is "handed over because of their sins" (διὰ τὰς ἁμαρτίας αὐτῶν παρεδόθη, 53:12). Isaiah 53, then, seemingly depicts a figure enduring the weight of Israel's guilt, taking their discipline onto himself in being handed over for their sins, to bring Israel peace and healing.[62]

So in predicting that he will be handed over to the nations to be put to death, Jesus is identifying with Israel's current plight, taking onto himself the yoke they currently experience, to effect the restoration he has heralded. In doing so, Jesus is entering into "cursed solidarity" with his people, as Rillera aptly puts it—entering into the covenant-curse plight Israel is *already experiencing*.[63] The discipline that hangs over them—their subjection to the

61. So Anthony R. Ceresko ("Rhetorical Strategy"), who argues that Isa. 53 "describes the Servant bearing in his own person the effect of these curses [of Deut. 28]" (50).

62. On the figure's action in Isa. 53 as a non- or extra-sacrificial act on Israel's behalf, see Moffitt, "Isaiah 53." He states, "The servant's vicarious death reboots that covenant relationship when it is so broken that no sacrifices can be offered" (48). See also Janowski, "He Bore Our Sins," whose account Moffitt credits.

Features of Isa. 53 that have been taken to indicate the "sacrificial" nature of the servant's death are his being "slaughtered" (53:7) and his being an אָשָׁם (*ʾāšām*, 53:10), often understood as Lev. 5's "guilt offering." However, as Moffitt notes, "Neither the Hebrew nor the Greek nouns denoting 'slaughter' . . . in Isa. 53:7 are used with reference to Levitical sacrifices in either the MT or LXX" ("Isaiah 53," 51–52), and "the Greek cognate verb (σφράζω) is used in LXX for sacrificial and nonsacrificial slaughter" (52n21). Notably, the latter Greek verb is not used in Isa. 53, and the next clause in Isa. 53:7 "compares the servant to a sheep before its shearers. Sheep were not taken to the temple to be sheared" (52). Regarding Isa. 53:10's "guilt," Moffitt notes that "this word is also used outside of cultic contexts, where it refers not to a guilt offering but to being guilty or to eliminating guilt (e.g. Gen. 26:10; 42:21; 2 Chron. 19:10; Isa. 24:6)" (53). As the servant has the iniquity or guilt of others placed upon him (Isa. 53:6, 11), "the point seems to be that God planned to eliminate the guilt of the people . . . by having the servant take the guilt and die" (53).

63. Rillera, *Lamb*, 256, 274, 284. Rillera employs the term "cursed solidarity" when discussing Paul, especially Gal. 3:13, though it also applies to the Synoptic situation, as Rillera argues, stating that "the Gospels construe Jesus' death as the embodiment of Jerusalem's judgment" and that a purpose of his death was "to share in and identify with Israel and Judah's covenant

nations—will be endured by him in his crucifixion at the hands of Roman soldiers. But importantly, crucifixion and torture in themselves are *not* the "necessary" plight. Israel's divinely ordained plight is being handed over to the nations, who put Israel to death. But the crucifixion is what "the nations" do, for which they will be judged. Like Assyria in Isa. 10, Rome acts as "the rod of [God's] anger" (10:5), but the nations do not intend this: they act out of expedience and ruthlessness. As shown below, this theme is retrieved in Isaiah, Zechariah, and the Animal Apocalypse of 1 Enoch. God hands Israel over to the nations for punishment, *but the nations overdo it*, transgressing the punitive limits set by God, for which the nations will be punished.

According to Isaiah, God was "angry" with his people, Judah, and "gave them into" the hand of Babylon, but Babylon "did not show mercy to them." Therefore, God will bring disaster on Babylon "for which [Babylon] cannot atone" (Isa. 47:6–7, 11). Or again, in God's anger he exiled his people, but after their seventy years of captivity, God states, "But I am very angry with the nations who are carefree, for while I was only a little angry [at Judah], they [the nations] furthered the disaster" (Zech. 1:15). The Animal Apocalypse of 1 En. 85–90 is especially noteworthy: Judah (the sheep) strays from God, and the people reject the prophets sent to them (89.51–53); consequently God "abandoned them into the hands of the lions" (the nations), and God "abandoned that house [temple] of theirs" (89.55–56).[64] God then "summoned seventy shepherds" (angels/divine beings),[65] and "he left those sheep to them" (89.59). God tells the angels, "I will tell you which of them [the sheep] are to be destroyed. Destroy them" (89.60). God then tells another angel to observe the punitive activity of the seventy shepherds and record every excess as testimony, for which the seventy shepherds (angels) will be punished after their tenure (89.61, 64; 90.22–25). The angels now "tending" Judah "began to kill and destroy many more than they had been commanded, and they abandoned those sheep [Judah] into the hands of the lions [nations]" (89.65). The point should be clear: God's punitive discipline is occasioned by Israel's disobedience and expressed in handing Judah over to the nations and angelic rulers. These angelic rulers execute God's punishment in the form of subjugation to the nations, but these rulers transgress the punitive limits set by God and thus are punished. However, the latter should not occlude the fact that Judah's

---

curse" (173). He clarifies that this is not "substitutionary," dying *instead* of his disciples, who must still bear their crosses, but a death *ahead of* and in "solidarity" with Israel's plight (174). See also Watts, "Jesus' Death," 143.

64. The translations of 1 Enoch are by Nickelsburg and VanderKam, *1 Enoch*.

65. See Tiller, *Animal Apocalypse*, 51–54, concerning the identity of the shepherds as "angels." See also Nickelsburg, *1 Enoch 1*, 389–91.

deliverance to the gentiles is (a) divine punishment that is (b) superintended by angels who execute that punishment (however treacherously).[66]

In the context of the Gospels, then, Jesus voluntarily submits to the punitive discipline, being handed over to the nations who are themselves ruled by Satan (Matt. 4:8–9; Luke 4:5–7; cp. Mark 3:22–27),[67] and the weight of this plight crushes him. But God will vindicate his obedience by resurrecting Jesus and granting him authority over the powers and the nations (Matt. 28:18; Luke 24:26, 46–47; Acts 2:32–36; 5:30–31; 17:31). For additional support, I turn to one of Jesus's interpretations of his impending death.

Ransoming the Captives

In Matthew and Mark, en route to Jerusalem with a clear-eyed vision of his rejection, Jesus states, "The Son of Man did not come to be served, but to serve, and to give his life as a ransom [λύτρον] in exchange for many [ἀντὶ πολλῶν]" (Mark 10:45; Matt. 20:28).[68] Several commentators detect a reference to Isa. 53, wherein the servant's actions benefit "many" (Isa. 53:11, 12).[69] While an allusion to Isa. 53 cannot be substantiated by this one word alone, the factors described above regarding Jesus being handed over support the interpretation; however, my argument does not depend on this allusion. More significant is the probable reference to the logic of the Jubilee in this payment of a "ransom" (λύτρον). Three points should be grasped.

First, the Year of Jubilee legislates the reversion of ancestral land to its original owner and the release of slaves (Lev. 25:8–13, 35–55). If one had leased land for their crops or to pay off debt, the land reverted to the ancestral owner in the Jubilee (25:10, 13–16, 25–28). If an Israelite sold himself into

66. God employing "angels" or other nations to execute his wrath or judgments is common in Jewish texts. Angels: Gen. 19:13; Exod. 12:23; 2 Sam. 24:16; Isa. 37:36; Jer. 51:1; 4Q387, frag. 2, 3.4; 4Q390, frag. 2, 1.7; 1 En. 89.60; Jub. 49.2; 1 Cor. 10:10; Rev. 6:1–8. Nations: Lev. 26:17; Deut. 28:49–50; Isa. 10:5–6; 1 En. 89.65; 2 Macc. 7:30–37.

67. As Mark 3:22–27 implies that Satan rules over Jews, a fortiori he rules the nations.

68. NASB, modifying "for many" to "in exchange for many," interpreting ἀντί + genitive as "in the place of" (cp. LXX: Num. 3:12, 41; 8:16; 1 Sam. 2:20; Isa. 61:3; Bar. 3:19) or "in exchange for" (Josh. 2:14; Amos 8:6; Joel 3:3 [4:3 LXX]; Heb. 12:16). Luke's omission of this saying does not imply disagreement; on the contrary, the theme of redemption is pronounced in Luke. Zechariah and Anna claim that through Jesus God is now accomplishing "redemption" (λύτρωσιν) for his people and Jerusalem (Luke 1:68; 2:38). On the road to Emmaus, two disciples tell Jesus they had hoped he "was going to redeem [λυτροῦσθαι] Israel" (24:21), employing a verbal form of the related noun in Mark 10:45/Matt. 20:28 (λύτρον). Jesus's answer indicates that he was the one to do so, but through his suffering.

69. See, e.g., Marcus, *Mark 8–16*, 750, 756–57; Shively, *Apocalyptic*, 228–30. For criticism of the notion that Isa. 53 informs this and other Gospel sayings, see Hooker, *Jesus and the Servant*; Hooker, "Use of Isaiah 53." For response to such criticisms, see Watts, "Jesus' Death."

servitude to another Israelite, he was released in the Year of Jubilee (25:35–41). Significantly, if an Israelite becomes so impoverished that he sells himself into servitude to a *non-Israelite* in the land, either the Israelite goes free in the Jubilee year of "release" (τῆς ἀφέσεως, 25:54 LXX), or "after he has been sold" (μετὰ τὸ πραθῆναι αὐτῷ), a fellow Israelite may pay the value of his remaining years of debt-servitude to "redeem him" (λυτρώσεται αὐτόν) from captivity to the foreign master (25:48). The payment due for his redemption is termed his "ransom" (λύτρα, 25:51–52 LXX, the plural form of λύτρον).

Second, because Israel's plight due to their covenant violation was described in terms of their exile (i.e., the forfeiture of their ancestral land) and subjugation (i.e., captivity to non-Israelites), some Jewish texts employ the releases granted by the Jubilee (return to the land and liberation from foreign captors) to depict Israel's restoration as an eschatological Jubilee. Such an idea may be latent in Josephus's interpretation of the noneschatological Jubilee when he says: "That fiftieth year is called by the Hebrews the Jubilee, wherein debtors are freed from their debts, and slaves are set at liberty; which slaves became such, though they were of the same stock, by transgressing [παραβάντας] some of those laws the punishment of which was not capital, but they were punished by this method of slavery [δουλείας]" (*Ant.* 3.282). On his reading, subjection to captivity was the punishment for transgression, and such punishment was relieved in the Jubilee. Given that he claims being "sold into slavery" (πραθέντας δουλεύειν) to the nations was the punishment for "transgressing" (παραβάντες) the laws (*Ant.* 4.312–13), it would not be surprising if Josephus considered the relief from such punishment as a kind of national Jubilee. This configuration is especially pronounced in Isaiah, in which Israel is sent into exile for their sin (5:13; 27:9), which is characterized as a "debt" that must be repaid (40:2; cp. Lev. 26:41, 43),[70] and they are "sold because of [their] wrongdoings" (ταῖς ἁμαρτίαις ὑμῶν ἐπράθητε, Isa. 50:1). Their exile, then, is characterized as a penal debt-servitude paid by their endurance of captivity to the nations.[71] But in the restoration, a spirit-anointed

70. Blenkinsopp, *Isaiah 40–55*, 180; Anderson, *Sin*, 73.

71. See full discussion in Anderson, *Sin*, 27–94. Israel's sin as a "debt" that must be / has been paid by their endurance of the covenant discipline is stated in Lev. 26:41; Isa. 40:2; Dan. 9:24 (see Anderson, *Sin*, 85–86); CD-A 3.10–12; 4Q504, frags. 1–2, 6.5–6; 11QMelch 2.1–6. These texts variously describe sin as a "debt" that is paid through endurance of the covenantal punishment, or they similarly describe the endurance of the punishment as a "payment" of the debt. Jesus tells a related parable in Matt. 18, wherein the one who received release from a debt but did not offer it to his fellow was so treated by his master: "And his master, moved with anger, handed him over to the torturers until he would repay all that was owed him. My heavenly Father will also do the same to you, if each of you does not forgive his brother from your heart" (18:34–35). The failure of one to forgive/release another's debt results in God not cancelling *his* debt, requiring him to pay it off in a debt prison.

figure is appointed to "proclaim release [ἄφεσιν] to captives" (Isa. 61:1), using the term employed to refer to debt release and release from captivity in the Jubilee.[72] As already discussed, 11QMelch combines debt-release texts (Deut. 15; Lev. 25; Isa. 61) in its characterization of Israel's iniquities as "debts," which they pay off by their captivity to Belial, the spiritual captor.[73] As Anderson summarizes, "Israel's sins have put her in the position of a slave sold into slavery because expenses could no longer be covered."[74] But in the day of salvation, Melchizedek, assuming the role of Isa. 61's herald proclaiming "release to the captives," releases Israel from these debts, thereby liberating them from their captor, Belial (11QMelch 2.1–13).[75] In the eschatological Jubilee, then, the Israelites enslaved to foreign captors (the nations and their gods) are to go free because they have been "redeemed" by God (Isa. 35:9–10; 43:1, 3–4; 44:22; 48:20; 52:3, 9; 59:20; 63:4). The Israelites were to heed the prophetic announcement of restoration, in other words, and walk out free!

Third, returning to the Gospels, Jesus is depicted as this herald of the eschatological Jubilee, the year of release (Luke 4:18–19; Matt. 11:4–5; implicitly in Mark).[76] His people are enslaved. Roman forces occupy the land, and the people are subject to their "enemies" and "the hand of all who hate us" (Luke 1:71). But as in 1 En. 89, discussed above, Israel is subject not just to the nations but also to the spiritual powers who rule them. They are captive to Satan, "the strong man," from whom Christ intends to deliver them (Matt. 12:25–29; Mark 3:22–27; Luke 11:17–22). And according to Matthew and Luke, Satan holds authority not just over Israel but over all kingdoms of the world (Luke 4:5–6; Matt. 4:8–9). Moreover, Matthew and Luke depict sin as "debt" that requires "release" (Matt. 6:12; Luke 11:4; see also 13:4–5). Consequently, his people need forgiveness of sin-debt and deliverance from captivity. Therefore, Jesus calls to them, announcing that their year of release is at hand, and yet they do not repent. So they remain in captivity to the nations and their spiritual power(s).

It is within this context—Israel's perduring spiritual and human captivity due to their prior covenant violation and current nonrepentance—in which they have not accepted that Jesus truly heralds the eschatological Jubilee, that Jesus pays their redemption price, giving his life as a "ransom" (λύτρον) in exchange for many (Mark 10:45; Matt. 20:28). In so doing, he frames his

72. Deut. 15:1–3; Lev. 25:10, 28, 30–31, 40, 50, 52, 54.

73. See the previous discussion under "Retaliation" in chap. 3.

74. Anderson, *Sin*, 35.

75. See the discussion in Anderson, *Sin*, 35–38; Williams, "Melchizedek."

76. For the resonances of restoration *qua* Jubilee in Mark, see Williams ("Melchizedek") and my discussion of Matt. 5:38–39 under "Retaliation" in chap. 3.

death in terms of Lev. 25's logic of paying a ransom (λύτρον) to liberate a fellow Israelite from captivity to a foreign captor (Lev. 25:47–52).[77] The above framework helps explain the historically vexing relationship between Jesus's "forgiving sins" early in his ministry (Mark 2:10 and par.) and yet dying as a ransom later in the narrative. Because such forgiveness was pronounced upon "seeing their faith" (Mark 2:5), when such "faith" is lacking—that is, when his audience does not recognize him as the agent of the Jubilee—so also goes the pronouncement of "forgiveness." Instead, they remain in "debt," having rejected that it is the "Jubilee," and thus to secure their liberation, he must pay their "ransom," the price set for redemption according to the Jubilee legislation (Lev. 25:47–52).[78] Because Israel's captors put them to death,[79] realizing Moses's warning that disobedience leads to death,[80] Jesus pays the debt of their remaining servitude by dying for their benefit/release. His death, then, is a voluntary self-giving to liberate his people from their debt-slavery that consists of death. Their debt-servitude *qua* death at the hands of foreign captors (spiritual and human) is the "ransom" he pays. For this reason, Jesus does not simply die but dies at the hands of Israel's captors, the Romans, who are presumably led by foreign spiritual powers (see Luke 4:5–7; Matt. 4:8–9; cp. Luke 22:3, 53; 1 En. 89.59–66; Jub. 15.31–32).[81]

Equally, however, because this captivity is the promised punishment for their sin, the ransom he pays is a participation in their punishment, bringing it to an end. Consequently, Jesus's death as an endurance of their punishment and as an act that liberates them ought not be played off one another.[82] Their

77. On "ransom" as securing deliverance from captivity, see A. Collins, "Signification"; Stein, *Mark*, 488. On Christ's death as a ransom from Satan's captivity, see Shively, *Apocalyptic*, 228–51.

78. See further discussion in note 82 below.

79. Deut. 28:20, 22, 24, 45, 48, 51, 61, 63; Lev. 26:38–39; Pss. 44:22; 79:11; Isa. 22:14–18; Jer. 11:22; Ezek. 3:18–19; Bar. 2:25; 3:2–3.

80. Deut. 30:15, 18–19; cp. Ezek. 37:11.

81. Luke 22:53 refers to the "power/authority of darkness" (ἡ ἐξουσία τοῦ σκότους) as governing the Jewish authorities that arrest him. That these authorities so led will hand him over to the nations (18:32) implies that the nations are comparably led. Likewise, Judas's betrayal is inspired by Satan (22:3).

82. Rillera (*Lamb*, 112–15) rightly argues for the nonsacrificial, financial/economic nature of "ransom" in several legal texts. However, Rillera and I differ regarding the function of the "ransom" in the Synoptic Gospels' situation. Rillera rightly compares the redemption wrought by Jesus to the deliverance from Egypt, but concludes, "This idea of Jesus's blood as a currency cannot be taken too far. Especially when we keep the scriptural exodus in mind, we realize that the use of 'ransom' was never 'literal,' even for the first exodus. Neither Pharaoh, nor Egypt, nor their gods were paid a ransom for Israel's liberation. God just freed them" (203). Consequently, "just as no one thinks that when God ransomed Israel from Egypt (or was to repeat this type of salvation in a new exodus from the nations) neither Egypt, or the nations, or God himself were being 'paid off,' so too we should not think that the use of 'ransom' imagery in the NT is conveying that Jesus's blood 'paid off' anything or anyone"

debt-slavery to the nations and their gods is a punishment, the expression of God's wrath, and Jesus co-enduring this punishment ends it for those who submit to his authority, thereby liberating the enslaved from their foreign captor, Satan.[83] Those who reject his "ransom" remain captive. However, those who join Christ are not released from suffering, and the temple will not after all be saved from its impending fate because of his self-giving. Rather, because the foreign captor is ultimately Satan, those who join Christ, who has received dominion and authority from his Father after his death and resurrection (Matt. 28:18; Luke 24:26; Acts 2:33; 5:31), are freed from their former captor/captivity. Thus, the benefit that his ransom secures is freedom from captivity to Satan (see Acts 26:18), and the "release" (ἄφεσιν) from the captivity that their sins incurred (Matt. 26:28; Luke 24:47; Acts 5:31; 13:38; 26:18).[84]

---

(204). Additionally, because all of Jesus's teaching about forgiveness using economic terms is about "debt forgiveness" rather than "debt satisfaction," Rillera concludes, "The notion that 'Jesus paid my debt' to God or the devil lacks any scriptural basis and contradicts Jesus's own teachings" (205). However, these conclusions neglect that the redemption from exile, though typologically comparable to the first exodus, is not identical to it. Though sin / covenant breach was not the occasion for their captivity in Egypt, it is the occasion for their captivity to the nations. Thus, liberation from the exilic captivity entails dealing with the sins that resulted in such captivity. Israel's sins are construed as debts that led to their debt-slavery to other powers/nations; rescue from those nations/powers implies that such (punitive) debts have been paid. Relatedly, though Jesus declared the time of release from debts, his people rejected the offer, resulting in their continued captivity. (As stated, this also helps explain the distinction between Jesus forgiving sins when "seeing their faith" [Mark 2:5] and his having to pay their debt when they lack such faith. Without such faith, they are not released from their sins.) Therefore, Jesus pays their remaining debt. Thus, that he teaches debt forgiveness does not preclude the "ransom" saying from functioning as a debt payment. On the contrary, it fits hand in glove with the narrative situation in which Israel refuses his offer of debt forgiveness, thereby remaining captive, because of which he explicitly claims that his death is a "ransom," the price paid to liberate from captivity. Once the notion that Israel's captivity to the nations/powers is itself superintended by God, the question "To whom does Jesus pay the ransom?" may comprehensibly be answered as either God, who holds the debt, or Satan, whom God superintends. If the latter, a payment made to Satan is itself still a payment made to God, who employs Satan to execute certain judgments (in this case, the debt-captivity of Israel). For an early attestation of this reading, see Origen, *Commentary on Romans* 2.13.29. I agree with Rillera, though, that this "ransom" is not "sacrificial" (*Lamb*, 249–51), that it is a participation in Israel's judgment (173), and that his resurrection is instrumental in effecting the liberation.

83. On liberation from Satan in Mark, see Shively, *Apocalyptic*, 228–51. Powell ("Plot and Subplots") notes that Jesus's death on the cross "defeats the will of Satan" (198), referring to Peter's "satanic" objection to Jesus's being killed. Inflecting Powell's observation within the scheme I've presented, Satan may want to stop Christ's crucifixion in Matthew because he recognizes it as the activity that would ransom and thereby liberate those Satan holds captive.

84. For a related (but distinct in nuance) discussion of the "ransom" within Matthew's broader context of sin and debt, see Eubank, *Wages of Cross-Bearing*.

"My Blood, Poured Out for You"

While eating the Last Supper with his disciples, Jesus provides an interpretative frame for his impending death. Each Gospel records the saying over the wine slightly differently:

> Mark 14:24: This is my blood of the covenant, which is being poured out for many [ὑπὲρ πολλῶν].
>
> Matt. 26:28: For this is my blood of the covenant, which is poured out for many [περὶ πολλῶν] for forgiveness of sins.
>
> Luke 22:20: This cup, which is poured out for you [ὑπὲρ ὑμῶν], is the new covenant in my blood.

Common to each is associating the blood with "covenant." Luke clarifies that it is the "new covenant." This is probably implicit in Mark and Matthew, given the restoration eschatology basic to both. Matthew adds "for forgiveness of sins," further supporting that "the covenant" refers to the new covenant, because it is in the making of the new covenant, according to Jer. 31:34, that God promises to "forgive" Israel's iniquity and forget their "sin."

Commentators regularly note that "blood of the covenant" echoes Exod. 24,[85] wherein Moses took blood from the peace offerings (24:5) and sprinkled half on the altar (24:6) and half on the people (24:8) to ratify the covenant, uniting God and Israel in fellowship.[86] Combined with Jesus's declaration to those present that this blood is "poured out" (ἐκχυννόμενον) for them, scholars have interpreted the Gospels' "blood of the covenant poured out" in a sacrificial register, taking "poured out" to refer to sacrificial practice.[87] But two things should be noted. First, the blood of the covenant in Exod. 24, which derives from a peace offering (24:5), is not for atonement or forgiveness.[88] If Jesus is echoing this phrase, it must be to signal that as that blood ratified a covenant, so his blood inaugurates a (new) covenant, presumably the covenant promised by Jeremiah for the time of restoration.[89] But it is not obvious that "blood of the covenant" in itself, in either context, refers

85. Inter alia, Healy, *Mark*, 286; Luz, *Matthew 21–28*, 280; Shauf, *Jesus the Sacrifice*, 118.

86. Sarna, *Exodus*, 152.

87. E.g., Cole, *Mark*, 299; Kimbell, *Atonement*, 35; Healy, *Mark*, 286; Culpepper, *Mark*, 495; Nolland, *Matthew*, 1079, though Nolland regards the expression as a secondary allusion to the notion of "murder."

88. See Shauf, *Jesus the Sacrifice*, 123; Rillera, *Lamb*, 179.

89. And as Rillera notes, the prophetically promised new covenant brings the forgiveness of sins "apart from any *kipper* sacrifice" (*Lamb*, 179). This comports with my previous analysis

to an atoning sacrifice. Second, relatedly, "poured out" does occur in a few sacrificial texts, but the overwhelming majority of scriptural instances refer not to sacrifice but to bloodshed in the sense of murder: "innocent blood" being "poured out." In sacrificial contexts, blood is "poured" in two instances of ordination offerings (Exod. 29:12; Lev. 8:15), once for atonement in the priests' inaugural offering (Lev. 9:9), and in the "purification offering" for atonement and forgiveness in Lev. 4 (4:7, 18, 25, 30, 34).[90] The other forty-five passages refer to acts of violence in nonsacrificial contexts.[91] For such acts of bloodshed, no sacrifice can be made. Numbers 35:33 spells this out: "So you shall not defile the land in which you live; for blood defiles the land, and no atonement can be made for the land for the blood that is shed on it [ἀπὸ τοῦ αἵματος τοῦ ἐκχυθέντος ἐπ' αὐτῆς], except by the blood of the one who shed it." Consequently, it may be that Jesus is shedding his blood (τὸ αἷμά μου . . . ἐκχυννόμενον, Matt. 26:28) as a representative endurance of the guilt for the shed blood (πᾶν αἷμα δίκαιον ἐκχυννόμενον, 23:35) of which Israel is guilty (23:30–31, 35–36; Luke 11:47–51).[92] Naturally, the above statistics are not determinative, but other clues suggest that here Jesus's blood shedding is not presented as an atoning "sacrifice" in the technical sense.

First, sacrifices are given to God in his sacred space, presented by a sacred officiant. David Moffitt has persuasively argued that the directionality of the gift—from common to sacred, from the owner's possession to God's—constitutes whether it is a sacrifice.[93] But Jesus's death occurs in profane space, is not performed by a priest, and is not presented to God in his sacred

that sacrifice neither averts discipline occasioned by covenant-violating sins nor relieves it. It simply was not given with that function (a conclusion also reached by Rillera).

90. However, Rillera (*Lamb*, 185–86) argues that even these references are not relevant to the Last Supper saying: the blood "poured out" in these OT sacrificial contexts has no atoning function but is instead mere disposal of extra blood.

91. Gen. 9:6; 37:22; Lev. 17:4; Num. 35:33; Deut. 19:10; 21:7; 1 Sam. 25:31; 1 Kings 2:31; 2 Kings 21:16; 24:4; 1 Chron. 22:8 (2×); 28:3; 2 Chron. 36:5d LXX; 1 Macc. 1:37; 7:17; 2 Macc. 1:8; Pss. 79:3, 10; 106:38 (13:3; 78:3, 10; 105:38 LXX); Prov. 1:16; 6:17; Sir. 28:11; 34:27 (34:22 LXX); Pss. Sol. 8.20; Joel 3:19 (4:19 LXX); Zeph. 1:17; Isa. 59:7; Jer. 7:6; 22:3, 17; Lam. 4:13; Ezek. 16:38; 18:10; 22:3, 4, 6, 9, 12; 36:18; Matt. 23:35; Luke 11:50; Acts 22:20; Rev. 16:6.

92. As Rillera notes, Num. 35:33 proscribes sacrificial atonement as the means of atoning for shed blood (*Lamb*, 113), but as argued above and below, Jesus's death is not construed as a sacrifice. Numbers 35 also forbids the murderer from making a monetary payment to wipe away bloodguilt (35:31–32). For this reason, I suggest that Jesus's "blood poured out" is a participation in their judgment, a representative undertaking of the punishment due those who shed blood (see 35:33), rather than an act that rescues Jerusalem from destruction. See the discussion in Rillera, *Lamb*, 187. For a study of "innocent blood" in Matthew, see C. Hamilton, *Death of Jesus*, though I disagree with her sacrificial interpretation of Jesus's poured-out blood (222). See also Setzer, "Innocent Blood Traditions."

93. Moffitt, "Observations on Directional Features."

space. Second, the offerings are presented to God unblemished, but Jesus is thoroughly "blemished" by his torture prior to his death. Third, "death" in itself does not constitute a sacrifice. Deaths occur routinely outside the context of the temple cult, and they are not regarded as sacrifice. Indeed, to treat something profane (death outside the cult) as a sacrifice fails to distinguish as required between the common and the holy (Lev. 10:10–11). When death is a part of sacrifice, it is but one step among many. That the animal's slaughter may be done by the nonpriest (4:24) suggests it is not treated as a sacred component of the ritual;[94] further, without the portage of the blood, which carries the animal's life (17:11), into God's presence, the death/slaughter of the animal would not be efficacious for atonement.[95] If you simply slaughter a bull, you wouldn't have forgiveness, just a dead animal and a mess.

The mistake often made, I think, is in interpreting common effects to signal identical means. The argument goes as follows: Jesus's death brings forgiveness of sins. Sacrifices bring the forgiveness of sins. Therefore, Jesus's death must be a sacrifice. But this interprets common effects (forgiveness) to imply identical means (sacrifice), which is illogical. Time with friends and writing this book both make me happy, but that does not mean that time with friends is identical to writing this book. An example from the Law is purification: water and the arrival of sundown purify (e.g., Lev. 15:8), and blood from an animal purifies (e.g., 16:19), but materially, water is not blood, and teleologically, one is a sacrifice (blood) while the other is not (water/sundown). Of course, Jesus's death is associated with Passover and the (new) covenant, which to many suggests that his death is an atoning sacrifice.[96] However, the association with the Passover meal is likely not to claim that his death is an atoning sacrifice, but to invest his death with the significance of liberation from foreign and spiritual oppression, which Passover commemorates (Exod. 12:14).[97] Just as Israel was protected from the "destroyer" and liberated from Egypt and their gods by virtue of the divinely commanded "blood" on the doorposts (12:7, 12–14), so now Israel will be liberated from their enemies by the blood (death) of Jesus because his death is the price paid as their ransom (in the jubilean sense above). To identify Jesus's shed blood with sacrifice, then, fallaciously collapses comparable purposes (forgiveness) into identical means (sacrifice) and mistakenly collapses a bloody execution performed by nonpriests in a profane space into sacrifice. Everything about Jesus's death

94. So also Shauf, *Jesus the Sacrifice*, 32.

95. For discussion of why death by itself does not atone within the Jewish sacrificial system, see Moffitt, *Logic of Resurrection*, 256–77; Eberhart, *Sacrifice of Jesus*, 96; Rillera, *Lamb*, 15–22.

96. See note 87 above.

97. On Jesus and Passover, see also Rillera, *Lamb*, 171–89.

in the Synoptic Gospels, in other words, signals that it is not an atoning sacrifice. Ironically, clinging to the metaphorical domain of "atoning sacrifice" to interpret Jesus's death in the Synoptic Gospels signals a misinterpretation of both sacrifice and Jesus's death.

Moreover, unhitching Jesus's death from sacrifice in the Synoptic Gospels is relevant to Israel's plight and how it relates to the Law, or rather, how the Law relates to Israel's plight, in at least two ways. First, not all sins have a sacrificial amelioration.[98] Sacrifices can cleanse the sanctuary, but some sins, especially murder and sexual transgression, defile the land (Num. 35:33; Lev. 18:24–28) and have no sacrificial remedy. So if Jesus's death were regarded as a "sacrifice," it would greatly limit the positive effect it could have given his accusation of "bloodshed" (Matt. 23:34–37; Luke 11:49–51).

Second, aside from the inaugural sacrifices, which likewise must be unblemished, offered by priests in sacred spaces, and are not reducible to killing the animal or pouring out its blood, the function of the sacrifices is, broadly speaking, covenant maintenance—that is, maintaining the intact covenant by offering the required offerings at the right time. But sacrifices do not mend a breached covenant.[99] That is simply not their purpose. Once the covenant is broken, sacrifices are not accepted—at least not for restoration—and Israel has no recourse but to endure their punishment (exile, subjugation), which is not described in sacrificial terms. This point requires expanding.

In Israel's Scriptures, an act of God (in this case, the redemption from Egypt) precedes the inaugurating sacrifice, which seals the covenant agreement and unites the people to God. In Exod. 19, for example, God states that he has rescued Israel from Egypt, and so they should "obey my voice and keep my covenant" (19:4–5). Israel agrees (19:8), after which God enumerates the commandments that constitute the covenantal stipulations (Exod. 20–23). Moses recounts these, and the people agree to them (24:3). He then seals the covenant with a sacrifice of peace offerings (24:4–8), uniting the people to the Lord. Once they construct the tabernacle and inaugurate it with offerings, the sacrificial system is operational. While the covenant is maintained—that is, while the people keep the covenant's requirements—sacrifices are acceptable. However, God warns the people that if they "reject [his] statutes . . . so as . . . to break [his] covenant [ὥστε διασκεδάσαι τὴν διαθήκην μου]" (Lev. 26:15), he will discipline the people in various ways, one of which is the desolation of the sanctuaries and God's rejection of their offerings: "I will . . . make

98. See "Discipline and Sacrifice" in chap. 2. See also Rillera, *Lamb*, 95–96, 132–36.

99. On sacrifices as covenant maintenance and the inability of sacrifice to mend the covenant breach, see Moffitt, "Wilderness Identity"; Moffitt, "Isaiah 53."

your sanctuaries desolate [ἐξερημώσω], and I will not smell your soothing aromas" (26:31). This punishment is well rehearsed in the prophetic literature (see chap. 2 above). Because Israel and Judah have "broken [God's] covenant [διεσκέδασαν . . . τὴν διαθήκην μου]" (Jer. 11:10), disaster is coming that "sacrificial flesh" cannot avert (11:15). In other words, sacrifice is a benefit of, and means of maintaining, the kept covenant. But once the covenant is broken, sacrifice itself cannot mend the breach. Only the endurance of the promised punishment, to which they agreed, remedies the disaster, after which sacrifice is acceptable again. Consequently, in light of the two broader points above, were Jesus's death to have the effects of a "sacrifice," it would not meet the need Israel was facing and would leave them subject to the punitive discipline.

In the context of the Gospels, then, in view of the broken covenant—why else would a new covenant be needed?—and the nonacceptance of the herald who called for repentance, Israel remains in a state of punitive discipline from which sacrifice is incapable of delivering. Moreover, in pivotal moments in Luke and Matthew, Jesus accuses the Pharisees and scribes/lawyers of sins for which there is no sacrificial expiation and for which judgment that is not avertable through sacrifice will come. In Matt. 23:23, Jesus states: "Woe to you, scribes and Pharisees, hypocrites! For you tithe mint and dill and cumin, and have neglected the weightier provisions of the Law: justice and mercy and faithfulness [τὴν κρίσιν καὶ τὸ ἔλεος καὶ τὴν πίστιν], but these are the things you should have done without neglecting the others." Significantly, Hosea 4:1 names the lack of "mercy" and "faithfulness" as the reasons for God's approaching judgment (see 4:3–6), and it is in the context of such judgment that God says, "I desire mercy [ἔλεος] and not sacrifice [καὶ οὐ θυσίαν]" (6:6). That is, sacrifice does not fix the problem of impending judgment caused by a lack of faithfulness.

Moreover, just as Hosea 4 accuses the people of "murder" (φόνος) and "bloodshed" (αἵματα, 4:2), for which they will be punished (4:3–6), Jesus in Matthew and Luke proceeds to accuse the Pharisees and scribes of complicity in Israel's past and present "murder" and "bloodshed" of the prophets, saying: "Woe to you, scribes and Pharisees, hypocrites! For you build the tombs of the prophets . . . and you say, 'If we had been living in the days of our fathers, we would not have been partners with them in shedding the blood of the prophets [ἐν τῷ αἵματι τῶν προφητῶν].' So you testify against yourselves, that you are sons of those who murdered [φονευσάντων] the prophets" (Matt. 23:29–31; cp. Luke 11:47–51). Thus the guilt and punishment resulting from "all the righteous blood shed on the land" (AT, πᾶν αἷμα δίκαιον ἐκχυννόμενον ἐπὶ τῆς γῆς) will fall on "this generation" (Matt. 23:35–36; Luke 11:51). Because Jerusalem was "unwilling" to be "gathered"—a term referring to the end of their exile—by Jesus (Matt. 23:37; cp. Luke 13:34), he declares, "Behold, your house is being left to you desolate [ἔρημος]" (Matt. 23:38; cp. Luke 13:35), using the term employed by Lev. 26:31 to refer to the promised punishment of the divine "desolation" (ἐξερημώσω) of the sanctuary and the consequent rejection of their sacrifices.[100]

In the context of Matt. 23 (and Luke 11:42–52), Jesus's discourse is the rhetoric of intramural, prophetic critique,[101] not unlike Josephus's comments to the Zealots occupying the temple before its destruction. Josephus indicts them of heinous sins (theft, betrayal, adultery, sexual assault, murder; *J.W.* 5.402), because of which "this divine place is polluted" (5.402), before concluding: "I cannot but suppose that God has fled out of his sanctuary and stands on the side of those against whom you fight" (5.412). Though not identical, this scenario captures well Jesus's woes against the Pharisees and scribes in Matt. 23, in which he names grave transgressions (23:16–36) on account of which "your house is being left to you desolate" (23:38).[102]

Significantly, Jesus does not delight in the coming judgment; he laments and weeps that destruction will come on Jerusalem (Matt. 23:37; Luke 19:41). However, he indicts the Pharisees of sins, especially "bloodshed," for which

100. For a similar reading of Jesus's death relative to the vacant temple, see Runesson, *Divine Wrath*, esp. 101–12, 191–99. Runesson rightly interprets the temple's judgment to be the result of sins that led to the temple's desolation, including the people's unrepentance. And he sees Jesus's death as the means of saving the people, given this impending judgment. However, *pace* Runesson, I do not think Jesus's death is a "sacrifice" in the technical sense as Runesson calls it in his book (e.g., 197, 199).

101. See the discussion in A. Collins, "Polemic against the Pharisees." For contextualization of Matt. 23 within rabbinic and early Christian evidence, see Reed, "When Did Rabbis?"

102. A comparable, if not more extreme, example of intramural rhetoric criticizing the Pharisees for their transgression of the Law and their leading astray the masses may be found in 4Q169, the Nahum pesher. By coordinating events and agents described in this pesher with accounts from Josephus, many suspect that those who "seek easy interpretations" referred to in this pesher are the Pharisees (for the data, see VanderKam, "Pharisees"). For example, frags. 3–4, col. 3, lines 3–5 read as follows: "Its interpretation concerns those looking for easy interpretations, whose evil deeds will be exposed to all Israel in the final time; many will fathom their sin, they will hate them and loathe them for their reprehensible arrogance. And when the glory of Judah is re[ve]aled the simple people of Ephraim will flee from among their assembly and desert the ones who misdirected them and will join . . . [I]srael." Earlier it states, "[Its] interpretation [con]cerns those who misdirect Ephraim, who with their fraudulent teaching and lying tongue and perfidious lip misdirect many; kings, princes, priests and people together with the proselyte attached to them" (frags. 3–4, col. 2, lines 8–9). Like Matt. 23:13–15, the author of this scroll accuses the "seekers" (probably the Pharisees) of misdirecting the people and proselytes through their teaching. My point is not to pile criticism on the Pharisees but to highlight that Jesus was not alone in regarding them as transgressors who led their audiences astray. Moreover, Jesus, like the author of this scroll, does not think the Pharisees' issue is that they are too "strict"—quite the opposite. Such was the stuff of some intramural discourse over the Law and eschatology in late Second Temple Judaism.

there is no sacrificial expiation (Num. 35:33; cp. Jub. 7.33; 21.18–20, 22; 33.18). Thus, in light of the coming judgment on Jerusalem, the sins that occasion it, and the general state of perduring covenant discipline, there is no sacrifice that may be given. For this reason, Jesus's death is best interpreted not as a sacrifice but as a voluntary submission to God's punitive discipline as a "ransom for many." The death is nonsacrificial in nature, being a profane execution performed by nonpriests in common space. Jesus submits to this execution in order to bring "forgiveness of sins" (Matt. 26:28; Luke 24:47) and to liberate the people from the punitive captivity (Mark 10:45; Matt. 20:28; Luke 24:21; cp. Acts 20:28) occasioned by their commission of sins for which there is no sacrificial atonement.

"If This Cup Cannot Pass"

I turn finally to the "cup" saying prior to his arrest. Each Synoptic Gospel records a prayer of Jesus before his arrest in which he petitions that "this cup [ποτήριον]" be removed from him, all contextualized by the caveat "Yet not what I will, but what you will" (Mark 14:36; cp. Luke 22:42; Matt. 26:39). Matthew alone adds this statement: "My Father, if this cup cannot pass away [παρελθεῖν] unless I drink from it [ἐὰν μὴ αὐτὸ πίω], your will be done" (26:42).

Commentators regularly and rightly point out the widespread usage of "cup" as a metaphor to refer to the "cup" of God's punitive wrath that he causes Israel or the nations to drink.[103] In these texts, a given nation is subject to divine punishment due to sin (transgression of God's Law or the nations' violence against Israel). The experience of this divine punishment, often termed God's "wrath," is manifest in subjugation to some hostile nation, and it is expressed as "drinking the cup" of God's affliction or wrath.

For example, Jer. 25 states that after Judah endures captivity to Babylon for seventy years, God will punish Babylon (25:12). God then addresses Jeremiah, "Take this cup of the wine of wrath from my hand and give it to all the nations to whom I send you, to drink from it" (25:15 [32:15 LXX]). Jeremiah then states, "So I took the cup from the Lord's hand and gave it to all the nations to whom the Lord sent me, to drink from it: To Jerusalem and the cities of Judah, and its kings and its officials, to make them places of ruins, objects of horror, hissing, and a curse, as it is this day" (25:17–18 [32:17–18 LXX]). God then tells Jeremiah, "And if they refuse to take the cup from your hand to drink, then you shall say to them, 'This is what the Lord of armies says: "You shall certainly drink!"'" (25:28 [32:28 LXX]). Israel's judgment for

103. E.g., Keener, *Matthew*, 638.

covenant violation is described as drinking from the cup of God's "wrath," manifest in the destruction wrought by "the sword" (25:29 [32:29 LXX]).[104]

Isaiah's usage is especially telling. In Isa. 51, God promises that he will soon liberate Israel from their captivity (51:14), declaring that "the redeemed [λελυτρωμένοις] of the Lord will return" (51:11). God then addresses captive Israel, "Arise, Jerusalem! / You who have drunk [ἡ πιοῦσα] from the Lord's hand the cup [τὸ ποτήριον] of his anger; / The chalice of staggering you have drunk to the dregs" (51:17). In view of his promise to rescue, God states, "Behold, I have taken from your hand the cup [τὸ ποτήριον] of staggering, / The chalice of my anger. / You will never drink [πιεῖν] it again" (51:22). As in Jeremiah, Israel's captivity is understood as God's punishment for Israel's sin, manifest in the promised curses of "devastation and destruction, famine and sword" (Isa. 51:19), and it is described as Israel's drink from the "cup of his anger" (51:17, 22). Additional Jewish texts attest to such usage.[105]

What then shall we say? Given the well-attested use of this image to refer to God's general judgment and punitive wrath manifest in subjection to the nations, and given that Israel's plight, which Jesus predicts he will experience, is just such a deliverance into the hands of the nations, he likely envisions his coming death at the hands of the nations as the endurance (the "drinking") of God's punitive judgment falling upon Israel due to their sin and current unrepentance. Isaiah 51 may inform the language and logic of Jesus's Gethsemane prayer when read against the wider narrative of Jesus's goal to "ransom" his people. In Isa. 51, Jerusalem's experience of captivity was described as their "drinking" the "cup" of God's wrath. But having drunk it (51:17), they will leave their captivity as "the redeemed" (λελυτρωμένοις) people of God (51:11, 17, 22). Within the Gospel narratives, Israel rejects the herald of salvation and thus remains in captivity, in need of "ransom" (Mark 10:45; Matt. 20:28; Luke 24:21), meaning that the cup of God's wrath remains theirs to drink. Knowing this, Jesus prays that this cup might pass, but he is determined to do as God wills. Realizing that this cup will not pass away unless he drinks it (τοῦτο παρελθεῖν ἐὰν μὴ αὐτὸ πίω), he obediently submits himself to the will of his Father: "Your will be done" (Matt. 26:42). "In Gethsemane the die has been cast."[106] He is prepared to endure Israel's fate with them and on their behalf so that "the redeemed of the Lord will return" (Isa. 51:11).

If these comments are on target, the Synoptic Gospels present Jesus as voluntarily undergoing Israel's punitive discipline, the covenant wrath of God

104. In Jeremiah, see also 49:12 (30:6 LXX); 51:7 (28:7 LXX).

105. Pss. 11:6; 60:1–3; 75:8; Isa. 63:6; Hab. 2:16; Lam. 2:13 LXX; 4:21; Zech. 12:2; Pss. Sol. 8.14; Rev. 14:10; 16:19; 18:6. See Raabe, "Drinking the Cup."

106. France, *Matthew*, 1006.

expressed in their/his being handed over to Israel's captors (i.e., the nations and their powers), to bring to an end such discipline in himself. This he does by dying at the hand of Israel's enemies as a ransom to liberate those captive to such enemies, of whom Satan is the chief. This death is punitive (or "penal") in that Jesus experiences Israel's punitive discipline occasioned by their past and current transgression, including their unrepentance despite Jesus's summons. But this notion of "punishment" should be contextualized within the Deuteronomic/Levitical matrix of Israel's covenant curses, which the nation is already experiencing. It would be misleading to abstract the "penal" component from its storied position and simply assert that God punished Jesus by killing him on the cross. Rather, Israel is already experiencing punitive discipline in the form of captivity to the nations and their powers, and Jesus enters into "cursed solidarity" with his people, enduring the plight they are under.[107] His subjection to the nations is his willing act, knowing that they will put him to death. Further, his death is liberative in that his death pays the punitive debt held and exercised by Israel's captors, thereby liberating those held captive due to this debt. So though his death is not strictly a sacrifice, it is nonetheless salvific.

Jesus's story does not end there. Having endured this fate, God vindicates the obedience of his Son by raising him from the dead. In view of Ezekiel's image of Israel as "dead" (punished) due to their sin, but "resurrected" (restored) when God delivers them from exile (Ezek. 37:1–14), Jesus's resurrection symbolizes, embodies, and initiates the inauguration of Israel's restoration.[108] Newly resurrected, Matthew claims that Jesus now possesses "all authority . . . in heaven and on earth" (28:18). Similarly, Luke claims that, having suffered, the Messiah has entered "into his glory" (24:26), probably

107. The phrase "cursed solidarity" is Rillera's (*Lamb*, 256) in reference to Gal. 3:13, but it aptly describes the Synoptic presentation as well, as Rillera's argument suggests (173–75, 274–75, 284). Rillera states that in his death Jesus experiences "the curses of the covenant for grave sins." As Rillera knows and argues, the curses are penal. Therefore, readers who correctly note that Rillera (rightly) argues against an abstract form of penal substitutionary atonement, whose proponents occasionally misinterpret Christ's death as a "sacrifice" and then attach related misunderstandings to Levitical sacrifice itself, should not regard Rillera's refutation of abstracted forms of penal substitutionary atonement as an argument against any "penal" components related to the cross. The only difference between Rillera's position and mine, as far as I can tell, is the notion of ransom as "debt payment." But just as he argues that penal components should not be abstracted from the covenantal situation, so I argue that debt payment occurs within the same narrative matrix for which he argues in his book, though I highlight the Jubilee context, which is less prominent in his configuration.

108. See further discussion in Kinzer, *Jerusalem Crucified, Jerusalem Risen*, 21–22, 54–55, 222–23; Rillera, *Lamb*, 187–89.

referring to his dominion over all the nations.[109] With this newly possessed authority over all the nations, Jesus sends his disciples once more to Israel, and now to the nations as well, to summon them to repentance (Luke 24:46–47) and to make them into disciples of Israel's Messiah (Matt. 28:19). That this post-resurrection summons does not replace following Jesus's interpretation of the Law for something else ("faith" in him, reductively) is made plain by Matt. 28 and Luke's sequel, Acts. In the former, the disciples are to teach "all the nations" to "follow all that I commanded you" (Matt. 28:20). In Acts, repentance, faith, and "doing deeds consistent with repentance" (Acts 26:20) are named as normative, and the Jerusalem Council (Acts 15) assumes that Jews still keep the Law and rules that gentiles keep select regulations prescribed in Lev. 17–18. I will discuss Acts 15 further in the next chapter, but a brief word on Matt. 28:19–20 is necessary here.

Teaching the Nations

Matthew 28:18–20 states, "All authority in heaven and on earth has been given to me. Go, therefore [οὖν], and make disciples of all the nations, baptizing them in the name of the Father and the Son and the Holy Spirit, teaching them to follow all that I commanded you." The commission to go to "all the nations" is connected logically (οὖν) to Jesus's possession of complete authority in heaven and on earth due to the assumed cosmology that the other nations were temporarily ruled by other powers (e.g., Deut. 4:19; 32:8–9; Ps. 82; Zeph. 2:11; Matt. 4:8–9), but that God has now subordinated such rule to his own Son, to whom he's given it. Having authority over the nations and the powers that governed them, Jesus commissions his disciples to summon the nations to allegiance to the God of Israel. Two major questions often discussed from these verses are: (1) Does "all the nations" include Israel[110] or refer only to non-Israelite nations?[111] And (2) Do the baptized gentiles become part of Israel and so become obligated to all the Law that obligates Israel,

109. Compare the temptation, where Satan possesses all the "authority" and "glory" of all the world's kingdoms (Luke 4:5–6). Newly resurrected and soon to be enthroned (Acts 2:30–33), Israel's Messiah, Jesus, now possesses all the "authority" of the nations. On the comparable pattern between Christ's enthronement and the consequent liberation from Satan and 11QMelch's reference to Melchizedek (an enthroned figure according to Ps. 110), who liberates captives from Belial, see Garrett, *Demise of the Devil*, 52–53.

110. So Dormeyer, "Die Rollen von Volk"; Stuhlmacher, "Zur missionsgeschichtlichen"; Konradt, *Israel*, 311–17; Novakovic, "Matthew and Paul," 114. See bibliography in Konradt, *Israel*, 311–12n252.

111. So Donaldson, "'Nations,'" 173–88; Runesson, "Aspects of Matthean Universalism."

or do they join the assembly as gentiles and do only what the Law requires of them as gentiles?[112]

Regarding the first question, if "all the nations" refers only to gentiles, either Israel is excluded from Jesus's future saving intent (highly improbable given Matt. 1:21 and 10:6) or the former prohibition not to go to the gentiles (Matt. 10:5–6) is now lifted, meaning that he is simply adding the gentiles to the ongoing mission to Israel.[113] In the latter case, even if Matt. 28's "all the nations" refers only to gentiles, Israel is still included. Supporting the position that Israel is included in "all the nations" is (a) Israel is a nation, thus "all the nations" would include them; (b) Jesus now possesses universal authority in heaven and earth (Matt. 28:18, alluding to Dan. 7:14),[114] suggesting authority over Israel and implying that they are included in his commission; (c) though rare according to Donaldson,[115] some texts do include Israelites within the label "(all) the nations";[116] and (d) as ancillary support, Luke 24:47's commission includes Jews in the label "all the nations." But Donaldson justifiably argues that "all the nations" indicates gentiles based on inter- and intratextual data; however, he rightly concludes that Israel is not thereby wholly excluded, since Matt. 28's commission, on his reading, simply adds gentiles to the still-ongoing mission to Israel.[117] For my purposes, it is not necessary to decide firmly since, regardless, Israel is still included in Jesus's saving intent.[118]

The second question is more pertinent: Are baptized gentiles incorporated into Israel and thus obligated to keep all the Law,[119] or do they stay gentiles and keep only parts of the Law?[120] There are three reasons why I think that the second answer is correct. First, Jesus's universal authority "in heaven and on earth" (Matt. 28:18) implies that he rules over all the nations (including Israel). Requiring the gentiles to "Israelize" would seem to compromise this

112. On these issues, see Meier, "Nations or Gentiles"; Sim, "Matthew, Paul, and the Origin"; Willitts, "Friendship"; White, "Eschatological Conversion"; Konradt, *Israel*, 311–17; Runesson, *Divine Wrath*, 30–36, 378–80; Runesson, "Aspects of Matthean Universalism"; Donaldson, "'Nations'"; Novakovic, "Matthew and Paul," 112–18.

113. Donaldson, "'Nations,'" 173–88. See also Konradt, *Israel*, 74–84, 316–17.

114. See Konradt, *Israel*, 284.

115. Donaldson, "'Nations,'" 181–83.

116. Ps. 113:4; Isa. 25:7; 52:10; Jer. 1:5, 18; 25:15–18; Dan. 3:2–8; 7:14; Matt. 24:14; Luke 24:47.

117. Donaldson, "'Nations,'" 173–88.

118. So also Konradt, *Israel*, 316.

119. Sim, *Matthew*, 251–54; Runesson, *Divine Wrath*, 30–36, 350, 378–80; Novakovic, "Matthew and Paul," 115–16.

120. Willitts, "Friendship"; and cautiously, conceding the ambiguity, Donaldson, "'Nations,'" 190–93. Konradt (*Israel*, 319–20) argues that the gentiles do not formally convert to Judaism—i.e., they do not receive circumcision—but they do follow Jesus's interpretation of the commandments.

authority over all the nations. Moreover, Dan. 7:14, to which Matt. 28:18 alludes, claims that "all the . . . nations . . . will serve him," implying that they stay nations. Or does the Son of Man have authority over Israel only? Does he not have authority over the gentiles? Yes, the gentiles also. Second, if Matt. 28:19–20 expects proselytization by circumcision and thereafter full Law observance, why is there no mention of circumcision in Matt. 28 or anywhere else in the Gospel? Although this is an argument from silence, that silence is loud. Third, Matt. 12:21 quotes Isa. 42:4 LXX with respect to Jesus and the nations, saying "and in his name the Gentiles will hope." Given that Matt. 28:19 requires the gentiles to be baptized "in the name" of the Father, Son, and Holy Spirit in conjunction with the quoted prophecy of Isa. 42:4, it seems probable that Matthew expects the nations to stay nations. Consequently, they observe the Law *as nations* and thus are obligated to only parts of it.

That Jesus requires these gentiles to "follow all that [he] commanded" (Matt. 28:20) does not entail that they do every commandment in the Law. Rather, what Jesus has programmatically commanded is to observe all the commandments and not nullify even the least of them (Matt. 5:19). Importantly, the commandments themselves regulate who is obligated. For example, the Law commands that foreskinned men may not eat the Passover (Exod. 12:48). Thus a gentile keeping the Law in this case means *not* eating the Passover. Additionally, the Law obligates Israel to the dietary laws (Lev. 11; Deut. 14) and permits gentiles to eat food forbidden to Israelites (Deut. 14:21; see also Gen. 9:3). Therefore, a gentile keeping the Law *as a gentile* is permitted to eat food forbidden to Israel. Donaldson detects what he considers an ambiguity "that cannot be resolved in any univocal resolution of the tensions"[121] in the fact that gentiles stay gentiles and yet are commissioned to do all that Jesus commanded. However, the "tension" is resolvable by recognizing that (a) Jesus requires doing all the commandments, (b) the baptized and discipled gentiles stay gentiles, and (c) the Law itself conditions the keeping of its commandments based on the ethnicity of the agent, so (d) baptized gentiles who observe Jesus's requirement to keep all the Law will follow the Law's own instructions on what they may or may not do as gentiles. For example, these baptized gentiles need not keep all of Israel's dietary restrictions.

Whether Matt. 28's assumption about what parts of the Law these baptized gentiles should observe coincides with the decision in Acts 15 is underdetermined.[122] I think Matthew's Jesus would agree with at least the commandments given in Acts 15, since they are drawn from Lev. 17–18, which requires the

121. Donaldson, "'Nations,'" 192–93.
122. See the discussion in the next chapter.

keeping of its commandments by both Israelites and foreigners in their midst. It also seems clear that these gentiles would be obligated to follow the legal instruction in the Sermon on the Mount for two reasons. First, excluding the legal justifications Jesus gave for his own practices, Matt. 5–7 is the sole body of positive instruction of the Law in Matthew. Presumably its instructions would be included in what Jesus refers to as "all that I commanded you" (Matt. 28:20). Second, related to this, Jesus asserts that all the Law and the Prophets hang on love of God and neighbor (Matt. 22:37–40). Because such neighbor treatment is extended to benefit non-Israelites in the land (Lev. 19:34), and because the commandments interpreted in Matt. 5 revolve around neighbor treatment (as argued in chap. 3), Matt. 28's baptized gentiles ought to follow the instructions given in the Sermon.[123] The Gospel of Matthew, therefore, expects Jewish and gentile followers of Jesus to keep the Law of Moses.[124]

Conclusion

Because of their rejection of Jesus's summons, Jerusalem and the temple will be judged. Because of their unrepentance, Israel remains in a state of punitive captivity, but determined to liberate his people, Jesus gives his life as a ransom for their deliverance. Though not strictly sacrificial, his death at the hands of the nations participates in Israel's punitive discipline, which he bears with them and on their behalf. Having done so out of obedience to his Father's will for Israel and himself, Jesus is vindicated through his resurrection, which embodies Israel's restoration. Now possessing authority over Israel and the nations as Israel's Messiah, Jesus commissions his disciples to summon Israel and the nations to repentance to receive the forgiveness of sins and the liberation offered through the new covenant inaugurated by his death and resurrection. Those who respond to this message are summoned to obey the Law of God as taught by his Son, Jesus.

123. Jesus in Matt. 5:21–48 exposits laws related to murder (5:21), adultery (5:27), and divorce (5:31), the last of which I take as a subset of his teaching on adultery and sexual immorality, vows (5:33), eye for eye (5:38), and love of neighbor (5:43). Laws concerning murder, adultery, sexual immorality, and eye for eye obligate both Israelites and foreigners (Lev. 24:21; 18:20, 26; 24:20–22, respectively). The vows in question are voluntary; thus their prohibition would seem to extend to non-Israelites. Finally, love toward a neighbor is extended to benefit non-Israelites in Lev. 19:34.

124. Space precludes discussion of the judgment scene in Matt. 25:31–46, though it does not affect the conclusions above regarding the expectation of Law observance among disciples. On this passage, see France, *Matthew*, 957–67; Runesson, *Divine Wrath*, 414–28. Both interpret the "saved sheep" as nondisciples who acted mercifully toward disciples of Jesus. Thus, their "salvation" is still wrapped up in activity directed toward Israel's Messiah, who was present in those they helped, whether they knew it or not.

Conclusion

The Law in the New Testament

The topic of Jesus and the Law is vast, and this book has only scratched the surface. For centuries, interpretation of the Law in the Gospels has labored under false presuppositions of Jewish legalism, works righteousness, and compassionless nationalism and particularism. I have tried to show the numerous shortcomings of such interpretations and to offer an alternative that takes seriously the restoration-eschatological framework of the Synoptic presentation of Jesus and the interpretation of the Law that results. Jesus, like Isaiah or Jeremiah, called for repentance and adherence to his divinely authorized message, warned of discipline for nonrepentance, and yet firmly believed that the God of Israel would not abandon his people and would restore those who returned to him. I have not examined the person of Jesus exhaustively but have instead focused on his depiction as the Son of God acting as a prophet summoning Israel to repentance in view of the coming restoration and judgment. Within this framework, Jesus's interpretation of the Law should be understood as his instruction in the way of doing God's will that characterizes those who participate in the restoration. Legal controversies arise when other teachers disagree with his conclusions, and when his halakhic conclusions are based on his eschatological mission and identity, these teachers question Jesus's authority to teach and act as he does. His action in the temple is now understood to represent not his distaste for external rituals, sacrifice, or a supposed violent nationalism but instead signals the impending punitive destruction of the temple as a result of Israel's grave sin (Matt. 23) and their rejection of the message of repentance proclaimed by John and

Jesus. The Jerusalem temple failed to be the eschatological temple promised for the age of restoration. Though Israel remained in punitive captivity due to their nonacceptance of his announcement of the eschatological Jubilee, Jesus was determined to liberate his people, volunteering his life as the "ransom" paid toward Israel's remaining punitive debt because of their prior covenant violation and current unrepentance. Resurrected, Jesus initiates and embodies the restoration and renewed covenant he formerly heralded, and with his acquired authority over heaven and earth, he commissions his disciples to summon Israel and the nations to allegiance to him and his interpretation of the Law as the world's appointed ruler and judge.

In what follows, I want briefly to address a few potential implications of my conclusions and to clear up some conceptual loose ends, such as continuity and discontinuity between "Old" and "New" Testaments, legal questions in Acts, and congruity between Jesus and Paul on the question of the restoration and the Law.

Continuity between Old and New Testaments

Determining what distinguishes the "covenants" is a perennial question among students of the Bible attempting to find coherence in God's dealings with Israel and the nations, especially those who read both Testaments as Scripture. It seems to me that a great deal of continuity is to be found when comparing the "Old" and the "New" or, more specifically, the Law and the Gospels. It is not the case that the Law only makes demands that the Gospels relieve, or that the graceless Law is resolved by the compassion of Jesus, or that the Law requires the earning of salvation while Jesus offers it without conditions, or that the Law is exclusionary and Jesus is not. Rather, the Law's commands operate within a covenantal agreement in which obedience is required and yet transgression is assumed, requiring and providing both divine and human forgiveness. So also with Jesus's instructions: obedience is demanded, and yet he assumes that humans will continue to need and be able to obtain both divine and human forgiveness. Moreover, both the Law and the Prophets anticipated in the restoration the divine transformation of the heart to enable the keeping of God's commandments (Deut. 30:6; Jer. 31:33–34; Ezek. 36:25–27). Such texts depict this divinely empowered obedience as characteristic of those who would participate in the restoration. Relatedly, when questioned about how one "enters eternal life," Jesus answers in terms of keeping the commandments (Matt. 19:16–17; Mark 10:17–21; Luke 18:18–22), affirming specifically the love of "the Lord your God with all your heart, and with all your soul" and the love of neighbor (Luke 10:27), stating, "Do this, and you will live [τοῦτο ποίει καὶ ζήσῃ]" (Luke 10:28). Here Luke's Jesus likely alludes to the restoration assurance in Deut. 30:6, where God promises to circumcise the heart so that they "love the LORD your God with all your heart and with all your soul, in order that you may live [ἵνα ζῇς σύ]." Jesus does not present these answers as impossibly high standards to prove instead the need for grace. Rather, with the Law and the Prophets, Jesus answers that in the restoration, God's people will keep the commandments. And with the Prophets, the Gospels and Acts assume or positively depict the divine transformation of the heart necessary for such obedience.[1] Although the mode of covenant maintenance is largely preserved, what of its precise contents? Here again I have tried to demonstrate that there is a high degree of continuity.

Jesus keeps and teaches his fellow Jews to keep all aspects of the Law, from the Ten Commandments and the love of neighbor to the purity regulations and tithing requirements. When Jesus and his disciples behave differently from what his interlocutors view as permissible, his defense denies neither the validity of the Law nor that his disciples are "breaking" the command. Instead, it centers on their capacity to ostensibly break a command because of an authorized duty that overrides the requirement. Moreover, as briefly discussed, his divine authorization, manifested at the transfiguration when God said "Listen to him!" (Mark 9:7; Matt. 17:5; Luke 9:35), alludes to Deut. 18:15.[2] In that passage, the people are commanded to listen to the prophet whom God would appoint. Thus, by listening to and obeying Jesus, the people are also thereby obeying a Pentateuchal command. Consequently, Jesus's telling people to keep the commandments and contextualizing his mission authorization in light of Deut. 18:15 means that heeding Jesus's mission/instruction ought to be construed not as independent of Torah but as obeying it.

However, there are instances that some may label "discontinuity," such as Jesus's prohibition of something the Law permits (e.g., vows, retaliation, and some instances of divorce). However, it would be incorrect to infer from these distinct practices an objection to the Law itself. As I argued above, the case of "eye for eye" being replaced by "turn the other cheek" is based not reductively on a "progressive" ethic that sees the Law as outdated but on a

1. On Matt. 6:9's relation to Ezek. 36:21–27 and the transformation of the heart, see the introduction to chap. 2. On the transformation of the heart in Acts, compare LXX Deut. 30:6's "heart purification" as the sign of the restoration and Acts 15:9. Mark assumes the activity of "the Holy Spirit" in Jesus's absence (Mark 13:11), plausibly implying the divinely wrought anthropological effects basic to many depictions of the restoration.

2. Marcus, *Mark 8–16*, 634; France, *Matthew*, 650.

conviction that the new time (eschatological Jubilee) has altered the acceptability of actions formerly permitted.

Regarding vows and divorce, prohibiting a permission is not the same as permitting a prohibition. Matters legislated by the Law but prohibited by Jesus are often set within casuistic settings. That is, the Law does not require divorce or the making of vows, but it legislates their execution if undertaken. Jesus, on the other hand, in agreement with many other Jewish voices, prohibits the use of such permissions based on a scriptural ethic of peacemaking, fidelity, and truthfulness to which God calls his people. In the case of divorce as recounted in Mark 10, Jesus's interlocutors concede that Moses only "permitted" (ἐπέτρεψεν) divorce (10:4); he did not require it. Jesus then asserts that they received this commandment because of their "hardness of heart" (10:5) and calls them to an ideal in continuity with the original divine intention expressed in the Law: "But from the beginning of creation . . ." (10:6).

Moreover, this interpretative move is not unique to Jesus. The Damascus Document likewise interprets God's will for marriage in view of creation rather than based reductively on the Mosaic permission (CD 4.21). Because it is all "Torah" (i.e., divine instruction), some parts—here Gen. 1:27—may override or "weigh more" than others.[3] Moreover, Matthew notes the permissibility of divorce in cases of "sexual immorality" (5:32; 19:9), depicting Jesus's instruction as his interpretation of the permission legislated in Deut. 24:1–4, coinciding with a Pharisaic interpretation of that legislation expressed in m. Git. 9.10. Thus Jesus's instruction is presented as in keeping with the Law. And this is not mere historical coincidence; rather, I have tried to show that calling Israel back to fidelity to God and his Law (as interpreted by Jesus) was basic to his mission.

The Gospels and Acts

But what about Acts 10? And Acts 15? After teaching about the Law in the Gospels, these are typically the first questions my students ask. In Acts 10, so the argument often goes, the food laws are abolished, so doesn't that mean God changed the laws that Jesus just taught as good and necessary? And in Acts 15, gentiles who believe the gospel don't have to do all the Law, so did the apostles change Jesus's message? The answer to both questions is no, but this requires some unpacking.

Acts 10:10–16 is the account of Peter's vision:

3. See the discussion in Forderer, "'What God Has Joined'"; Klawans, "Prohibition of Oaths," 35–40.

> He became hungry and wanted to eat; but while they were making preparations, he fell into a trance; and he saw the sky opened up, and an object like a great sheet coming down, lowered by four corners to the ground, and on it were all kinds of four-footed animals and crawling creatures of the earth and birds of the sky. And a voice came to him, "Get up, Peter, kill and eat!" [ἀναστάς, Πέτρε, θῦσον καὶ φάγε]. But Peter said, "By no means, Lord, for I have never eaten anything defiled or impure [κοινὸν καὶ ἀκάθαρτον]." Again a voice came to him a second time, "What God has cleansed [ἐκαθάρισεν], no longer consider defiled [κοίνου]." This happened three times, and immediately the object was taken up into the sky. (NASB, with modifications)[4]

From this scene, interpreters have routinely understood Acts 10:15's "what God has cleansed" to indicate the cleansing of all foods, dissolving the Law's

4. NASB translates κοινὸν καὶ ἀκάθαρτον as "unholy and unclean" (10:14) and κοίνου as "unholy" (10:15), but "unholy" (NASB) or "common" (ESV) would suggest that Peter only ever ate sacred food, which is implausible. Moreover, the LXX uniformly uses βέβηλος, not κοινός, when referring to profane (i.e., nonsacred) items. I here translate Acts 10:14–15's κοινόν as "defiled," referring to common, permissible ("clean") food that has become unclean (cp. NIV). As Logan Williams pointed out to me in conversation, impurity can be "shared," which makes sense of texts employing κοιν- terminology; such terminology often indicates commonality, communion, or fellowship when referring to items that may have shared in the impurity of something else. (Any errors in the following are my own.) For example, see Mark 7:15: "There is nothing outside the person which can defile him [κοινῶσαι αὐτόν] if it goes into him" (i.e., no permissible food that has become unclean can make the eater a participant in that impurity). However and whenever κοιν- came to refer to defilement in the sense of "sharing impurity," the sense is reflected in rabbinic texts. For example, m. Eduyyot 2.4 states, "Concerning a beaten egg placed upon vegetables of *terumah*—that . . . is a connective; but if it is like a cap—that . . . is not a connective." Regarding "connective," Shaye Cohen notes, "If a source of light impurity (e.g. a *tevul yom*) touches the egg, even though the egg itself does not become impure, it conveys impurity to the *terumah* beneath" (Cohen, Goldenberg, and Lapin, *Oxford Annotated Mishnah*, 2:641). The point for our purposes is that "connective" translates חִבּוּר (from חָבַר). In the MT, the cognate verb often means "join" or "unite"; the noun, "companion" or "partner"; and the adjective, "joined" or "shared." Significantly, Septuagintal passages regularly translate this root with κοινωνέω ("to join" or "to partner"; 2 Chron. 20:35; Eccles. 9:4) or κοινός ("shared"; Prov. 21:9; 25:24) or κοινωνός ("companion"; Prov. 28:24; Isa. 1:23). Though using a different term, Philo (*Spec. Laws* 3.208) expresses this understanding of impurity's transmissibility by one object "participating" in another object's impurity: "And the law says, 'Let everything which a man that is unclean [ἀκάθαρτος] has touched be also unclean [ἀκάθαρτα], being polluted [μιαινόμενα] by a participation [μετουσίᾳ] in that which is unclean [μὴ καθαροῦ].'" Elsewhere Philo uses μετουσία ("participation") in relation to κοινωνέω/κοινωνία ("sharing," "participating in"). See also Philo, *Allegorical Interpretation* 3.171; *Sacrifices* 1.33; *Life of Joseph* 1.220; *Spec. Laws* 4.100; *Rewards* 87. Therefore, when Peter denied having eaten anything κοινὸν καὶ ἀκάθαρτον (Acts 10:14), he meant that he had never eaten forbidden ("unclean") food (ἀκάθαρτον) or defiled food (κοινόν)—i.e., permissible ("clean") food secondarily defiled by having "shared" (κοινόν) in the impurity of another impure substance. On κοινόν pertaining to "defilement by association," see House, "Defilement by Association."

distinction between clean and unclean food.[5] This is often seen as an extension of the (mis)interpretation of Mark 7:19, where Jesus supposedly "declared all foods clean,"[6] and to be in continuity with (a misinterpretation of) Rom. 14, where Paul supposedly considers all foods clean (14:14, 20). Mark 7 has already been interpreted, and Rom. 14 will have to wait for another day.[7] However, there are four reasons suggesting that such an interpretation misreads Acts 10.

First, Acts 10 records a vision. Items in visions regularly do not correspond one to one with the same items outside of the vision. Thus, because there are "animals" in the vision does not indicate that the vision instructs about animals *outside the vision*. Daniel likewise sees a vision of "beasts" (Dan. 7:3), but he does not therefore expect Israel to be attacked by a literal winged lion. The beasts *in the vision* refer to gentile kings (7:17). Similarly, Peter's visionary unclean animals likely do not correspond to actual unclean animals in the world outside Peter's vision (i.e., animals forbidden for consumption in Lev. 11 and Deut. 14).[8]

Second, as both Thiessen and Staples have argued, Jewish texts use animals, especially "unclean" ones, to depict gentiles.[9] Daniel 7 and the Animal Apocalypse (1 En. 85–90) are prime examples. In these, gentiles are depicted as hybrid animals (Dan. 7) or animals described as unclean in Lev. 11 (cp. 1 Enoch). This evidence suggests that Peter's vision of unclean animals plausibly refers to gentiles, not Israel's dietary laws.

Third, the above is certified by the subsequent account in Acts 10, in which the vision is interpreted to refer to God's acceptance of the formerly "unclean" gentiles.[10] Two observations support this. First, following the vision, three men summon Peter to visit Cornelius, a gentile (10:19, 22). As Peter is considering

5. Bruce, *Acts*, 256; Longenecker, *Acts*, 388; Tyson, "Dietary Regulations," 146; Polhill, *Acts*, 254–56; Larkin, *Acts*, 473–76; Marguerat, *Les Acts des apôtres*, 406; Bock, *Acts*, 389–90.

6. Bruce, *Acts*, 256; Longenecker, *Acts*, 388; Polhill, *Acts*, 255–56; Larkin, *Acts*, 474; Bock, *Acts*, 382.

7. Logan Williams and I argue that all of Rom. 14 pertains to food sacrificed to images rather than to a Pauline subordination of all the dietary laws and Sabbath regulations. In short, some fear that meat purchased on or near a Roman festival "day" (cp. 14:5–6) would likely be sacrificial food and thus may make them a participant in idolatry if they eat it, and thus they eat only vegetables in those times. Others do not consider the day and so eat meat, not fearing that they are thereby committing idolatry because they eat in service to the Lord (14:6). Paul permits such action because he is convinced that nothing is automatically "connected" (κοινόν, 14:14) to an idol or demon. In this way, his argument is akin to his reasoning in 1 Cor. 8–10. For conference presentations on this thesis, see Sloan and Williams, "Neither Sabbath nor Kashrut" and "Avodah Zarah" (article in preparation).

8. See also Oliver, *Torah Praxis*, 324, 344.

9. Thiessen, *Contesting Conversion*, 136–37; Staples, "'Rise, Kill, and Eat.'"

10. Oliver, *Torah Praxis*, 352–55.

the vision, the Spirit speaks to him, "Arise, descend and go [ἀναστὰς κατάβηθι καὶ πορεύου] with them without misgivings" (10:20 AT). The command and its syntax corresponds to that of the vision concerning the animals:

Acts 10:13 (AT): "Arise, Peter, kill and eat" (ἀναστάς, Πέτρε, θῦσον καὶ φάγε).

Acts 10:20 (AT): "Arise, descend and go" (ἀναστὰς κατάβηθι καὶ πορεύου).

In the former, Peter is presented with unclean animals and given a command, "Arise, kill and eat," to which Peter responds with trepidation, and his trepidation is answered: "What God has cleansed, no longer consider defiled." In the latter, Peter is presented with unknown men (presumably gentiles) and given a command by the Spirit: "Arise, descend and go," and his implicit trepidation is answered: go "without misgivings, for I have sent them myself" (10:20). The comparable command while contemplating the vision alerts the reader that here the explanation is at hand. Just as God has cleansed the animals in the vision, answering Peter's potential objection to eating them, so now Peter is to go to the gentiles without misgivings because this is of God.[11]

Furthermore, when Peter arrives at the house of Cornelius and sees this centurion and "many people assembled," he says, "You yourselves know how uncustomary [ἀθέμιτον] it is for a Jewish man to associate intimately with or visit a foreigner;[12] and yet God has shown me [ὁ θεὸς ἔδειξεν] that I am not to call any person [ἄνθρωπον] defiled or unclean [κοινὸν ἢ ἀκάθαρτον]" (10:28, NASB modified). Peter realizes that the point of the vision ("God has shown me") is that he may not consider any human "defiled or unclean," employing the precise language of Peter's speech in the vision concerning the animals.[13] These gentiles too are welcomed by God and enabled to participate in the "forgiveness of sins" enjoyed by Jews who believe the gospel (10:43).

11. See also Eschner, "Purity and Impurity of Food and People," 386.

12. I translate 10:28's ἀθέμιτον as "uncustomary" rather than "forbidden" (NASB) or "against our Law" (NIV); the latter translations suggest that a Pentateuchal law prohibits such action when in fact it does not. And I translate 10:28's κολλᾶσθαι as "associate intimately" because the bare "associate" (NASB, NIV) suggests a prohibition of even general contact, whereas the verb (from κολλάω) indicates a high degree of union or fellowship. For example, a man leaves his parents and is "joined" (κολληθήσεται) to his wife (Matt. 19:5; cp. Gen. 2:24). The term also indicates sole allegiance to God (Deut. 6:13; 10:20), intimate sexual relationships (1 Kings 11:2), and joining the assembly allied to Jesus (Acts 5:13). Thus Peter refers to close, intimate associations with gentiles rather than general contact, probably due to associations with idolatry rather than ritual impurity. He regards such intimacy as "uncustomary" but not as "forbidden by the Law of Moses" (provided the Jew does not actually commit idolatry). Contra Willimon (*Acts*, 97), who claims that Peter "breached Jewish law." See further discussion in Oliver, *Torah Praxis*, 358–59.

13. Oliver, *Torah Praxis*, 353–54.

Fourth, the reason given in the vision for why Peter was to "kill and eat" was that God had "cleansed" (ἐκαθάρισεν, 10:15) the animals. Correspondingly, when explaining his dining with gentiles to the Jewish "brothers" in Jerusalem (15:7–9), Peter states: "God, who knows the heart, testified to them [the gentiles] giving them the Holy Spirit, just as he also did to us [Jews], and he made no distinction between us [Jews] and them [gentiles], cleansing [καθαρίσας] their hearts by faith." Once again, the language of the vision is interpreted to refer to God's activity toward the gentiles. God has cleansed them too, so they may no longer be considered perpetually "defiled and impure."[14]

These four points make plain that Acts 10 pertains not to Israel's dietary laws but to the admission of gentiles into the people of God by the activity of the Spirit. As Thiessen notes, "Peter's speech in Acts 10:34–43 indicates that it is precisely the salvation of the Gentiles that is the crux here."[15] Additionally, the purification of these gentiles does not require an alteration of the Jewish dietary laws, since Jews could eat with gentiles without violating such laws if proper preparations were made. This should not be difficult to grasp, not least because evidence roughly contemporary with Acts demonstrates that Jews ate with gentiles without compromising their food laws.[16] Moreover, the Acts 15 debate about gentile obligations toward the Law assumes that Jews still keep all of it. Consequently, if the cleansing of the gentiles nullified the food laws for Jews, the believing Pharisees and the apostles did not get the message. Furthermore, when Jews hear of Peter's actions with Cornelius, they do not suppose he ate illicit food; they object to his having eaten with uncircumcised men (11:3). What is at stake in Acts 11 is the uncircumcised status of his dining partners, not the menu. Once Peter relates the divine revelation and the gentiles' reception of the Spirit, they concede (11:18). Moreover, Cornelius is described as both "a devout

14. On Luke's depiction of gentiles as "genealogically impure," a situation now rectified for those who receive the Spirit, see Thiessen, *Contesting Conversion*, 131–40. On the relation between Peter's recognition that God considers gentiles who fear him "acceptable" (δεκτός) (Acts 10:35) and his revelation that they are "cleansed," see Akagi, "Acceptability and Purity."

15. Thiessen, *Contesting Conversion*, 139. For a detailed treatment along the lines I have presented, see also Eschner, "Purity and Impurity of Food and People."

16. See Jdt. 12; Letter of Aristeas; m. Avodah Zarah 5.5. In these texts, Jews eat with gentiles (even gentile hosts) without compromising Jewish dietary laws. See E. P. Sanders, "Jewish Association." Larkin (*Acts*, 475), discussing Jewish dietary laws and the way they supposedly preclude association with gentiles, oddly asserts, "Rabbinic law extended the separation [of Jews from gentiles] by proscribing Jewish acceptance of hospitality in Gentile homes (*m. Avodah Zarah* 5:5; *m. Teharot* 7:6)." But these rabbinic passages do no such thing: rather than proscribing gentile hospitality, m. Avodah Zarah 5.5 assumes that Jews *are* eating with gentiles, and the passage discusses etiquette concerning gentile wine, given the fear that it was offered as a libation to a foreign god in the Jew's absence. And m. Tohorot 7.6 describes the potentially defiling effects of certain items by tax collectors, thieves, and gentiles upon entering Jewish homes. Gentile hospitality of Jews is not at stake.

man who feared God [φοβούμενος τὸν θεόν] with all his household; [who] gave alms generously to the people and prayed constantly to God" (10:2 NRSV) and "a righteous . . . man well spoken of by the entire nation of the Jews" (10:22). Elsewhere Acts refers to "god-fearers" as a body of people, presumably non-Jews, present in a synagogue on the Sabbath and hearing the Law explicated (13:16, 26). Cornelius's degree of Law observance is not stated, but it is highly doubtful that one so aligned with the God of Israel—who is charitable to the Jewish people, may attend synagogue meetings on the Sabbath, and is highly reputed by the Jews—would be so inhospitable as to serve food he knew to be prohibited for a Jewish guest he invited.[17] The contemporary assumption, then, that the cleansing of the gentiles necessarily entails the nullification of the food laws reflects a lack of historical imagination and a failure to integrate evidence that points in the opposite direction.

But if the dietary laws are not affected, why do they not become obligatory for "the Gentiles who are turning to God" (Acts 15:19)? And how does the Jerusalem Council decide on which commands to enforce (15:20)? The first is easy to answer. The Law itself does not obligate gentiles to Israel's food laws. Leviticus 11's restrictions are explicitly and repeatedly stressed to apply to Israel: "Speak to the sons of Israel" (Lev. 11:2), such and such animals "are unclean *to you*" (11:4 and throughout). These animals are unclean (forbidden) for Israel. A related point is made in Deut. 14:21: "You [Israel] shall not eat anything which dies of itself. You may give it to the stranger who is in your town, so that he may eat it, or you may sell it to a stranger, for you are a holy people to the Lord your God." Thus, food prohibited to an Israelite is not forbidden to gentiles, even those who live in the land. Therefore, even if the Jerusalem Council had concluded that gentiles must keep the whole Law, a gentile "keeping the Law" would still be permitted to eat "unclean" food, since such food was proscribed only for Israel. The second question, concerning the basis for the obligations for gentiles, requires unpacking.

Acts 15: Leviticus for Gentiles

At the time of the council in Acts 15, gentiles joining the family of God en masse is a new moment in God's eschatological plan. How the Law obligates them becomes an unavoidable question. When this question is addressed by

17. See further discussion of Peter staying with Cornelius in Oliver, *Torah Praxis*, 357–62. Oliver notes, "Luke *never* claims that Peter ate non-kosher food during his stay with Cornelius. He operates under the assumption that Jews and Gentiles, purified and sanctified, can enjoy fellowship together without leading the former to forsake their kosher diet" (362, italics original).

a council in Jerusalem, "some of the sect of the Pharisees who had believed stood up, saying, 'It is necessary to circumcise them and to direct them to keep the Law of Moses'" (15:5). This Pharisaic position is likely not based on a desire to "make it as hard on them as it has been on us." Rather, Law-keeping is Israel's manner of life and revered as the path of wisdom and life. Incorporating gentiles fully into Law-keeping would entail their participation in the joyous festival of Passover and the life of Israel.[18] Circumcising them and directing them to observe the Law of Moses need not be interpreted as a sign of ill will but can be seen as a desire for their full inclusion: gentiles are really joining the family, and so they must do all that the family does.

In any case, the Pharisees' opinion is not adopted by the council. After debate, James speaks:

> Simeon has described how God first concerned himself about taking a people for his name from among the Gentiles. The words of the Prophets agree with this, just as it is written:
>
> > "After these things I will return,
> > And I will rebuild the fallen tabernacle of David,
> > And I will rebuild its ruins,
> > And I will restore it,
> > So that the rest of mankind may seek the LORD,
> > And all the Gentiles who are called by my name,"
> > Says the LORD, who makes these things known from long ago.
>
> Therefore, it is my judgment that we do not cause trouble for those from the Gentiles who are turning [ἐπιστρέφουσιν] to God, but that we write to them that they abstain from things contaminated by idols, from acts of sexual immorality, from what has been strangled, and from blood. (Acts 15:14–20)

Two things are clear and one big thing is not. First, James interprets the influx of gentiles as a fulfillment of the prophetic expectation that the gentiles will turn to God after the restoration of Israel. Second, his quotation is an amalgamation of several prophetic texts that envisage this restoration and the consequent influx of gentiles. The quotation evidently combines Amos 9:11–12, Hosea 3:5, Jer. 12:15, and Isa. 45:20–22 due to lexical and thematic parity. The table below contains James's quotation beside the relevant portions of the quoted texts. Portions from the prophetic texts quoted in Acts 15 are italicized.

18. Willimon, *Acts*, 128–29.

Acts 15:16–18	Old Testament Texts (AT)
"After these things	*After these things* the sons of Israel will return and *seek the Lord* their God and David their king. (Hosea 3:5)
I will return,	And it will come about that after I have uprooted them, *I will return*, I will have mercy on them; and I will bring them back. . . . Then it will come about that if they [gentiles] will really learn the ways of my people, to swear by my name, "As the Lord lives," even as they taught my people to swear by Baal, then they will be built up in the midst of my people. (Jer. 12:15–16)
And I will rebuild the fallen tabernacle of David, / And I will rebuild its ruins, / And I will restore it, / So that the rest of mankind may seek the Lord, / And all the Gentiles who are called by my name," / Says the Lord,	"In that day I will raise up the *fallen booth of David. I will rebuild its fallen parts and its ruined parts*. I will also raise it up and *rebuild* it as in the days of old, *so that the rest of humans and all the nations upon whom my name is called may seek*," declares the Lord. (Amos 9:11–12)
who makes these things known from of old.	Gather yourselves and come. Draw near together, you fugitives of the nations. . . . Who has *announced this from of old*? Who has long since declared it? Is it not I, the Lord? . . . *Return* to me and be saved, all the ends of the earth. For I am God. (Isa. 45:20–22)

Much of the material quoted by James derives from Amos 9:11–12. However, both "after these things" and "seek the Lord" occur in Hosea 3:5, "I will return" appears in Jer. 12:15, and "made known / heard from of old" comes from Isa. 45:21.[19] These texts are combined due to mutual concern for the return of God, Israel's restoration, and an influx of "the nations."

What remains unclear is Acts 15:19's "therefore" (διό), leading to the named legal requirements for gentiles. What leads James from these prophetic texts to those legal requirements? Richard Bauckham provides a persuasive solution.[20] In addition to the textual legwork enabling the production of the table above,[21] Bauckham argues that a portion of Jer. 12 that is unquoted in Acts 15 supplies the logic for the selection of the various legal obligations. Acts 15:16 quotes from Jer. 12:15 in saying "I will return." The next verse, Jer. 12:16, states that the incoming gentiles will be "built up" (see Acts 15:16's emphasis on "rebuilding") "in the midst of my people" (בְּתוֹךְ עַמִּי) if they "really learn

19. I italicize "return" (ἐπιστράφητε) in Isa. 45:22 due to James's summary of these nations as those "who are turning [ἐπιστρέφουσιν] to God" (Acts 15:19).

20. Bauckham, "Jerusalem Church," esp. 450–62.

21. Bauckham, "Jerusalem Church," 453–58.

the ways of my people." Bauckham argues two points: first, that "learning the ways of my people" entails gentiles doing things legislated by Israel's law; and second, that Jeremiah's "in the midst of my people" functions as the lexical link to the Law that informs which commandments become obligatory for them. He notes that the equivalent of the above phrase ("in your midst" or "in their midst") occurs five times when referring to laws in Leviticus that obligate both Israel and "the sojourner in their midst [בְּתוֹכָם]" (Lev. 17:8, 10, 12, 13; 18:26). For both groups, 17:8 prohibits illicit sacrificial offerings; 17:10, 12, and 13 prohibit consumption of blood and declare the requirement to drain it (and thus not to kill the animal only by strangling); and 18:26 summarily prohibits Lev. 18's named acts of illicit sex. These texts, Bauckham argues, provide the basis for the council's decision that gentiles turning to God ought to abstain from food contaminated by images (illicit offerings), sexual immorality, strangling, and consumption of blood (Acts 15:20).[22] As Oliver

22. See also Jervell, *People of God*, 143–44; Kinzer, *Jerusalem Crucified, Jerusalem Risen*, 220–24; Oliver, *Torah Praxis*, 370–98; Willimon, *Acts*, 130–31. *Pace* Marguerat ("Paul and the Torah," 110), the lack of "strangled" (πνικτοῦ, Acts 15:20) in Lev. 17–18 does not hinder the conclusion that Acts 15:20's directives derive from Leviticus. A strangled animal cannot easily be exsanguinated as Lev. 17:13–15 requires. Moreover, Oliver (*Torah Praxis*, 381) has shown that Philo (*Spec. Laws* 4.119–23), "undoubtedly" interpreting Lev. 17:13–15, "condemns those who eat meat that has not been ritually slaughtered. . . . He condemns them for strangling and throttling [ἄγχοντες καὶ ἀποπνίγοντες] creatures, for burying their blood in their bodies." Thus Philo, interpreting Lev. 17's requirement for releasing the animal's blood, condemns "strangling," using a cognate (ἀποπνίγοντες) of Acts 15:20's requirement (πνικτοῦ), because it keeps the blood in the dead animal's body. However, Simon Butticaz ("Acts 15," 126) considers it "unthinkable, without falling into incoherence, to see this [the council's prescriptions] as a ritual *halakhah* with regard to non-Jews," and he argues that these decisions do not derive from Leviticus for three reasons: (1) the basis for the decree is "not the Torah, but the Holy Spirit and the Apostles" (127); (2) the prohibitions of Lev. 17–18 are limited to the land, lacking universal application, whereas this rule will apply to gentiles in the diaspora; (3) any connection of Acts 15:20 to Lev. 17–18 is "imprecise and vague" (127). However, point 1 is false and a non sequitur. James arrives at his judgment after quoting prophets said to "accord" with Peter's testimony (Acts 15:15). As Bauckham shows in his essay (not engaged by Butticaz), the words of the quoted passages serve to connect the prophecies concerning these nations now turning to God to the requirements in Lev. 17–18. Thus the judgment by James in Acts 15 is plausibly exegetical. Moreover, the basis of the decree being the apostles would not preclude the apostles from applying Torah in forming their conclusion. Point 2, circumscribing the prohibitions of Lev. 17–18 to the land, is also false. On Butticaz's reading, Israel would be permitted to make offerings to God away from the tent, provided they were out of the land, or to worship other gods/idols in other lands, both of which are highly improbable. On the contrary, subjection to "idols" in exile is a punishment, not a permission (Deut. 28:36, 64). Additionally, the prohibited sexual acts named in Lev. 18 are prefaced, "You shall not do what is done in the land of Egypt" (Lev. 18:3), implying that such practices are condemnable wherever they occur. Butticaz evidently misinterprets the defiling effect on the land resultant from violating such prohibitions (Lev. 18:27) to imply that these prohibitions apply only in the land. By this logic, murder, which defiles the land (Num. 35:33), would be prohibited only in

rightly notes, a correlation between Acts 15 and Lev. 17–18 "can account for the choice and number of regulations outlined in the decree, four in total, which are listed in Acts 15:29 and 21:21 in the same order as the 'parallel' commandments given to the Israelite and the *ger* in Lev 17–18."[23]

Significantly, though, not all laws obligating non-Israelites are singled out in Acts 15. Recognizing the connection between Jer. 12:16's "in your midst" and the Pentateuchal laws with that same terminology thus helps explain why *those* laws from Lev. 17–18 were selected and not all the laws for foreigners generally. For example, Sabbath legislation is conspicuously missing from Acts 15:20, despite the Law obligating Sabbath keeping for non-Israelites who live in the land of Israel (Exod. 20:9–10; Deut. 5:14). However, the latter legislation does not include "in your midst" as do Lev. 17:8, 10, 12, 13; 18:26. Thus it is not strictly accurate to say that Acts 15 obligates believing gentiles to all that the Law required of non-Israelites; rather, it decides for laws obligating the foreigner "in your midst." This further elucidates Acts 15:21, which is a notorious *crux interpretum*.[24] It states: "For [γάρ] from ancient generations Moses has those who preach him in every city, since he is read in the synagogues every Sabbath." What's the significance of the γάρ, and how does verse 21 relate to verse 20? I think the sense is this: if Jews are in every city, gentiles are always "in the midst" of Jews, and thus laws obligating foreigners "in [their] midst" are reasonably applied to such gentiles.[25] Not only does this explain the "for" (γάρ) opening Acts 15:21, which grounds the justifiable application of the content of the decree (15:20) in the fact of Jews being present everywhere (15:21), but it also serves as a response to one who might object that such laws should not be applied to diaspora gentiles. On the contrary,

---

the land. Finally, the blood prohibition applies to any "from the house of Israel" (Lev. 17:10, 12–13), connecting the prohibition to a genealogical category rather than presence in the land. However, even if Lev. 17's prohibition of blood consumption were bound to the land, Gen. 9:4 prohibits the sons of Noah from consuming meat with blood, indicating such a prohibition is not confined to the land of Israel (see Milgrom, *Leviticus 1–16*, 705). Thus Lev. 17, if read together with Gen. 9, simply repeats and particularizes a prohibition already regarded as universal. Also, Oliver (*Torah Praxis*, 393) argues that rabbinic literature predominantly interprets Gen. 9:4 to forbid not the consumption of blood as an object but the consumption of an animal with its blood still flowing in it, indicating that the prohibition of "blood" as an object of consumption likely derives from Leviticus. Philo (*Spec. Laws* 4.119–23) evidently takes Leviticus's prohibition as universal. Point 3, declaring the connection to Lev. 17–18 to be "imprecise and vague," is a subjective judgment and reflects a failure to recognize the exegetical connection between the quoted prophetic texts and Lev. 17–18. Butticaz's claim that such a connection is "unthinkable" ("Acts 15," 126) should therefore be rethought.

23. Oliver, *Torah Praxis*, 370.

24. Dibelius (*Studies*, 97) called it "one of the most difficult verses in the New Testament."

25. So also Zellentin, *Law beyond Israel*, 63.

James could respond that they apply to gentiles "in [Israel's] midst" and "Jews are in every city," thus the council's decision is exegetically defensible.

Whether my interpretation of Acts 15:21 is sound is of course debatable, but it aside, two major conclusions follow from the council's decision. First, because the debate concerns whether gentiles must keep all of the Law, the debate assumes that believing Jews continue to observe all of it. Second, the obligations that fall to gentiles derive from Leviticus. This means that the council implemented a decision consonant with the Law itself in that the Law already distinguishes the obligatory status of laws based on one's ethnicity. The totality of the Law obligates Israel uniquely in that the Law addresses Israel primarily. Laws such as Lev. 11:4 and Deut. 14:21, as described above, make plain that most dietary laws obligate only Israel. But certain laws obligate both Israel and the foreigner "in [Israel's] midst," and it is these laws that the council applies to the gentiles turning to God. Evidently they found no issue in concluding that God saved Jews and gentiles on the same basis—through the grace of Jesus (Acts 15:11)—and that the distinct groups were governed by overlapping but not coterminous laws.[26] Acts, therefore, presents the Jews in Jerusalem (15:22) and Paul and his team (15:22, 25–29) as requiring believing gentiles to keep certain Levitical commandments.[27]

Paul, Jesus, and the Law

Paul and the Law, not to mention the question of continuity between Jesus and Paul, is an immense topic. I will not pretend to answer it fully here, and I will certainly "let Paul be Paul." Here I will simply gesture toward a few points that suggest a high degree of congruity between Jesus and Paul on the Law.

First, readers must account for the ethnic distinction of Jesus's and Paul's audience. Jesus is speaking almost exclusively to Jews, for whom Law-keeping is assumed and normative. Paul, on the other hand, is often speaking exclusively to gentiles in his letters, and the arguments he makes about the Law are not identical to the features of Jesus's (or the Gospels') setting. Paul routinely emphasizes that the gentiles are incorporated into God's covenant family and addresses how, having been admitted, they are to conduct themselves in the interim between Christ's enthronement and gift of the Spirit, on the one hand, and Christ's/God's return, on the other. He explicitly requires that believing gentiles fulfill the Law (Rom. 13:8, 10), referring to actions of

26. See also Thiessen, *Contesting Conversion*, 140–41.

27. On Paul and the council's decree, see Nanos, *Mystery of Romans*, 166–238.

Spirit-led obedience whereby they keep Leviticus's requirement "You shall love your neighbor as yourself" (13:9). And he refers to such love as an obligation (13:8), whose performance entails the implicit keeping of "any other commandment" of the Law (13:9).

To be sure, fulfilling the Law through love of neighbor is not identical to, say, the assumption in the Gospels that Jews are observing even the minutest details, such as tithing (Luke 11:42; Matt. 23:23) and washing dishes properly (Matt. 23:26). But again, the ethnic distinction of Paul's audience must be kept in mind. Recall that the Law does not obligate gentiles to all its commands. When the Law obligates Israel and the non-Israelite in the land, it makes this expectation explicit. As discussed, even if Matt. 28:19–20 were to require that gentiles keep all of the Law, they would presumably do so as gentiles. If so, what does gentile Law-keeping of Deut. 14:21, which distinguishes food permissible to Israel and gentiles, look like? A gentile keeping the Law would not be obligated to such dietary restrictions.[28] So even if Paul were to conclude that gentiles should keep all the Law as gentiles, they would be obligated to only a fraction of what obligates Israel.[29] Moreover, the Jerusalem Council decided that the legal obligations for believing gentiles amount to abstaining from foods contaminated by images, sexual immorality, and consumption of blood. Except the blood prohibition, which may well be absent due only to the occasional nature of Paul's letters,[30] these decisions are also expressed in Paul's letters: he warns gentiles to abstain from sexual immorality[31] and fellowship with demons, which might result from eating food in an image's temple (1 Cor. 10:14–21).

Regarding image food, Paul agrees that gentiles should avoid such contamination. He simply argues about how such contamination obtains. His

28. See "Teaching the Nations" in the previous chapter.

29. Moreover, it may not simply be that the gentiles are "not obligated." Thiessen ("Paul's So-Called Jew") has argued that Paul plausibly objected to full Law adherence by gentiles because some Jews may have viewed it as appropriating privileges granted to Israel alone.

30. So also Bockmuehl (*Jewish Law*, 170), who notes that non-Jews also typically drained the animal's blood in the slaughtering process. See further discussion in Oliver, *Torah Praxis*, 389, esp. note 89 and the bibliography there.

31. In 1 Cor. 5:1, Paul expresses shock that "someone has his father's wife" (γυναῖκά τινα τοῦ πατρὸς ἔχειν), probably echoing the prohibition in Deut. 23:1 LXX (22:30 ET): "A man shall not take his father's wife" (οὐ λήμψεται ἄνθρωπος τὴν γυναῖκα τοῦ πατρὸς αὐτοῦ). See also Deut. 27:20; Lev. 18:8. He then states, "Remove the evil person from among yourselves" (ἐξάρατε τὸν πονηρὸν ἐξ ὑμῶν αὐτῶν, 1 Cor. 5:13), quoting the Deuteronomic refrain to punish one guilty of violating a prohibition: "So you shall eliminate the evil from your midst" (ἐξαρεῖς τὸν πονηρὸν ἐξ ὑμῶν, Deut. 21:21). See also Deut. 13:5; 17:7, 12; 22:21; and discussion in Fee, *First Epistle to the Corinthians*, 198–228. Consequently, Paul holds a gentile liable for violating a sexual taboo named in Leviticus and Deuteronomy and employs Deuteronomy's expression of punishment. The nature of the punishment in Paul is much debated.

point is not that such contamination cannot occur but that it does not happen automatically. Though gentiles might unknowingly buy meat for private consumption that had been sacrificed to an image, Paul argues that the intention of the eater governs whether such food establishes fellowship with the demon. In this, Paul is not unlike an opinion espoused in m. Avodah Zarah that regards the intention of relevant agents as a determining factor regarding whether an action is "idolatrous" or not.[32] Consequently, Paul permits gentiles to eat whatever they buy in the market, provided they thank God (1 Cor. 10:25–26, 30). Paul probably regarded the enthronement of Christ above the powers as having evacuated the powers' ability to haunt automatically meat that may have been previously offered, but such meat must be consumed away from the image's temple and with the intention that it is "for the Lord" (Rom. 14:6; cp. 1 Cor. 10:31). Paul forbids eating in an image's temple on two grounds: the failure to love your "brother" who might stumble at seeing this (8:1–3, 7–13), and the failure to love God, whom they would provoke by eating at the "table of demons" (10:21–22). Paul's reasoning on image food is thus plausibly informed by the requirements to "love God" and "love your neighbor as yourself."[33]

Whether Paul knew and employed the council's decision is not my point (though I am willing to accept this on the testimony of Acts 15:25–29). My point is simply that from Paul's letters alone, his requirements for gentiles are consonant with the decision made at the Jerusalem Council. Consequently, a description of Paul's mission as "Law-free" is overdue for mandatory retirement,[34] and the place of the Law in Paul's moral reasoning should continue to be explored in the ways initiated by several scholars.[35]

Why, then, do we find seemingly negative language about the Law in Paul? Four brief points should be noted. First, in view of the imminent arrival of

32. See m. Avodah Zarah 3.4. See the discussion in Tomson, *Jewish Law*, 189–220; Bockmuehl, *Jewish Law*, 168–69. See also b. Hullin 41a (4), where two rabbis conclude that wine poured as a libation by a gentile away from the object of worship is permissible to a Jew on two grounds: (1) such idolatrous libations are typically poured in the presence of the image, and thus its absence suggests that it is not really a libation; and (2) the Jew can conclude that it is not within the gentile's power "to render my wine forbidden against my will," indicating that, for these two rabbis, the intention of the Jew is the relevant factor.

33. See Cheung, *Idol Food*, 297. On Paul's legal reasoning in 1 Cor. 8–10 generally, see also Tomson, *Jewish Law*, 189–220; Fotopoulos, *Food Offered to Idols*.

34. See Fredriksen ("Mandatory Retirement"), who uses this phrase regarding "conversion," "nationalism," "*religio licita*," and "monotheism." Staples rightly claims that Paul "does not present his gospel as 'law-free' but rather as 'law-implanted'" (*Paul and the Resurrection*, 89). On the deficiencies of a "Law-free" apostle or mission, see Nanos, "'Law-Free' Paul"; Fredriksen, "Judaizing the Nations"; Fredriksen, "Why Should?"; Novakovic, "Matthew and Paul," 107–12.

35. Inter alia, Tomson, *Jewish Law*; Bockmuehl, *Jewish Law*.

God and his kingdom, humans need to be equipped to stand in his presence. Human mortality—weak, frail, and subject to decay—is unable to endure the sudden approach of God. In view of the plight of human mortality, what humans need is resurrection, an imperishable body able to withstand the glory of God when it floods creation. And this resurrection is precisely what the Law could not provide. If the Law could resurrect people, then Paul thinks righteousness would come through the Law. As he says in Gal. 3:21: "Is the Law then contrary to the promises of God? Far from it! For if a law had been given that was able to resurrect [ζῳοποιῆσαι], then righteousness would indeed have been based on Law" (NASB modified). Translations of Gal. 3:21 that render ζῳοποιῆσαι as "impart life" (NASB; see also NIV and ESV) obscure the fact that all other Pauline uses of the term ζῳοποιῆσαι and cognates indicate not life in the abstract, but resurrection, life from the dead (Rom. 4:17; 8:11; 1 Cor. 15:22, 36, 45; 2 Cor. 3:6). In other words, what the Law could not do was transform mortal humans into immortal ones. For that reason, Paul states, righteousness is not from the Law.

Second, like many Jews of his period, Paul regarded the punitive discipline occasioned by Israel's historic transgression still to be operative until Christ.[36] This is the sense of his "curse" language in Galatians: Jews were "under the curse of the Law" (Gal. 3:13)—that is, the curse pronounced by the Law for Israel's transgression.[37] As discussed from the Prophets, additional Law-keeping in itself (especially the performance of sacrifices) would not obviate the curse. This sense is intended in Gal. 2:19: "For through the Law I died to the Law." Through the Law's condemnation, Paul "died," echoing the Mosaic and prophetic claim that Israel "dies" when they violate the covenant (Deut. 30:15–19; Ezek. 37:1–12). Consequently, he did not consider Law-keeping *by itself* as the means of restoration; Paul "died to the Law" as having this function. What was needed was the endurance of the curse, which Christ did "for us" (Gal. 3:13). Because Christ has redeemed us from the "curse of the Law," Jews and gentiles ought to die with Christ (Gal. 2:20; 6:14; Rom. 6:3–11; 2 Cor. 5:14–15), ensuring that the curse is exhausted in them, to thereby participate in Christ's resurrection (Rom. 6:3–8; 2 Cor. 5:14–17). Thus one reason the Law by itself cannot justify is that outside of Christ, it dispenses "curse" (Gal. 3:10) and "wrath" (Rom. 4:15). But having exhausted the curse's effects, believers now live with one foot in the eschatological age and thus are obligated to live under the Law

36. See Wright, *Climax of the Covenant*, 141–56; P. Sloan, "Law Will Testify"; Staples, *Paul and the Resurrection*, 52–63.

37. Rillera, *Lamb*, 256.

of the Messiah (Gal. 6:2) and to fulfill, by the Spirit, "the righteous decree of the Law" (Rom. 8:4).

Third, Paul takes seriously the verbiage of God's promise to Abraham. God promises Abraham that in him "all the nations" will be blessed (Gal. 3:8). But if Law-keeping by gentiles *Judaizes* them (2:14), requiring gentile Law-keeping would entail that gentiles become Jews, and then God could not keep his promise to bless the nations as nations. For this reason, inheritance in Abraham's blessings is not through the Law; if it were, God's promise could not obtain for all of Abraham's descendants (Rom. 4:16), and his promise to Abraham that he would be "the father of many nations" would fail (4:17). If all the nations become Jews through Law-keeping, Abraham cannot be the father of many nations, and God would be seen to be the God of Jews only (Rom. 3:28–29).

Fourth and finally, in the interim between Christ's enthronement and return, Paul evidently expects various groups to keep the commandments that govern them within their respective social status. As others have argued, this is probably Paul's meaning when he says, "Circumcision is nothing, and foreskin is nothing, but what matters is the keeping of the commandments of God [τήρησις ἐντολῶν θεοῦ]. Each person is to remain in that state in which he was called" (1 Cor. 7:19–20).[38] Paul recognizes that the commandments of God apply differently to various groups, with the circumcised keeping the commandments applicable to them and the gentiles keeping the commandments applicable to them.[39] Foreskinned believers should not seek circumci-

38. NASB, modifying "uncircumcision" to "foreskin." On the point from 1 Cor. 7, see Tomson, *Jewish Law*, 271–72; Rudolph, *Jew to the Jews*, 82–85; Tucker, *"Remain in Your Calling,"* 77–80; Thiessen, *Gentile Problem*, 8–11; Collman, *Apostle*, 41–45; Novakovic, "Matthew and Paul," 109; Collman (*Apostle*, 42) also cites Eisenbaum, *Paul Was Not a Christian*, 62–63; Bockmuehl, *Jewish Law*, 170–72; and Runesson, "Paul's Rule," 216–19.

39. Contrary to widespread opinion, 1 Cor. 9 does not deny Paul's Law observance. See Rudolph, *Jew to the Jews*; P. Sloan, "Jewish Law-Observance in Paul." In short, Paul's exposition of his relation to the Law in 1 Cor. 9:20–22 is fully explicable within the kind of halakhic reasoning expounded in Matt. 12:1–8, in which one who is commissioned is exempt from other commandments that might hinder the commissioned duty when so engaged. Moreover, those engaged in life-saving activity were exempt from commands that might hinder that activity (m. Yoma 8.6–7). Both factors are present in 1 Cor. 9, where Paul prefaces the description of his task when among various groups with the fact that he was commissioned by Christ to preach the gospel (9:14–17) and claims that all his activity is to "save" people (9:22). Thus when with the Jews, he acts like a Jew, and when with transgressors of the Law (τοῖς ἀνόμοις, 9:21), he becomes as a transgressor, though not being transgressive himself (μὴ ὢν ἄνομος θεοῦ, 9:21). Rather, because Christ has commissioned him, Paul's activity that might present as transgression is actually "lawful"; hence his claim that he is "lawful before/because of Christ" (ἔννομος Χριστοῦ, 9:22). Here he does not claim that he is not under the Law of Moses but under the Law of Christ; rather, he says that he's not a transgressor of the Law, even if his commissioned work requires that he forfeit some commands when engaged in his mission, since he is "lawful"

sion. Rather, having been incorporated into God's people, what matters is that they keep the commandments that apply to them, which, as we have seen, entails (negatively) the avoidance of idolatry and sexual immorality and (positively) Leviticus's requirement to love one's neighbor and thereby fulfill the Law's commandments.

Paul will be Paul, and scholars must respect the differences between him and Jesus, but such respect should not come at the expense of congruity when a supposed incongruity may be the result of failing to read either individual properly.

(Truly) Concluding Remarks

For centuries, NT scholars have (inadvertently or not) maligned or misinterpreted Jews, Judaism, and the Law in the process of explaining the supposed uniqueness of Jesus's legal or ethical instruction. Such interpretations (which often ignored, intentionally or not, the work of Jewish scholars whose expertise greatly aided the writing of this book) often lamentably traded in misrepresentations of Jewish literature and the Gospels, depicting a Judaism and a Jesus available in neither. Undoubtedly, errors remain in my own presentation, but being mere flesh and blood, I don't yet know what they are. Thus, while much else could and will be said about Jesus and the Law, I hope this interpretation at least causes a fresh look at the Gospels' portrait of Jesus, who, when asked "What shall I do to inherit eternal life?" responded: "What is written in the Law? How does it read to you?" (Luke 10:25–26).

because of the Messiah's commissioning of him. In this way, he is like the priest who profanes the Sabbath innocently due to his divinely required work of offering. So also Paul, when doing his divinely required work of preaching, may be exempt from certain commandments that might hinder that activity. Thus it is not that he "keeps" the Law only as a missiological strategy. The opposite is true: he "breaks" the Law only when on mission, but even then he clarifies that it isn't lawbreaking due to his commissioned status.

Bibliography

Achenbach, Reinhard, Rainer Albertz, and Jakob Wöhrle, eds. *The Foreigner and the Law: Perspectives from the Hebrew Bible and the Ancient Near East*. BZABR 16. Wiesbaden: Harrassowitz, 2011.

Ackroyd, Peter. *Exile and Restoration: A Study of Hebrew Thought of the Sixth Century B.C.* London: SCM, 1968.

Adler, Yonatan. *The Origins of Judaism: An Archaeological-Historical Reappraisal*. New Haven: Yale University Press, 2022.

Ådna, Jostein. "Jesus and the Temple." Pages 2635–75 in *The Historical Jesus*. Vol. 3 of *Handbook for the Study of the Historical Jesus*. Edited by Tom Holmén and Stanley E. Porter. Leiden: Brill, 2011.

———. *Jesu Stellung zum Tempel: Die Tempelaktion und das Tempelwort als Ausdruck seiner messianischen Sendung*. WUNT 2/119. Tübingen: Mohr Siebeck, 2000.

———. "Temple Act." Pages 947–52 in *Dictionary of Jesus and the Gospels*. Edited by Joel B. Green, Jeannine K. Brown, and Nicholas Perrin. 2nd ed. Downers Grove, IL: IVP Academic, 2013.

Akagi, Kai. "Acceptability and Purity in Acts 10:35." *NovT* 66 (2024): 309–20.

Akiyama, Kengo. *The Love of Neighbor in Ancient Judaism: The Reception of Leviticus 19:18 in the Hebrew Bible, the Septuagint, the Book of Jubilees, the Dead Sea Scrolls, and the New Testament*. AJEC 105. Leiden: Brill, 2018.

Allison, Dale C. *The Sermon on the Mount: Inspiring the Moral Imagination*. New York: Crossroad, 1999.

Andersen, F. I. "2 (Slavonic Apocalypse of) Enoch: A New Translation and Introduction." Pages 91–213 in vol. 1. of *OTP*. Edited by James H. Charlesworth. New York: Doubleday, 1983.

Anderson, Gary A. “From Israel’s Burden to Israel’s Debt: Towards a Theology of Sin in Biblical and Early Second Temple Sources.” Pages 1–30 in *Reworking the Bible: Apocryphal and Related Texts at Qumran*. Edited by Esther G. Chazon, Devorah Dimant, and Ruth A. Clements. Leiden: Brill, 2005.

———. “How Does Almsgiving Purge Sins?” Pages 1–14 in *Hebrew in the Second Temple Period: The Hebrew of the Dead Sea Scrolls and of Other Contemporary Sources*. Edited by Steven E. Fassberg, Moshe Bar-Asher, and Ruth A. Clements. Leiden: Brill, 2013.

———. *Sin: A History*. New Haven: Yale University Press, 2009.

Balberg, Mira. *Purity, Body, and Self in Early Rabbinic Literature*. Los Angeles: University of California Press, 2014.

Banks, Robert. *Jesus and the Law in the Synoptic Tradition*. SNTSMS 29. Cambridge: Cambridge University Press, 1975.

Bartos, Michael, and Bernard M. Levinson. “‘This Is the Manner of Remission’: Implicit Legal Exegesis in 11QMelchizedek as a Response to the Formation of the Torah.” *JBL* 132.2 (2013): 351–71.

Bauckham, Richard. “James and the Jerusalem Church.” Pages 415–80 in *Palestinian Setting*. Edited by Richard Bauckham. Vol. 4 of *The Book of Acts in Its First Century Setting*. Grand Rapids: Eerdmans, 1995.

———. “Jesus’ Demonstration in the Temple.” Pages 72–89 in *Law and Religion: Essays on the Place of the Law in Israel and Early Christianity*. Edited by Barnabas Lindars. Cambridge: James Clarke, 1988.

Bergsma, John Seitze. *The Jubilee from Leviticus to Qumran: A History of Interpretation*. Leiden: Brill, 2007.

Betz, Hans Dieter. *The Sermon on the Mount: A Commentary on the Sermon on the Mount, Including the Sermon on the Plain (Matthew 5:2–7:27 and Luke 6:20–49)*. Hermeneia. Minneapolis: Fortress, 1995.

Blenkinsopp, Joseph. *Isaiah 1–39: A New Translation with Introduction and Commentary*. AB 19. New York: Doubleday, 2000.

———. *Isaiah 40–55: A New Translation with Introduction and Commentary*. AB 19A. New York: Doubleday, 2002.

Blomberg, Craig L. *Jesus the Purifier: John’s Gospel and the Fourth Quest for the Historical Jesus*. Grand Rapids: Baker Academic, 2023.

———. “The Law in Luke-Acts.” *JSNT* 22 (1984): 53–80.

Boccaccini, Gabriele. “The Covenantal Theology of the Apocalyptic Book of Daniel.” Pages 39–44 in *Enoch and Qumran Origins: New Light on a Forgotten Connection*. Edited by Gabriele Boccaccini. Grand Rapids: Eerdmans, 2005.

Bock, Darrell L. *Acts*. BECNT. Grand Rapids: Baker Academic, 2007.

Bockmuehl, Markus. *Jewish Law in Gentile Churches: Halakhah and the Beginning of Christian Public Ethics*. Grand Rapids: Baker Academic, 2000.

———. "'Leave the Dead to Bury Their Own Dead': A Brief Clarification in Reply to Crispin H. T. Fletcher-Louis." *JSNT* 26.2 (2003): 241–42.

———. "'Let the Dead Bury Their Dead' (Matt. 8:22/Luke 9:60): Jesus and the Halakhah." *Journal of Theological Studies* 49.2 (1998): 552–81.

Booth, Roger P. *Jesus and the Laws of Purity: Tradition History and Legal History in Mark 7*. JSNTSup 13. Sheffield: JSOT Press, 1986.

Borg, Marcus J. *Conflict, Holiness, and Politics in the Teachings of Jesus*. Rev. ed. Harrisburg, PA: Trinity Press International, 1998. 1st ed., 1984.

Bovon, François. *Luke 2: A Commentary on the Gospel of Luke 9:51–19:27*. Translated by Donald S. Deer. Hermeneia. Minneapolis: Fortress, 2013.

Boyarin, Daniel. *The Jewish Gospels: The Story of the Jewish Christ*. New York: New Press, 2012.

———. "Mark 7:1–23—Finally." Pages 19–34 in *Re-making the World: Christianity and Categories; Essays in Honor of Karen L. King*. Edited by Taylor G. Petrey. Tübingen: Mohr Siebeck, 2019.

Brown, Jeannine K., and Kyle Roberts. *Matthew*. THNTC. Grand Rapids: Eerdmans, 2018.

Brown, Raymond E. "The Pater Noster as an Eschatological Prayer." *Theological Studies* 22.2 (1961): 175–208.

Bruce, F. F. *The Acts of the Apostles: Greek Text with Introduction and Commentary*. 3rd ed. Grand Rapids: Eerdmans, 1990. 1st ed., 1951; 2nd ed., 1952.

Bryan, Steven M. *Jesus and Israel's Traditions of Judgement and Restoration*. SNTSMS 117. Cambridge: Cambridge University Press, 2002.

Bultmann, Rudolf. *Primitive Christianity in Its Contemporary Setting*. Translated by R. H. Fuller. New York: World, 1956.

———. *Theology of the New Testament*. Translated by Kendrick Grobel. New York: Scribner, 1951. Repr., Waco: Baylor University Press, 2007.

Butticaz, Simon. "Acts 15 or the 'Return of the Oppressed'? The Church and the Law in Acts." Pages 118–32 in *Torah in the New Testament*. Edited by Michael Tait and Peter Oakes. LNTS 401. London: T&T Clark International, 2009.

Carter, Joe. "Survey: Majority of American Christians Don't Believe the Gospel." The Gospel Coalition. August 9, 2020. https://www.thegospelcoalition.org/article/survey-a-majority-of-american-christians-dont-believe-the-gospel/.

Ceresko, Anthony R. "The Rhetorical Strategy of the Fourth Servant Song (Isa. 52:13–53:12): Poetry and the Exodus-New Exodus." *CBQ* 56 (1994): 42–55.

Cheung, Alex T. *Idol Food in Corinth: Jewish Background and Pauline Legacy*. JSNTSup 176. Sheffield: Sheffield Academic, 1999.

Cohen, Shaye J. D., Robert Goldenberg, and Hayim Lapin, eds. *The Oxford Annotated Mishnah: A New Translation of the Mishnah with Introduction and Notes*. 3 vols. Oxford: Oxford University Press, 2022.

Cole, R. Alan. *Mark*. TNTC. 2nd ed. Downers Grove, IL: InterVarsity, 1989. 1st ed., 1961.

Collins, Adela Yarbro. "Jesus' Action in Herod's Temple." Pages 48–53 in *Antiquity and Humanity: Essays on Ancient Religion and Philosophy Presented to Hans Dieter Betz on His 70th Birthday*. Edited by A. Y. Collins and Margaret M. Mitchell. Tübingen: Mohr Siebeck, 2001.

———. "Polemic against the Pharisees in Matthew 23." Pages 148–63 in *The Pharisees*. Edited by Joseph Sievers and A.-J. Levine. Grand Rapids: Eerdmans, 2021.

———. "The Signification of Mark 10:45 among Gentile Christians." *HTR* 90.4 (1997): 371–82.

Collins, John J. *Daniel, First Maccabees, Second Maccabees, with an Excursus on the Apocalyptic Genre*. OTM 15. Wilmington, DE: Glazier, 1981.

Collins, Nina L. *Jesus, the Sabbath and the Jewish Debate: Healing on the Sabbath in the 1st and 2nd Centuries CE*. LNTS 474. London: T&T Clark, 2014.

Collman, Ryan D. *The Apostle to the Foreskin: Circumcision in the Letters of Paul*. BZNW 259. Berlin: De Gruyter, 2023.

Crossley, James G. *Jesus and the Chaos of History: Redirecting the Life of the Historical Jesus*. Oxford: Oxford University Press, 2015.

———. "Mark 7.1–23: Revisiting the Question of 'All Foods Clean.'" Pages 8–20 in *the Torah in the New Testament*. Edited by Peter Oaks and Michael Tait. LNTS 401. London: T&T Clark, 2009.

———. "Matthew and the Torah: Jesus as Legal Interpreter." Pages 29–52 in *Matthew within Judaism: Israel and the Nations in the First Gospel*. Edited by Anders Runesson and Daniel M. Gurtner. Atlanta: SBL Press, 2020.

———. *The New Testament and Jewish Law: A Guide for the Perplexed*. London: T&T Clark, 2010.

Crossley, James, and Robert J. Myles. *Jesus: A Life in Class Conflict*. Winchester, UK: Zero Books, 2023.

Culpepper, R. Alan. *Mark*. SHBC. Macon, GA: Smyth & Helwys, 2007.

Daube, David. *The New Testament and Rabbinic Judaism*. London: Athlone, 1956.

Davies, W. D. *The Setting of the Sermon on the Mount*. BJS 186. Cambridge: Cambridge University Press, 1964. Repr., Atlanta: Scholars Press, 1989.

Davies, W. D., and Dale C. Allison Jr. *The Gospel according to Saint Matthew*. Vol. 1. ICC. Edinburgh: T&T Clark, 1988.

———. *Matthew: A Shorter Commentary*. London: T&T Clark International, 2004.

Davis, James. *Lex Talionis in Early Judaism and the Exhortations of Jesus in Matthew 5:38–42*. JSNTSup 281. London: T&T Clark International, 2005.

Dibelius, Martin. *Studies in the Acts of the Apostles*. Translated by Mary Ling. London: SCM, 1956.

Dimant, Devorah. "The Book of Tobit and the Qumran Halakhah." Pages 193–211 in *From Enoch to Tobit: Collected Studies in Ancient Jewish Literature*. FAT 114. Tübingen: Mohr Siebeck, 2017.

———. "Israel's Subjugation to the Gentiles as an Expression of Demonic Power in Qumran Documents and Related Literature." *RevQ* 22.6 (2006): 373–88.

Doering, Lutz. "'Much Ado about Nothing?' Jesus' Sabbath Healings and Their Halakhic Implications Revisited." Pages 217–41 in *Judaistik und neutestamentliche Wissenschaft*. Edited by Lutz Doering, Hans-Günther Waubke, and Florian Wilk. FRLANT 226. Göttingen: Vandenhoeck & Ruprecht, 2008.

———. "Sabbath Laws in the New Testament." Pages 207–54 in *The New Testament and Rabbinic Literature*. Edited by Reimund Bieringer, Florentino García Martínez, Didier Pollefeyt, and Peter J. Tomson. JSJSup 136. Leiden: Brill, 2010.

———. *Schabbat: Sabbathalacha und -praxis im antiken Judentum und Urchristentum*. TSAJ 78. Tübingen: Mohr Siebeck, 1999.

Donaldson, Terence L. "'Nations,' 'Non-Jewish Nations,' or 'Non-Jewish Individuals': Matthew 28:19 Revisited." Pages 169–94 in *Matthew within Judaism: Israel and the Nations in the First Gospel*. Edited by Anders Runesson and Daniel M. Gurtner. Atlanta: SBL Press, 2020.

Doran, Robert. *2 Maccabees: A Critical Commentary*. Hermeneia. Minneapolis: Fortress, 2012.

Dormeyer, Detlev. "Die Rollen von Volk, Jüngern und Gegnern im Matthäusevangelium." Pages 105–28 in *"Dies ist das Buch . . .": Das Matthäusevangelium; Interpretation—Rezeption—Rezeptionsgeschichte*. Edited by Rainer Kampling. Paderborn: Schöningh, 2004.

Dunn, James D. G. *Jesus, Paul, and the Law: Studies in Mark and Galatians*. Louisville: Westminster John Knox, 1990.

———. *The Partings of the Ways: Between Christianity and Judaism and Their Significance for the Character of Christianity*. 2nd ed. London: SCM, 2006. 1st ed., 1991.

Dvořáček, Jiří. *The Son of David in Matthew's Gospel in the Light of the Solomon as Exorcist Tradition*. WUNT 2/415. Tübingen: Mohr Siebeck, 2016.

Eberhart, Christian A. *The Sacrifice of Jesus: Understanding Atonement Biblically*. Minneapolis: Fortress, 2011.

Ego, Beate. "The Book of Tobit and the Diaspora." Pages 41–54 in *The Book of Tobit: Text, Tradition, Theology*. Edited by Géza G. Xeravits and József Zsengellér. JSJSup 98. Leiden: Brill, 2005.

Eisenbaum, Pamela. *Paul Was Not a Christian: The Original Message of a Misunderstood Apostle*. San Francisco: HarperOne, 2009.

Ermakov, Arseny. "The Salvific Significance of the Torah in Mark 10.17–22 and 12.28–34." Pages 21–31 in *Torah in the New Testament*. Edited by Michael Tait and Peter Oakes. LNTS 401. London: T&T Clark International, 2009.

Eschner, Christina. “Purity and Impurity of Food and People in Acts 10:1–11:18: Is the Abolition of Jewish Food Laws at the Center of the Cornelian Narrative?” Pages 359–94 in *Purity in Ancient Judaism: Texts, Contexts, and Concepts*. Edited by Lutz Doering, Jörg Frey, and Laura von Bartenwerffer. WUNT 528. Tübingen: Mohr Siebeck, 2025.

Eshel, Hanan. “4Q390, the 490-Year Prophecy, and the Calendrical History of the Second Temple Period.” Pages 102–10 in *Enoch and Qumran Origins: New Light on a Forgotten Connection*. Edited by Gabriele Boccaccini. Grand Rapids: Eerdmans, 2005.

Eubank, Nathan. *Wages of Cross-Bearing and Debt of Sin: The Economy of Heaven in Matthew’s Gospel*. BZNW 196. Berlin: De Gruyter, 2013.

Evans, Craig A. “Aspects of Exile and Restoration in the Proclamation of Jesus and the Gospels.” Pages 263–93 in *Jesus in Context: Temple, Purity, and Restoration*. By Bruce Chilton and Craig A. Evans. AGJU 39. Leiden: Brill, 1997.

———. “Jesus’ Action in the Temple: Cleansing or Portent of Destruction?” *CBQ* 51 (1989): 237–70.

———. “Jesus and Zechariah’s Messianic Hope.” Pages 373–88 in *Authenticating the Activities of Jesus*. NTTSD 28.2. Leiden: Brill, 1999.

———. *Matthew*. NCBC. Cambridge: Cambridge University Press, 2012.

Feder, Yitzhaq. *Purity and Pollution in the Hebrew Bible: From Embodied Experience to Moral Metaphor*. Cambridge: Cambridge University Press, 2022.

Fee, Gordon D. *The First Epistle to the Corinthians*. NICNT. Grand Rapids: Eerdmans, 1987.

Feldman, Ariel. “New Light on the Ten Jubilees of 11QMelchizedek (11Q13).” *DSD* 25 (2018): 178–84.

Feldman, Liane M. *The Story of Sacrifice: Ritual and Narrative in the Priestly Source*. FAT 141. Tübingen: Mohr Siebeck, 2020.

Fitzmyer, Joseph A. *The Gospel according to Luke I–IX: A New Translation with Introduction and Commentary*. AB 28. New York: Doubleday, 1981.

———. *Tobit*. CEJL. Berlin: De Gruyter, 2003.

Fletcher-Louis, Crispin H. T. “The Destruction of the Temple and the Relativization of the Old Covenant: Mark 13:31 and Matthew 5:18.” Pages 145–69 in *Eschatology in Bible and Theology: Evangelical Essays at the Dawn of a New Millennium*. Edited by Kent E. Brower and Mark W. Elliott. Downers Grove, IL: InterVarsity, 1997.

———. “‘Leave the Dead to Bury Their Own Dead’: Q 9.60 and the Redefinition of the People of God.” *JSNT* 26.1 (2003): 39–68.

Flusser, David. “The Half-Shekel in the Gospels and the Qumran Community.” Pages 327–33 in *Qumran and Apocalypticism*. Vol. 1 of *Judaism of the Second Temple Period*. Translated by Azzan Yadin. Grand Rapids: Eerdmans, 2007.

Forderer, Tanja. "'What God Has Joined Together, Let No Man Pull Asunder'? The Prohibition of Divorce in Mark's Gospel in the Context of the Controversy between Jesus and the Pharisees." *NovT* 66 (2024): 1–17.

Fotopoulos, John. *Food Offered to Idols in Roman Corinth: A Socio-Rhetorical Reconsideration of 1 Corinthians 8:1–11:1*. WUNT 2/151. Tübingen: Mohr Siebeck, 2003.

France, R. T. *The Gospel of Mark: A Commentary on the Greek Text*. NIGTC. Grand Rapids: Eerdmans, 1996.

———. *The Gospel of Matthew*. NICNT. Grand Rapids: Eerdmans, 2007.

Fredriksen, Paula. "Compassion Is to Purity as Fish Is to Bicycle." Pages 55–67 in *Apocalypticism, Anti-Semitism and the Historical Jesus: Subtexts in Criticism*. Edited by John S. Kloppenborg and John Marshall. LNTS 275. London: T&T Clark International, 2005.

———. "Did Jesus Oppose the Purity Laws?" *BRev* 11.3 (1995): 27–40.

———. *Jesus of Nazareth, King of the Jews: A Jewish Life and the Emergence of Christianity*. London: Macmillan, 1999.

———. "Judaizing the Nations: The Ritual Demands of Paul's Gospel." *NTS* 56 (2010): 232–52.

———. "Mandatory Retirement: Ideas in the Study of Christian Origins Whose Time Has Come to Go." *SR* 35.2 (2006): 231–46.

———. *Paul: The Pagans' Apostle*. New Haven: Yale University Press, 2017.

———. "Why Should a 'Law-Free' Mission Mean a 'Law-Free' Apostle?" *JBL* 134.3 (2015): 637–50.

Friebel, Kelvin G. *Jeremiah's and Ezekiel's Sign-Acts: Rhetorical Nonverbal Communication*. JSOTSup 283. Sheffield: Sheffield Academic, 1999.

Furstenberg, Yair. "Controlling Impurity: The Natures of Impurity in Second Temple Debates." *Dine Israel* 30 (2015): 163–96.

———. "Defilement Penetrating the Body: A New Understanding of Contamination in Mark 7.15." *NTS* 54.2 (2008): 176–200.

———. "Jesus against the Laws of the Pharisees: The Legal Woe Sayings and Second Temple Intersectarian Discourse." *JBL* 139.4 (2020): 769–88.

———. *Purity and Identity in Ancient Judaism: From the Temple to the Mishnah*. Translated by Sara Tova Brody. Bloomington: Indiana University Press, 2023.

Gane, Roy. *Cult and Character: Purification Offerings, Day of Atonement, and Theodicy*. Winona Lake, IN: Eisenbrauns, 2005.

García Martínez, Florentino, and Eibert J. C. Tigchelaar, eds. *The Dead Sea Scrolls Study Edition*. 2 vols. Leiden: Brill; Grand Rapids: Eerdmans, 1997–98.

Garland, David E. *Luke*. ZECNT. Grand Rapids: Zondervan, 2011.

Garrett, Susan R. *The Demise of the Devil: Magic and the Demonic in Luke's Writings*. Minneapolis: Fortress, 1989.

Goldstone, Matthew. "The Structure of Matthew's Antitheses in Light of Early Jewish, Christian and Rabbinic Sources." *JSNT* 40.2 (2017): 214–35.

Gray, Alyssa. "Redemptive Almsgiving and the Rabbis of Late Antiquity." *JSQ* 18 (2011): 144–84.

Green, Joel. *The Gospel of Luke*. NICNT. Grand Rapids: Eerdmans, 1997.

Guggenheimer, Heinrich W. *The Jerusalem Talmud: Translation and Commentary*. Berlin: De Gruyter, 1999–2015.

Gurtner, Daniel M. *Second Baruch: A Critical Edition of the Syriac Text, with Greek and Latin Fragments, English Translation, Introduction, and Concordances*. Jewish and Christian Texts in Contexts and Related Studies. New York: Continuum International, 2009.

Halpern-Amaru, Betsy. "Exile and Return in Jubilees." Pages 127–44 in *Exile: Old Testament, Jewish, and Christian Conceptions*. Edited by James M. Scott. JSJSup 56. Leiden: Brill, 1997.

Hamilton, Catherine Sider. *The Death of Jesus in Matthew: Innocent Blood and the End of Exile*. SNTSMS 167. Cambridge: Cambridge University Press, 2017.

Hamilton, Neill. "Temple Cleansing and Temple Bank." *JBL* 83.4 (1964): 365–72.

Hammer, Reuven. *Sifre: A Tannaitic Commentary on the Book of Deuteronomy*. YJS 24. New Haven: Yale University Press, 1986.

Harrington, Hannah K. "Did Pharisees Eat Ordinary Food in a State of Ritual Purity?" *JSJ* 26 (1995): 42–54.

Hartman, Louis F., and Alexander A. Di Lella. *The Book of Daniel*. AB 23. New York: Doubleday, 1978.

Hayes, Christine E. *Gentile Impurities and Jewish Identities: Intermarriage and Conversion from the Bible to the Talmud*. Oxford: Oxford University Press, 2002.

Hays, Richard B. *Echoes of Scripture in the Gospels*. Waco: Baylor University Press, 2016.

Healy, Mary. *The Gospel of Mark*. CCSS. Grand Rapids: Baker Academic, 2008.

Hellerman, Joseph. *Jesus and the People of God: Reconfiguring Ethnic Identity*. Sheffield: Sheffield Phoenix, 2007.

Henderson, Suzanne Watts. "Was Mark a Supersessionist? Two Test Cases from the Earliest Gospel." Pages 145–68 in *The Ways That Often Parted: Essays in Honor of Joel Marcus*. Edited by Lori Baron, Jill Hicks-Keeton, and Matthew Thiessen. Atlanta: SBL Press, 2018.

Hengel, Martin. *The Charismatic Leader and His Followers*. Translated by James C. G. Greig. Edinburgh: T&T Clark, 1981.

Hieke, Thomas, and Tobias Nicklas, eds. *The Day of Atonement: Its Interpretations in Early Jewish and Christian Traditions*. TBN 15. Leiden: Brill, 2012.

Hofmann, Norbert. "Die Rezeption des Deuteronomiums im Buche Tobit, in der Assumptio Mosis und im 4 Esrabuch." Pages 311–42 in *Das Deuteronomium*. Edited by Georg Braulik. ÖBS 23. Frankfurt am Main: Lang, 2003.

Holladay, William L. *Jeremiah 1: A Commentary on the Book of the Prophet Jeremiah, Chapters 1–25*. Hermeneia. Minneapolis: Fortress, 1986.

Hooker, Morna. "Did the Use of Isaiah 53 to Interpret His Mission Begin with Jesus?" Pages 88–103 in *Jesus and the Suffering Servant: Isaiah 53 and Christian Origins*. Edited by William H. Bellinger Jr. and William R. Farmer. Harrisburg, PA: Trinity Press International, 1998.

———. *Jesus and the Servant*. London: SPCK, 1959.

Horsley, Richard A. "Popular Prophetic Movements at the Time of Jesus: Their Principal Features and Social Origins." *JSNT* 26 (1986): 3–27.

House, Colin. "Defilement by Association: Some Insights from the Usage of κοινός/κοινόω in Acts 10 and 11." *AUSS* 21.2 (1983): 143–53.

Hultgren, Stephen. *From the Damascus Covenant to the Covenant of the Community: Literary, Historical, and Theological Studies in the Dead Sea Scrolls*. STDJ 66. Leiden: Brill, 2007.

Jacobs, Mignon R. *The Books of Haggai and Malachi*. NICOT. Grand Rapids: Eerdmans, 2017.

Janowski, Bernd. "Das Geschenk der Versöhnung: Leviticus 16 als Schlussstein der priesterlichen Kulttheologie." Pages 3–31 in *The Day of Atonement: Its Interpretations in Early Jewish and Christian Traditions*. Edited by Thomas Hieke and Tobias Nicklas. TBN 15. Leiden: Brill, 2012.

———. "He Bore Our Sins: Isaiah 53 and the Drama of Taking Another's Place." Pages 48–74 in *The Suffering Servant: Isaiah 53 in Jewish and Christian Sources*. Edited by Bernd Janowski and Peter Stuhlmacher. Translated by Daniel P. Bailey. Grand Rapids: Eerdmans, 2004.

Jervell, Jacob. *Luke and the People of God: A New Look at Luke-Acts*. Minneapolis: Augsburg, 1972.

Johnson, Luke Timothy. *The Gospel of Luke*. SP. Collegeville, MN: Liturgical Press, 1991.

Jonge, Henk Jan de. "The Cleansing of the Temple in Mark 11:15 and Zechariah 14:21." Pages 87–100 in *The Book of Zechariah and Its Influence*. Edited by Christopher Tuckett. Burlington, VT: Ashgate, 2003.

Joseph, Simon. *Jesus and the Temple: The Crucifixion in Its Jewish Context*. SNTSMS 165. Cambridge: Cambridge University Press, 2016.

Josephus. Translated by H. St. J. Thackeray et al. 10 vols. LCL. Cambridge, MA: Harvard University Press, 1926–65.

Kampen, John. *Matthew within Sectarian Judaism*. New Haven: Yale University Press, 2019.

Kazen, Thomas. "Concern, Custom, and Common-Sense: Discharge, Handwashing, and Graded Purification." Pages 181–216 in *Impurity and Purification in Early Judaism and the Jesus Tradition*. RBS 98. Atlanta: SBL Press, 2021.

———. "Jesus and the *Zavah*: Implications for Interpreting Mark." Pages 112–43 in *Purity, Holiness, and Identity in Judaism and Christianity: Essays in Memory of Susan Haber*. Edited by Carl S. Ehrlich, Anders Runesson, and Eileen Schuller. Tübingen: Mohr Siebeck, 2013.

Keener, Craig S. *A Commentary on the Gospel of Matthew*. Grand Rapids: Eerdmans, 1999.

Keith, Chris. *Jesus against the Scribal Elite: The Origins of the Conflict*. Grand Rapids: Baker Academic, 2014.

Kimbell, John. *The Atonement in Lukan Theology*. Newcastle upon Tyne: Cambridge Scholars, 2014.

Kinzer, Mark S. *Jerusalem Crucified, Jerusalem Risen: The Resurrected Messiah, the Jewish People, and the Land of Promise*. Eugene, OR: Cascade Books, 2018.

Kister, Menahem. "Leave the Dead to Bury Their Own Dead." Pages 43–56 in *Studies in Ancient Midrash*. Edited by James L. Kugel. Cambridge, MA: Harvard University Center for Jewish Studies, 2001.

———. "Plucking on the Sabbath and Christian-Jewish Polemic." *Immanuel* 24/25 (1990): 35–51.

Kiuchi, Nobuyoshi. *Leviticus*. ApOTC. Downers Grove, IL: IVP Academic, 2007.

Klawans, Jonathan. *Impurity and Sin in Ancient Judaism*. Oxford: Oxford University Press, 2000.

———. "The Prohibition of Oaths and Contra-Scriptural *Halakhot*: A Response to John P. Meier." *JSHJ* 6 (2008): 33–48.

———. *Purity, Sacrifice, and the Temple: Symbolism and Supersessionism in the Study of Ancient Judaism*. Oxford: Oxford University Press, 2005.

Klein, Ralph W. *2 Chronicles: A Commentary*. Hermeneia. Minneapolis: Fortress, 2012.

Klijn, A. F. J. "2 (Syriac Apocalypse of) Baruch: A New Translation and Introduction." Pages 615–52 in vol. 1 of *OTP*. Edited by James H. Charlesworth. New York: Doubleday, 1983.

Klinzing, Georg. *Die Umdeutung des Kultus in der Qumrangemeinde und im Neuen Testament*. SUNT 7. Göttingen: Vandenhoeck & Ruprecht, 1971.

Knibb, Michael. "The Exile in the Literature of the Intertestamental Period." *HeyJ* 17.3 (1976): 253–72.

Kohn, Risa Levitt. *A New Heart and a New Soul: Ezekiel, the Exile and the Torah*. JSOTSup 358. London: Sheffield Academic, 2002.

Konradt, Matthias. *Christology, Torah, and Ethics in the Gospel of Matthew*. Translated by Wayne Coppins. Waco: Baylor University Press, 2022.

———. *Israel, Church, and the Gentiles in the Gospel of Matthew*. Translated by Kathleen Ess. Waco: Baylor University Press, 2014.

———. "'Nehmt auf euch mein Joch und lernt von mir!' (Mt 11,29): Mt 11,28–30 und die christologische Dimension der matthäischen Ethik." *ZNW* 109.1 (2018): 1–31.

Laansma, Jon. *I Will Give You Rest: The Rest Motif in the New Testament with Special Reference to Mt 11 and Heb 3–4*. WUNT 2/98. Tübingen: Mohr Siebeck, 1997.

Lambert, David A. *How Repentance Became Biblical: Judaism, Christianity, and the Interpretation of Scripture*. Oxford: Oxford University Press, 2016.

Larkin, William J. *Acts*. Cornerstone Biblical Commentary. Carol Stream, IL: Tyndale, 2006.

Levine, Amy-Jill. "Matthew and Anti-Judaism." *Currents in Theology and Mission* 34.6 (2007): 409–16.

———. *The Misunderstood Jew: The Church and the Scandal of the Jewish Jesus*. New York: HarperOne, 2006.

———. "A Pharisee and a Tax Collector Walk into a Parable: Questioning the Sources of Anti-Jewish Interpretations." *PRSt* 49.3 (2022): 241–55.

Levine, Baruch A. *Leviticus*. JPSTC. Philadelphia: Jewish Publication Society, 2003.

Loader, William R. G. *Jesus' Attitude towards the Law: A Study of the Gospels*. Grand Rapids: Eerdmans, 2002.

Lohmeyer, Ernst. *The Lord's Prayer*. London: Collins, 2005.

Longenecker, Richard N. *Acts*. EBC. Grand Rapids: Zondervan, 1981.

Luz, Ulrich. *Matthew 8–20: A Commentary on the Gospel of Matthew*. Hermeneia. Translated by James E. Crouch. Minneapolis: Fortress, 2000.

———. *Matthew 21–28: A Commentary on the Gospel of Matthew*. Hermeneia. Translated by James E. Crouch. Minneapolis: Fortress, 2005.

Maccoby, Hyam. "How Unclean Were Tax-Collectors?" *BTB* 31.2 (2001): 60–63.

———. *Ritual and Morality: The Ritual Purity System and Its Place in Judaism*. Cambridge: Cambridge University Press, 1999.

———. "The Washing of Cups." *JSNT* 14 (1982): 3–15.

Marcus, Joel. "The Enigma of the Antitheses." *NTS* 69 (2023): 121–37.

———. *John the Baptist in History and Theology*. SPNT. Columbia: University of South Carolina Press, 2018.

———. *Mark 1–8: A New Translation with Introduction and Commentary*. AB 27. New Haven: Yale University Press, 1999.

———. *Mark 8–16: A New Translation with Introduction and Commentary*. AB 27A. New Haven: Yale University Press, 2009.

———. "No More Zealots in the House of the Lord: A Note on the History of Interpretation of Zechariah 14:21." *NovT* 55 (2013): 22–30.

———. "'The Time Has Been Fulfilled!' (Mark 1.15)." Pages 49–68 in *Apocalyptic and the New Testament: Essays in Honor of J. Louis Martyn*. Edited by Joel Marcus and Marion L. Soards. JSNTSup 24. Sheffield: JSOT Press, 1989.

Marguerat, Daniel. *Les Acts des apôtres (1–12)*. CNT. Deuxième série. Geneva: Labor et Fides, 2007.

———. "Paul and the Torah in the Acts of the Apostles." Pages 98–117 in *Torah in the New Testament*. Edited by Michael Tait and Peter Oakes. LNTS 401. London: T&T Clark International, 2009.

Mason, Steven. "Jews, Judaeans, Judaizing, Judaism: Problems of Categorization in Ancient History." *JSJ* 38 (2007): 457–512.

———. "Josephus's Pharisees: The Narratives." Pages 3–40 in *In Quest of the Historical Pharisees*. Edited by Jacob Neusner and Bruce D. Chilton. Waco: Baylor University Press, 2007.

———. "Josephus's Pharisees: The Philosophy." Pages 41–66 in *In Quest of the Historical Pharisees*. Edited by Jacob Neusner and Bruce D. Chilton. Waco: Baylor University Press, 2007.

McCane, Byron R. "'Let the Dead Bury Their Own Dead': Secondary Burial and Matthew 8:21–22." *HTR* 83.1 (1990): 31–43.

McConville, J. G. "Ezra-Nehemiah and the Fulfilment of Prophecy." *VT* 36.2 (1986): 205–24.

McGrath, James F. *Christmaker: A Life of John the Baptist*. Grand Rapids: Eerdmans, 2024.

McKnight, Scot. *A New Vision for Israel: The Teachings of Jesus in National Context*. Grand Rapids: Eerdmans, 1999.

McManigal, Daniel W. *A Baptism of Judgment in the Fire of the Holy Spirit: John's Eschatological Proclamation in Matthew 3*. LNTS 595. London: Bloomsbury T&T Clark, 2019.

Meier, John P. "Did the Historical Jesus Prohibit All Oaths? Part 1." *JSHJ* 5 (2007): 175–204.

———. "Nations or Gentiles in Matthew 28:19?" *CBQ* 39 (1977): 194–202.

Milgrom, Jacob. *Leviticus 1–16: A New Translation with Introduction and Commentary*. AB 3. New York: Doubleday, 1991.

———. *Leviticus 17–22: A New Translation with Introduction and Commentary*. AB 3A. New York: Doubleday, 2000.

———. *Leviticus 23–27: A New Translation with Introduction and Commentary*. AB 3B. New York: Doubleday, 2001.

Milik, Josef. "Milki-sedeq et Milki-resha' dans les anciens écrits juifs et chrétiens." *JJS* 23 (1972): 95–144.

Moffitt, David M. *Atonement and the Logic of Resurrection in the Epistle to the Hebrews*. SNT 141. Leiden: Brill, 2013.

———. "Isaiah 53, Hebrews, and Covenant Renewal." Pages 47–71 in *Rethinking the Atonement: New Perspectives on Death, Resurrection, and Ascension*. Grand Rapids: Baker Academic, 2022.

———. "Observations on Directional Features of the Incarnation and Jesus' Sacrifice in Hebrews." Pages 159–80 in *Rethinking the Atonement: New Perspectives on Death, Resurrection, and Ascension*. Grand Rapids: Baker Academic, 2022.

———. "Wilderness Identity and Pentateuchal Narrative: Distinguishing between Jesus' Inauguration and Maintenance of the New Covenant in Hebrews." Pages 29–45 in *Rethinking the Atonement: New Perspectives on Jesus's Death, Resurrection, and Ascension*. Grand Rapids: Baker Academic, 2022.

Moore, George Foot. "Christian Writers on Judaism." *HTR* 14.3 (1921): 197–254.

Moss, Candida. "The Man with the Flow of Power: Porous Bodies in Mark 5:25–34." *JBL* 129.3 (2010): 507–19.

Motyer, J. Alec. *The Prophecy of Isaiah: An Introduction and Commentary*. Downers Grove, IL: IVP Academic, 1993.

Mussner, Franz. *The Miracles of Jesus*. Notre Dame: Notre Dame University Press, 1968.

Nanos, Mark D. *The Mystery of Romans*. Minneapolis: Fortress, 1996.

———. "The Myth of the 'Law-Free' Paul Standing between Christians and Jews." *SCJR* (2009): 1–21.

Neusner, Jacob. "'First Cleanse the Inside': The 'Halakhic' Background of a Controversy-Saying." *NTS* 22 (1976): 486–95.

———. *The Tosefta: Translated from the Hebrew with a New Introduction*. 2 vols. Peabody, MA: Hendrickson, 2002.

Nickelsburg, George W. E. *1 Enoch 1: A Commentary on the Book of 1 Enoch, Chapters 1–36; 81–108*. Hermeneia. Minneapolis: Fortress, 2001.

Nickelsburg, George W. E., and James C. VanderKam. *1 Enoch: The Hermeneia Translation*. Minneapolis: Fortress, 2012.

Nolland, John. *The Gospel of Matthew: A Commentary on the Greek Text*. NIGTC. Grand Rapids: Eerdmans, 2005.

———. *Luke 9:21–18:34*. WBC. Waco: Word, 1993.

Novakovic, Lidija. "Matthew and Paul on Torah Observance: Is Matthew's Gospel Anti-Pauline, Pro-Pauline, or Un-Pauline?" Pages 104–21 in *"To Recover What Has Been Lost": Essays on Eschatology, Intertextuality, and Reception History in Honor of Dale C. Allison, Jr.* SNT 183. Leiden: Brill, 2021.

———. *Messiah, the Healer of the Sick: A Study of Jesus as the Son of David in the Gospel of Matthew*. WUNT 2/170. Tübingen: Mohr Siebeck, 2003.

Novenson, Matthew V. *Paul and Judaism at the End of History*. Cambridge: Cambridge University Press, 2024.

Oliver, Isaac W. *Luke's Jewish Eschatology: The National Restoration of Israel in Luke-Acts*. Oxford: Oxford University Press, 2021.

———. *Torah Praxis after 70 CE: Reading Matthew and Luke-Acts as Jewish Texts*. WUNT 2/355. Tübingen: Mohr Siebeck, 2013.

Parke-Taylor, Geoffrey H. *The Formation of the Book of Jeremiah: Doublets and Recurring Phrases*. SBLMS 51. Atlanta: Society of Biblical Literature, 2000.

Penner, Ken M. "Philo's Eschatology, Personal and Cosmic." *JSJ* 50.3 (2019): 383–402.

Pennington, Jonathan T. *The Sermon on the Mount and Human Flourishing: A Theological Commentary*. Grand Rapids: Baker Academic, 2017.

Perrin, Nicholas. *Jesus the Temple*. Grand Rapids: Baker Academic, 2010.

Peters, Dorothy M. "The Dead Sea Scrolls and Exile's End." Pages 183–200 in *Exile: A Conversation with N. T. Wright*. Edited by James M. Scott. Downers Grove, IL: IVP Academic, 2017.

Philo. Translated by Francis H. Colson, George H. Whitaker, and Ralph Marcus. 12 vols. LCL. Cambridge, MA: Harvard University Press, 1929–62.

Pitre, Brant. *Jesus, the Tribulation, and the End of the Exile: Restoration Eschatology and the Origin of the Atonement*. WUNT 2/204. Tübingen: Mohr Siebeck, 2005.

Plant, R. J. R. *Good Figs, Bad Figs: Judicial Differentiation in the Book of Jeremiah*. LHBOTS 481. New York: T&T Clark, 2008.

Plummer, Alfred. *A Critical and Exegetical Commentary on the Gospel according to St. Luke*. 5th ed. ICC. Edinburgh: T&T Clark, 1922. 1st ed., 1896.

Poirier, John C. "Why Did the Pharisees Wash Their Hands?" *JJS* 47 (1996): 217–33.

Polhill, John B. *Acts*. NAC. Nashville: Broadman, 1992.

Powell, Mark Allan. "The Plot and Subplots of Matthew's Gospel." *NTS* 38 (1992): 187–204.

Przybylski, Benno. *Righteousness in Matthew and His World of Thought*. SNTSMS 41. Cambridge: Cambridge University Press, 1980.

Puech, Émile. "Notes sur le manuscrit de 11QMelkisedeq." *RevQ* 12 (1987): 483–514.

Raabe, Paul R. "Drinking the Cup of God's Wrath: A Biblical Metaphor." Pages 45–56 in *"Hear the Word of Yahweh": Essays on Scripture and Archaeology in Honor of Horace D. Hummel*. Edited by Dean O. Wenthe, Paul L. Schrieber, and Lee A. Maxwell. St. Louis: Concordia, 2002.

Reed, Annette Yoshiko. "When Did Rabbis Become Pharisees?" Pages 331–60 in *Jewish-Christianity and the History of Judaism*. Minneapolis: Fortress, 2022.

Reinhartz, Adele. "The Temple Cleansing and the Death of Jesus." Pages 100–111 in *Purity, Holiness, and Identity in Judaism and Christianity: Essays in Memory of Susan Haber*. Edited by Carl S. Ehrlich, Anders Runesson, and Eileen Schuller. WUNT 1/305. Tübingen: Mohr Siebeck, 2013.

Ridlehoover, Charles Nathan. *The Lord's Prayer and the Sermon on the Mount in Matthew's Gospel*. LNTS 616. London: T&T Clark, 2020.

Rillera, Andrew Remington. *Lamb of the Free: Recovering the Varied Sacrificial Understandings of Jesus's Death*. Eugene, OR: Cascade Books, 2024.

Rosenblum, Jordan. *Food and Identity in Early Rabbinic Judaism*. New York: Cambridge University Press, 2013.

Roth, Cecil. "The Cleansing of the Temple and Zechariah XIV 21." *NovT* 4.3 (1960): 174–81.

Rudolph, David J. *A Jew to the Jews: Jewish Contours of Pauline Flexibility in 1 Corinthians 9:19–23*. Eugene, OR: Wipf & Stock, 2016.

Runesson, Anders. "Aspects of Matthean Universalism: Ethnic Identity as a Theological Tool in the First Gospel." Pages 103–33 in *Matthew within Judaism: Israel and the Nations in the First Gospel*. Edited by Anders Runesson and Daniel M. Gurtner. ECL 27. Atlanta: SBL Press, 2020.

———. *Divine Wrath and Salvation in Matthew: The Narrative World of the First Gospel*. Minneapolis: Fortress, 2016.

———. "Paul's Rule in All the *Ekklēsiai*." Pages 214–23 in *Introduction to Messianic Judaism: Its Ecclesial Context and Biblical Foundations*. Edited by David Rudolph and Joel Willitts. Grand Rapids: Zondervan, 2013.

———. "Purity, Holiness, and the Kingdom of Heaven in Matthew's Narrative World." Pages 144–80 in *Purity, Holiness, and Identity in Judaism and Christianity: Essays in Memory of Susan Haber*. Edited by Carl S. Ehrlich, Anders Runesson, and Eileen Schuller. WUNT 1/305. Tübingen: Mohr Siebeck, 2013.

Runesson, Anders, Donald D. Binder, and Birger Olsson. *The Ancient Synagogue from Its Origins to 200 C.E.: A Source Book*. AJEC 72. Leiden: Brill, 2008.

Sanders, E. P. *The Historical Figure of Jesus*. London: Penguin, 1993.

———. *Jesus and Judaism*. Philadelphia: Fortress, 1985.

———. "Jewish Association with Gentiles and Galatians 2:11–14." Pages 287–308 in *Comparing Judaism and Christianity: Common Judaism, Paul, and the Inner and the Outer in Ancient Religion*. Minneapolis: Fortress, 2016.

———. *Jewish Law from Jesus to the Mishnah: Five Studies*. London: SCM, 1990.

———. *Paul and Palestinian Judaism: A Comparison of Patterns of Religion*. Philadelphia: Fortress, 1977.

———. *The Question of Uniqueness in the Teaching of Jesus*. Ethel M. Wood Lecture, February 15, 1990. London: University of London, 1990.

Sanders, James A. "Sins, Debts, and Jubilee Release." Pages 84–92 in *Luke and Scripture: The Function of Sacred Tradition in Luke-Acts*. By Craig A. Evans and James A. Sanders. Minneapolis: Fortress, 1993.

Sarna, Nahum M. *Exodus*. JPSTC. New York: Jewish Publication Society, 1991.

Scott, James M. "Restoration of Israel." Pages 796–805 in *Dictionary of Paul and His Letters*. Edited by Gerald F. Hawthorne, Ralph P. Martin, and Daniel G. Reid. Downers Grove, IL: InterVarsity, 1993.

Segal, Michael. *The Book of Jubilees: Rewritten Bible, Redaction, Ideology and Theology*. JSJSup 117. Leiden: Brill, 2007.

Setzer, Claudia. "Sinai, Covenant, and Innocent Blood Traditions in Matthew's Blood Cry (Matt. 27:25)." Pages 169–83 in *The Ways That Often Parted: Essays in Honor of Joel Marcus*. Edited by Lori Baron, Jill Hicks Keeton, and Matthew Thiessen. Atlanta: SBL Press, 2018.

Shauf, Scott. *Jesus the Sacrifice: A Historical and Theological Study*. Lanham, MD: Lexington Books, 2022.

Shedd, Nathan L. *A Dangerous Parting: The Beheading of John the Baptist in Early Christian Memory*. Waco: Baylor University Press, 2021.

Shively, Elizabeth E. *Apocalyptic Imagination in the Gospel of Mark: The Literary and Theological Role of Mark 3:22–30*. BZNW 189. Berlin: De Gruyter, 2012.

———. "Purification of the Body and the Reign of God in the Gospel of Mark." *Journal of Theological Studies* 71.1 (2020): 62–89.

Sievers, Joseph, and A.-J. Levine, eds. *The Pharisees*. Grand Rapids: Eerdmans, 2021.

Sigal, Phillip. *The Halakhah of Jesus of Nazareth according to the Gospel of Matthew*. New York: University Press of America, 1986.

Sim, David C. *The Gospel of Matthew and Christian Judaism: The History and Social Setting of the Matthean Community*. SNTW. Edinburgh: T&T Clark, 1998.

———. "Matthew, Paul, and the Origin and Nature of the Gentile Mission: The Great Commission in Matthew 28:16–20 as an Anti-Pauline Tradition." *TS* 64.1 (2008): 377–92.

Sloan, Paul T. "Jewish Law-Observance in Paul." *Religions* 16.1 (2025): 1–14.

———. "The Law Will Testify against You: Deuteronomy 28–32 and the Restoration of Israel in Romans 3." Pages 140–64 in *The Beginning of Paul's Gospel: Theological Explorations in Romans 1–4*. Edited by Nijay K. Gupta and John K. Goodrich. Eugene, OR: Cascade Books, 2023.

———. *Mark 13 and the Return of the Shepherd: The Narrative Logic of Zechariah in Mark*. LNTS 604. London: T&T Clark International, 2019.

Sloan, Paul T., and Logan A. Williams. "Avodah Zarah and the Roman Messiah-Assembly: Anxieties over Pagan Holidays and Food Offered to Images in Romans 14:1–23." Paper presented at the Annual Meeting of the Society of Biblical Literature. San Diego, CA, November 2024.

———. "Neither Sabbath nor Kashrut but a Demonic Third Thing: Pagan Holidays and Food Sacrificed to Idols in Romans 14:1–23." Paper presented at the Annual Meeting of the Institute for Biblical Research. San Antonio, TX, November 2023.

Sloan, Robert B. *The Favorable Year of the Lord: A Study of Jubilary Theology in the Gospel of Luke*. Austin: Schola, 1977.

Smith, Joshua Paul. *Luke Was Not a Christian: Reading the Third Gospel and Acts within Judaism*. BIS 218. Leiden: Brill, 2024.

Smith, Steve. *The Fate of the Jerusalem Temple in Luke-Acts: An Intertextual Approach to Jesus' Laments over Jerusalem and Stephen's Speech*. LNTS 553. London: Bloomsbury T&T Clark, 2017.

Staples, Jason A. *The Idea of Israel in Second Temple Judaism: A New Theory of People, Exile, and Israelite Identity*. Cambridge: Cambridge University Press, 2021.

———. *Paul and the Resurrection of Israel: Jews, Former Gentiles, Israelites*. Cambridge: Cambridge University Press, 2024.

———. "'Rise, Kill, and Eat': Animals as Nations in Early Jewish Visionary Literature and Acts 10." *JSNT* 42.1 (2019): 3–17.

Steck, Odil Hannes. *Israel und das gewaltsame Geschick der Propheten: Untersuchungen zur Überlieferung des deuteronomistischen Geschichtsbildes im Alten Testament, Spätjudentum und Urchristentum*. Neukirchen-Vluyn: Neukirchener Verlag, 1967.

Stein, Robert H. *Mark*. BECNT. Grand Rapids: Baker Academic, 2008.

Steinsaltz, Adin Even-Israel. *The Babylonian Talmud*. Edited by William Davidson. https://www.sefaria.org/texts/Talmud.

Stone, Michael E. *Ancient Judaism: New Visions and Views*. Grand Rapids: Eerdmans, 2011.

Stuckenbruck, Loren T. *1 Enoch 91–108*. CEJL. Berlin: De Gruyter, 2007.

Stuhlmacher, Peter. "Zur missionsgeschichtlichen Bedeutung von Mt 28,16–20." *EvT* 59 (1999): 108–30.

Tan, Kim Huat. *The Zion Traditions and the Aims of Jesus*. SNTSMS 91. Cambridge: Cambridge University Press, 1997.

Taylor, Joan E. *The Immerser: John the Baptist within Second Temple Judaism*. Grand Rapids: Eerdmans, 1997.

Telford, William. *The Barren Temple and the Withered Fig Tree: A Redaction-Critical Analysis of the Cursing of the Fig-Tree Pericope in Mark's Gospel and Its Relation to the Cleansing of the Temple Tradition*. JSNT 1. Sheffield: JSOT Press, 1980.

Thiessen, Matthew. *Contesting Conversion: Genealogy, Circumcision, and Identity in Ancient Judaism and Christianity*. Oxford: Oxford University Press, 2011.

———. *Jesus and the Forces of Death: The Gospels' Portrayal of Ritual Impurity within First-Century Judaism*. Grand Rapids: Baker Academic, 2021.

———. *Paul and the Gentile Problem*. Oxford: Oxford University Press, 2016.

———. "Paul's So-Called Jew and Lawless Lawkeeping." Pages 59–83 in *The So-Called Jew in Paul's Letter to the Romans*. Edited by Rafael Rodríguez and Matthew Thiessen. Minneapolis: Fortress, 2016.

Tigay, Jeffrey H. *Deuteronomy*. JPSTC. Philadelphia: Jewish Publication Society, 1996.

Tiller, Patrick A. *A Commentary on the Animal Apocalypse of 1 Enoch*. Atlanta: SBL Press, 1993.

Tomson, Peter J. "Jewish Food Laws in Early Christian Community Discourse." *Semeia* 86 (1999): 193–211.

———. *Paul and the Jewish Law: Halakha in the Letters of the Apostle to the Gentiles*. Leiden: Brill, 1990.

Trocmé, Étienne. "L'expulsion des marchands du Temple." *NTS* 15.1 (1968): 1–22.

Tucker, J. Brian. *"Remain in Your Calling": Paul and the Continuation of Social Identities in 1 Corinthians*. Eugene, OR: Wipf & Stock, 2011.

Tyson, Joseph B. "Acts 6:1–7 and Dietary Regulations in Early Christianity." *PRSt* 10 (1983): 145–61.

VanderKam, James C. *Jubilees 1: A Commentary on the Book of Jubilees, Chapters 1–21*. Hermeneia. Minneapolis: Fortress, 2018.

———. "The Pharisees and the Dead Sea Scrolls." Pages 225–36 in *In Quest of the Historical Pharisees*. Edited by Jacob Neusner and Bruce D. Chilton. Waco: Baylor University Press, 2007.

van Henten, J. W. *The Maccabean Martyrs as Saviours of the Jewish People: A Study of 2 and 4 Maccabees*. JSJSup 57. Leiden: Brill, 1997.

van Houten, Christiana. *The Alien in Israelite Law*. JSOTSup 107. Sheffield: Sheffield Academic, 1991.

Van Maaren, John. "Does Mark's Jesus Abrogate Torah? Jesus' Purity Logion and Its Illustration in Mark 7:15–23." *Journal of the Jesus Movement in Its Jewish Setting* 4 (2017): 21–41.

———. *The Gospel of Mark's Judaism and the Death of Christ as Ransom for Many*. WUNT 1/534. Tübingen: Mohr Siebeck, 2025.

Wassén, Cecilia. "Jesus' Table Fellowship with 'Toll Collectors and Sinners': Questioning the Alleged Purity Implications." *JSHJ* 14 (2016): 137–57.

———. "The Jewishness of Jesus and Ritual Purity." *Scripta Instituti Donneriani Aboenis* 27 (2016): 11–36.

———. "Moral Impurity in the Gospel of Matthew." Pages 285–308 in *Matthew within Judaism: Israel and the Nations in the First Gospel*. Edited by Anders Runesson and Daniel M. Gurtner. Atlanta: SBL Press, 2020.

Watts, Rikki E. *Isaiah's New Exodus in Mark*. Grand Rapids: Baker Academic, 2000.

———. "Jesus' Death, Isaiah 53, and Mark 10:45: A Crux Revisited." Pages 125–51 in *Jesus and the Suffering Servant: Isaiah 53 and Christian Origins*. Edited by William H. Bellinger Jr. and William R. Farmer. Harrisburg, PA: Trinity Press International, 1998.

Webb, Robert L. *John the Baptizer and Prophet: A Socio-Historical Study*. JSNTSup 62. Sheffield: Sheffield Academic, 1991.

Weber, Max. *The Sociology of Religion*. Translated by Ephraim Fischoff. Boston: Beacon, 1963.

Wellhausen, Julius. *Prolegomena to the History of Israel: With a Reprint of the Article "Israel" from the Encyclopaedia Britannica*. Translated by J. Sutherland Black and Allan Menzies. 1885. Repr., New York: Meridian Books, 1957.

Weren, Wim J. C. "Marriage, Adultery, and Divorce: Interpretations of Old Testament Texts in Matthew 5:27–32 and 19:3–12." Pages 143–61 in *Studies in Matthew's Gospel: Literary Design, Intertextuality, and Social Setting*. BIS 130. Leiden: Brill, 2014.

Werrett, Ian C. *Ritual Purity and the Dead Sea Scrolls*. STDJ 72. Leiden: Brill, 2007.

White, Benjamin L. "The Eschatological Conversion of 'All the Nations' in Matthew 28.19–20: (Mis)reading Matthew through Paul." *JSNT* 36 (2014): 353–82.

Williams, Logan. "Melchizedek, the Son of Man, and Eschatological Jubilee: The Sin-Forgiving Messiahs in 11QMelchizedek and Mark." *JSNT* 46.2 (2023): 111–49.

———. "The Stomach Purifies All Foods: Jesus' Anatomical Argument in Mark 7.18–19." *NTS* 70.3 (2024): 371–91.

Willimon, William H. *Acts*. Interpretation. Louisville: Westminster John Knox, 2010.

Willitts, Joel. "The Friendship of Matthew and Paul: A Response to a Recent Trend in the Interpretation of Matthew's Gospel." *TS* 65.1 (2009): 150–57.

———. *Matthew's Messianic Shepherd-King: In Search of "The Lost Sheep of the House of Israel."* BZNW 147. Berlin: De Gruyter, 2007.

Wintermute, O. S. "Jubilees: A New Translation and Introduction." Pages 35–142 in vol. 2 of *OTP*. Edited by James H. Charlesworth. New York: Doubleday, 1985.

Wright, N. T. *The Climax of the Covenant: Christ and the Law in Pauline Theology*. Minneapolis: Fortress, 1992.

———. "In Grateful Dialogue." Pages 244–77 in *Jesus and the Restoration of Israel*. Edited by Carey C. Newman. Downers Grove, IL: IVP Academic, 1999.

———. *Jesus and the Victory of God*. Christian Origins and the Question of God 2. Minneapolis: Fortress, 1996.

———. "The Letter to the Romans." Pages 393–770 in vol. 10 of *The New Interpreter's Bible*. Edited by Leander E. Keck. Nashville: Abingdon, 2002.

———. *The New Testament and the People of God*. Christian Origins and the Question of God 1. Minneapolis: Fortress, 1992.

———. *Paul and the Faithfulness of God*. Christian Origins and the Question of God 4. Minneapolis: Fortress, 2013.

Yang, Yong-Eui. *Jesus and the Sabbath in Matthew's Gospel*. JSNTSup 139. Sheffield: Sheffield Academic, 1997.

Yinger, Kent L. *The Pharisees: Their History, Character, and New Testament Portrait*. Eugene, OR: Cascade Books, 2022.

Zellentin, Holger M. *Law beyond Israel: From the Bible to the Qur'an*. Oxford Studies in the Abrahamic Religions. Oxford: Oxford University Press, 2022.

Author Index

Scripture Index

Old Testament

Genesis

Exodus

Leviticus

Numbers

Deuteronomy

Jeremiah

Lamentations

Ezekiel

Daniel

Hosea

Joel

Amos

Micah

Nahum

Habakkuk

Zephaniah

Haggai

Zechariah

Malachi

New Testament

Matthew

Mark

Luke

John

Acts

Romans